HIROHITO

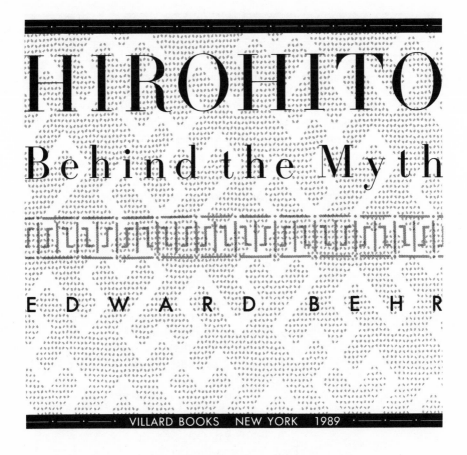

HIROHITO
Behind the Myth

EDWARD BEHR

VILLARD BOOKS   NEW YORK   1989

All rights reserved under International and Pan-American Copyright Conventions. Published in the United States by Villard Books, a division of Random House, Inc., New York, and simultaneously in Canada by Random House of Canada Limited, Toronto. Originally published in Great Britain by Hamish Hamilton Ltd.

Library of Congress Cataloging-in-Publication Data

Behr, Edward
Hirohito: behind the myth / by Edward Behr
p.   cm.
ISBN 0-394-58072-9
1. Hirohito, Emperor of Japan, 1901-1989. 2. Japan—Emperors-Biography. I. Title.
DS889.8.B44 1989
952.03'3'0924—dc19
[B]   89-5677

Manufactured in the United States of America
9 8 7 6 5 4 3 2
First American Edition

Book Design by Guenet Abraham

FOR P.B. AND C.B.

FOREWORD

It was while researching *The Last Emperor* that I determined that my next book had to be a biography of Emperor Hirohito.

Pu-yi, the puppet emperor of Manchukuo, and Emperor Hirohito had much in common: both were prisoners of an extremely rigid court routine; both were treated, in their youth, like "living gods"; and both were singularly ill equipped physically to assume the roles they were made to play. But whereas Pu-yi's whole life was a tragicomic failure, the saga of Hirohito is a barely credible one for its ironies: one of the "three most hated men in the world" alongside Hitler and Mussolini, according to Allied wartime propaganda, he went on to become a universally respected constitutional monarch, his prewar and wartime past certainly forgiven, if not forgotten. Not only the sheer longevity of his reign but the way he managed to extricate himself from responsibility for any of the prewar and wartime decisions leading to millions of deaths make him without doubt the ultimate survivor of all time.

Many of the events described in this book have been only partially reported outside Japan: the rise of Japanese imperialism was overshadowed, in Western eyes, by the rise of fascism in Italy and Hitler's domination of Germany. Pearl Harbor came as a horrifying shock to most Americans, even though the prospect of war between the United States and Japan had seemed inevitable to President Roosevelt and his advisers.

This book would not have been possible without the invaluable source material provided by two key books: the two-volume Kido diaries and the two-volume *Sugiyama Memorandum.* From the moment he became confidential secretary to the Lord Privy Seal, a post he eventually assumed himself, Koichi Kido kept a detailed diary. After his arrest as a Grade A war criminal suspect, he decided, on the advice of his son-in-law, to turn over this diary to the prosecution staff of the International Military Tribunal of the Far East (IMTFE), which eventually sentenced him to life imprisonment. It has since been published in Japanese, but never in translation. Many earlier books about Hirohito and the rise of the Greater East Asia Co-Prosperity Sphere quote selected portions of Kido's diaries, but to my surprise I discovered much in them that had never been utilized before.

The *Sugiyama Memorandum,* another seminal work about the period, is a diarylike record of all meetings held during the time General Hajime Sugiyama was army chief of staff; so detailed are the day-to-day entries that at times they read like tape-recording transcripts.

For chapters 3 and 4, I have relied heavily on that monumental piece of research the *Brocade Banner* report; for chapter 5, I am indebted to Jerrold M. Packard's *Sons of Heaven* for the description of the wedding and coronation ceremonies; for chapters 8, 9, 10 and 11, to the *Honjo Diaries* and *Brocade Banner.* From chapter 12 onwards, I have drawn heavily on the Kido diaries and the *Sugiyama Memorandum,* State Department and OSS records, and the SCAP Archives at Suitland, Maryland.

My thanks, above all, to those who patiently translated thousands of pages of documents, diaries, books and newspaper articles for me—Fuyuko Nishisato, Motoko Suzuki and Yukiko Shimahara, my interpreter; to the BBC's Anthony Geffen and Janet Williams, in London and Tokyo; and to the numerous experts on the period and subject who were kind enough to submit themselves to lengthy interrogations: Faubion Bowers, General MacArthur's former aide; Robert Fearey, formerly with MacArthur's SCAP, Tokyo; Robert Donihi, former prosecution staff, IMTFE; Dr. Ikuhiko Hata, professor of history at Tokyo's Takushoku University, Tokyo, and author of *The Emperor's Five Decisions;* Professor Kyoshi Inouye, author of *The Em-*

peror's Responsibilities; Dr. Roger Buckley, associate professor, International University of Japan, Tokyo; Dr. D.C.S. Sissons, Department of International Relations, Research School of Pacific Studies, Australian National University, Canberra; and H.I.H. Prince Takamado.

John Taylor of the National Archives, Washington, D.C., gave me invaluable guidance, and the staffs of both the National Archives and the Military Archives in Suitland were unfailingly helpful and patient, as were the staffs of the libraries of the School of Oriental and African Studies, at London University, of the Correspondents' Club and of the *Japan Times,* Tokyo.

Among veteran experts on Japan's prewar and wartime period who talked to me I want particularly to thank Robert Guillain, Havas correspondent in Tokyo from 1938 to 1945 and *Le Monde* correspondent there from 1948 to 1971; Ambassador Jacques Baeyens; Ambassador Bernard Dorin; Sir John Pilcher; Rear Admiral George C. Ross (retired); General Eiku Arisue; Morio Tateno, formerly of NHK (Japan Broadcasting Company); Torahiko Nagazumi, a Peers' School contemporary of Emperor Hirohito and later one of his chamberlains; Peter McGill, Tokyo correspondent of the *Observer;* Masaki Shimosato of *Akahata;* Taro Kimura; Shizuto Haruna, formerly of NHK; Toshiya Matsuzaki of *Josei Jishin;* Tetsuya Chikushi, *Asahi Shimbun;* Kyo Naruse, president of the Hara Shobo publishing house; Mrs. Yoshiko Yashimoto; *Newsweek*'s Ted Slate; Walter Harris and many others. Finally, I would like to thank Mrs. Penny Bergamini, for generously allowing me to use her late husband's archives and source materials, and Ed Victor, for his continued support and encouragement.

Edward Behr
Paris, 1989

INTRODUCTION

On September 27, 1945, an extraordinary event took place, marking the end of an invincible era that had lasted in Japan for over twenty-six hundred years. On that day the oldest serviceable imperial limousine (an ancient Mercedes) was coaxed into life in the Imperial Palace garage, and at 10:00 A.M. an unusual motorcade emerged through the palace gates, crossed the moat, and wended its way up the hill through flattened, charred, war-ravaged Tokyo. There were five cars in all (two of them filled with police and palace bodyguards) and two motorcycle outriders, a modest enough attendance by imperial standards.

Inside the Mercedes (which later became known to American forces, after its frequent appearances, as "the cement mixer," and now has pride of place in West Germany's Mercedes museum) sat a small, dapper man with a neat mustache and a slightly receding chin, dressed in a black morning coat, striped trousers and top hat. The clothes, a witness noted, were almost as old as the Mercedes—and indeed, for the next three years, Emperor Hirohito would make it a practice to wear shabby, ill-fitting suits, to share, symbolically, the hardships and penury of his people. That September morning, Emperor Hirohito was on his way to meet General MacArthur, the supreme commander,

Allied powers (SCAP), the new American "shogun," in the main reception room of the United States Embassy residence in Tokyo—a meeting that symbolized both Japan's defeat and the emperor's own determination to render obeisance to the new master of Japan.

The encounter, immortalized in a faintly comic picture taken by a U.S. signals-photographer sergeant, emphasized the difference between the two men. MacArthur, tieless, hands in pockets, in simple tan army shirt and trousers, stands next to the emperor, who barely comes up to his shoulder. MacArthur is stern, unsmiling, his jaw set in something of a snarl. Emperor Hirohito's features are fixed in a somewhat nervous half-smile; he has a fatalistic but slightly apprehensive air, and looks incredibly young. The photographer, recalled ex-Major Faubion Bowers, MacArthur's personal aide, was allowed only a few seconds to operate. MacArthur wanted only one picture. As a good professional, the sergeant begged for two, "in case the first doesn't come out," and MacArthur agreed, with a curt nod. (It was a wise decision: in the first picture, the emperor's eyes are closed, and it would have been unusable.)

Japanese editors were appalled by the contrast between the towering MacArthur and their tiny emperor, and were at first reluctant to publish the photograph, but SCAP directives prevailed. Paradoxically, the photograph did more to endear the emperor to the Japanese public than any of his later proclamations because he looked so vulnerable, and so clearly shared his people's predicament.

MacArthur's informal attire scandalized not only editors but almost all Japanese readers as well. They felt that the general should at least have dressed up in his full general's uniform for the occasion. In MacArthur's eyes, there was nothing disrespectful about his appearance—his was, after all, the standard dress of all U.S. personnel in U.S.-occupied Japan. He was surprised later to learn of these Japanese reactions, for he believed he had done his utmost to protect the emperor from embarrassment: there was no advance notice to the press of the visit, no mention of the appointment ever found its way into the MacArthur agenda, nor did the Honor Guard at the embassy residence gates know whom to expect when the Mercedes, followed by two other cars, entered the small driveway. All they had been told was to "present arms" with exceptional "panache" to an expected VIP delegation. Even the U.S. Army photographer who took the historic photograph had no inkling of the visitor's identity until he actually saw him. MacArthur deliberately stuck his hands in his pockets, Bowers feels, "to show who was boss."

Emperor Hirohito must have found the whole morning's experience somewhat baffling. From the start there was a studied informality about it. An aide, General Bonner Fellers, greeted the emperor with a hearty handshake. "Welcome, it's a pleasure to meet you, sir," he said. The nine palace aides who accompanied the emperor caused MacArthur's staff something of a problem. "We expected him to come alone, or accompanied by only one equerry," Bowers remembered. Instead, the nine most senior officials of the Imperial Household Ministry, including Tsuneo Matsudaira, the Imperial Household minister, and Marquis Koichi Kido, the Lord Privy Seal and also the emperor's closest adviser and lifelong friend (they had prepared together for the meeting the previous day for nearly three hours), remained downstairs in a tiny sitting room. Conversation was difficult. Bowers, MacArthur's personal interpreter as well as his military aide, did his best to amuse them with desultory small talk. An expert on kabuki theater, he tried to steer the conversation round to his pet subject. The palace officials were polite but their minds were evidently elsewhere.

The emperor's nervousness was apparent and well founded. He was, understandably, terrified. On the day of the signing of Japan's unconditional surrender aboard the *Missouri,* only some three weeks previously, the elderly Japanese foreign minister, Mamoru Shigemitsu, exhausted from his climb up the gangway of the battleship—an exceedingly painful ordeal for a seventy-year-old with only one leg (he had lost the other in a bomb explosion in Shanghai in the thirties)—had asked for a glass of water, and Admiral William Halsey had refused. Hirohito did not know what to expect. His request to see MacArthur had been curtly granted ("About time, too," the "Supremo" had told his staff), and he did not know whether he would be humiliated, as his foreign minister had been aboard the *Missouri,* or perhaps even be arrested on the spot.

For all these reasons, Bowers recalled, Hirohito "looked frightened to death. As I took his top hat I noticed his hands were trembling. On meeting MacArthur on the threshold of the drawing room he bowed low, very low, a servant's bow." MacArthur shook hands with the emperor, and said, "You are very, very welcome, sir." He added that an American interpreter, Bowers, was standing by, but if he preferred, the emperor could use his own interpreter, and MacArthur would not insist on a second one being present. Hirohito immediately commanded his own interpreter, Katuzo Okamura, to remain by his side. Sitting on straight-backed Louis XV–style chairs around a low table decorated with valuable Japanese ceramics, the three of them talked in apparent secrecy. The emperor's insistence on his own interpreter was understandable: what he had to say was so delicate, so difficult to express, that the idea of allowing a foreigner to translate would have been intolerable. He would have been mortified to know that Jean MacArthur, the general's wife, was listening to every word behind a curtain.

Later, MacArthur was to tell his staff that the emperor was both nervous and tense, but determined not to show it. "I tried to make it as easy for him as I could, but I knew how deep and dreadful must be his agony and humiliation," MacArthur said. "How painful it is to see someone raised so high brought so low." At one point he offered the emperor a cigarette, and Hirohito "was so nervous his hands shook." MacArthur lit it for him. The cigarettes had been an afterthought. "Does he smoke?" MacArthur asked Bowers minutes before the emperor's arrival. MacArthur, of course, smoked only his corncob pipe. Bowers gave the general his own pack of Lucky Strikes.

If anyone on the American side could put the emperor at ease, it was Douglas MacArthur, who, as aide-de-camp to his father, General Arthur MacArthur, had accompanied him on a visit to Japan just after the 1905 Russo-Japanese War, during the reign of Emperor Meiji. MacArthur reminded the emperor of this, and actually made him smile, thus breaking the ice. The new Supremo told Hirohito how preoccupied Emperor Meiji had been about a serious cholera epidemic that had broken out among the army units which had taken part in the campaign. The trouble was, the emperor had told MacArthur's father, the soldiers simply refused to take their anticholera pills.

"My father," MacArthur told Hirohito, "had a piece of advice for your grandfather. He suggested that inside each box of pills there should be a notice: 'The Emperor requests that each soldier take one capsule every four hours.' My father's advice was followed—and the cholera epidemic ceased."

From then on it was clear sailing, although there were a few awkward moments. Hirohito recognized the good conduct and restraint of the U.S. occupation troops; MacArthur congratulated Hirohito on the conduct of the Japanese people in this difficult time. The generalities then became a little less formal. After MacArthur had praised Hirohito for ending the war, the emperor replied that others, too, deserved credit. "The peace party did not prevail," said Hirohito, "until the bombing of Hiroshima created a situation which could be dramatized."

MacArthur then asked a question many people have asked since. How was it that an emperor powerful enough to end the war had been unable to prevent it? "I felt my heart was breaking," said Hirohito, adding that the worst part of it was reflecting on the consequences of the war on the British royal family, "who had treated me with great kindness when I visited them as Crown Prince. But the idea of gainsaying my advisers in those days never even occurred to me. Besides, it would have done no good. I would have been put in an insane asylum or even assassinated."

"A monarch must be brave enough to run such risks," said MacArthur.

But Hirohito had another, unexpected rejoinder, and, considering the circumstances, it showed him to be both a stubborn man and a brilliant poker player. "It was not clear to me that our course was unjustified," he said. "Even now I am not sure how historians will allocate the responsibility for the war." He then, in what must have been an excruciatingly difficult speech to make, told MacArthur that he came before him "to offer myself to the judgment of the powers you represent as the one to bear the sole responsibility for every political and military decision made and action taken by my people in the conduct of the war."

It was, of course, an empty gesture: the emperor knew full well by this time, nearly two months after Hiroshima, that on the whole MacArthur was against his indictment as a war criminal, and that his status as emperor, though likely to change, would not be ended outright, as he would almost certainly not be asked to abdicate. MacArthur knew that the emperor knew that he knew this. But "bellytalk" is an essential part of formal Japanese social intercourse, and the emperor, in offering himself up as a scapegoat, was in fact making the point that the occupation authorities should not lean too hard on Japan, especially where "war criminals" were concerned. If they were determined to spare the emperor, how could they possibly punish his loyal and devoted servants?

MacArthur, too, was at pains to tell the emperor that America did not intend to behave as a colonizing power. In all, the meeting lasted thirty-five minutes. After it was over, according to Paul Manning, a veteran U.S. correspondent who had covered the war in the Pacific, flown on bombing missions over Japan and witnessed the surrender aboard the *Missouri* and had privileged access to MacArthur's staff, "both knew they could work together to rehabilitate Japan and its people. Their respect was mutual, their courtesy and empathy marked. . . . They knew they were to be partners in the task of occupation that lay ahead." For Hirohito, the dreaded meeting had turned into a personal triumph. As he told Marquis Kido later, MacArthur had actually asked him for advice! As Kido recorded in his diaries, MacArthur had said "that the Emperor of Japan knows best about the important men in the Japanese political world. Therefore I want to get your advice from now on, on various matters. . . ."

As he left, Emperor Hirohito was heard to ask Marquis Kido for the name of the general who had ushered him into the embassy, and later sent Bonner Fellers a photograph, signed in English. It was a surprising gesture on the part of a still-divine emperor, and proof that Hirohito, for all his palace seclusion, was fully aware of Western-style public relations techniques. More tokens of esteem followed: shortly after the meeting, Empress Nagako sent Jean MacArthur a huge basket of flowers, which she acknowledged in a thank-you letter addressed to "Your Majesty." And shortly after that came another gift, from the emperor this time: a gold and lacquered writing box, for General and Mrs. MacArthur. Mrs. MacArthur promptly had it appraised and was slightly disappointed to learn that, though valuable, it wasn't all that old, probably dating back to the nineteenth-century Tokugawa era.

MacArthur was quick to acknowledge the emperor's first postwar victory. He told his aides that Hirohito "was an Emperor by inherent birth but at that instant I knew I faced the first gentleman of Japan in his own right." He said to a visitor that at first "I came here with the idea of using the Emperor more sternly. But it hasn't been necessary. He is a sincere man and a genuine liberal." At no time did MacArthur ever write to his titular chief, President Truman, an account of what had gone on in the embassy residence between himself and Hirohito. This apparent dereliction of duty was deliberate: MacArthur, in this and all subsequent conversations with the emperor (there were to be ten in all before the occupation ended), respected Hirohito's wish that they be not only off the record but completely private, even though, after subsequent meetings, the Japanese Foreign Ministry immediately debriefed the emperor's interpreter, with Hirohito's consent. Besides, as Faubion Bowers recalled many years later, "anti-Japanese feeling ran so high in Washington at the time that had MacArthur reported back that the Emperor claimed full responsibility for the war, the pinkos in the State Department would have clamoured: fine, let's try him." (The substance of their subsequent talks has remained in a top-secret file inside the Ministry, with the exception of one deliberate leak, engineered by the Japanese Foreign Ministry, which led to the dismissal of one of Hirohito's interpreters, at MacArthur's request.)

Three months after his first meeting with MacArthur, Emperor Hirohito renounced his "godliness" in a carefully prepared text he had mulled over for days. "The bondage between Us and you, the people," he said, "is constantly tied with mutual trust, love and respect. It is not brought about by mere mythology and legends. It is never founded on a chimerical conception which ascribes the Emperor as a living deity, and, moreover, [regards] the Japanese as superior to all other races of people, hence destined to rule the world." All pictures of him showed him in civilian clothes, and a new spirit prevailed within SCAP. MacArthur's deputy chief of the government section, Colonel C. L. Kades, said MacArthur felt that "the Emperor had atoned for any past errors by his wholehearted support of the Occupation." General Courtney Whitney, MacArthur's chief aide, told reporters, "I would consider it a gross breach of faith if the Emperor were to be tried as a war criminal after all the services he has rendered to the allies."

The story of Hirohito is a complicated one to unravel, not least because, in the short space of time between the emperor's decision to surrender and the arrival of the American occupying force, almost all Japanese confidential documents were destroyed. The Imperial Household minister ordered the elimination of all "sensitive" palace papers shortly before Japan's surrender, and the foreign, army and navy ministers, as well as the army and navy chiefs of staff, gave similar instructions, which were obeyed with rigorous thoroughness, so that when the time came for prosecutors of Japanese war criminal suspects to gather evidence they found almost no documents to work on, in marked contrast to the mass of papers left behind by the Nazi bureaucracy. This is why, on the whole, the image of a passive, blameless monarch has prevailed.

At this remove in time, it is strange, however, to realize that back in August 1945 there was a very real possibility of Emperor Hirohito standing trial as a war criminal for his responsibility in the events leading up to Pearl Harbor. It was not just the Soviet Union (for reasons that had everything to do with furthering the cause of the Japanese Communist party, which had so long lain underground, and nothing to do with justice per se) that sought his trial and the abolition of the Japanese monarchy. Australia wanted to identify Hirohito as the man who had condoned the summary execution of Australian prisoners of war and the systematic ill-treatment of tens of thousands of prisoners in defiance of all clauses of the Geneva Convention; New Zealand shared the Australian view; a strong current of opinion in the United States felt that Hirohito, who had done nothing to save the lives of the earliest American aircrews captured on bombing raids over Japan, some of whom were executed as "war criminals," deserved to suffer the same fate. In September 1945, a joint resolution in Congress declared that "it is the policy of the United States that Emperor Hirohito of Japan be tried as a war criminal." Many individual members of the U.S., British Commonwealth and Chinese prosecution teams preparing for the International Military Tribunal of the Far East (IMTFE, otherwise known as the Tokyo Trials) believed he deserved to be indicted. So of course did the surviving prisoners of war, who emerged in August 1945, their lives shattered by years of privation and sadistic treatment. Their indignation was nothing compared with that of the Chinese and *their* case against Hirohito for millions of Chinese deaths, starting with the Mukden Incident of September 1931 (which placed Manchuria under Japanese control in a carefully prepared putsch engineered by Japanese army officers) and encompassing the Shanghai Incident of 1932, the later China Incident, which led to the wholesale invasion of China in 1937, the infamous "rape of Nanking" and horrendous experiments on Chinese prisoners used as guinea pigs in chemical and bacteriological warfare experiments in Japanese camps and laboratories in "Manchukuo" and on the Chinese mainland. Eisenhower even sent MacArthur a "Joint Chiefs of Staff Directive," drafted by the State/War/Navy Coordinating Committee (SNWCC) in Washington, reminding MacArthur that

Hirohito was not necessarily immune from prosecution as a war criminal and that SCAP Headquarters was to collate evidence to be forwarded to Washington, to enable officials there to decide whether or not he should stand trial.

In almost any other political context, the supreme ruler of a country that had perpetrated such behavior would have been tried and perhaps even executed. Indeed, there is a case for saying that many of those tried at Nuremberg were punished for far less, that their responsibilities, though major, nevertheless fell short of Hitler's. There is an even greater case for maintaining that the fate of the Japanese war criminals sentenced in the Philippines in 1945 and at the close of the "Japanese Nuremberg trials" in 1947 was a travesty of justice.

The view that Hirohito was a war criminal—prevalent at the close of World War II—has since become shockingly unfashionable, and even to raise the subject is enough to provoke a storm of indignation, especially in the United States. Nowadays, any hint that Emperor Hirohito may deserve even a small portion of the blame for the events that led to Pearl Harbor and tens of millions of Western and Asian deaths is regarded as unwarrantable. The only major English-language "revisionist" book to question the accepted view of Hirohito as a peace-loving, powerless prisoner of his entourage, David Bergamini's *Japan's Imperialist Conspiracy,* was so violently attacked by a cohort of academic experts that Bergamini became a pariah, reviled, ridiculed and driven to an early death by the weight of negative critical abuse. Bergamini's error was to attempt to discover a conspiratorial pattern in Hirohito's behavior, from his earliest years as crown prince, and to try to prove that he deliberately placed a handful of key supporters in top positions in order to plan Japan's militaristic expansionism, ruthlessly suppressing those who disagreed with the "Strike South" option (the conquest by force of Southeast Asia) and favored, instead, the "Strike North" option (a move against the Soviet Union that would have recovered part of Siberia, which had once belonged to China). It was a flawed view, for Bergamini failed to grasp the difference between the emperor's formal, "abstract" powers and their practical limits, and this failure was compounded by erratic scholarship, an attempt to twist all available facts to prove his theory. Bergamini also had a somewhat paranoid attitude toward Japan in general, perhaps as a result of his own experiences as an adolescent civilian internee in

Japanese hands in the Philippines during the war years, his ordeal as searing as that of Jim in J. G. Ballard's autobiographical novel, *Empire of the Sun.*

I am not a professional historian. Nor do I have an ax to grind. In Southeast Asia at the close of World War II, as a teenage subaltern in the Indian army, I did catch glimpses of Japanese servicemen, but by that time they were cooperative, disciplined prisoners of war. As a veteran journalist and witness of the major events that have shaken the world since the early fifties, I have, however, developed something of a "lie detector" flair for anything that smacks of orchestrated propaganda exercises, of the kind even democratic institutions indulge in so freely, and I was struck by the extraordinarily skilled campaign designed to insulate Hirohito from responsibility for all the traumatic events that took place during the first twenty years of his reign. It was not an exclusively Japanese phenomenon: MacArthur's own attitude toward the emperor was a determining factor. He had been quick to come to the conclusion, even before the end of the war, that the Japanese social fabric might well disintegrate were the emperor's title to be abolished. Joseph C. Grew, a close wartime adviser to Roosevelt and America's ambassador in Tokyo prior to Pearl Harbor, thought the same, and the cold war that followed on the heels of Japan's surrender, with the Korean War starting a mere five years later, led him—and other key policy-makers—to the conclusion that because Japan was a necessary bulwark in Asia against Communism in general and Soviet territorial ambitions in the East in particular, it was fruitless, and counterproductive, to harp too much on the past. What had gone before was to be exorcised by the sentences imposed on Japan's war criminals by the IMTFE. A clean sweep of the past was needed.

This view persisted through the years, starting with the Korean War and culminating during the Vietnam war: during both conflicts the United States used Japan as a rear-echelon base. It is, today, widely accepted that the emperor was a virtual prisoner of the militarists who, from 1931, effectively seized power and led Japan on its expansionist march toward Pearl Harbor and the invasion of the Philippines and Malaysia. In the minds of most people throughout the world, Emperor Hirohito remains the passive, withdrawn monarch-scientist, the marine biologist, who was kept inadequately informed of his government's decisions and was in any case unable to control the military, who, while invoking the imperial will, in fact imposed their own.

The meeting with MacArthur, however, that September day in 1945, reveals qualities, and determination, that make nonsense of the passivity theory. MacArthur's question to him, asking why a man of such qualities had been unable to prevent the war in the first place, remains astonishingly relevant. As the encounter showed, here was a shrewd and skillful manipulator at work, who knew what was going on. That he was capable of decisive and ruthless action was shown on February 28, 1936, when, almost single-handedly, he dealt with a serious army uprising that nearly toppled the regime. In August 1945, again almost single-handedly, he decided to end the war.

Yet at other times, during the Mukden Incident, and the later China Incident, and during some of the events leading up to that fateful December 7, 1941, Hirohito's behavior *was* strangely, uncharacteristically passive, his statements in direct contradiction to the policies that prevailed. There are two possible explanations: either Hirohito was, as his own propagandists have, so far successfully, claimed, a mere stooge of the military (and this is belied by his decisive behavior in two key events) or else there was, in Hirohito's makeup, an ambivalence toward the military, along with a combination of guile, ruse and a passion for secrecy that enabled him to "ride the tiger" of militarism when it suited him while at the same time insulating himself from any concomitant blame for the militaristic expansionism that marked the 1931–41 decade.

The "official" Japanese line that Hirohito could not be held responsible for any of the steps that led to World War II because he was unaware of what was going on behind the scenes and was, in any case, lacking any real power, seems to me incredible. On the evidence of what actually happened, it is clear to me that for all his occasional verbal disapproval of the militarist expansionists, their aims and goals—if not always their methods—had his wholehearted approval.

He endorsed Japan's full-scale war against China from 1937 onward, his only complaint to his generals being that they had misled him by promising him quick victories and were not winning them fast enough. He believed, without any apparent reservations, in the Japanese "Monroe Doctrine" (prevalent from 1940 onward) that gave his country the untrammeled right to hegemony in Asia, and he certainly believed, until events proved him wrong, that the Italian and German Axis powers had similar rights over Europe—the Western Hemisphere remaining America's legitimate sphere of interest so long as she respected both the Japanese and the Axis rights to dominate *their* "legitimate" spheres of interest after Germany's final and, in Hirohito's view, inevitable victory in Europe.

It has become fashionable among historians to underline the limited nature of his "discretionary" or veto powers. But the plain fact is that no major decision, promotion or troop movement could occur without Hirohito's seal of approval, and that such an approval could be, and sometimes was, withheld—without any one of his army or navy staff either objecting or threatening to rebel. Instilled into every Japanese was the notion of blind obedience to the emperor, and it is inconceivable that any decision taken by him, or any opinion expressed by him, not even necessarily in forceful terms, would have been ignored. As Tojo—the leading war criminal judged at IMTFE— let drop during the court proceedings, Hirohito was the ultimate arbiter of the situation, for "no Japanese subject would go against the will of His Majesty."

Despite his ineffectual and, almost certainly, deliberately half-hearted verbal reservations, Hirohito allowed the Manchukuo and China "incidents" to happen, promoted those responsible for them, and was fully aware of preparations for World War II without ever making one concrete move that would have reversed the trend toward confrontation. As diaries of his most intimate staff have revealed, he not only was aware of the key step taken in advance of Pearl Harbor— the establishment of Japanese army and air force bases in what was then French Indochina in 1941—but also openly questioned whether this should not also be accompanied by an invasion of Thailand. And it is hard to claim, as some apologists still do, that Hirohito had no advance warning of Pearl Harbor when records exist of his debate with his military chiefs of staff about December 8—Monday in Japan but Sunday, December 7, in Hawaii—and of his being told that Sunday was the best possible day for the attack because U.S. navy and military personnel generally tended to overindulge on Saturday nights, and that they would therefore be "tired." Hirohito openly exulted in the early Japanese victories, although, after the war, he told a visiting clergyman (himself involved in last-minute attempts to prevent war from breaking out) that had he received Roosevelt's personal letter in time, he would have "called off Pearl Harbor," a statement implying that it had been within his power to do so. But as early as 1946, when the Tokyo Trials started, Hirohito—and his imperial family—were off limits to war crimes prosecutors, for by this time the fiction had been established that the only persons responsible for the events leading up to Pearl Harbor were the twenty-seven individuals arraigned at the trial; neither President Truman nor MacArthur wanted to know otherwise.

All this means that Hirohito escaped the consequences of his actions with total impunity. After a decent interval he resumed his state visits to major countries, was greeted with cordial courtesy by both Queen Elizabeth and President Ford. He is respected by many Japanese as "the man who stopped the war." Since 1945, and until his death, in 1989, he became a highly regarded constitutional monarch, and the Japanese monarchy is, along with Britain's and Spain's, the only real going concern; the notion that the monarchical system might one day come to an end is regarded not just as lèse-majesté but as aberrant nonsense, as Crown Prince Akihito's accession to the throne proved. The official line concerning Hirohito's responsibilities in the events leading up to war is accepted not only by the overwhelming majority of Japanese themselves but by the mass of academic expert opinion, at any rate in the United States. Because of Japan's huge postwar wealth and influence as a world power, it has become ill advised to question Hirohito's role or go behind the "chrysanthemum curtain."

In contrast, other monarchs similarly caught up in wars not always entirely of their own choosing have fared badly: Kaiser Wilhelm II ended his days in exile after the collapse of Germany in 1918, and King Leopold III of the Belgians was compelled to abdicate simply because he chose to remain during the German occupation instead of fleeing to Britain—even though he scrupulously avoided the taint of collaboration.

Hirohito not only survived but lived on to become not merely the "last emperor" but also the longest-living monarch in contemporary history. Here was a ruler who became regent in 1921, and emperor in 1926. It was as though Winston Churchill were still at the helm in the eighties, or Raymond Poincaré still a power in Mitterrand's France. The biography of Emperor Hirohito encompasses so many changes, and so much history, that it makes the life story of any other twentieth-century statesman appear ephemeral in the extreme. Hirohito rode down the Mall in a carriage with King George V in 1921, and in his lifetime became familiar with the France of President Alexandre Millerand (1859–1943) as well as with that of President Mitterrand. For all his failing health, he was still carrying out formal duties in April 1988, nine months before his death. On the grounds of longevity alone, Hirohito's story is unique. But even more fascinating than his staying power is the nature of his controversial role while Japan was on its expansionist, militaristic rampage. Hirohito not only survived defeat, his country's near-total physical destruction and the ignominious end of the Greater East Asia Co-Prosperity Sphere, but became a born-again constitutional emperor, revered by his people, and respected if not admired all over the world. Time has been good to Emperor Hirohito, and in the interests of realpolitik, everyone has been impressively kind. Too kind, perhaps?

This book may restore the balance.

HIROHITO

CHAPTER ONE

Japan at the time of Hirohito's birth in 1901 was a country that had experienced incredible change in the previous fifty years after centuries of isolation in a seventeenth-century time warp.

As a small child, Hirohito grew up at the court of Emperor Meiji, his grandfather and Japan's first modern ruler. It was under Meiji that the "great leap forward" had taken place. Before that, for over two hundred sixty years, the emperors had been mere figureheads, virtual prisoners of the shoguns, the hereditary overlords and real rulers of Japan. The emperors did not even reside in Tokyo—or Edo, as it was then called—but were confined to the religious capital, Kyoto, where they were respected as religious leaders of Shintoism but denied any temporal power. The Tokugawa, the family of shoguns who ruled Japan in the nineteenth century, imposed police-state techniques and tried to seal the country off from the outside world. Conventional historical wisdom is that they did so with considerable success; the building of oceangoing ships was banned, and those unfortunate Japanese who were shipwrecked off Japan's coast and rescued at sea by foreign ships were not allowed to return to their country. But the new school of Japanese historians now believes that despite this ban foreign ideas and techniques seeped through on a larger scale than was once commonly believed.

The end of the Tokugawa shogunate was hastened by the arrival of Commodore Matthew Perry's "black ships" in 1853. Initially, the civil wars that terminated Tokugawa rule were inspired by xenophobia, and the rallying cry was "Revere the emperor! Expel the barbarians!" But the uprising was social and economic too: Kyoto silk merchants sided with Emperor Komei, Meiji's father, and so did the ronin, the masterless samurai reduced to lawlessness after the shogun's brutal repression of local feudalism. Two leading noble families, the Choshu and the Satsuma, supported the emperor. Japan was still in turmoil when Meiji, a mere boy of fifteen, succeeded to the throne.

Under Meiji, Japan at last came of age. The first few years of his reign were marked by a series of wars, initially against the last shogun, Keiki, who despite his personal oath of allegiance to the new emperor was persuaded to attack Kyoto and rid him of "evil advisers." He failed, but the notion that it was morally acceptable to try to eradicate the emperor's henchmen on the grounds that they were providing him with bad advice was one that would plague Meiji's grandson, Hirohito, throughout the 1930s. Keiki survived, after handing over his Tokyo palace to the young emperor, and many years later, in 1902, after Meiji's many victories and his fundamental reorganization of Japanese society, he was received in audience, and subsequently granted the title of prince.

From 1868 onward, Japan underwent the same breathtaking modernization that characterized Napoleonic France and Kemal Atatürk's Turkey: no sooner had the young emperor settled in Edo, now renamed Tokyo (the eastern capital), in 1869 than he realized that he needed the barbarians—or at any rate the skills they brought with them—in order to become, in time, strong enough to expel them. Foreigners were hired to run harbors, railways, schools. The ban on foreign travel for Japanese was eased. Japan was put under modern, centralized rule, with prefects in each province responsible to a home minister. Western dress became fashionable, and sword carrying was outlawed in 1870. There was a cult of all things foreign, so much so that by 1880 a popular children's song, sung to the accompaniment of a bouncing ball and entitled "The Civilization Ball Song," recorded the ten most worthwhile Western inventions. In order of priority, they were railway engines, gas lamps, cameras, telegrams, lighting conductors, newspapers, schools, a postal system, steamships and cabs. And, in every domain, the Japanese started to prove they were superlatively good at copying the West, whether in administrative systems, engineering or armaments, especially after compulsory education was established early in the Meiji period.

With modernization and increased travel abroad came a growing awareness of life beyond Japan's own frontiers, especially on the mainland closest to the nation—China. Here, Meiji's advisers soon realized, was a state of affairs to be avoided at all costs: China was becoming a virtual colony of the foreign powers at the very same time that Japan was becoming part of the modern world. Because of her weakness and ungovernability, China was in the process of surrendering chunks of her sovereign territory to Britain, France and Germany. Foreign concessions were springing up all over China, and Japan— after providing half the relief troops that broke the Boxer rebellion in 1901—was, in time, to ask for her share of these. She was determined, moreover, never to be compelled, as China had been, to accept for any length of time a foreign presence on her soil enjoying extraterritorial rights. There were in fact many similarities between China and Japan—the imperial tradition, the writing of ideograms, Confucianism and Buddhism—except in the matter of patriotism, which the Chinese lacked. Increasingly, from the Meiji era on, most Japanese were to regard China not as a nation but more as a culture, a state of mind.

It was an age when navies assumed the importance that nuclear forces have today, when China was the last frontier left for aggressive, industrial Western powers, so dominant on the world scene that Britain, France, Germany, Russia and the United States were known simply as "the powers." Japan was beginning to qualify, and soon showed she was determined to become a member of this exclusive club.

The reason why Japan succeeded where China failed was, in part, the foresightedness of Japan's leading families, including those who had destroyed the Tokugawa shogunate. During the Meiji era, from 1868 to 1912, China was destabilized by a series of revolutions and civil wars, a prey to warlords, unable to establish for long a unified, centralized rule of any kind under the discredited *fin de race* Ching dynasty that was finally overthrown in 1912. Japan might well have suffered the same fate, but her ruling families, after overthrowing the shogun, voluntarily surrendered their power to the emperor. "There is no soil within the Empire that does not belong to Him," their memorial read, recalling that "Imperial Power had declined, and military classes usurped power in the recent past. Now that Imperial power is restored, how can we retain possession of land that belongs to the Emperor and govern people who are his subjects? We therefore reverently offer up all our feudal possessions so that a uniform rule may prevail throughout the Empire. Thus the country will be able to rank equally with the other nations of the world."

Without this act of allegiance the Meiji Restoration would have been short-lived, and Japan would not have been able to play an active role on the world scene so soon after emerging from her isolation. It was fear of becoming another China that was behind this statesmanlike impulse, along with the determination to deny the Western powers a monopoly role in the acquisition of Chinese "international concessions." As a comparatively small nation, a cluster of islands close to China, Japan could not stand by and watch Britain consolidate her enclaves along the China coast, France move into Cochin China and Cambodia, and Russia annex part of Chinese Manchuria, without fearing for her own integrity. The best defense was offense, which explains why, under Meiji, Japan countered the encroaching Western powers first by extending her influence over Korea, after a lightning war with China, then by providing a huge contingent for the relief of Peking during the Boxer rebellion of 1900 (Japanese troops were the only ones who refrained from looting) and, finally, by challenging Russia over Manchuria.

Emperor Meiji had taken personal command of his new, modernized army in the 1894 war with China, and his terms were harsh: Korea became a virtual Japanese protectorate, Taiwan became Japanese, China was made to pay a large "indemnity" and Japan moved into the southeastern part of Manchuria known as the Liaotung (later Kwangtung) peninsula. So dramatic was Japan's emergence as the rising power in the East that, deeply alarmed, France, Germany and Russia joined together in a "triple intervention" to put pressure on Japan to be less greedy. Emperor Meiji reluctantly gave in—the war had left Japan financially exhausted—but the memory of such "colonialist" behavior, and suspicion that the West would always try to prevent Japan from reaping her just rewards, was to rankle in the Japanese collective subconscious for generations.

In the late nineteenth century, rail communications were as important to a nation's prestige as the mastery of space is today, and Russia's completion of the trans-Siberian railway was, in a way, as noteworthy a feat as the first launching of *Challenger* or of permanent orbital stations. The shortest route to Vladivostok was through Manchuria; the Russians set up the Chinese eastern railway with a Chinese name, but it was in fact a Russian railway crossing China. All of a sudden Manchuria became an area of huge strategic importance, and the Russians, three years after forcing Japan out of the Liaotung peninsula, moved in themselves, leasing enclaves, including Port Arthur, running a railway from Port Arthur to Harbin, and gradually turning the whole of Manchuria into a Russian sphere of influence.

These were the days of Kipling's "great game," with Russia constantly threatening British hegemony over India through the buffer state of Afghanistan—and to Japan the Russian push into Manchuria was a Japanese version of the "great game," one she was determined to resist. Britain had refused to be part of the "triple intervention" powers—her suspicions of Russia were too great—and it was the new Russian threat to Japan, through Manchuria, that led first to the British-Japanese friendship treaty of 1902, then to the Russo-Japanese War of 1904–1905.

It was a war that astonished the whole world: before it started, it was known that Japan had a first-class army and navy, with thirteen divisions, brand-new artillery, and some seventy-six warships. But no Western specialist believed she could take on a major European power and win. Even in Japan there were doubts: the Constitutionalists, Japan's first major political party, were against the war, and Emperor Meiji himself ensured against a humiliating defeat by secretly obtaining from the United States the assurance that she would prevent Russia's outright invasion of Japan.

Though Japan severed diplomatic relations with Russia on February 5, 1904, she did not formally declare war until February 10. On February 8 the Japanese navy launched a surprise attack on Russia's Far Eastern Fleet, near Port Arthur (later renamed Lushun), with devastating results. It was a prefiguration of Pearl Harbor: in the samurai tradition, all was fair in war, and attacking the enemy by stealth, and without warning, was not merely acceptable strategy but part of the cruel Japanese rules of the game. Admiral Heihachiro Togo scattered the Russian fleet again at the battle of Tsushima, on May 27–28, 1905. "Gallant little Japan," so inferior to Russia in size, was so much the underdog that—in contradiction to world opinion after Pearl Harbor later—the sneak attack was condoned. "The Japanese Navy has opened the war by an act of daring which is destined to take a place of honor in naval annals," wrote the London *Times.*

At the start of the war the remnants of the Russian fleet sought refuge in Port Arthur while another Baltic-based fleet set out to relieve them and lift the siege. Loyally implementing the friendship treaty, Britain denied the czar's navy the right of passage through the Suez Canal, forcing it to sail round the world, and France compounded its difficulties by denying it bunkering rights in French Indochina.

It was vital for the emperor to overwhelm the Russian garrison in Port Arthur before the reinforcements arrived, and he ordered his favorite general, Maresuke Nogi, to capture it at all costs. Nogi in turn told his soldiers to be prepared to die for the emperor. Officers were not expected to survive, and anyone leaving the battlefield without reason was shot out of hand. For months, wave upon wave of Japanese infantry attempted to break through the Russian defenses. Nogi watched through binoculars as his two sons went into battle, waving their samurai swords at the head of their troops. They were both killed, and Nogi made it known he intended to commit suicide. Meiji, to whom he was devoted, forbade him to do so. "As long as I am alive," he told Nogi, "you must remain alive also."

General Nogi became a figure in the world press, as did Admiral Togo. *The Times* waxed lyrical about Japan's final victory: "The attitude of the Japanese people in the presence of this epoch-making triumph is a sight for men and gods," it wrote on June 7, 1905. "No noisy and vulgar clamour, no self-laudation, no triumph over a fallen enemy, but deep thankfulness, calm satisfaction, and once more reference of the cause of victory to the illustrious virtues of the Emperor of Japan."

The British press had another reason for being blatantly pro-Japanese: the new Japanese navy was largely the product of British engineers, naval dockyards and Royal Navy advisers and instructors. When Admiral Togo, the "father of the Japanese navy," virtually wiped out the relieving Russian fleet at Tsushima in the most decisive naval encounter of modern times, he became, overnight, the leading authority on modern naval warfare, and a hero to the British.

The Treaty of Portsmouth (New Hampshire) gave Japan uncontested rights over Korea and territorial rights in Manchuria, which she was this time determined to preserve. The new South Manchuria Railway Company, soon to become a tentacular industrial and trading corporation along the lines of the old British East India Company, was protected by a permanent force of Japanese troops stationed in Manchuria known as the Kwangtung Army.

While Japanese politicians inflamed public opinion, claiming that Japan should have gained more from the war, including a Russian indemnity, the emperor knew that the war's end, and the providential American peacemaking role between Japan and Russia, had come not a moment too soon: once more, Japan was impoverished, almost bankrupted by the costly series of campaigns on land and sea and by the invasion of Manchuria. It was the first time an Asian country had decisively beaten a major Western power, but the cost, in terms of casualties and sheer financial deficit, had been enormous.

It is impossible to overestimate the impact of the Japanese victory over the Russian giant on the Japanese psyche: the *bushido* qualities of its army and navy, the stories of legendary heroism in the face of overwhelming odds told and retold in the Japanese press and history books, the new self-confidence and pride and, above all, the image of the emperor Meiji himself as a godlike commander, influenced Japanese from all walks of life. Army and navy careers became more sought after than ever, and for the first time began attracting youngsters from the lower middle class and the peasantry; Japan's superiority over one of the largest powers on earth, now made evident, encouraged notions of Japan's "civilizing mission" in the rest of Asia.

Two Japanese officers were, in different ways, indelibly marked by the Russo-Japanese War: aboard the *Nisshin,* one of Admiral Togo's warships, a young naval officer called Isoroku Yamamoto, a tough, humorous runt of a man, had two fingers amputated and was left with scars all over his body when one of the guns aboard his warship misfired, its recoil all but killing him. In later years Admiral Yamamoto, architect of Pearl Harbor and, for all that, one of the sanest, most levelheaded, farsighted and likable members of the Japanese armed services oligarchy, was to brag that he had been wounded by a Russian shell. His early experience as an admiring disciple of Admiral Togo made him conscious of the need for surprise in battle and for ultramodern weaponry—the new Japanese torpedo boats had played a determining role in the Russian defeat.

The war made a similar impact on another young officer, Hideki Tojo, who was too young to see active service in it (when it started he was still a student at the Military Academy), but owed his lightning promotion to the vacancies resulting from Japan's severe casualties. All his life, until he was hanged as a war criminal in 1948, Tojo was to remember the lessons of the Russo-Japanese War, especially the way a smaller power, provided it was bold and unscrupulous and sufficiently organized, could humiliate a giant empire.

Hirohito was only four at the time of the Russo-Japanese War, a lonely, introspective boy with none of the normal comforts of a family life. He was already surrounded by adults and formal priests and courtiers inculcating in him the notion that as a future "living God" he was different from all others. Most of his childhood companions were older, already highly motivated nationalists, fully aware of the unfolding drama at sea and on the Manchurian battlefields, hero-worshiping the emperor's victorious generals and admirals, whom they were occasionally able to glimpse at close quarters. Perhaps inevitably, given the jingoistic climate brought about by the war and its aftermath, they too grew up thinking that Japan not only had a special role to play, but was uniquely qualified to lead the Asian world because of the superior quality of its armed forces.

Significantly, Hirohito's first public appearance, at Emperor Meiji's side, in 1905, at the Tokyo railway station (to greet Prince Arthur of Connaught, come to invest Emperor Meiji with the Order of the Garter), was in the uniform of a Japanese army officer.

It was in the imperial tradition for the heir to the throne to be brought up by outsiders. Originally this had been inspired by security reasons, and the custom remained: it was supposed to instill toughness and guard against excessive sycophancy. At the age of only seventy days, Hirohito was taken away from his mother and brought up by a series of wet nurses in the house of a retired admiral, Count Kawamura. The count took his duties seriously. He consulted an English governess, in the employ of another princely family, who had three basic rules for successful child-rearing: inducing in her charge "an independent spirit, a sympathetic heart and a sentiment of gratitude."

Count Kawamura was seventy at the time, a traditionalist who was determined to impart, also, a "dauntless spirit to withstand all hardships" and to eradicate "traces of arrogance and egotism." Once during dinner the tiny Hirohito threw a tantrum. He flung down his chopsticks and said, "I won't eat that." He was reprimanded by the Count, who said sternly, "You don't have to eat, but you will be served no more food." Hirohito quietly sobbed, then said, "in a subdued voice, 'I'll eat it, I'll eat it.' " Court Chamberlain Osanaga Kanroji wrote that when Kawamura saw him eating the food he had rejected, "with his chubby fingers grasping the chopsticks, he turned his face to one side and wept."

Hirohito was not quite four years old when the count died (in 1904). He returned to the Akasaka Palace, where his father, the crown prince, lived, but not to the bosom of his family. In a separate small house he was surrounded by chamberlains and courtiers, and attended a special "imperial" kindergarten with princely children of his own age. The school was run by a former teacher of the Peers' School who was something of a martinet. Another teacher, Tsuchiya, though also a strict disciplinarian, was deeply interested in marine life and plants, and Hirohito's lifelong passion for marine biology originated with after-school sessions with him. Another kindergarten teacher was Mrs. Takako Suzuki, a naval officer's wife whose husband, many years later, was to become Hirohito's last wartime prime minister.

The tough kindergarten routine, with plenty of homework and calligraphy lessons, included one monthly outing outside the palace. Invariably, Hirohito chose to visit the Ueno Park zoo. But even here he was not allowed to behave like ordinary children, but was endlessly lectured on animal life by the zoo superintendent. In his portrait of young Hirohito the court diarist Osanaga Kanroji recalls that the sight of a newly captured badger, trembling with fear in its small cage, depressed the small boy almost to tears. "I don't want to look at it any more," he wailed. "I want to go home."*

"Home" was precisely what he lacked: Hirohito and his younger brother, Prince Chichibu, one year his junior, living in a separate compound (where they shared the same room) saw their mother only once a week, their father much less often. Life was hard for Hirohito, harder than for Chichibu, an athletic extrovert, who rapidly became

---

*Osanaga Kanroji, *Hirohito: An Intimate Portrait of the Japanese Emperor* (Los Angeles: Gateway Publishers, 1975).

the natural leader of the kindergarten group. Hirohito was isolated from the other children, partly because of his status as future emperor and "living God," but also because of his physical disabilities: he walked with a slight shuffle, a hereditary defect he had inherited from his grandfather, had poor posture (a curved spine), suffered from myopia (but was denied glasses for several months because "an emperor does not wear spectacles"), and was generally weaker, smaller and less aggressive than other children of his own age. He was also exceedingly clumsy, and Chichibu made fun of him. "When Hiro falls down," he said, "he doesn't know how to get up." Needless to say, Kanroji makes no mention of sibling rivalry (though there is evidence of this in other court writings), painting instead an idyllic and somewhat false picture of Hirohito "clutching Chichibu's hand or looking at picture books with him." The situation did not improve when a second younger brother, Prince Takamatsu, joined them, for he too was livelier and more outgoing than Hirohito. One of Hirohito's few surviving contemporaries, Torahiko Nagazumi, recalls that the emperor was far more introspective than his two "lively" brothers, but always, in childish war games played out in the Hayama Palace gardens, insisted on being "the commander in chief." "Chichibu," he says, "was almost always the commander of Hirohito's advance guard, and the two brothers were always on the same side, for Chichibu never wanted to play at being 'the enemy.' " Hirohito was not entirely insulated by his rank from the rough-and-tumble of war games. Nagazumi recalls that his own father told him: "If you wrestle with Hirohito, don't lose on purpose simply because he is going to be the emperor one day."

But Hirohito was denied small pleasures accessible to others: his tutor saw to it, for example, that he did not jump off walls, for fear of his breaking a royal leg. At a ridiculously early age, Hirohito was imbued with a sense of gravity—a melancholy recognition of his inherent differentness. There were a few minor compensations: he could assume responsibility for the childish misdemeanors of his companions (like making holes in paper screens) without being punished.

So determined is Kanroji, in his memoirs, to make Hirohito a paragon of all the virtues that when he admits to the prince's clumsiness, one infers that Hirohito must have been very clumsy indeed. The prince also had to submit to grim routines designed to improve his posture and his eyesight. For hours on end he was made to stare into space. Some trees were cut down so that he could look at the distant Shinagawa coastline—concentrating on distant objects was supposed to cure myopia. He was also made to sit for hours at a time in a specially designed chair, grasping handles on either side to keep his spine erect, with a reading stand fourteen inches from his eyes—all in a vain attempt to improve his posture.

The imperial court under the great Meiji was a strange place to grow up in: the atmosphere—despite the pace of change outside the palace—remained medieval, something from an epic Kurosawa film. The emperor himself, a thickset, commanding figure with a short beard, piercing eyes and, very probably, a clubfoot, was hardly the epitome of the jolly, indulgent grandfather; though Hirohito saw him more often than he saw his own father, Crown Prince Yoshihito (later Emperor Taisho), Emperor Meiji scarcely lavished any affection on the small boy.

Hirohito, Kanroji wrote, "snuggled up to Emperor Meiji and called him granddaddy," but Meiji, "because of his position as Emperor, and because of the nature of his temperament, showed his affection only by smiling at the little prince." Meiji behaved in exactly the same way toward his son. At the Japanese court, the notion that children should be seen and not heard was even more prevalent than in upper-class Victorian Britain. Kanroji wrote that Meiji saw his son Prince Yoshihito "only on formal occasions," when the crown prince would "bow low," while Meiji, "though nodding in acknowledgment, would remain silent throughout the audience." Though Kanroji was Prince Yoshihito's constant childhood companion, the only time, he recalls, that Emperor Meiji actually spoke to them was during archery practice along a palace corridor. Meiji came across the two boys, and, unobserved, watched them. After a particularly good hit, he boomed, "Excellent!" The boys turned, bowed low, and went on with their practice; Emperor Meiji stayed to watch, shouting "Good . . . excellent!" whenever they scored a bull's-eye.

Hirohito did not get even that small measure of encouragement from his own father. Kanroji hardly mentions him, and with good reason: Crown Prince Yoshihito was almost never there, and when he was, he was prone to fits of drinking and debauchery, neglecting his family for days on end. He hated Tokyo in the winter, and sought warmth elsewhere. Even by the standards of Japan, where husbands tend to live their own lives and wives (especially in those prewar days) are confined to rigid domesticity, Crown Prince Yoshihito behaved exceptionally badly. What young Hirohito did see of court ways left an indelible mark on him: drunkenness was common, and Hirohito, early on, became a teetotaler. Both his grandfather and his father were promiscuous; Hirohito, from adolescence, was prim, monogamous and puritanical.

Emperor Meiji himself remained, in his habits, a profoundly conservative Japanese noble lord, enjoying vintage claret, the writing of poetry and beautiful women, in that order. A dozen concubines, euphemistically termed ladies-in-waiting, nightly awaited the drop of the imperial handkerchief at their feet to follow him into his quarters, out of bounds to all but a handful of specially chosen page boys and furnished in the Japanese style. Meiji slept, however, not on a tatami mat but in a comfortable Western-style bed. He also mastered the mysteries of capitalism with remarkable ease. Under Meiji, the Mitsuis, Sumitomos and Iwasakis (of Mitsubishi fame) became familiar figures at court, and as these founder members of the zaibatsu, the huge industrial conglomerates that were soon to dominate Japan economically, grew, so did the imperial fortune.

Kanroji's portrait of Meiji is that of a roistering extrovert with Falstaffian appetites, surrounded by drunken cronies. He describes a marathon drinking bout the emperor indulged in with his palace chamberlains, ending with Meiji ordering a horse to be brought and telling one of his drinking companions to mount it. "No matter how many times the tipsy chamberlain tried, he would invariably slip down from the saddle, causing Emperor Meiji to roar with laughter. Apparently Emperor Meiji too sometimes got so intoxicated that he was unable to return to his palace on horseback."

Drunkenness was as excusable then as it is now in Japanese society, and the impression Kanroji conveys of palace life in the Meiji era is of a perpetual overhanging alcoholic haze. Chamberlains sent on errands by the emperor would return intoxicated, but "Emperor Meiji would listen to them with a smile on his face, with never a rebuke for their breach of etiquette."

Crown Prince Yoshihito introduced Hirohito to drink at the age of five, with traumatic results: he plied his son with sake, forcing him to drink large quantities and respond to toasts, until the obedient boy keeled over in a drunken stupor. Hirohito never forgot the humiliation, or the prodigious hangover that followed. From that day on, he later told his court, he never touched alcohol in any form.

Like his contemporary, the Prince of Wales who later became Edward VII, Yoshihito led a futile existence in the shadow of a glorious parent. He developed a passion for uniforms, especially the "Death's Head" German Uhlan variety, waxed his mustache, like Kaiser Wilhelm, and was determined to be "modern," which meant, in practice, collecting Impressionists and building himself a miniature replica of Versailles, the Akasaka Palace, which was crammed with glittering candelabra and neo–Louis XV brocaded furniture. Meiji found it in atrocious taste, and went there only once.

For all his outward "modernism," Crown Prince Yoshihito had bowed to his father's wishes, obediently marrying the emperor's choice, a girl from the aristocratic Fujiwara clan, a princely family that had provided brides for the imperial family for centuries. Princess Sadako was intelligent and beautiful, and had been groomed since childhood for such a marriage. She was only sixteen when Hirohito was born on April 29, 1901—the first Japanese emperor since 1758 not to be born of an imperial concubine. In his early childhood she played almost no part, for she was seldom allowed to see him.

The surrogate for Hirohito's father—and mother—was General Nogi, the war hero, whom Meiji appointed head of the Peers' School. He became, to all intents and purposes, Hirohito's tutor. Nogi not only epitomized the old-fashioned samurai virtues but was also that rare breed in Japan—a soldier who was also an intellectual, a skilled calligraphist, a bonsai (miniature tree) expert and a moralist. It was Nogi who instilled in young Hirohito the notion that there was nothing—neither physical weakness nor inherent clumsiness and faulty coordination—that could not be overcome through the assertion of will and practice. Because he worshiped Nogi and desperately sought his approval, Hirohito became, from the age of ten onward, a competent athlete, a strong swimmer, an above-average golfer and sumo wrestler. He also took lessons in fencing—a sport that had cost Nogi an eye in his youth—and embarked on a grueling routine of cold showers, exhausting physical training, and long hours of study. Nogi succeeded in bringing young Hirohito out of his shell, getting rid, as he put it, of his "hunchback mentality."

He also acquired something of Nogi's puritanical contempt for the pleasures of the flesh as well as his sense of thrift. Nogi's house, still standing in central Tokyo and surrounded on all sides by high-rise offices and apartment houses, is a plain two-story wooden building looking very much like a small Japanese farmhouse. Now a shrine and little-known museum, it is one of the few houses in the Aoyama district of Tokyo spared by wartime B-29 bombing; it reflects the general's taste for plain living, its only extravagance being its huge stables, for Nogi was a great horseman and lavished considerable care on his thoroughbreds. Otherwise his life-style was unassuming, almost parsimonious. One of his "house rules" was: Be ashamed of torn clothes, never of patched ones. It was a lesson Hirohito was to remember all his life. During his years at the Peers' School, Nogi made him wear coarse cotton underwear and kimonos—he never knew the touch of silk next to his skin. Hirohito started hoarding things, using his pencils till they were too small to hold, erasers till they were the size of a pea.

In the normal course of events, Hirohito's younger brother Prince Chichibu would have become Nogi's favorite. Handsome, bright, athletic, he was clearly more of a natural leader than Hirohito. But Nogi, as a soldier, believed that Hirohito would improve through emulation, and it was the brothers' almost pathetic desire to please their foster father that caused Hirohito to shed some of his inhibitions, though he remained withdrawn, a listener rather than a speechmaker, a strangely inscrutable child.

In 1911 Emperor Meiji chose Nogi as his representative to attend the coronation of King George V. Nogi absented himself for several months, and it was during this period that Emperor Meiji's cancer took a fatal turn, leading to his death on July 29, 1912, at the early age of fifty-nine.

Kanroji wrote that Hirohito, in a nightmare, had a premonition of his grandfather's death. He was to have a far more traumatic experience on the day of his grandfather's funeral, which took place after six weeks of official mourning.

On the eve of the funeral Hirohito had been summoned to General Nogi's study at the Peers' School. "I am not dissatisfied with your progress while I have been away," he told Hirohito, "but I ask you to study harder. You are now the crown prince, the youngest of the officers of the Army and Navy, and the future commander of the nation. I beg you to attend to your military duties, and to take care of your health, no matter how busy you are. Please remember that my physical presence is not necessary for me to be with you in your work. I shall always be watching you and your welfare will always be my concern. Work hard, for your sake and the sake of Japan." They bowed to each other and Hirohito left the room.

The following morning, while Japanese guns boomed their salute to the dead emperor, General Nogi and his wife bathed, dressed themselves in white kimonos, and solemnly bowed to an autographed portrait of Emperor Meiji. Countess Nogi died first, cutting her throat with a razor-sharp dagger. Nogi himself then committed ritual *seppuku,* or disembowelment, with an equally sharp short sword. In a note, he called on every patriotic Japanese to abide by the ancient Japanese virtues, deploring the current laissez-faire in morals. He had fulfilled his pledge to the emperor made on the battlefield after his two sons' deaths, in a way that ensured his place in history.

The impact on Hirohito, aged twelve, can only be imagined: Nogi had been the object of his admiration as well as the father figure he had craved in the absence of his own, despised father.

Outwardly, he showed an almost frightening composure on learning the news. "Japan has suffered a regrettable loss," he said, with no apparent emotion.

CHAPTER TWO

Emperor Meiji's death meant little immediate alteration to Hirohito's daily routine, but considerable change in the attitudes of those around him. He was now officially crown prince, with a commission in both the army and navy, and he wore his new uniforms proudly. He now had a room to himself. More important still, his younger brothers were compelled to treat him with the respect due to a future "living God." But he continued to attend the Peers' School for nearly two more years, walking to it from the palace with his brothers every morning unless it rained, when he was allowed to take a carriage. Later, a room in his father's Akasaka Palace was turned into a schoolroom and he acquired a set of private tutors, selected for him by palace chamberlains with his father's approbation.

The new overall supervisor of Hirohito's studies was Admiral Heihachiro Togo, who, like Nogi, was a hero of the Russo-Japanese War. But Togo was totally unlike Nogi, and there was no rapport between him and the crown prince. The admiral had been a bold naval strategist and an undoubted leader of men. In everyday life, however, he was surprisingly uninspiring, with none of Nogi's mystical samurai fervor—a run-of-the-mill, pleasure-loving officer whose success had infuriated several navy colleagues. Nogi's life-style had been almost obsessively austere. Togo was a prodigious (and messy) eater, something that devalued him in Hirohito's eyes. It was impossible for Hirohito not to contrast his new teacher's ordinariness (and relative lack of interest in Japan's hegemony over Asia) with the dead Nogi's outstanding virtues.

Hirohito's tutors were drawn from the cream of Japan's academic world. So awed were they by the honor conferred on them that they failed to make the most of their opportunities. Hirohito's French teacher, for example, could never bring himself to correct any of his royal pupil's faults, so Hirohito's knowledge of French would never compare, in later life, with that of Prince Chichibu, who spoke the language almost flawlessly. Hirohito's ethics teacher, Dr. Jugo Sugiura, who had a degree in chemistry from London University, proved to be a very odd choice indeed. Sugiura's lectures were a hodgepodge of Shintoist superstitions and clichés about Japanese national virtues. A great believer in the superiority of the Aryan race, he viewed the Japanese as the Aryans of Asia, racially far superior to the "degenerate Chinese," but Japan, he cautioned, should be wary of European ways, even those of "Aryan" nations, for in every respect the Japanese way of life was better—even its religion was superior to any other. Sugiura also had the disconcerting habit of bursting into occasional song, quoting from classical Noh plays or Chinese opera, to make his point. He sang atrociously, but seemed unaware of this. Hirohito observed, patiently but listlessly. It would have been bad form to ask his chamberlains to replace any of the tutors they had chosen for him—loss of face for them and the tutors alike. But their uninspiring, excessively formal relations with their royal pupil had the effect of inhibiting him even further.

The teachings of Isaburo Wada, a graduate of Johns Hopkins and MIT, provided something of an antidote to Sugiura's. He lectured on mechanics, aerodynamics, chemistry. The sessions would have been even more interesting to Hirohito had they taken place in a workshop or laboratory. But protocol required that teacher and pupil face each other across a tatami mat, rigidly motionless, with frequent bows and expressions of mutual respect.

The teacher who made the greatest impact on Hirohito was Dr. Hirotaro Hattori, who instructed him in natural science and biology. Hirohito did voice the mildest of complaints to his chamberlains that most of his lecturers were as bland as *jagaimo,* the potatoes recently introduced into Japan from the West, but Hattori was different. A believer in teaching by doing, he took Hirohito out to the country on field trips, and when Hirohito objected to the cortege of chamberlains and palace hangers-on trailing behind him and his teacher wherever they went, Hattori not only reduced the size of the party but started taking Hirohito on boat trips in fishing vessels too small to accommodate any officials at all. Hirohito was by this time a strong swimmer, and when Hattori hired a couple of pearl divers to collect underwater specimens, Hirohito joined them, insisting on bringing in his share. These excursions mostly took place at Hayama, the seaside resort where the imperial family owned a secluded house that was more cottage than palace. Hattori later became Hirohito's scientific aide, and his entire life was spent in the emperor's service, looking after his laboratory in later years.

In his own memoirs, Prince Chichibu recalled that Hirohito, even as a small boy, always had a meticulous collector's approach to things. Whereas Chichibu had little patience, Hirohito, from the age of ten, kept a careful record of his own collections of butterflies, insects and wildflowers. They have been preserved, dated and signed in his neat hand, and his contribution to marine biology, though later exaggerated by hagiographers, was real enough: at the age of seventeen, at Numazu, Hirohito wandered down to the beach after a storm to collect shellfish and spotted a red prawn, about eight centimeters long. Back in his villa, he pored over reference books, and was intrigued to discover that his find was not catalogued in any of them. This was the famous *Sympathiphae imperialis,* whose identification caused a stir when it was revealed to the academic world in 1919. The discovery filled Hirohito with pride, and turned him into a lifelong marine biologist. A special boat was built for him, and trawling for specimens became not just a hobby but a passion. He never duplicated his early success, though he did find several rare specimens of shellfish, including the *Genebis argenteonitens,* off the coast at Hayama.

Hirohito's passion for invertebrate specimens may have reflected his introspection, aloofness and inhibitions. Some of the court chamberlains deplored in private the fact that he was not more interested in manlier sports like hunting, and some army generals were bold enough to draw Emperor Taisho's attention to the crown prince's outlandish pastime. They could hardly complain, however, about the fact that Hirohito also showed, as an adolescent, an almost equally passionate interest in military history. Moreover, on one occasion, he satisfied another of Emperor Taisho's requirements. Sexual puritanism plays no part in the *bushido* creed, and Taisho dispatched one of his young concubines to Hirohito's quarters, who reported back that the fifteen-year-old crown prince had been at first somewhat bewildered, but had displayed a certain scientific curiosity in sex, leading in time to a perfectly normal conclusion. The emperor was relieved that his eldest son, for all his other curious pleasures, was also capable of indulging in what was, in his own case, an almost full-time occupation. This, Hirohito's first sexual experience, did not stimulate a consuming interest in sex. Instead, in his performance with the gifted concubine, he was apparently an obedient adolescent once again bowing to imposed traditions.

While Hirohito listened to boring lectures, trawled for shellfish and learned about the Napoleonic wars, Japan was experiencing the consequences of her new status as a major power. Emperor Taisho, by temperament, was an interventionist, with a marked pro-German bias, blissfully unaware of Kaiser Wilhelm's own views about the "yellow peril." World War I, however, saw Japan side with Britain, France and Russia, with Taisho reluctantly bowing to his advisers' arguments that Japan's interests, strategic and financial, were better served by this alliance.

The real reason, of course, was China, still neutral, though she too was later to enter the war against Germany. Japan, without waiting for Allied approval, invaded the German concession of Tsingtao, on the Chinese coast, and also occupied the tiny Pacific island of Yap, a German colony. As a commissioned officer in both the army and the navy, and as crown prince, Hirohito was regularly briefed on international affairs, and Japan's reasons for entering the war were made clear to him.

Japan's actual fighting contribution to the war was negligible: the Japanese navy patrolled the Mediterranean, and "protected" Hong Kong and Britain's Shanghai concession. But Japan exacted a huge price in return. Her Twenty-one Demands, submitted to China's new president, Yüan Shi-k'ai, in 1915, amounted to formal Japanese overlordship over the whole of China. In addition to increased territorial concessions in Shantung Province and in Manchuria, on ninety-nine-year leases, Japan demanded that China formally pledge she would not give away any more concessions to any other power, and would not

only turn to Japan for economic development in Manchuria and Tsingtao, but also make Japan her exclusive banker for any future loans. A
further set of demands, which Japan insisted the Chinese keep secret
(though they were immediately and deliberately leaked to the press in
Peking by the indignant Chinese president), required Peking to use
Japanese technical advisers for all its major industrial and armaments
projects, to grant Japan the monopoly to build all railways in China, to
buy 50 percent of its military supplies from Japan, and to allow Japanese
advisers to play a special role in Chinese political affairs.

Hirohito was only fifteen when these demands were made, and
of course had no responsibility for them. His tutors presented them
in the most favorable light, arguing that Japan was, geographically
and historically, destined to play the part of China's "big brother."
Yüan Shi-k'ai, China's "strong man," was obliged to accept them
under duress. After the war, thanks largely to British and U.S. pressure at the Versailles Conference, all but the Tsingtao and Manchurian
clauses were dropped.

The Twenty-one Demands were, however, a watershed, not only
in Sino-Japanese but in U.S.-Japanese relations: in American eyes, as
early as 1915, the image of "gallant little Japan" began to be replaced
by a perception of Japan as a bullying, predatory nation.

The demands also contributed to Japan's rising militarism, for they
put into concrete form the growing nationalism of the new generation
of officers who had been fed on the mystique of the Russo-Japanese
War. Of all its clauses, it was the Manchuria issue that mattered most.
The Russo-Japanese War had wrested concessions in Manchuria from
Russia that most nationalistic Japanese believed had not been sufficient. Among Hirohito's small group of aristocratic "uncles," most of
them career officers in the army and navy who endorsed the views of
the militarists and briefed him about Japan's new role in Asia, Manchuria was regarded as a legitimate prize—not just the existing concessions, but the entire province. Bound up with the Manchurian issue
was the whole question of Communist Russia, for with the 1917
October Revolution Russia's presence in Manchuria, even in a reduced form, took on a completely new dimension and was seen as a
completely new threat. Among Hirohito's aristocratic coterie, fear of
Communism, and hatred of all left-wing organizations, dominated.
The almost irrational fear that Communism might spread like a cancer-

ous growth throughout Asia afflicted the young Hirohito as much as it did his companions.

The other major event taking place during Hirohito's adolescence was the growing confrontation between the Choshu and Satsuma clans. Both had helped rid the imperial dynasty of the shoguns. Now both were jostling for power, and it was proof of Japan's transformation into a modern nation-state that their quarrel was resolved in a series of political confrontations, rather than, as in the past, open warfare. One clan issue, however—the choice of Hirohito's bride— was settled only after a series of court intrigues reminiscent of medieval times, but harnessing the forces of the "new" Japan—the media, the political parties and even the underworld—with Hirohito a vitally concerned but passive spectator.

One of the few survivors of the glorious Meiji era was the former army chief of staff, General Aritomo Yamagata. This brutal but politically astute samurai had been the real founder of the modern Japanese army that had crushed the Russians in 1905. He had become a *genro*, a permanent personal counselor, to Emperor Taisho—and like other *genro*, past and present, his aim had been not only to advise the throne, but also to advance the fortunes of his clan and put his own nominees in key positions. Another *genro*, Prince Kinmochi Saionji, was to outlast him, providing Hirohito with advice, often neglected, right up to his death in 1940.

Saionji—a leader of the Satsuma clan—and Yamagata between them manipulated not only prime ministerships (they designated likely candidates to the emperor, who was in theory bound to abide by their advice) but also senior military commands. Yamagata first realized that his supremacy was being challenged when a non-Choshu appointee, just before World War I, reduced the size of the army by two divisions to cut defense expenditure. In the confused infighting that followed, the cuts were restored, but transferred to the navy. Yamagata was not pleased, for the navy was dominated by Satsuma- clan appointees.

Premierships continued to change hands almost with the frequency of those in postwar Italy, with real power in the hands of the *genro*, but there were further signs of Yamagata's waning influence: in 1916, following the Twenty-one Demands, Japan moved into southern Manchuria, and Yamagata, a cautious tactician, urged moderation. He was

well aware that the Western powers saw in Japan an aggressive, bullying nation. But while Yamagata was establishing cordial relations with
the Chinese warlord of the north, the Manchu general Chang Tso-lin,
whose "capital" was Mukden, and promising him Japan's support,
other Japanese "interventionists," encouraged by the emperor, were
fomenting uprisings in Mongolia and were determined to crush
Chang Tso-lin. The Manchu warlord narrowly escaped a Japanese
assassination trap in Mukden, and rallied his troops to oust the Japanese from Mongolia.

This confused, unedifying episode showed how directionless
Japan's foreign policy had become; the reason, though never openly
referred to in the Japanese press, and only discussed in hushed voices
elsewhere, was that Emperor Taisho was becoming, by fits and starts,
increasingly eccentric, unstable and unfit to rule.

It was a secret shared by the *genro,* the empress and Hirohito himself, though he never mentioned it, even to his closest adolescent
friends. It explained the growing contempt shown by Yamagata for
the emperor, contrasting him to his legendary father. On good days,
as Saionji remembered later, Taisho was capable of brilliance and
"shrewd decision-making at least as remarkable as that of Meiji himself." He was sexually promiscuous, and his chamberlains had great
difficulty keeping track of his liaisons with various concubines (for
each sexual encounter was supposed to be recorded in a kind of
imperial studbook so that concubines' pregnancies could be properly
registered), but this was not regarded as a major flaw in an emperor's
character. What was embarrassing was his erratic behavior, so much
so that the *genro* were reluctant to let him appear in public at all. On
one occasion, during a military parade, he slashed at soldiers with a
riding crop, then embraced an officer, ordered another soldier to
unpack his gear, and then insisted on repacking it himself. At a ceremonial opening of the Diet (the parliamentary system was not yet
based on universal suffrage—only some three million property own-
ers could vote) in 1915, he rolled up his prepared speech and peered
quizzically at the Diet members, as through a telescope. What might
have passed for mild eccentricity in any other country was unacceptable in Japan, where the "divine" emperor's every gesture was closely
observed.

Inevitably, as Emperor Taisho's condition (variously thought to have been due to a stroke or an undiagnosed cerebral hemorrhage, but probably stemming from the aftereffects of meningitis in childhood) deteriorated, the *genro* assumed increasing power, and so did the empress, who, like any loyal Japanese wife, rallied to her husband in his hour of need, overlooking his scandalous past treatment of her. Such was the climate at court as Hirohito gradually emerged from adolescence to manhood. It was clear to both the empress and the *genro* that, with the emperor unlikely to recover, his eldest son would have to bear the de facto burden of office far earlier than expected. This meant that the choice of a wife assumed even more importance than usual. Hirohito was having adulthood thrust on him whether he liked it or not. Not for him the carefree bachelorhood of his princely friends and relatives. It would have been unthinkable for him to resist moves to marry him off, for both his father and grandfather had unquestioningly accepted the wedding arrangements made for them, aware they were vital to the continued survival of the dynasty. Their acceptance of their brides was probably conditioned by the awareness that marriage had nothing to do with monogamy. Hirohito's mother, Empress Sadako, who herself had married Taisho without ever setting eyes on him, was a levelheaded, "modern" woman, who wanted to let her son have at least a partial say in the matter. The court, and the *genro,* drew up a list of suitable girls, and she invited them to tea ceremonies, with Hirohito observing them unseen, like Polonius behind an arras.

There were some charming, good-looking girls from the leading Choshu, Satsuma and Fushimi families, including one remarkable princess who later was to marry a member of the Korean royal family, and later still devote her twilight years to a charitable foundation for Korean-Japanese orphans, but Hirohito, surprisingly, chose none of the prettier ones. Instead, he asked his mother to select Nagako, a bright but certainly not beautiful girl whom he had known since childhood—a short, squat, sturdy fourteen-year-old, of impeccable but impoverished lineage.

She was the daughter of Prince Kuni, of the Fushimi house, whose family had intermarried with emperors for centuries. Prince Kuni's wife was a member of the Satsuma clan, and he had nineteen offspring in all, thirteen of them (but not Nagako) the sons and daughters of concubines. Professor Sugiura, Hirohito's ethics lecturer, who also taught at the girls' wing of the Peers' School, where she was a pupil, had spotted her as a possible candidate, and was delighted with his royal pupil's choice.

It also pleased the empress, who was finding the elderly *genro* Yamagata increasingly overbearing, but it infuriated the crotchety general, who had been convinced that the new empress would be a Choshu, and needed a representative of his clan at the highest pinnacle of the Court in order to restore its fortunes. At first, he extended his congratulations to Prince Kuni on the imperial choice. In the wings, he started to plot to have the betrothal annulled, and in the process enlisted the support of Baron Nakamura, also a Choshu, and minister of the Imperial Household.

The suspense lasted six years, and during that time Nagako and Hirohito met only nine times, always very briefly. The first meeting took place shortly after the fateful tea ceremony. The two adolescents were allowed to take a walk in the palace grounds alone, but what might have been a romantic moment was marred by a torrential downpour. The second meeting, three weeks later, was for a formal betrothal photograph duly published in the press. Nagako by this time had been removed from school, subjected to grueling medical examinations, and set up in a separate pavilion on the grounds of her father's house, where, with seventeen assorted tutors and two adolescent companions, she was to remain until marriage, carefully groomed by the tutors and her solicitous father to fulfill her duties as an empress. She studied English, French and international relations under special tutors, and there were courses on the history of Japan and its relations with Europe. The betrothal was a long one, as it was intended to be, for only if Emperor Taisho's health took a dramatic turn for the worse would it be necessary for Hirohito to ensure that he could sire an heir to the throne.

Yamagata's offensive, four years after the betrothal, was both unexpected and masterly. He was eighty-five by now, but shrewdly used a thoroughly modern medium: the press. In a medical journal, a Japanese doctor and expert on heredity wrote a learned article on the transmission of color blindness from one generation to the next, and the need to reform the conscription law to exclude such sufferers from military service. But the article also examined color blindness from the vantage point of one of Japan's best-known aristocratic families, the Shimazu. It so happened that, on her mother's side, Nagako was herself a Shimazu.

Hardly coincidentally, the former surgeon general of the Japanese army, who happened to be Yamagata's personal physician, drew the general's attention to the article, and to evidence of color blindness in the Shimazu family. While on the face of it color blindness might not appear to be a serious defect, even in empresses, the issue was an important one, for every male member of the imperial family was expected to enter the armed forces. Showing every sign of hypocritical distress, and listening only to his soldier's conscience, Yamagata, as the oldest living *genro,* found it impossible to ignore this warning, which implied that the emperor's heirs might themselves be born with such an affliction. He asked a group of leading Japanese specialists to study the article and comment on it. When they decided it was scientifically sound, Yamagata approached his Choshu clansmen, Baron Nakamura, the Imperial Household minister, and the prime minister, Takashi Hara, and asked them for their advice.

Hara's reaction was that the matter must be hushed up at all costs: the imperial family could not be shown to have made a mistaken choice, for this in itself was an act of lèse-majesté. Precisely, said Yamagata. That was why he proposed confronting Nagako's father with the evidence, to ask him to cancel the engagement. The aged Prince Fushimi was cajoled into the role of go-between, for the Choshu clansmen believed it would be unthinkable for Prince Kuni to go against the wishes of his eminent father.

They were wrong. The meeting degenerated into a noisy family row. "Do you come from the Empress?" Prince Kuni shouted. "Do *they* want the engagement annulled?" Reminding his father that it was the empress, and Hirohito himself, who had selected his daughter, Kuni told Fushimi it was up to them to break off the match, but if they did, the affront was such he would kill both his daughter and himself.

Kuni began his own counteroffensive: first, he enlisted the support of Professor Sugiura. Sugiura assured him that breaking off the engagement would be a breach of ethics. As one of Nagako's "discoverers," Sugiura had a vested interest in the match. In turn, he threatened to commit *seppuku* if it was annulled.

Prince Kuni then wrote a personal letter to Emperor Taisho, whose affairs, by this time, were handled by the empress. This masterly document, eloquent yet restrained, made no direct allusion to Choshu clan intrigue. It enclosed a full report of cases of color blindness in his family, together with the findings of another group of specialists, contradicting the findings of the first. It came, like all correspondence for the emperor, into the hands of Baron Nakamura, who, before forwarding it, sent General Yamagata a copy.

At this stage the general made the fatal mistake of intervening directly. In a letter to Prince Kuni he clearly revealed his own dynastic ambitions.

> Of course Prince Kuni is right in insisting that the engagement should be adhered to once entered into. But it should not be forgotten that the engagement was arranged, so to speak, behind our back. If we had been advised of the negotiations, we would have been able to offer our humble point of view beforehand. We are deeply distressed at the way things have turned out.

After questioning the validity of the dissenting doctors' findings, he called for further medical expertise. "In the last part of your memorandum," he concluded,

> you say that if you were convinced that the marriage would be to the detriment of the Imperial Family you would gladly cancel your daughter's engagement to the Crown Prince. That is the best witness to your loyalty to the Imperial Family and the cancellation of the engagement would certainly bring public applause. Your reconsideration is sincerely urged.

At the same time, through intermediaries, he let Prince Kuni know that if he did the sensible thing, he would not regret it financially. Kuni, in turn, informed the empress of both the offer and the letter. Yamagata, realizing he was dealing with a wily adversary, put pressure on his clansman the Imperial Household minister to speed up preparations for a long trip that Hirohito, as crown prince, was due to make abroad, in order to get him out of the way.

This was the opportunity to bring the conflict out into the open. The Black Dragon Society, like other ultranationalist associations, was against any such foreign travel, on the grounds that exposure to unfamiliar customs might make the divine emperor-to-be look ridiculous, and Professor Sugiura, for all his lifelong devotion to ethics, was on intimate terms with Mitsuro Toyama, the Black Dragon leader and one of the most influential men in Japan. (Ultimately, it was Japan's underworld that was to rout the Choshu clan and enable Hirohito to wed the girl of his choice.)

Sugiura gave Toyama a detailed account of the crisis, and the underworld leader bristled with indignation at General Yamagata's "disrespect" for the emperor. He began mobilizing his considerable forces, planting a story in the Japanese press that "a delicate situation had arisen between the Imperial Family and the Imperial Household Minister."

There were also articles criticizing Hirohito's trip abroad, and such was the fear Toyama inspired that Choshu clansmen now mounted guard on General Yamagata's residence. Toyama's masterstroke was his use of the Tokyo mob on National Foundation Day, February 11, the commemoration of the founding of the imperial dynasty by Emperor Jimmu in 660 B.C. It was a national holiday (Empire Day) devoted to visits to shrines and prayers for the continued prosperity of Japan and the imperial family. Toyama's men distributed tracts supporting Hirohito's betrothal to Nagako; muscular young men paraded through the streets shouting "Death to Yamagata" and "Nakamura insults the emperor." Hara, the prime minister and leader of the Constitutionalist party, panicked: his worst fears had materialized. He told Nakamura to obtain an immediate and unequivocal ruling from the emperor. Did he intend to allow Hirohito to marry Nagako or not?

As a member of the Imperial Household later revealed, Nakamura bowed deeply toward Taisho and the empress and apologized for his failure to discover in time that there had been cases of color blindness in Princess Nagako's family. "Now that it is generally known," he asked, "what is Your Imperial Majesty's wish?"

Already briefed by his wife, the emperor said haltingly, "I hear that even science is fallible." The empress impatiently motioned Nakamura to rise and leave the room. That night the engagement was officially confirmed, and Nakamura resigned his post. *The Times* of London said that "a very remarkable demonstration of the power of public opinion" had been responsible for the betrothal. Nowhere was there a mention of Toyama or his men. The Black Dragon leader was surprisingly quick to call off his agitation against Hirohito's foreign trip. The British Foreign Office was now told that Crown Prince Hirohito would arrive in London a week ahead of schedule, and that his trip would last longer than originally planned, which caused the British Government considerable annoyance, since, then as now, state visits were a carefully prepared ritual brooking no last-minute changes, especially when Buckingham Palace was involved. The haste to get Hirohito out of the country as soon as possible, now that the drama was over, was probably due to anxiety that Toyama might change his mind, and not stay "bought."

Hirohito's behavior revealed a degree of self-control that was daunting in one so young: he had been kept informed of the crisis, but had refused to intervene, even though his own choice of bride was being criticized and his entire domestic future was at stake. Not once during the crisis did he contact Nagako, to reassure her or to express his confidence in its eventual outcome, nor did he visit her before leaving Japan.

CHAPTER THREE

Hirohito left Yokohama aboard the battleship *Katori* on March 3, 1921, with a handful of aides and officers in attendance. There were no important members of the Choshu clan among them. The escort vessel was the battleship *Kajima,* and both his future father-in-law, Prince Kuni, and Professor Sugiura, the matchmaker, were there to see him off.

For the first time he was free: protocol was less rigid, since most of his court attendants had been left behind. There were certain unavoidable rituals: Hirohito bowed in the direction of the coast, to the emperor and empress, and toward Mount Fuji, as the convoy left Yokohama Bay, and the ships shuddered to a standstill one afternoon while he performed Shinto rites on a religious anniversary day.

He wrestled, swam, played quoits, watched films and studied English and French. A firsthand account of the trip exists, written by two palace secretaries who accompanied Hirohito to Europe. Even in the leisurely annals of the imperial court their slow pace was something of a record, for their work did not appear for four years. It was not, however, altogether their fault. The first edition was entirely destroyed in the 1923 Tokyo earthquake.*

Their hagiographic prose is unintentionally comic, but this kind of flattery was de rigueur at the time:

> The subject itself is too great and august for our humble pen. We found him a prince worthy of our profound admiration and wholehearted devotion. His lofty and noble character, his manliness, his intellectual brilliance, his manifold interests, his sympathetic mentality, his wonderful memory, his fine sportsmanship, his most natural and unassuming character, his peace-loving disposition and charming demeanour, his strength of will; the happy union of all these fine qualities never elsewhere found together was revealed to us in full light. It occurred to us that such a joy and pleasure must by no means be monopolized, and that it was our bounden duty to share it with our fellow-countrymen by putting down in black and white the impressions of the most memorable tour ever recorded in the annals of our country.

Hirohito was also praised for his democratic spirit in ordering crew members to sit closer to him during film shows so they could get a better view. But an explosion aboard the *Kajima,* in which three stokers died, and another engine-room accident aboard Hirohito's own flagship, killing two sailors, are dismissed in the book in a couple of paragraphs, as a mildly irritating contretemps.

Hirohito stopped on his way to London at Hong Kong, Singapore, Colombo, Cairo, Malta and Gibraltar, receiving on the way the enthusiastic homage of overseas Japanese. Field Marshal Edmund Allenby threw a huge garden party for him in Cairo, which was disrupted by a violent sandstorm; in Malta he attended an Italian opera company's rendering of Verdi's *Otello,* and his first Western cultural experience left him somewhat baffled; in Gibraltar he went to the races, was asked to bet on a horse, and chose one at random, which won. Everywhere, he visited architectural sites, botanical gardens and natural history museums.

During the twenty-eight-day cruise, he learned and memorized

---

*The Crown Prince's European Tour, Osaka Mainichi, 1925.

phrases in French and English, rehearsed the speeches and toasts he would have to make, and perused the lists of foreign guests whose names he would be expected to recognize. With typical Japanese thoroughness, a diplomat from the embassy in London joined the crown prince in Gibraltar with an updated schedule. This was Shigeru Yoshida, later Japan's durable postwar prime minister. On arrival at Spithead, the Prince of Wales was there to greet Hirohito, and the Royal Navy put on an impressive display.

He was amazed by the spontaneous welcome he received in London. "Such a great crowd uncontrolled by the police," he remarked. He was also surprised, and delighted, by the informal cordiality shown by the British royal family.

This was the time of privileged Anglo-Japanese relations, and the links between the two navies were still strong. While Hirohito was a guest at Buckingham Palace, King George V entered his bedroom suite one evening, unannounced and half dressed. Hirohito was amazed that the king of England should wander the corridors of his palace unescorted, tieless, and clap him on the shoulder like an old friend. "I hope, me boy, that everyone is giving you everything you need," said the king. "I'll never forget how your grandfather treated me and me brother when we were in Yokohama. No geishas here, though, I'm afraid. Her Majesty wouldn't allow it."

The member of the British royal family he most admired, Hirohito told aides, was the Prince of Wales, for his "casual elegance" and relaxed approach to his duties. What impressed him was the prince's languid, mocking, aristocratic contempt for protocol, and his masterful handling of the more pompous palace officials.

Hirohito spent three days at Buckingham Palace, eight days in Chesterfield House as a guest of the government, and a week in Scotland shooting with the Duke of Atholl at Blair Castle. He was astonished to discover that the Duke and Duchess used their castle only for formal occasions, living almost servantless in a nearby cottage, and that the hundreds of servants waiting on them and organizing the shoots were in fact clan locals who had volunteered their services free. He was even more amazed when the locals joined in the Highland reels, dancing with the duke and duchess with affectionate familiarity. Here, Hirohito told an aide, was "genuine democracy without class distinctions."

He spent a further week in England as a private visitor, toured arms factories, shipyards, Manchester, Glasgow, the Bank of England, Oxford University and Eton College. There was an embarrassing moment when his aides discovered an irreverent piece of prose about him in the *Eton College Chronicle* and tried to have it suppressed. The only unfavorable article was an ill-informed diatribe against Japan in the *Church Times.* Hirohito watched a performance of Pavlova's *Dying Swan,* had his portrait painted by Augustus John, and entertained European-based diplomats, businessmen and military attachés. Such was the importance of the occasion that some Japanese socialites had traveled all the way to England in the hope of being invited.

In his talks with George V, Hirohito put his knowledge of recent military history to good use: much of their conversation had to do with the Great War, still a vivid, traumatic memory. He amazed one British general by his familiarity with the British order of battle, correcting him on a point of detail. Later, visiting Belgian battlefields, he cabled King George that the "impressive and edifying scene reminded me of the words in which Your Majesty explained to me the sanguinary character of the struggle on this field of honour at Ypres."

The recent war was one of the few subjects of interest he and King George had in common, but the king may have had another purpose in mind: to remind Hirohito of the huge losses suffered by the Allies, implicitly contrasting them with Japan's negligible contribution.

With Lloyd George, the prime minister, topics of mutual interest were fewer. As the authors of *The Crown Prince's European Tour* somewhat condescendingly put it, "One could only marvel at the coming together of the Heir to the most ancient and historic throne in the world and the nephew of a cobbler from an obscure Welsh village—an incongruity furnishing food for thought to philosophers."

The next leg of the crown prince's trip was France, and here too Hirohito's passion for military history was gratified by the grizzled French heroes of *la grande guerre.* He went through the immutable routine of any important foreign guest—lunching at the Elysée Palace with President Millerand, laying a wreath at the tomb of the Unknown Soldier, visiting the Eiffel Tower and getting lost on the Paris métro. He took in a brief tour of the Louvre (*Le Temps* noted that it was at a jogger's pace) and a lengthy one of Napoleon's tomb at the Invalides.

From the protocol point of view, his visit was a private one, but he was treated like a sovereign on a state visit. For the first time, he went shopping and handled money, buying an indifferent oil painting (which he later gave his aide-de-camp, General Shigeru Honjo, as a parting gift) and a bust of Napoleon, to put in his study next to those of his other two heroes, Lincoln and Darwin. He also made a generous contribution to the upkeep of the tomb.

He saw Versailles, again briefly, went to the Opéra, and took in a performance of *Macbeth* by an American touring company. He shopped at fashionable stores, ate snails at Lapérouse, and, in an exclusive interview with the United Press correspondent in Paris, praised America's "noble ideals and patriotism," expressing the hope and desire to visit the United States soon. "I know to what point justice and freedom are valued in America and that no efforts are ever spared by her people in the cause of humanity," he said. "I hope that America and Japan will always be found working hand in hand not only to our mutual benefit but to ensure lasting peace throughout the world."

Marshal Pétain, the victor of Verdun, took him to the grim battlefield. Hirohito also attended army maneuvers in Alsace, visited the French Military Academy at Saint-Cyr, and watched French army maneuvers at Metz.

So many Japanese officers flocked to Paris to see him that the Sûreté, France's counterespionage organization, became interested. It was Prince Higashikuni, a member of the Fushimi clan and a close kinsman of Hirohito himself (he had married one of Meiji's daughters) who came under particular suspicion. He was "studying" in Paris at the advanced age of thirty-five, and the Sûreté was convinced that he ran Japan's intelligence network in Europe.

A "familiarization tour" of Europe, America or Asia, often lasting as long as three years, was the standard reward for all promising young officers, and espionage was required experience for anyone earmarked for promotion to the top. In Asia, as China was shortly to find out to its cost, Japanese intelligence would in time establish devastating "fifth column" networks, inventing a new form of warfare later copied by Franco and the Axis powers.

In Europe, Japanese agents stood out like sore thumbs, but worked with enormous diligence; not having actually fought in the Great War, the Japanese armed forces had fallen behind technically, and there was great interest, in army and navy GHQs, in the European forces' latest weaponry and tactics. Japanese troops had been sent to Siberia in the wake of the 1917 Russian revolution and had been aghast to find that the Communist troops there had been anything but soft. Higashikuni introduced Hirohito to some of the promising junior officers on missions abroad.

Before returning to Japan, Hirohito toured Belgium (more battlefields) and the Netherlands, meeting both the Belgian and Netherlands royal families, before taking a private train to Toulon to board his flagship there. On the way back, the fleet anchored at Naples, and Hirohito visited Rome and the Vatican (where he had an audience with Pope Benedict XV) and more arms factories. He also met Czechoslovakia's President Tomáš Masaryk, himself on a visit to Italy.

Time and again, Hirohito was to refer to this trip as "the happiest time of his life." Court officials noted that it changed him. "He blossomed," one chamberlain said, "and stood taller on his return."

The crowds greeting him in Japan showed the trip had been a public relations success at home as well as in Europe, focusing attention on an up-and-coming country and on a young emperor-to-be, who might be expected to transform the relationship between the imperial system and the people. He brought back some bagpipes for his future father-in-law, Prince Kuni, and a cask of malt whisky—a gift from the Duke of Atholl—for himself; this he stored away for a celebration party.

No sooner was he home than he was immediately plunged into a series of crises. The first was provoked by the expected and relatively unmourned death of General Yamagata, the *genro* who had opposed his choice of a bride. Both Hirohito and his court came to the conclusion that there was no need to replace him: henceforth, Prince Saionji would be the sole surviving *genro*. Another death, far more preoccupying because it renewed the tradition of political violence, was the murder of Emperor Taisho's prime minister, Takashi Hara, stabbed by a right-wing extremist. Though the Black Dragon leader, Toyama, had not been directly involved, the murderer's motives showed how crazily susceptible some Japanese were where military matters were concerned. Hara died because a fanatic felt he had shown disrespect for the navy by assuming the vacant Navy Ministry portfolio while the previous incumbent was away in Washington negotiating the terms of a treaty limiting ceilings of U.S., British and Japanese navy tonnage. His murderer later told his judges in court that he had no regrets, because the dead man had insulted not only the navy but the emperor as well. After serving a relatively light twelve-year sentence, the killer would get a pension for life from a rightist group. The court's leniency implied that politically motivated murder carried "extenuating circumstances."

These were interesting times for Japan, but anxious ones for Hirohito, the princely oligarchy and conservatives in general. Largely as a result of the personal liberal and "internationalist" convictions of Prince Saionji, who had headed the Japanese delegation to Versailles for the peace treaty conference, Japan had not only adhered to the League of Nations but seemed prepared to play a leading role in it. This was almost entirely Saionji's own doing, for the majority of the government, in 1920–21, was only mildly in favor of such involvement. Saionji, an exceptional statesman and Francophile, who had spent ten years in France studying law before entering the Foreign Ministry (and spoke perfect French with a curious Marseillais accent, because he had been in the South of France) was, in those heady early twenties, a formidably influential figure at court. By this time one of the few links with the Meiji past (he had served both Emperors Meiji and Taisho) this witty, urbane aesthete was convinced that Japan's future lay in her close cooperation with the West and in the rejection of her militarist past. In a flowery piece of prose at the time of Versailles, he had outlined his convictions in an article addressed to the favorite paper of his student youth, *Le Petit Marseillais:*

> In the age of staggering progress in which we live, it is the duty of men of all walks of life and of all races to help in the destruction of all those elements, like Prussian militarism, that could halt or even delay civilization's progress. . . . This message cannot lend itself to any ambiguity. . . . The peace that must emerge from the [Versailles] conference must not be just a European peace, but well and truly world peace and it must be kept forever. Humanity must be able to draw lessons from the mistakes of the past, if it is to live in happiness in rich and eternal peace.

One of the reasons why Hirohito, as crown prince, was regarded as a promising, liberal-minded monarch-to-be was the constant presence at his side of Prince Saionji, who had been, at Emperor Meiji's court, the first nobleman to wear Western dress and cut his hair short, Western style, had met and befriended Georges Clemenceau, the

Goncourt brothers and Liszt, and had a passion for Houbigant soaps and scents and for Vichy water. Saionji saw in the Versailles Peace Treaty and the establishment of the League of Nations Japan's only hope of breaking with her isolationist past. As he wrote to Emperor Taisho in 1920 (a letter actually read by Hirohito because by this time the emperor's illness had robbed him of most of his mental faculties):

> the results of the [Versailles] Conference will have a profound effect on the position of Japan in international politics. Japan has joined the ranks of the five great powers and this is the beginning of our participation in European politics. Furthermore, since we occupy an important place in the League of Nations, we have acquired the right to participate in future in all East-West matters.

The note was designed to convince Hirohito that Japan could exert her influence far more efficiently through peaceful diplomacy and close cooperation with the West than through the pursuit of militaristic Asian adventures. Saionji's own reward for his role at Versailles— the title of prince and the highest-ranking Grand Order of the Chrysanthemum—implied that his was now the message the palace was hearing most attentively.

The early twenties were years of promise but also of economic hardship and disillusion. World War I prosperity had ended suddenly, and Japan was conscious, as never before, of the cost of her military infrastructure and of her new role as a major power. It was a time marked by a serious agricultural crisis, leading to an influx of farmers' sons and daughters into the towns, a weakening of family ties and urban unemployment; by worsening employer-worker relations, and the beginning of a class war; by a proliferation of avant-garde and "leftist" clubs, frequently raided by the police, causing the palace, and the conservative right generally, to apprehend a "Communist millennium," of which the Soviet phenomenon had been, in their view, the forerunner. Socialism and Marxism, though virtually outlawed, were spreading from struggling, semiclandestine trade union leaders to the offspring of prosperous middle-class families, so that "Marx boy" now became part of the Japanese vocabulary. So did *moga* (modern girl) and *mobo* (modern boy). Japan had her "flappers" and "jazz age" enthusiasts. Japanese historians labeled these times the years of "ero," "guro" and "nonsensu"—eroticism, grotesquerie and nonsense.

The avant-garde and leftist clubs, however, were nowhere near as numerous as the mushrooming right-wing "nationalist" clubs and secret societies that formed, re-formed, split up and came together again with bewildering frequency from the early twenties onward.

According to the authoritative *Brocade Banner* study* (carried out by U.S. intelligence experts in the immediate postwar period), such secret societies reached the staggering figure of "between 800 and 900" by 1941. Though these societies differed enormously in importance, their "basic premise was that the Emperor, by virtue of his divine origin, should rule not only Japan but all peoples of the earth." They all had one thing in common: a fanatically professed devotion to the emperor as the bulwark against lax behavior of all kinds, political and moral.

Hirohito himself, after observing freer societies at work and play in Europe, was in tune with the new spirit of liberalism, becoming— briefly—a *mobo* himself. He went to the races in Tokyo for the first time, was seen at nightclubs, ordered tweed plus fours (of the kind he had seen the Prince of Wales wearing) for golf, and became addicted to bacon-and-egg breakfasts. He reduced the size of the court, streamlining it, and, determined to be the first truly monogamous emperor in Japanese history, sent all "ladies-in-waiting" packing, except those in attendance on his mother the empress. He told his chamberlains to remove his traditional kimonos from his wardrobe— never again would he wear them, except for the occasional religious ceremony and after bathing.

He tried to emulate the free and easy spirit he had witnessed while staying with the Atholls—with disastrous results. In December 1921 he threw his first and last informal party in the Akasaka Palace to celebrate his return. There were geishas as well as his princely coterie and childhood friends (males only); jazz records were played, there was dancing and a good deal of drinking. Some of his guests (mostly Peers' School old boys or boyhood friends from his kindergarten days) took literally his command to treat him not as crown prince but

---

The Brocade Banner: The Story of Japanese Nationalism, Civil Intelligence Section, GHQ Far Eastern Command, 1946.

as friend. The Duke of Atholl's whisky went to their heads. They became overfamiliar, either embarrassingly maudlin or mildly disrespectful. The informality of it all shocked the chamberlains. Scandalized court officials informed Prince Saionji, who immediately boarded the train for Tokyo from his country retreat. At the palace he gave Hirohito a stern talking-to. Deferentially but firmly, he told a contrite crown prince that the worst aspect of it all had been "the appalling familiarity towards His Royal Highness."

It was not the drinking or the geishas to which Saionji objected: Hirohito's illustrious grandfather had been addicted to both, and he himself was no puritan either. What really worried him, for all his liberalism, was the fear that Hirohito might start questioning traditional values that alone had ensured the unbroken continuity of the royal house. Privacy had to be maintained at all costs if imperial prestige was to survive the hazards of these changing times. Hirohito promised it would not happen again.

In Japan's armed forces, too, a new spirit prevailed. On the face of it, Japan's army and navy were still highly regarded institutions, but, with time, memories of the Russo-Japanese War had faded, and the Chiefs of Staff faced both a recruitment problem and politicians' demands for retrenchment. This only made the career officers of both services more determined than ever not to compromise. On the contrary, their leaders argued, what was required was not less but more expenditure, for Japan's armed forces were now old-fashioned compared with those of countries that had participated in major Great War campaigns.

At this time there were two maverick intellectuals who were to play a leading part in the dramatic events on the road to Pearl Harbor: Dr. Shumei Okawa, a strong personality in close touch with key palace officials (Okawa was scheduled to go on trial for war crimes in Tokyo after World War II but won release after brilliantly faking temporary insanity), and Ikki Kita, his erstwhile friend and guru (who was shot by a Japanese firing squad in 1936). Both men influenced not only the army and navy nationalists, but also imperial family members, including Prince Chichibu, who was briefly attracted to socialism in general, and in particular to Kita's brand of national socialism, which advocated not only ceilings for individual and corporate fortunes, profit sharing and an eight-hour working day, but also the nationalization of all assets owned by the imperial family. Though this worried some palace advisers, their alarm was tempered by the knowledge that Prince Chichibu's enthusiasms, though intense, were generally short-lived.

Another prominent aristocrat "infected" in his youth with avant-garde ideas was Prince Fumimaro Konoye, later to become prime minister three times in the crucial years leading up to Japan's "Great Asian War." Konoye, after graduating from Tokyo Imperial University, wrote a much discussed article attacking the terms of the Versailles Peace Treaty and the establishment of the League of Nations as mere window dressing for continuing Western colonialism. Having established himself as a left-wing nationalist, Konoye, whose own father was president of the House of Peers and whose lineage was almost as illustrious as that of Hirohito himself, then scandalized palace officials by hinting that he might emigrate to the United States permanently because he was bored with old-fashioned, conservative Japan and its excessively antiquated court ritual.

Dr. Okawa, a brilliant Tokyo University graduate and Chinese-language scholar who had spent years in China on various secret intelligence assignments, was a protégé both of Count Nobuaki Makino, the Satsuma clansman who had accompanied Hirohito on his European trip (and was soon to become high chamberlain), and of Hirohito's future father-in-law, Prince Kuni. He also had extremely close relations with the Black Dragon Society, and was Toyama's favorite intellectual. It was to Okawa that Makino turned when Hirohito, shortly after his return, decided to transform the Palace Meteorological Observatory into a privately subsidized think tank, variously known as the Social Problems Research Institute, the University Lodging House, or the Daigaku (the title was derived from the Confucian analect of that name), with Makino in nominal charge.

Inspired by similar institutions in Europe, Hirohito probably intended it to supplement the more formal Staff College and the school for junior diplomats run by the foreign ministry. It became, in the four years of its ephemeral existence, a select and secretive club, where bright young bureaucrats mingled with up-and-coming staff officers and policemen, and heard lectures by Confucian scholars, members of the Imperial Household, and prominent generals and War Ministry officials. "The place," noted *The Brocade Banner,* "was frequented by imperialistic young army and navy officers who were later to play a prominent part in the attempted coups d'etat of the thirties." Hirohito may have envisaged it as a Japanese Chatham House or Council on Foreign Relations, but with coopted members only. It also acquired the reputation of being an "intelligence university," providing contingency plans on anything from naval rearmament to undercover operations in China and Manchuria, and its members, long after its demise, stuck together and regarded themselves as part of a privileged, secretive clan in close touch with the palace and the Emperor—able and ready to do his bidding, clandestinely if need be.

The University Lodging House also became the sounding board for Dr. Okawa's own pet theories, a blend of right-wing national socialism and the kind of ultranationalist mysticism embodied in the French poetry of Charles Péguy and the writings of the right-wing nationalist French ideologue Charles Maurras. Since Okawa was a brilliant debater as well as a formidable operator, it is no wonder that many of the graduates emerged as arrant nationalists.

It is not clear why Hirohito closed the house down in 1924. The pretext was that the building had become, after the earthquake, structurally unsound, but this was not the real reason. It may be that Dr. Okawa had turned out to be a somewhat embarrassing figure. Hirohito, always frugal, may also have balked at the continued expense. Perhaps he felt that the house had served its purpose, bringing together the best and the brightest of Japan's military elite and administrative establishment and instilling in them a common sense of purpose. Hirohito cannot have been unaware of the content of the University Lodging House seminars, for it was out of character for him to take an initiative and then lose interest in it. There was a schoolmasterly side to him: seminars on all sorts of subjects, from Zen philosophy to ancient Chinese history, continued to be staged inside the palace even during the darkest moments of World War II.

Dr. Okawa was not the only ideologue to preach the dogma of authoritarian nationalism and the need for territorial expansion. There were, within the Japanese establishment, three conflicting views on Japan's role, and Hirohito, with his interest in strategy and military history, again cannot have been unaware of them.

One view was reflected by a powerful lobby which believed that Soviet Russia represented Japan's greatest permanent threat, both because of her physical presence in Manchuria and because her leaders openly preached world revolution. The very Japanese qualities of respect for authority and unquestioning discipline, the argument ran, made the Japanese rank and file vulnerable to Communism. Therefore, Japan's long-term aim should be to confront the USSR in Siberia, to gain territory there and ensure that Soviet influence was eradicated in Manchuria and in Asia in general. This concept became known as the Strike North theory.

Another school of thought focused on Japan's need to take the lead in Asia, to help the Chinese overcome their many problems and drive out the Western colonialists there. At its best, and most idealistic, this policy was pro-Chinese, and implied real friendship and equality. Japan was uniquely placed to witness the decay of Chinese institutions and the predatory nature of Western powers. This "positive attitude" toward China took many forms: it was embodied in the brutal Twenty-one Demands, but it also explains why both Sun Yat-sen, and, later, Chiang Kai-shek, potential Japanese allies, were initially given a cordial welcome in Japan. Both Chinese leaders, in their day, embodied change. It was Japan's misfortune that Sun Yat-sen was very quickly removed from power, and shortly afterward fell ill and died. Chiang Kai-shek was also seen, at first, as a possible ally and collaborator in a Japanese "grand design" for Asia.

Finally, there were those who believed that Japan, a "developed" country on a par with the Western powers, could not afford to limit her sphere of influence to China but must compete, on world terms, with the same Western powers not only in China but elsewhere. This meant that Japan must not let Britain, France and the Netherlands assume that their colonial possessions in Asia were secure forever. This came to be known as the Strike South theory.

If Japan was to be a major world power, she had to be treated as an equal. She also had to have the means to defend herself against other world powers. Hence the indignation shown by many Japanese at alleged discrimination over the number of warships Japan was to be allowed to build and the maximum size and range of the naval guns. Hence, too, Japan's anger at the refusal of the "white races" at the Versailles Peace Conference to agree on a text calling for legal equality among nations "without racial distinctions." This was compounded by a U.S. Supreme Court ruling preventing any Japanese from becoming U.S. citizens, and by the de facto immigration ban on the Japanese ruthlessly enforced by Canada, Latin America, Australia, New Zealand and the United States. For all Hirohito's friendly statement in Paris to the United Press, American attitudes toward Japan—

some Japanese were already arguing in 1921—were profoundly hypo-critical.

All these issues were certainly discussed at the University Lodging House, and at Dr. Okawa's later "school," as well as in a noted best-seller by a retired lieutenant general, Kojiro Sato, published in 1921, entitled *If Japan and America Fight*. A Russo-Japanese War veteran, Sato reflected in print the anger and resentment felt by Japanese officers who believed that Japan's legitimate claims embodied in the Twenty-one Demands had been unfairly quashed by the major powers at Versailles.

As a British officer, Captain Malcolm Kennedy, who spent some time with the Japanese army in the early twenties, was to write, Japanese officers felt that "just as Japan was getting really skilful at the game of grab, the other powers, most of whom had all they wanted anyway, suddenly had an access of virtue and called the game off." Their vision of America, he wrote, was of "a selfish meddler, interfering unreasonably with Japan's national aspirations," and they saw Japan as a beleaguered fortress facing a hostile world.* They were relatively tolerant, at this time, of both Germany's and Britain's axis of influence, referred to, in the military jargon of the time, as the "three Bs" (Berlin-Budapest-Baghdad) and the "three Cs" (Cairo-Capetown-Calcutta). It was the "three As," the America-Alaska-Asia axis, that were seen as the real threat to Japan. Dr. Okawa, in 1924, in a book called *Asia, Europe and Japan*, which also considered the possibility of war with the United States, wrote: "These two countries, the U.S. and Japan, are destined to fight each other as Greece had to battle Persia and Rome Carthage. O Japan, will that be in a year, 10 years, 30 years? No one can tell. Prepare yourselves for that heavenly call."

Sato claimed that the United States had "insolently" revealed her imperialistic ambitions "while professing the open door." Her anti-immigration policy had "insulted the Japanese race." He advocated lightning raids on strategic American centers by Japanese "special forces" in a blitzkrieg that would terrify the United States into submission and a more understanding attitude toward Japan. This, the least credible part of his book, was studded with appeals to the Japanese to

---

*M. D. Kennedy, *The Military Side of Japanese Life* (Boston: Houghton Mifflin, 1923).

remember that in the past they had overcome insuperable odds through their "indomitable will," and that in the long run it was this almost mystical determination that would be required to challenge, and overcome, an enemy of such size. He also strongly urged Japan's education minister to institute compulsory military training in Japan's schools and called for a general militarization of Japanese society. If his advice was followed, Japan could win, "for in the point of mentality, the Japanese are rather superior than inferior to the Americans."

Though eventually he was to reject the Strike North theory in its entirety, show considerable impatience with those who caused Japan to be embroiled in a protracted war with China, and clearly favor the Strike South option, Hirohito had not made up his mind on any of these issues when, after a further deterioration in Emperor Taisho's health, he became regent on November 25, 1921. Memories of his European trip were still vivid, and they were revived by the Prince of Wales' return visit to Japan in 1922. Hirohito played golf with Edward, and showed himself to be in every sense a modern, enlightened monarch-to-be. Japanese newspaper editors, however, were shocked by a photograph showing the Prince of Wales dressed up for fun as a ricksha-man.

To the Japanese, the first day of September is traditionally the equivalent of Friday the thirteenth. Superstition was hugely bolstered when, on September 1, 1923, the worst natural calamity in the history of Japan struck. Just before noon a giant earthquake hit Tokyo, Yokohama and the whole surrounding area known as Kanto. At the Tokyo Seismological Institute, readings went right off the Richter scale. An initial "tidal wave on land" undulated through towns, villages and fields, leaving devastation in its wake; concrete blocks and shantytowns alike were flattened, and only those few buildings specially designed to withstand earthquakes, including Frank Lloyd Wright's Imperial Hotel (one of the imperial family's prized pieces of property) and a few other office buildings in the center of Tokyo, designed by American architects, remained unscathed.

The charcoal hibachi stove was then in use in most Japanese homes, which were generally built of wood. Since most Japanese housewives were preparing their midday meal at the time, the earthquake was followed by a gigantic series of conflagrations, wiping out most of the Tokyo and Yokohama residential areas. In Yokohama, huge oil storage vats collapsed into the sea, and burst into flames. When the fires finally died out, over half a million homes in the Kanto area had been destroyed, and official casualties ranged from 100,000 to 150,000 dead.

The emperor and empress, in the hill resort of Nikko, were unharmed, and so was Princess Nagako. The Imperial Palace buildings suffered only minor damage, and Hirohito, at work in his office, did not leave his desk until urged to do so. Japan was in the grip of another cabinet crisis, and the incoming premier, the retired Admiral Yamamoto (unrelated to the man who was to mastermind the attack on Pearl Harbor) was slightly injured by falling masonry as he was holding a party conference inside the Navy Club. Power cuts were general, and electricity was not restored for days. Most radio communications went dead, and no newspapers could be published.

In Japanese folklore, the earthquakes that had ravaged that part of the coast since time immemorial were the work of giant catfish living at the bottom of the sea, which only stirred when the Japanese race misbehaved. This perhaps explains the absurd reaction of Japanese officialdom: whereas the natural reaction of almost any government would have been to make its plight public and appeal for international aid, Japanese officials tried their best to keep the news from leaking out, jamming what few radio communications still functioned and denying, until it was no longer possible to do so, that anything untoward had happened.

A young Royal Navy officer, George C. Ross, was aboard a British warship that entered Yokohama with medicine and blankets shortly after the earthquake. He recalls that survivors complained to him that the captains of Japanese navy vessels at anchor there behaved with extreme callousness: thousands of survivors tried to escape the fires raging on land by swimming out to sea, "but were generally not allowed to board the ships." The Japanese attempt to keep the calamity secret from the outside world was "incomprehensible," he added.

Some of the palace grounds in Tokyo were opened to survivors as first-aid stations, and Hirohito set up an improvised command post in the gardens. The investiture of Premier-elect Yamamoto took place inside Akasaka Palace the following day, and a few days later martial law was proclaimed. But neither Hirohito nor the new government took the necessary steps to reassure and comfort the dazed survivors. Though Hirohito was eventually to visit the damaged zones, there was no immediate informal royal tour of the city. The weight of protocol was such that palace officials were incapable of reacting to unforeseen situations such as this one, and Hirohito himself seems to have lacked the imagination, or social concern, to insist on making an immediate public appearance, although he did, weeks later, tour the ruined capital on horseback and contributed ten million yen to the relief fund.

What followed showed that however much Japan had moved with the times since the Meiji Restoration, its Western veneer was only skin-deep: old atavistic fears and superstitions remained strong. Korean immigrants were Japan's lumpenproletariat, and had an execrable reputation. Rumors spread throughout Tokyo and Yokohama that the hated Koreans and the leftists had offended the spirits of Japan's ancestors by their conduct and provoked the earthquake. Instinctively, Tokyo survivors turned on them, blaming them not only for the looting but for the earthquake itself. Thousands were massacred, while police and army units stood by.

The earthquake was not the only calamity of the year: on December 27, in Toranomon, Hirohito was in a carriage on his way to open the new Diet session when he was shot at by a disgruntled member of the Choshu clan, Daisaku Namba. The official version was that Namba was a pro-Communist revolutionary. He was also the son of a well-known politician, and the weapon he used was a pistol concealed in a stick, originally purchased in London by a prominent Choshu dignitary, Hirobumi Ito. There were no "extenuating circumstances," and Namba was executed. Police reported that he died shouting Marxist slogans.

A month almost to the day after the assassination attempt, on January 26, 1924, Hirohito was married. There had already been one postponement, because of the earthquake. Some palace officials wanted the ceremony delayed again so that guests would not be reminded of the recent calamity, but Nagako insisted: she had been engaged for five years, and felt she had waited long enough.

CHAPTER FOUR

A royal wedding is always a great morale booster; Hirohito's was no exception. The traumatic events of the previous three months were forgotten in the excitement, and loyal Japanese—already avid newspaper readers thanks to a half-century of compulsory education—were able to enter into the festive spirit. Japanese press coverage almost equaled that of Britain's popular newspapers in its wealth of detail and gossipy, but always deferential, handling of every conceivable aspect of the hugely publicized event.

January was not the ideal month, but January 26, 1924, turned out to be a fine, mild day. A national holiday was proclaimed, and there were celebrations all over Japan. Large crowds gathered outside the palace walls and along the route taken by the royal couple. Hirohito left the Akasaka Palace for the Imperial Palace grounds, alone and in a closed horse-drawn carriage, wearing a lieutenant colonel's uniform. The bride, in another, similarly closed carriage, arrived at the Imperial Palace in a separate procession. Those who stood patiently for hours outside the grounds and along the route of the procession cheered and shouted *"Banzai,"* but all but the boldest continued to avert their gaze in religious awe. It was not wholly unlike a British royal wedding, with all the excitement of watching the distinguished

Japanese guests arrive for the religious ceremony, and, later, the diplomatic corps for a separate afternoon reception.

But the ceremony itself, from beginning to end, took place within the palace, and even the most privileged guests caught only a glimpse of the actual rites. These took place inside the imperial family shrine, a small, secluded temple hidden by a screen of trees and strictly out of bounds to all but the imperial family and a handful of Shinto priests. The seven hundred guests, all Japanese—they included the notorious underworld boss Toyama, who had done so much to make the marriage possible, but not Emperor Taisho, who was "too sick" to attend—waited outside the shrine. Apart from a few priests, Princess Nagako and Hirohito himself, only Prince Kujo, the "master of the rites," was present at the actual ceremony.

Preparations had taken several hours, for both Hirohito and his bride had to change into heavy, cumbersome ceremonial dress. Hirohito's was an orange robe and skirt, and he carried a scepter and wore a black lacquered hat. His part in the proceedings, in addition to the marriage vows themselves, consisted of addressing the spirits of his ancestors in the court language used only for such rites—a language totally incomprehensible to ordinary Japanese—informing them of his decision to marry Nagako. Then came the relatively simple exchange of vows. Hirohito, then Nagako, in a scarlet and lilac kimono, drank three times from a goblet of sacred wine. A hundred-and-one-gun salute marked the end of the ceremony, after which they emerged from the shrine and briefly faced the bowing guests. There was no immediate secluded honeymoon: the newly married couple spent the night in Akasaka Palace, and the following day Hirohito and his bride visited Emperor Taisho, in Numazu, to pay their respects.

Loyal subjects eagerly awaited news of Nagako's pregnancy, but not till the spring of 1925 was such an announcement made, and the disappointment, when Nagako finally gave birth to a baby girl, Shigeko, was palpable: only male heirs could ensure the dynasty's continuity. Princess Nagako's pregnancy did, however, quash a nationwide rumor that the late General Yamagata had cursed Nagako on his deathbed and vowed that she would be barren. After this first birth, the older palace chamberlains and Prince Saionji, the *genro,* felt that Hirohito would be luckier next time. If not, they hinted—but never in his presence—a royal concubine could always be brought into play.

This showed how out of touch they were with Hirohito's state of mind. For all his aloofness during the engagement years, Hirohito immediately proved to be a model and affectionate, if somewhat formal and predictable, companion. Memories of the licentious Meiji court and his own father's excesses turned him into an uxorious, primly monogamous husband. What had been extreme, almost obsessive, orderliness in childhood now manifested itself in rigid routine. There were timetables for everything. Court officials knew precisely when Hirohito was likely to be out riding, or playing golf, or feeding the birds and swans in the palace gardens, what afternoons he would spend studying marine biology with Dr. Hattori, now one of his aides-de-camp. So methodical was the imperial routine that there were probably set dates and times for procreation. Princess Nagako very quickly adjusted to her new life and appeared to enjoy it: in the early years of their married life, the diarist Kanroji noted, their "attentive intimacy was a beautiful thing to see."

Hirohito's honeymoon years were also something of a honeymoon for Japan herself. From 1924 to 1927, the country enjoyed an unprecedentedly liberal spell: universal suffrage for all males of twenty-five and over was introduced, the size of the army was slightly reduced, and the Japanese press became more lively and more openly critical than at any other time in its history. The two main political parties, Minseito and Seiyukai, ruled alternately, as if by tacit agreement. Politically they were practically indistinguishable (Minseito was perhaps a shade more liberal), but in both camps supporters were swayed more by personalities than by issues. Both parties were heavily dependent on the large industrial conglomerates, the zaibatsu, with Minseito financed by Mitsubishi and Seiyukai by Mitsui. Corruption was widespread, the conglomerates dictated economic policy, and, with a few outstanding exceptions, politicians' reputations were low. For all that, Japan seemed to be moving toward a form of parliamentary democracy. On the diplomatic front, she was a signatory to the nine-power treaty guaranteeing not only the independence and integrity of China but the equal rights of those countries wishing to invest there.

Briefly, in the mid-twenties, it looked as if Japan under its new emperor might after all normalize her relations with China and forget about her dreams of overlordship and the iniquitous Twenty-one Demands. But for all this "runaway liberal movement of the urban middle class,"* there remained an undercurrent of intolerance and xenophobia. Tokyo's daily *Nichi-Nichi* published a "strong warning to the undesirable foreign elements in Japan . . . who commit in the dark detestable crimes." Though the first part of Tokyo to be rebuilt after the earthquake was its huge brothel area, the Yoshiwara district, it was the "immorality of foreigners" that attracted editorial comment, and in hotels and restaurants foreigners' behavior was monitored and put on file by Japan's secret police. At a banquet held in a Tokyo hotel by the Minseito party, its organizers complained that one of the waiters was a police spy. The manager replied that this particular spy had become such a fixture, listening to foreigners' conversations, that he was regarded as part of the staff. Foreign diplomats in Tokyo were routinely spied on by their Japanese employees and servants, and "espionitis" would eventually reach absurd levels.

A. Morgan Young, a British journalist and editor, resident in Tokyo at the time, later wrote that in 1927 there was "independent civilian thinking which five years later would be inconceivable,"† for the liberal mood did not outlast the twenties. Liberalism was dealt a huge blow when, in 1927, a series of bank failures sparked off a predepression crisis leading to business collapses among the new middle class and extreme poverty among the farmers, still the bulk of Japan's population. The zaibatsu, unscathed, bought up everything in sight. The antiparliament, antibusiness wave that followed fueled the lunatic-fringe nationalists, the militarists, and the authoritarian Secret Society bosses. A new Maintenance of Public Peace bill, voted into existence shortly afterward, drastically curbed civil liberties and freedom of speech; an imperial decree, signed by Hirohito without debate in parliament—almost certainly at the request of Prince Konoye, the emperor's kinsman and friend, now a member of the House of Peers and no longer a radical—increased the maximum penalty for convicted offenders from ten years in jail to a possible death sentence. A huge purge began shortly afterward in schools and universities, as well as a wave of arrests of Communists, socialists and suspected leftists at all levels of society. By mid-1928, said Morgan Young, "every liberal professor had been driven out of the universities."

---

*Edwin O. Reischauer, *Japan's Past and Present* (London: Duckworth, 1947).
†A. Morgan Young, *Imperial Japan* (New York: William Morrow, 1938).

By now, another of General Sato's demands (put forward in *If America and Japan Fight*) had been fulfilled: in 1926 military drill and education began in preparatory and middle schools and were soon extended to the entire educational system. The "emperor cult" in schools was given an additional, military fillip, with schoolchildren parading in uniform before photographs of Hirohito—himself invariably in the uniform of commander in chief. This had been one way of coping with manpower cuts in the army, for many superannuated or redundant army officers found employment as military instructors in schools throughout the country. The decrease in the size of the army (a reduction of some four infantry divisions) was compensated for by the creation of new tank and antitank units, a signals corps, and, later, a chemical and bacteriological warfare center. These last two were, in part at least, the brainchild of the scientifically minded Prince Kuni, Hirohito's father-in-law, and Hirohito himself, with his passion for science and marine biology, took a keen interest in both centers.

Emperor Taisho, in seclusion ever since his embarrassing public lapses, died on December 18, 1926—but the news of his death was made public only on Christmas Day. Hirohito, warned that the end was near, had mounted a bedside vigil in the seaside resort of Hayama, where Taisho had lived for the last five years, but he was actually asleep when his father died. There was little real grief among the people—the emperor had been out of the public eye for so long, and Hirohito, as regent, had already assumed all his father's powers, with the exception of the actual title. The death was marked by a minor but significant crisis within the media, which showed to what extent secrecy prevailed where palace decisions were concerned.

Every Japanese emperor has two names, one for his lifetime, the other for posterity. Until their deaths, Emperor Meiji had been known as Emperor Mutsuhito, and Taisho as Emperor Yoshihito; only posthumously were they referred to as Emperor Meiji and Emperor Taisho (which meant "great righteousness"). On his father's death, Hirohito now had to choose the name under which he himself would go down in history. The daily *Mainichi* correctly announced that the Hirohito era would be known as Kobun (meaning "light and literary attainments"), the news having leaked from the Imperial Palace several weeks previously, when it was clear that the emperor was dying.

Hirohito was furious, and decided to punish the *Mainichi* by changing the name to Showa, meaning "peace and enlightenment." In *Fifty*

Years of Light and Dark, a book published on the fiftieth anniversary of Hirohito's reign, the *Mainichi* revealed that at the time the emperor's decision caused a huge crisis within the paper's staff, compelling several editors to resign. It added that, in the light of what was to happen later, to call Hirohito's reign the "age of enlightenment and peace" was "a dour irony unmatched in the nation's history."

The title Hirohito now assumed had been transmitted, in more or less unbroken succession, since the year 660 B.C., the year his glorious ancestor, Jimmu, first appears in the earliest annals of Japan. In fact Emperor Jimmu may have "reigned" within several hundred years of this somewhat arbitrarily chosen date, and there is even doubt cast on his existence. Jimmu himself, the "divine" son of a whole series of divine mythological ancestors, or someone like him, was in all probability the first of a series of tribal chiefs to leave his mark on one of the islands of the Japanese archipelago, inhabited at the time by primitive tribes of Chinese-Korean descent who had themselves displaced and eliminated its original Ainu inhabitants.

The myth of Jimmu, a direct descendant of the sun goddess Amaterasu, herself related to a whole series of gods and goddesses who gave birth to matter, oceans, heat and light as well as to other deities (they had life spans of five hundred years and more), became dogma only in Emperor Meiji's time, as a useful underpinning of the newly restored emperor's authority through Shintoism. The holy attributes of the emperor—the mirror, the sword and the necklace—were, officially at least, believed to be truly authentic holy relics of the heroic prehistoric age. The copper mirror was the device one of the gods had used to tempt the goddess Amaterasu out of her cave, where she had fled, condemning the entire world to darkness; handing her the mirror, a relative compelled her to come out of the cave to contemplate her features in the light. The sword was an equally mythic attribute, supposedly plucked from a dragon's tail; the necklace, actually composed of crudely carved stones, was perhaps the only truly authentic relic of the three. The mirror remained in the Japanese Holy of Holies, the shrine of Ise, where emperors went twice a year to commune with their ancestors; the other relics were kept in the imperial family shrine.

Young Japanese were taught to believe in these heroic mythological tales in the same way that fundamentalist Christians are taught to believe in the literal truth of the Bible. Needless to say, the "crude and bawdy tales" of the origins of the Japanese gods, who became, by stages, human beings and the rulers of Japan, were regarded by nearly all highly educated Japanese as myths. Hirohito, with his passion for marine biology and a keen interest in Darwinism, refused to take them seriously. In his youth, his refusal to listen patiently to specially appointed professors expounding them as though they were historical truths had led them to complain to Prince Saionji that their royal pupil was remiss in studies concerning his own divinity. Saionji, the French-speaking hedonist, composer and poet who admired Voltaire and French eighteenth- and nineteenth-century erotic literature, a cynic who fully understood Hirohito's reservations, agreed with the young prince privately that the myths were probably nonsense, but said that they happened to be useful nonsense: why deprive believers of their faith, especially when this faith made them implicitly obedient to the emperor's will, and facilitated to a considerable degree the ruler's task? It was a lesson Hirohito immediately understood.

The jurists who had drafted the 1889 constitution, drawing heavily on its Prussian model, maintained the fiction that it had been a "gift from the throne." In theory at least, every emperor, from Meiji onward, was an absolute ruler, since the constitution proclaimed not only that "the Empire shall be reigned over and governed by a line of Emperors unbroken for ages eternal," but that the emperor was "sacred and inviolable . . . combining in Himself the rights and the exercise of sovereignty," as well as supreme command of the armed forces.

As defined in the *Japan Yearbook,* "the Emperor . . . cannot be removed from the Throne for any reason, and he is not to be held responsible for over-stepping the limitations of law in the exercise of his sovereignty." All such responsibility "must be assumed by the Ministers of State and other organs. Thus no criticism can be directed against the Emperor but only against the instruments of his sovereignty. Laws are not to be applied to the Emperor as a principle, especially criminal laws, for no court of law can try the Emperor himself and he is not subject to any law."

This doctrine of imperial infallibility was in practice hedged about with tacit limitations, for both the jurists who drafted the constitution and the oligarchs who helped the emperor run the country realized that no government could be perfect, that errors would invariably occur, and that the same infallibility doctrine—if it was to be respected as part of the emperor's religious attributes—required that he should have only indirect responsibility in the day-to-day running of the country. The reason was that only by letting others take the decisions could the emperor remain unsullied by the possibility of human error. By Emperor Taisho's time, the direct exercise of the emperor's powers was formalistic: he apposed his seal on government decrees, but the day-to-day decision-making process was the responsibility of the cabinet. The Privy Council acted as an advisory body, and while the Diet's powers were more illusory than real, the two most powerful figures in Japanese life were neither "imperial" nor elected: they were the army and navy chiefs of staff, both, in practice, more powerful even than the prime minister. They had the right to consult with the emperor without the presence of any other minister or court official; the tacit ruling—nowhere referred to in the constitution—that army and navy ministers should be drawn from the ranks of serving officers was to give the military veto powers over the composition of successive ministries.

Hirohito fully understood, from the moment he became regent, that he was "above politics" and that his "margin of maneuver" was limited. But these restrictions did not mean that the emperor was a puppet in the hands of a series of overlapping oligarchical institutions: far from it, for the emperor, in the last resort, wielded the ultimate, albeit limited, weapon—the power of the veto. His seal was needed on any document promulgating any decision of importance; by refusing or delaying its apposition he could effectively block any measure he was determined to oppose, from the appointment of a prime minister to the dispatch of an army unit abroad. All of these had to have his official sanction.

And because no decision of even minor importance was implemented without first being scrutinized by the emperor, his behind-the-scenes influence was huge: there could be no single individual better informed on the state of Japan than a hard-working Japanese emperor. Hirohito was exceptionally industrious, methodical and almost obsessively concerned with detail. A member of the imperial family confirmed in an interview that "the Emperor always read everything he put his seal to." For all these reasons, he knew at almost all times everything that was going on, not only within the Privy Council, the Supreme War Command and the cabinet but within the army and navy and the many ultranationalist clubs and secret societies as well. His personal "kitchen cabinet," consisting of the Imperial Household minister, the Lord Privy Seal, the chief aide-de-camp and the grand chamberlain, were his privileged "eyes and ears," and the information-gathering resources at their disposal were formidable.

There was another area where the emperor assumed enormous importance: because of his huge wealth, he could underwrite ventures that, for one reason or another, could not be charged to official government budgets. The emperor's private funds, right up to the end of World War II, served in a multitude of ways to accomplish what had to be kept secret. In the wartime diaries of some of the court officials closest to Hirohito, for example, there are tantalizing references to a "special weapons research center" that was clearly privately funded, through special palace intermediaries.

The extent, and limitation, of Hirohito's powers were well understood by those who were determined to turn Japan into an expansionist, authoritarian state. Such was the weight of tradition, and the aura of infallibility around a supposedly "divine" emperor, that even to talk of attempting to influence his thought was regarded as lèse-majesté. This also made the formulation of policy in the emperor's presence, even when relatively simple matters were concerned, difficult. For this reason, much of the vocabulary used at court and in the emperor's presence was circumlocutory, allusive and fully comprehensible only to an inside clique.

Among themselves, however, army officers spoke their minds. One such instance was reported by Ryukishi Tanaka, an intelligence officer who was later to achieve considerable notoriety as a prosecution witness for the International Military Tribunal (IMTFE) and a confidential aide to its chief prosecutor, Joseph B. Keenan.

Tanaka was in the company of a small, select group of officers, all members of the recently closed University Lodging House, who celebrated Hirohito's accession shortly after the news of Taisho's death. Dr. Okawa drank a toast to the conquest of Manchuria, only to be reminded by Lieutenant Colonel Tojo (he was later to be wartime premier) that "we can never move troops unless the Emperor says so."

Later the somewhat tipsy group went past the Imperial Palace, and saw Japanese families, some of them from the country, kneeling in the moonlight to pray to the new emperor. Tanaka remembered: "We felt relieved by the sight, as if the independence of Manchuria was already assured."

While Hirohito was mounting his round-the-clock watch over his dying father, two very different but equally colorful individuals were at the forefront of events in China, a country that would soon play a crucial role in determining Japan's drift into war. Both hoped to use Japan for their own ends. While Hirohito never met either personally, he was well aware of their respective strengths and weaknesses, followed their careers with unflagging interest, and—ultimately—betrayed them both.

One was Chiang Kai-shek, the ambitious, wily ex-broker who was determined to unify China and break the power of the warlords, if possible with Hirohito's active support. The other was General Chang Tso-lin, the "uncrowned king of Manchuria," who had fought with the Japanese against Russia during the 1905 war but had narrowly survived a Japanese assassination attempt in 1916.

Under Chang Tso-lin, a Manchu orphan pauper who had become, first, a Robin Hood brigand, and then the leader of a private army, Manchuria had been turned into the best-administered province in China. A diminutive wisp of a man with the looks of a slant-eyed Clark Gable and a deceptively soft-spoken manner, Chang Tso-lin was a ruthless, highly intelligent administrator. He had the White Queen's disconcerting habit of ordering "Off with their heads"—beheadings without benefit of prior trial were a regular feature of his rule. But his victims were mostly drug dealers, corrupt bankers, businessmen and black marketeers, and his summary executions made him popular with the common people. His Mukden palace was guarded by a fanatically loyal Praetorian guard of handpicked Manchus in Hollywood uniforms of his own creation. He was a compelling negotiator and an attentive host, and was extraordinarily attractive to women; he had a weakness for expensive furs and teenage concubines. He was also a sophisticated financial planner who early on understood the economic and strategic importance of railways, building his own to compete with the Japanese-owned line; though he still lived by the tough gangster code that had brought him to the pinnacle of power and wealth, he was, in his curious way, a patriot, determined to turn Manchuria into a prosperous, well-ordered province. He had the knack of inspiring loyalty among all who worked for him: an Italian adventurer, Amleto Vespa, who became one of his senior advisers and later wrote about his experiences in Japanese-occupied Manchuria, considered him one of the greatest men who ever lived.*

By treaty, Japanese forces in Manchuria at the time of Hirohito's accession were limited to a few thousand men: these were units earmarked for the protection of the South Manchurian railway, owned and operated by the Japanese, and the long-established Kwangtung Army under General Muto, which had its headquarters in Port Arthur.

Despite the presence of Japanese troops on Manchurian soil, Japan's relations with Chang Tso-lin were cordial. The Japanese lent him military advisers, and assured him of their everlasting support. Had he confined his sphere of influence to Manchuria and Mongolia, both the Japanese and Chiang Kai-shek would have found him a difficult nut to crack. But Chang Tso-lin believed that his was a national destiny: he hinted as much to Henry Pu-yi, the weak-willed, demoralized ex-emperor of China, then only twenty-one, who had taken refuge in the Japanese-run part of the Tientsin International Concession; and he made the huge mistake of seizing power in Peking, with only a token force, driving out Feng Yu-hsiang, the "Christian general," then Chiang Kai-shek's ally, whose Communist sympathies were well known.

Chiang Kai-shek, at the time of Hirohito's accession, had moved north from his Canton base and also saw himself as China's man of destiny. Though his allies included leftists as well as traditional warlords, Chiang had realized by this time that to obtain international recognition he would have to break with the Communists. When Chang Tso-lin, acting on a Japanese tip-off, had the Soviet embassy in Peking raided and found proof in documents discovered there of a Comintern plot to "sovietize" China, Chiang Kai-shek seized on the pretext he had been looking for: on April 12, 1927, Black Tuesday in the annals of China, he turned on his Communist allies with sudden, ruthless cruelty. Thousands were apprehended and executed. Chou En-lai, formerly one of Chiang Kai-shek's subordinates, who had taught at the Whampoa Academy, the staff college for budding Kuomintang leaders that Chiang Kai-shek had set up in the south with

---

*Amleto Vespa, *Secret Agent of Japan* (Boston: Little, Brown and Co., 1938).

Soviet funds, precipitately fled Shanghai. Soviet advisers dispersed, returning to Russia in haste. A few days later, Chiang Kai-shek established his provisional capital in Nanking, a halfway house on the way to Peking.

On April 20 another general, Giichi Tanaka, became Hirohito's new prime minister. As usual, the nomination had come from Prince Saionji, and had been approved by the Privy Council. After resigning from the army in 1925 (he had opposed military budget cuts), Tanaka had moved into politics and become president of the Seiyukai party. He succeeded an administration discredited by bank failures and corruption. As both an army man and a member of the Choshu clan, Saionji told Hirohito, Tanaka could not only speak to the military with authority, but help his disgruntled clansmen forget the past. A bluff, hearty, outgoing soldier, Tanaka had some of the requisite qualities for a prime minister. What he lacked was a statesman's long-term vision and the subtlety, and capacity for intrigue, of the born courtier.

Like all the other top military men, Tanaka believed Japan needed to consolidate her hold on Manchuria and Mongolia as a buffer between Communist Russia and a weak, divided China. He was disturbed by Chang Tso-lin's recent march into Peking, and advised the warlord to return to Manchuria, where he belonged—for Chang Tso-lin, a rabid anti-Communist, was the best possible insurance against Russian encroachment in that part of the world. But Chang Tso-lin refused. For all Chiang Kai-shek's new anti-Communism, he was not to be trusted, he argued. "My war [against Chiang Kai-shek] is Japan's war," he told Tanaka, deploring the fact that Japan maintained friendly relations with a man who until so recently had had Communist allies.

The situation was a complicated one, too complicated for Tanaka alone. In time-honored Japanese fashion, a consensus solution, based on extensive study, was sought. In the month following Tanaka's appointment, a working party convened to prepare for the Far Eastern Conference, which took place in Tokyo from June 1 to July 7, 1927. The middle-level specialists who sat on this preparatory committee included some of the brightest but also some of the most uncompromising advocates of Japanese expansionism and authoritarian nationalism in the ranks of the military and intelligence establishments. Hirohito was fully aware of the contents of its working papers, and may even have indirectly influenced them, for two of its members were his own ADCs—Viscount Machijiri, a former subordinate of Prince Higashikuni in Paris, and Major Anami, who later became Japan's last wartime defense minister. Nearly all its participants happened to be "graduates" of the late University Lodging House, and Anami was particularly close to Hirohito.

The Far Eastern Conference is rightly seen as the first clear evidence of Japan's "forward policy" in China under Hirohito's aegis, and of her determination to turn her huge but vulnerable neighbor into a Japanese vassal, by friendly persuasion if possible, by force if not. Attended by senior officers and diplomats (including the Japanese minister in Peking, Kenkichi Yoshizawa, and that up-and-coming embassy secretary who had boarded Hirohito's warship in Gibraltar and was now consul in Mukden, Shigeru Yoshida), the conference discussed the various alternatives open to Japan in her determination to increase her influence in Asia. These ranged from the outright conquest of Manchuria—one of the proposals drafted by the preparatory committee—to a mere reinforcement of Japan's economic presence there. Complaints were voiced that the Chinese, in defiance of the 1915 treaty with Japan (the famous Twenty-one Demands), were refusing to lease land to the Japanese. If they continued to do so, outright ownership was the only answer, the conference decided; it also suggested that Koreans, not viewed as first-class Japanese citizens by the Chinese, be brought in as convenient stalking horses for Japanese entrepreneurs.

Years later Chiang Kai-shek's propagandists would publicize the conclusions of the Far Eastern Conference in a booklet entitled *The Tanaka Memorial,* which, they claimed, was the text of a formal document submitted by Tanaka to Hirohito in 1927 as an "address to the throne," and was accepted by the latter as Japan's future master plan for her domination of Asia.

This document—nothing less than a blueprint for the military conquest of Manchuria and the whole of China, to be followed by the annexation of all of Asia and armed confrontation with the United States—was almost certainly a fake, though it was undoubtedly based on the preliminary reports submitted by the preparatory committee. Annexation of the whole of Asia—what came to be known later as the Strike South doctrine—was discussed at the conference. Though this was indeed what, in time, occurred, the claim that every twist and turn in Japanese policy that followed was based on this Nipponese *Mein*

Kampf does not stand up. For one thing, the *Tanaka Memorial* was far too long: rigid protocol required that any formal "address to the Throne" not exceed two pages. Also, Premier Tanaka, who had also assumed the Foreign Ministry portfolio, and the Kwangtung Army's commander in chief, General Muto, were well aware that any open military intervention in Manchuria might lead to reprisals on the part of the Western powers. For all that, most experts, including Morgan Young, who was in Tokyo at the time, agree that the tone of its deliberations corresponded to the substance of the *Tanaka Memorial,* even if its conclusions were not presented to Hirohito exactly in that form.

Shortly after the conference ended, Yoshizawa, at a rare press conference back in Peking, affirmed that "Japan has no intention whatever of adopting a decisive positive policy toward Manchuria, nor does she plan anything like invasion." But all the signs were that he was lying.

Chiang Kai-shek himself arrived in Japan on the heels of the Far Eastern Conference. It was not just a private visit, though he was courting Mei-ling Soong, the daughter of the Chinese banker C. J. Soong, who was in Japan at the time, and married her on December 1, 1927. After minor policy differences with his own colleagues, Chiang had temporarily relinquished the Kuomintang leadership, though it remained his for the asking.

His other purpose in coming to Japan was to sound out Japanese policy-makers on their attitudes toward a Kuomintang-ruled China, with himself at its head. Though it was out of the question for him to have an audience with Hirohito himself, he did (on November 5, 1927) meet Premier Tanaka privately. The Japanese prime minister, who wished to keep both Chiang Kai-shek and Chang Tso-lin in play, warned him against becoming entangled in "warlord politics" in the north. Japan, he said, was only too happy to assist him in his efforts, but not at the expense of such a proven anti-Communist as Chang Tso-lin. Chiang Kai-shek argued that his drive north was essential, and appealed for help to counteract the impression that the Japanese were Chang Tso-lin's allies.

It was an inconclusive—and, for Chiang Kai-shek, unsatisfactory—session, but he also met other powerful behind-the-scenes establishment figures, including the Black Dragon leader, Toyama, and it is likely that he also urged them to use their influence to topple Chang

Tso-lin. Toyama, despite his age (he was not to die until 1945 at age ninety) was still enormously powerful. He still had unrivaled access not just to diehard nationalist officers and intelligence specialists whose vocation was to destabilize Manchuria, but also to men close to Hirohito, like Prince Konoye, who had just founded the Tuesday Club, an informal working party of members of the House of Peers that advocated friendly relations with Chiang Kai-shek as a means of achieving a united Asia under Japanese leadership. It is inconceivable that Hirohito was not kept abreast of Chiang Kai-shek's "secret" talks in Japan: through his "kitchen cabinet" and close friends like Konoye, Chiang Kai-shek's wishes were certainly relayed to him. It is also probable that Chiang Kai-shek intended to let Hirohito know that should Japan eliminate Chang Tso-lin, he himself would not grieve too much if Japan extended her sphere of influence to Manchuria and Mongolia, provided this did not extend south of the Great Wall.

Hardly coincidentally, in December 1927, an army activist, Colonel Daisaku Komoto, a Manchurian-based staff officer of the Kwangtung Army, dynamited a bridge on a Manchurian railway line: the damage was attributed to "bandits." He repeated the experience several times, increasing the explosive charge, over the next few months, and each time "bandits" were blamed. It is not known whether the upper echelons of the Japanese General Staff knew for sure who the real protagonist was, or whether the news ever reached Hirohito's ears. But it is likely that Toyama, and perhaps some of his aristocratic cronies with palace connections, were aware of the purpose of these experiments. Prime Minister Tanaka certainly was not: he was to try, repeatedly, to save not only Chang Tso-lin's reputation but his life by urging him to give up Peking and return to Manchuria.

For in the spring and early summer of 1928 Chiang Kai-shek was on the march northward, and Chang Tso-lin's army was both outnumbered and outgunned. The progress of Chiang Kai-shek's troops was checked, briefly, south of Peking. Here, in Tsinan, Chiang Kai-shek's Kuomintang troops and Japanese army units from the Tientsin International Concession sent to protect Japanese civilians clashed violently in a series of sporadic skirmishes that commanders on both sides claimed were the fault of inexperienced junior officers acting without orders. These clashes escalated into a full-scale battle, with a massive attack on Tsinan by Japanese troops on May 8 in which atrocities were committed and at least one thousand Chinese soldiers and civilians were killed. Chiang Kai-shek requested investigation by the League of Nations, which took no action. The Tsinan "incident" certainly cooled Chiang Kai-shek's ardor for a rapprochement with Japan—for the first time he saw how viscerally anti-Chinese Japanese troops were—but his chief concern was to crush Chang Tso-lin, and he deliberately took no action to further provoke the Japanese.

Ten days later, after meeting Hirohito, Prime Minister Tanaka informed British, French, Italian and U.S. diplomats in Tokyo that he intended to deliver a memorandum to Chang Tso-lin the following day asking him to "withdraw quietly" from Peking. "If he fights on the way," said Tanaka, "we will prevent him from passing into Manchuria. . . . I look forward to Peking being evacuated and passing quietly into the hands of the Southerners [the Kuomintang]."

Japan's most senior diplomat in Peking, Yoshizawa, duly delivered the note, assuring Chang Tso-lin that Japan could save him if he agreed to leave. The Manchu warlord was trapped, though at first he refused to admit it. He had counted on Western support, failing to realize that the sole concern of the Western powers was the safety of European and American families in Peking and the Tientsin International Concession—on no account must any Western lives be lost in this remote, complicated mini–civil war. Chang Tso-lin's own officers knew the battle for Peking had been lost, and some of his troops began their withdrawal to Manchuria of their own volition. On June 1 Chang Tso-lin turned the city over to a Peace Preservation Committee and, in a farewell address, announced his return to Manchuria "in order to spare further bloodshed."

Ryukishi Tanaka, the same Japanese officer who had watched crowds outside the palace pray for the new emperor just after Taisho's death, was now an army intelligence agent in China, keeping close watch on Chang Tso-lin's comings and goings. As Manchuria's uncrowned king, Chang had private trains at his disposal, and the first of these, a seven-wagon decoy with some of his staff and his favorite concubine aboard, left Peking on the evening of June 2. Chang Tso-lin himself followed in another train, departing after midnight. Despite worsening relations with Japan, Chang Tso-lin still had a few Japanese liaison officers with him. Two left the train in Tientsin. The one remaining officer aboard, Major Nobuya Giga, kept him company, playing mah-jongg and drinking beer with him throughout the night. Chang Tso-lin felt that he was safe so long as even one Japanese officer stayed on the train.

Tanaka, the spy, had reported the departure of both trains to his superiors in Mukden. The first arrived there without mishap. About a couple of miles south of Mukden station, as Chang Tso-lin's journey was nearing its end, Major Giga casually retired to his own compartment on the pretext of collecting his belongings. What he did was to rush to the train's rear platform, curl up and pray he would be spared. As the train entered the last underpass a Japanese team trained by Major Komoto triggered the explosive device. There was a huge roar. Chang Tso-lin's compartment reared up in the air. He died instantly, along with eighteen other travelers (Major Giga survived). The outrage, the Japanese army staff in Mukden blandly reported, was undoubtedly the work of "bandits." Two bodies were conveniently put on show, allegedly caught by Japanese army railway troops. These were, of course, decoys, sacrificed for the occasion, but a third "bandit" managed to escape, and broke the news to Chang Tso-lin's son of what had really happened.

The "bandits" version of Chang Tso-lin's death remained, of course, the official version for years to come, and it was the only version dutifully reported in the Japanese press. Not until after World War II, when IMTFE prosecutors began investigating suspected Japanese war criminals' prewar careers, did some of the details actually come to light.

Premier Tanaka, of course, immediately suspected that Chang Tso-lin's convenient demise was the work of Japanese officers; indeed some activists later claimed, in sessions with U.S. interrogators,* that Tanaka himself had been perfectly aware all along of the plot to blow up the train. He certainly knew that a full investigation might have embarrassing consequences for people in high places.

Hirohito blandly advised him to make a full, no-holds-barred inquiry, probably aware that he was putting Tanaka in an impossible situation—for either Tanaka made only a token inquiry, in which case he was transgressing his emperor's orders while protecting individuals

---

*The Brocade Banner.

in key places, or else he went ahead and risked making public a major scandal, with possible ramifications too embarrassing to contemplate.

When rumors in Japan began to spread, hinting that Chang Tso-lin had died in an elaborately planned Japanese army plot, Tanaka asked the head of the Japanese secret police, General Komatsu Mine, to initiate a full, personal, on-the-spot inquiry. Inevitably, Mine's report turned out to be a risible travesty of the facts: bandits had been at work; the Japanese army unit responsible for patrolling the line had been guilty of negligence. He suggested that Major Komoto be reprimanded. In the event, two officers took the blame: a general (later reinstated) and Komoto himself were removed from the active list "for failing to place guards along the line."

Had Tanaka had the gall to accept the Mine report at its face value, he might have ensured his own political survival. But he was himself in an increasingly precarious position: heavily criticized for allowing Japan to become a party to the Briand-Kellogg Pact against war, he was also under fire in the Diet, where an opposition proposal for another probe of the Chang Tso-lin affair was defeated, but only by 220 to 198; Tanaka eventually sent Mine back to Manchuria, and this time Mine, assuming that Tanaka knew what he was doing, produced a report that told most of the story. Tanaka was shocked, and again went to the emperor for advice. After receiving assurances, once more, from palace chamberlains that Hirohito did indeed want the unvarnished truth, Tanaka was reassured. But the Japanese were about to celebrate their new emperor's formal enthronement ceremony, and all government business ground to a halt.

It was only in 1929 that the saga resumed, with Saionji hinting that if the second report was ever released, the emperor's "august face would be muddy." As it happened, Hirohito had already been briefed by his war minister on the contents of the second Mine report, though Tanaka was unaware of this. His nerve, in the last resort, failed him. He backtracked, telling the emperor that there were no sensational new revelations to come, after all. Hirohito immediately exploited this volte-face. "Does this not completely contradict what you told me previously?" he asked Tanaka. To his grand chamberlain, he said, "I cannot understand Tanaka. I do not ever want to see him again."

Tanaka had no choice but to submit his resignation. He died three months later. There were reports he had committed suicide as a protest against the slur on his good name. But the Tokyo grapevine had it that he died in a geisha's arms after a drinking bout.

Four years later, Hirohito told his chief aide-de-camp, General Honjo, that he had dismissed Tanaka not so much because he had lied but because he had gone about his lying in such a clumsy way. As Honjo recorded the conversation in his diary,* Hirohito said that "had he [Tanaka] made such a statement [i.e., a cover-up] on his own authority, then explained it had been necessary for political reasons, and *then* submitted his resignation," the Emperor's view was that "as a politician he probably had no other choice. . . . But he asked me to approve the statement beforehand; if I had given my approval it would have meant telling my people a falsehood." This was why Hirohito had found it necessary not only to get rid of Tanaka, but also to disgrace him.

Even now there are gray areas in the Chang Tso-lin assassination plot. It can never be proved that Hirohito was aware of the detailed ramifications of the "army plot" to get rid of Chang Tso-lin until he received a version of the second Mine report. On the other hand, many of the protagonists were personally known to him, and, in the aftermath of the war, several piquant details emerged. General Mine, whose investigation first whitewashed the army and then put it on the spot, was himself implicated in the plot up to the hilt. Colonel Kanji Ishihara, another top-level intelligence officer involved in the Chang Tso-lin assassination plot, was questioned by IMTFE prosecutors in May 1947. Completely unrepentant about any of Japan's war crimes, Ishihara—whose career came to a sudden end in 1941 owing to his personal hostility to Tojo and his later conviction that a protracted war with China was a mistake—affirmed that, contrary to general belief, Tanaka had indeed already told the emperor the truth about the circumstances of the Chang Tso-lin murder by the time he came before him, that final time, with the "cover-up" version.

If Ishihara's story is correct, then Tanaka's utter confusion, on being dismissed, is readily explained: the bluff soldier was only casting about for a version of events that he felt was the one Hirohito wanted to hear. Completely out of his depth, he floundered—and Hirohito brilliantly extricated himself from a personally embarrassing situation by

---

*The Honjo Diary, 1933–36, University of Tokyo Press.

taking a high moral stance and rebuking Tanaka for attempting to dissemble the truth. Scarcely coincidentally, Tanaka's disgrace was also that of the Choshu clan as a whole.

Ishihara also told IMTFE investigators that Tanaka had given the emperor the names of the three key "plotters"—Major Kenji Doihara, Colonel Seishiro Itagaki and Ishihara himself—who had masterminded the Chang Tso-lin murder. Had his moral indignation been as genuine as he made it out to be to the unfortunate Tanaka, Hirohito could then and there have put a stop to their careers. But Major Komoto, the explosives expert, was the only scapegoat, and was made to resign his commission. Very soon afterward, he became a leading businessman in Manchuria, amassing a considerable fortune. None of the others found their careers impeded. On the contrary, they remained in close touch with those palace officials and ADCs in daily contact with the emperor. Itagaki, later war minister, was to visit the palace in 1932, and was almost certainly received in person by the emperor.

Hirohito, for all his youth, displayed, throughout the Tanaka/Chang Tso-lin affair, considerable talent in distancing himself from individuals and events that might affect his reputation, letting others carry the burden of responsibility for their actions while insulating himself from any ensuing adverse consequences. It was a technique that would be perfected as time went on.

CHAPTER FIVE

While the Chang Tso-lin murder investigation was still marking time, Hirohito was formally enthroned as the one hundred twenty-fourth emperor in direct line of succession. The ceremonies symbolized the temporal and spiritual links between the age-old imperial dynasty and the emperor himself as titular head of Shintoism, Japan's state religion.

The rites surrounding the most important event in Hirohito's life actually began months in advance, with the symbolic planting of high-quality rice at specially chosen sites; this was the Great New Food Festival. Since the lushness of the newly planted rice would determine the prosperity and general quality of his reign, special care was taken to ensure its glorious maturing. Various other religious ceremonies took place throughout the year, leading up to Hirohito's actual November 1928 enthronement in the ancient city of Kyoto, the capital of his forebears, in a series of pageants, banquets and Shinto rites.

There was an unprecedented effort beforehand to personalize the ceremony and present Hirohito to the public as a modern, forward-looking emperor. Exceptionally, there were press kits and detailed explanations of the significance of the various rites involved, for the benefit of both the Japanese and the foreign press. Though the explanations were couched in language that was still, by modern Western standards, absurdly reverent and formal, they represented a marked departure from what had gone before, for the hallmark of everything involving the emperor and the imperial family generally was secrecy.

As anyone who has visited the Shinto Holy of Holies in Ise knows, the actual shrine where the supremely sacred (if fake) Amaterasu mirror is housed is completely hidden from view and never seen by anyone except the emperor himself. After a long walk up a hill through meticulously tended gardens, with rivers full of startlingly colored carp, one comes to a small proscenium, an open-air stage setting for an avant-garde Japanese play. The entrance to the shrine is entirely shrouded by an opaque white curtain. What lies right, left and beyond is out of bounds, and even as late as the nineteenth century the penalty for trying to glimpse beyond this curtain was death. In the same way, the actual palace grounds, occupying a huge area in the center of Tokyo, are protected from prying eyes by deliberate, man-made landscaping that screens all but the green copper roofs of a few buildings. The Akasaka Palace, that miniature Versailles, is fully visible from the street, but the rest of the 123-acre site, where the emperor's closest relatives live walled in (and these days subject to wraparound electronic surveillance from TV cameras), is not. The imperial buildings must be among the most discreetly secure homes anywhere in the world.

On November 6, 1928, the emperor and empress, in separate horse-drawn carriages, left the palace for the Tokyo railway station, then still a provincial-looking red-brick building, along a route lined with soldiers and cheering crowds. The journey to Kyoto took two days; the royal train proceeded at a deliberately slow pace, and crowds of villagers and schoolchildren, all officially convened, lined the track. The royal couple rested that first night in Nagoya.

In Kyoto, several thousand participants—princely relatives, government members, priests, dignitaries both Japanese and foreign—had already gathered. They included a glittering couple: dashing Prince Chichibu and his bride, the glamorous Setsuko, daughter of Japan's former ambassador in Washington, Baron Tsuneo Matsudaira. In many respects Chichibu and his beautiful bride were far more typical of the new, "smart" Japan than the reigning couple. Chichibu was just down from Oxford, and had a near-perfect command of English. He had met his bride while staying at the Japanese embassy residence in

Washington, during his Oxford undergraduate days. She was far more sophisticated and worldly-wise than the empress. Both Chichibu and Setsuko were avid American film and jazz fans, in touch with all the latest Western fads and fashions. By this time, Empress Nagako had given birth to two daughters, and both she and the Palace advisers around her impatiently hoped her next child would be male. If not, they told each other, something would have to be done.

The ceremonies were preceded by three days of intense rehearsals. As usual, the actual proceedings were witnessed only by a handful of participants within the Secret Purple Hall, the court buildings in the center of a huge park. The mass of privileged guests saw next to nothing, although, for the first time, some journalists were allowed to be present in the outer chamber. There was no actual crowning, but a series of purificatory rites, which took place behind an opaque white curtain. The royal couple's regalia made it difficult for them to move. Hirohito's costume, deliberately patterned on the earliest records of such rites, dating back at least a thousand years, consisted of a saffron silk robe illuminated with emblems and omens; with this he wore platform shoes and brocaded trousers, both red, and his headpiece was stiffened by black lacquer. He carried his personal emblem, a plain wooden scepter, in his right hand.

Empress Nagako's dress was even more complicatedly elaborate, a set of five stiffened, embroidered superimposed kimonos, weighing at least seventy-five pounds. Her face was chalk-white, her hair elaborately coiffed and surmounted by a golden crown. Their "thrones" were miniature temples, set on high platforms.

It was here that Hirohito issued his proclamation, invoking the spirits of his ancestors and the "wish to preserve world peace and benefit the welfare of the human race," to which Prime Minister Tanaka replied with a short congratulatory homily, ending with "Tenno heika, banzai!" (May the Lord Emperor live ten thousand years). With remarkable coordination in this pre-electronics age, the cry was taken up all over the country at that very minute, followed by the nationwide rendering of Japan's national anthem, "Kimigayo."

This was only the first of a series of celebrations lasting nearly two weeks, including banquets, further purification rites, ritual river immersion, contemplation ("soul quieting") and the mystical daijosai, the offering of symbolic food to the Shinto gods in an interminably complicated ritual lasting several nights. One of them Hirohito spent alone under a sacred quilt, in symbolic communion with his ancestor, the sun-goddess Amaterasu, being "reborn." In all these rites, Hirohito was both the object and performing high priest, anointer and anointee. The sacred nature of the proceedings can be gauged from the fact that after the whole thing was over, all the artifacts involved, as well as the building in which the ceremonies had taken place, were ceremonially burned.

Twenty days later Hirohito and the empress returned to the Imperial Palace in Tokyo, to the accompaniment of the same crowds, troops and formal welcomes. A 101-gun salute boomed out as they entered the palace, and that night the city was lit up by fireworks as the people rejoiced.

Only now, with the ceremonies completed, was Hirohito considered by the Shinto priesthood to be fully qualified, as their supreme religious leader, to act as the sole intermediary between the world of the living and the world of the spirits of his imperial ancestors.

As a full-fledged emperor, Hirohito now instituted an austere working schedule he would rarely depart from till the end of his life: protocol was even more rigidly observed, and his public appearances became less frequent. From 1929 onward, they were restricted to garden parties, Diet openings and inspections of his armed forces, including military maneuvers on land and sea. Hirohito regularly took the salute at march-pasts of students and notables, and he regularly received ambassadors, but the informal part of his life now took place, more than ever, far from the public gaze. A nine-hole golf course was laid out within the palace grounds, and the Imperial Household laboratory built so that Hirohito could indulge in his favorite pastime without leaving the palace enclosure.

Inside his father's palace Hirohito made a number of significant changes. He furnished his office in the Western style, displaying photographs of distinguished personalities he had met on his European tour—Marshal Pétain, King Albert of the Belgians, the Prince of Wales. There were busts of Lincoln, Darwin and Napoleon—and a couch, should he be required in an emergency to spend the night there. He had a personal telephone line installed, in August 1928, which gave him far freer access to subordinates, ministers and chiefs of staff: he never identified himself on the phone—those he called were sufficiently intimate to recognize his voice. The imperial library was put to more active use, for the more formal receptions. One of his first decisions, after Taisho's death, was to put an end to the habit of being presented on momentous occasions with gifts of dead fish. As a naturalist, he felt the only place for such creatures was the sea. He also reduced the amount of clothes handed down to courtiers. His forebears—taking their cue from the Chinese Ming and Ching dynasties—wore their robes only a few times. Hirohito, remembering General Nogi's thrifty precepts, changed all that.

Some time-honored rites and taboos were retained: protocol required that the emperor's body was not to be touched, not even by doctors or tailors. (Doctors wore silk gloves, but tailors had to guess the emperor's measurements, which perhaps explains why, in photographs, his suits and uniforms look either too big or too small.) There were still food tasters—two separate sets of meals, to guard against poison—and regular examination of the royal feces. But otherwise his daily life was that of any busy, hardworking twentieth-century statesman.

He rose early, at six, prayed, exercised (on horseback if the weather permitted) and breakfasted with the empress. He read the papers, including the English-language *Japan Times and Advertiser,* the Foreign Ministry's influential mouthpiece, and followed this with a brief informal conference with his grand chamberlain, reviewing the major appointments and activities of the day to come, or with his chief ADC, if there were meetings later with the military. From 10:00 A.M. to 2:00 P.M. he was almost always at his desk, reading, reviewing and ordering the imposition of the imperial seal. This was also the time he received visitors, either in his office or in the library. After a light, Japanese-style lunch, he exercised again, usually playing golf. Most of his court ministers were or became ardent golfers, especially Kido and Prince Konoye—proficiency was almost a requisite for a senior palace post.

Afterward he bathed. The palace was equipped with both European-style baths and the Japanese kind, and Hirohito used one or the other as the fancy took him. Later there was more office work, followed by private pursuits, reading, conversations with the empress, relaxation with his growing family, perhaps a spell in his marine biology laboratory. He went to bed early, in a Western-style bed, and no one, not even his most trusted palace servants, was allowed inside the imperial bedchamber unless specially summoned.

Four personally selected high officials—in effect, staff officers with enormous but somewhat loosely defined, overlapping powers—helped Hirohito run his private, his palace and his public life. First in importance, at any rate in salary terms, was the Imperial Household minister, with responsibility for all public functions and official engagements; next in importance came two men, the Lord Privy Seal and the emperor's chief aide-de-camp, with similar duties, one civilian, the other military. The Lord Privy Seal (like the Imperial Household minister, he had the rank of minister of state) was the emperor's political liaison officer, engaged in an exchange of information not just with cabinet ministers and politicians but with the Japanese establishment as a whole. The chief ADC was his military equivalent, with his own staff of eight more junior ADCs drawn from the navy as well as the army. Finally, the grand chamberlain handled palace staff administration and supervised the emperor's own vast fortune, in jewelry, land, bank and business holdings.

Because the grand chamberlain knew all about the emperor's personal wealth, he was also the unofficial link between the emperor and the zaibatsu, the large industrial conglomerates. Many of the imperial family's assets were in fact invested in the zaibatsu or kept in zaibatsu-controlled banks. The grand chamberlain was also the official "appointments secretary," and, like all those controlling access, immensely powerful for that reason alone.

Over the years the relative influence of these four men, all of whom saw the emperor several times a day, varied with circumstances. As the last surviving *genro,* Saionji, became older and less active, so his political advice tended to count less, and, as a result, that of the Lord Privy Seal increased. The chief ADC should by rights have become more powerful than any of the other three as the armed forces began playing an ever-increasingly important part in the life of Japan, but in fact he never assumed in military affairs quite the status a trusted, sophisticated Lord Privy Seal such as Marquis Kido enjoyed, for one very simple reason: both the army and navy chiefs of staff had privileged access to the emperor, alone if they so requested, provided the grand chamberlain found them a gap in the emperor's daily schedule.

There were special tasks for special days. Wednesdays were Privy Council days, when treaties, imperial ordinances and broad lines of both domestic and foreign policy were discussed. Since these were substantive meetings, Hirohito liked to leave the next day free, so that he could mull over the proceedings without being disturbed. Fridays were set aside for formal meetings with ambassadors, foreign guests and award-winning athletes or academics; Saturday mornings, for his beloved marine biology. Twice a month he saw the vice chiefs of staff, and several times a year the routine was shattered: Hirohito had to officiate in Shinto ceremonies, dressed in heavy white silk robes—the only time, apart from his enthronement ceremony, when he wore formal Japanese dress.

There were tacit regulations where both civilian and military audiences were concerned: it was a house rule, dating back to Emperor Meiji's times, that when postings were being discussed, no ADC or other outsider should be present. Meiji had heard that in imperial Russia ADCs listening in on such conversations would later claim that they had been responsible for intervening in favor of those promoted or nominated to new commands, and thus exert undue influence. Hirohito was always more at ease with military men than he was with civilians, or the military were less likely to spring unwelcome, unexpected petitions on him. The Lord Privy Seal invariably attended audiences with civilians. Hirohito reduced their frequency after a high official once had the temerity to raise with him an issue not on the official agenda. On occasion, even chiefs of staff had their audiences postponed if the grand chamberlain felt this was in line with the emperor's policies: after the Treaty of London regulating the tonnage of Japanese warships, the naval chief of staff attempted to see Hirohito to protest against such limitations, but the grand chamberlain (Kantaro Suzuki, an admiral and lifelong courtier, later to become the last wartime premier) found no place for him on the emperor's schedule. In this indirect way were the emperor's preferences known.

All four individuals held such key positions that the emperor had to be utterly convinced of their loyalty and discretion. Ever since the Choshu "plot" that tried to prevent his marrying the girl of his choice, Hirohito saw to it that he was surrounded by people he had known for years and trusted implicitly: in 1928 his grand chamberlain was Sutemi Chinda, an experienced, sophisticated diplomat who had accompanied him on his European tour, as had his chief ADC, General Akira Nara. Later, he was to draw on people who were either "family" (like Prince Konoye) or had been lifelong servants of the court, like Admiral Suzuki, whose wife had taught him in the palace kindergarten at the age of five, and Marquis Kido. Whenever the situation became threatening, Hirohito would close ranks and rely, ever more heavily, on princely relatives or those who had known him since boyhood.

Since several of the most senior palace officials were to keep detailed records of their conversations with Hirohito, and record his day-to-day timetable, it is surprising there are so few glimpses of his informal, "human" behavior. Even his poetry has a curiously formal, predictable stamp to it, if the court diarist Kanroji's selections are typical. His first *waka,* in 1921, went:

> *The day has begun*
> *with the twittering of birds*
> *calmly at dawn, gradually disclosing*
> *the shrine of Yoyogi.*

Another, much quoted poem, written on his return home after his European trip, read:

> *Would that all the world*
> *were as tranquil*
> *as this expanse of sea,*
> *flooded brightly*
> *with the warm sunshine at morn.*

There are a few—very few—instances of imperial humor: on one occasion, Kanroji fell heavily on a ski slope, and started swearing like a trooper. The emperor glided up to him, and said, with the ghost of a smile, "I wish I knew some of those words." Most of Hirohito's fun was at his staff's expense: he was amused by their falls while skiing, but, Kanroji adds, "His Majesty never laughed." His one recorded practical joke illustrates his naturalist's bent: knowing Kanroji's weakness for watermelon, he presented him with a pumpkin that looked just like one, and asked him repeatedly if he had tasted it. But he rarely, if ever, allowed others to see him behaving like an ordinary human being, and was almost completely devoid of small talk, except of the most stilted, banal kind. (The empress, foreign diplomats noted, was far more skillful in this respect.) A French diplomat recalls the excruciatingly formal exchanges between the French ambassador and the emperor on those rare occasions when they met formally, on National Day or its equivalent. The emperor invariably said, "And how is the health of my good brother, the distinguished French president of the republic?'' The ambassador would assure him that he was well. "In that case," Hirohito invariably answered, "please congratulate him on his good health and also convey my best wishes to the people of France." As the ambassador left the imperial presence, he could hear the emperor ask the ambassador behind him: "And how is the health of my good brother, the distinguished king of the Belgians?"

Kanroji gives endless examples illustrating Hirohito's conscientiousness as a monarch, never shirking his official duties, however boring, tiring or repetitive (there is a whole chapter headed "Thinking Ever of the People"). Like De Gaulle, Hirohito never allowed his aides to shield him from the rain when reviewing troops or saluting crowds; he seems to have had an infinite capacity for taking the salute for hours on end, and even, on one occasion, bowed to crowds he could not see when told they were massed on the shoreline to greet his flagship.

As an example of Hirohito's presence of mind, Kanroji cites his neatly phrased refusal after he had been offered a ride in a fighter plane during his visit to Britain as crown prince: "I'm sure it would be an interesting experience, but unfortunately it's impossible on today's tight itinerary." Kanroji's tone shows he regarded the off-the-cuff British proposal as an enormous protocol blunder.

Though the gulf between emperor and people remained huge, Hirohito's enthronement had been an excellent public relations operation, for him and for Japan. There was a remarkable consensus, among Western governments and Tokyo-based diplomats, that this young emperor—the only one ever to have traveled outside Japan—would usher in a new, progressive, "moderate" era. The choice of Showa (peace and enlightenment) as a hallmark of his reign was not yet perceived as ironic. His top four court officials and ministers were regarded by foreign observers as responsible, sophisticated moderates who would surely be able to restrain the military adventurists among the junior ranks of the services. The details of the Chang Tso-lin murder were still not generally known. The outside world was prepared not only to live with Japan as a major power but to look sympathetically on her coming of age.

Despite the purge of university liberals and the growing militarization of Japan's educational system, foreign observers were not unduly worried, in 1928, by the growth of military influence. Diplomats could not fail to notice that official portraits of Hirohito invariably showed him in uniform, but saw nothing sinister in this.

What worried observers far more was the economic crisis brought about by worldwide depression following the crash of 1929. Half of Japan's farmers relied on raw silk as a cottage industry to eke out their inadequate income, with America by far the biggest importer. Sales of this luxury commodity to the United States dropped catastrophically from 1930 on, causing real hardship. Japan was still a predominantly agricultural country, and there was overpopulation in agriculture—simply not enough land to go round. Some of the new military radicalism resulted from firsthand knowledge of the peasants' plight, for many army men now came from poor lower-middle-class or farming families. But Hirohito was not much concerned about his people's problems. Inevitably, perhaps, it was difficult for someone living on such a rarefied plane to grasp the nature of dire poverty. Even his chief ADC, Honjo, in a guarded, indirect sort of way, expressed some concern, in his diary, at the emperor's apparent indifference. In his conversations, later, with Honjo, there was a naive element in his apologia for the simple, rural life, the kind of life Hirohito claimed he would willingly have led had he not been born into the imperial family.

Army officers, and Japan's top technocrats, were fully aware of the crisis. The chief executive of the South Manchurian Railway Company openly campaigned for government-sponsored emigration by Japanese farmers to the Manchurian countryside as the only solution to Japan's economic and agricultural plight. (One officially sponsored plan called for emigration quotas of Japanese farmers to Manchuria on a yearly basis right up to 1956.) The widely believed, popular (and, needless to say, unsubstantiated) myth was that Manchuria, a kind of El Dorado, could accommodate millions of new settlers without displacing the native population or causing any hardship of any kind. Part of the Japanese expansionist push that came soon after the enthronement was in response to the cry for *Lebensraum.* Advocates of the colonization of Manchuria regarded such an operation not only as a sound economic proposition but also as a neat military solution. Trained ex-servicemen were to be given preference over civilian farmers, and local officials (doctors, nurses, harbormasters, railway officials) were also to be drawn from the ranks of the reservists, who would be able, in an emergency, to assume their army roles. In politicians' and generals' speeches, at this time, Japan was constantly referred to as a small potted tree struggling to extend its roots—and dying in the process.

Still, in contrast to both her Chinese and her Russian neighbors, Japan appeared immeasurably more stable. In Soviet Russia (recognized by Japan in 1928) these were the early Stalinist years, with forcible collectivization, widespread famine and the elimination of the kulaks; China was still far from united, with Chiang Kai-shek only beginning his struggle against the Communists, facing unrest and subversion in cities and provinces not fully under his control. The Manchurian situation remained volatile: Chang Tso-lin's son, Chang Hsueh-liang, called the "Young Marshal," had disappointed the Japanese plotters of his father's murder, proclaiming his allegiance to Chiang Kai-shek instead of becoming, as they had hoped, a docile Japanese puppet. Japan had not yet given up hope in him and, as a wry token of esteem, a Japanese dignitary had been sent to attend his father's funeral ceremonies. The Order of the Rising Sun was conferred on the Young Marshal in an attempt at ingratiation. This occurred despite a particularly dramatic bloodletting, which showed that Chang Tso-lin's son, for all his reputation as an opium addict, was a chip off the old block. He invited a Manchu general and the head of the Chinese Railways in Manchuria to a game of mah-jongg in his Mukden palace. Both men, he had discovered, were plotting with the Japanese to turn Manchuria into a Japanese-controlled puppet province. As they entered the room the Young Marshal had them gunned down, as an example to others.

The choice of the next prime minister after Tanaka had been another reassuring factor to foreign observers and liberal Japanese alike. Hirohito, again after consulting with Saionji, chose Osachi Hamaguchi (prime minister, 1929–1932), a highly respected leader of the Minseito party who looked a little like a tiny Oriental Einstein. The nomination of Baron Kijuro Shidehara, a man known for his moderation where China was concerned, as foreign minister was also seen as a victory for the liberals.

The only fire-eater in Hamaguchi's cabinet was Kenzo Adachi, the home minister, a man with a sinister past and a reputation for winning

elections by knocking heads. In his early days he had masterminded
a particularly horrible crime—the murder of the Korean queen, deliberately instigated by Japan's intelligence services, backed by Black
Dragon extremists, to facilitate Japan's increased hold on the country.
That Hamaguchi should find the need to include such a monster in
his otherwise impressive cabinet was a sad commentary on the state
of Japanese political parties, with their excessive reliance on bullyboys
and Tammany Hall–type bosses.

The issue most debated in 1929–30 was not the economy but
Japan's role as a naval power. After preparatory talks in Washington,
the leading naval powers met in London to decide on the respective
sizes of their navies. The purpose was to avoid an arms race, but in
Japan the conference was regarded as a deliberate racist slur. What
right, nationalists asked, did the Western powers have to interfere in
what was Japan's sovereign right to build what warships she needed?

Both in Washington and in London, the brunt of the work fell on
a relatively junior naval officer, Rear Admiral Yamamoto, the man
who had lost two fingers of his left hand during the 1905 Russo-
Japanese War. Yamamoto did not share the jingoistic views of some
of his colleagues. In advance of his time, he believed that to measure
a navy's strength solely by tonnage was hopelessly old-fashioned. He
believed in a force of speedy, highly maneuverable pocket battleships,
in submarines and, above all, in a strike force of carrier-based naval
aircraft. Privately, he felt a 10–10–6 ratio (six tons for Japan for every
ten tons for U.S. or U.K. navy vessels) more than adequate. Hirohito,
a military history enthusiast and sound amateur strategist himself,
agreed. For bargaining purposes, however, Hirohito felt, like his navy
chief of staff, that Japan should press for a 10–10–7 ratio.

In the event, after talks first in Washington, then in London in 1930,
Japan won a surprising victory. The final figure (6.9945 tons to Japan
for every 10 tons to the United States and the United Kingdom) was
far more than Hirohito or his naval experts had expected. Moreover,
America agreed to allow Japan 73 percent of parity till 1936, and also
announced she would delay the construction of three heavy cruisers.
More important still, naval aircraft were not even mentioned in the
deal.

Rear Admiral Yamamoto returned to Japan via the USSR and Manchuria. He met discreetly with Prince Konoye, the head of the Tuesday Club, and one of the few Japanese able to see Hirohito informally

at almost all times, regardless of the emperor's schedule. Konoye told Yamamoto that his performance had taken everyone by surprise. He congratulated him, assured him of a brilliant future, but warned him not to be surprised if some diehards, back in Tokyo, expressed their disappointment at the outcome. The parity issue had become a symbol for the lunatic-fringe nationalists. Nevertheless, both Yamamoto and his navy minister got an enthusiastic reception on their arrival. Hirohito received them in audience and formally thanked them for their work. But a Black Dragon activist presented another of the conference delegates with a wrapped dagger—a Mafia-like hint that he should commit suicide "for endangering national defense."

Hirohito shared Yamamoto's view that technical innovation, rather than tonnage, really determined naval power. What concerned him now, far more than international tonnage ratios, was the amount of money needed to make the Japanese navy one of the best in the world. With considerable infighting skill, he refused to sign the naval limitations treaty until his prime minister came up with a sufficiently large figure. This in turn sparked off an interservices quarrel, for the army was not at all pleased to see the navy get the lion's share of the military budget. The generals' eyes were on Manchuria, and a showdown there would be expensive. It would take place on land, not on sea. General Kazushige Ugaki, the war minister, took to his bed for months with an alleged ear infection. It was, Prince Chichibu inferred, with his newly acquired Oxford wit, really a "sick-down strike," a mute protest against excessive spending on the navy.

Though both Ugaki, the army chief of staff, and Prime Minister Hamaguchi eventually gave in to navy spending demands, there was some discreet intraservice politicking too: one of the trade-offs was a more tolerant attitude toward nationalist army "clubs" and secret societies of all kinds in return for acceptance of the navy's construction budget. The most important of these groups, founded in 1927, was the Cherry Blossom Society, with restricted membership (150 officers from captain to colonel), which not only became a breeding ground for military jingoists of all kinds but also played a leading role in the army putsch that was to put Manchuria under effective Japanese control through the Mukden Incident of September 1931. The new tolerance for this and other societies of the same kind turned out to be disastrous, since the Cherry Blossom Society—and its imitators—became the focal point for every kind of ideological military extremism, gaining strength and winning over new recruits year by year until the very hierarchical principle of the army was threatened. The time would soon come when a well-connected colonel, backed by the right kind of secret society or army "club," wielded far more real power than his actual superior.

The army General Staff also recognized that with so much money going to the navy any military operation involving Manchuria would now necessarily have to be carried out on the cheap. It began reexamining a plan, submitted by Lieutenant Colonel Ishiwara, one of the plotters of Chang Tso-lin's murder, which took this crucial cost factor into account, even turning it into an advantage. Hirohito had almost certainly studied this document. He was already taking an almost paternal interest in Ishiwara and Itagaki, both of them brilliant, unconventional staff officers of immense promise.

In October 1930, with some of the navy budget problems behind him, Hirohito attended naval maneuvers on a flagship in the Inland Sea. He was particularly impressed by Yamamoto's display of naval air power: his carrier-based planes wiped out the conventional battleships in the realistic war games laid on for the emperor. As early as 1921, George C. Ross, the young Royal Navy officer who later helped in the earthquake relief operations, had written home:

> Unless we start a naval construction programme soon, we will be left a long way behind Japan as a naval power. They work day and night in their dockyards. . . . What's more, they are right up to date in everything. It is alarming, as it seems they only started a few years ago.

Since then, Japan had become the most up-to-date naval air power in the world, and Yamamoto's secret naval air base, out of bounds to all but a handful of specialists, made the most of a lean budget: the takeoff and landing decks of imaginary aircraft carriers (Japan possessed only four aircraft carriers, though more were on the way) were simulated on the ground, and a special corps of naval air pilots, handpicked by Yamamoto, was becoming the most sought-after unit in the service.

To be "top gun" in the new naval air corps was to ensure entry into top families through marriage, and into the most exclusive geisha houses too: the socially conscious madams were well aware that the more these dashing, glamorous officers used their establishments, the more "face" they earned, and the more the reputation of their houses soared. For this reason, these prohibitively expensive places—clubs rather than brothels, where discretion was assured—often gave substantial discounts to elite army and navy officers on low salaries. Admiral Yamamoto, with no private means, spent practically all his leisure time in the company of geishas or gambling in geisha houses. He could not have done so on his salary, despite his frequent winning streaks. But in his case, as in others, the madams were shrewd enough to waive their usual fees, while the doors remained inexorably closed to those lacking the right social, financial or political connections. Word of mouth throughout the military, zaibatsu and government "establishments," to say nothing of the discreet but tentacular surveillance of Japan's secret police, ensured that those in the know were well aware of the off-duty geisha proclivities of "top people." Admiral Ross, Britain's assistant naval attaché in Tokyo from 1933 to 1936, was a frequent patron of some of these establishments. He recalls seeing Admiral Yamamoto surrounded by geishas in one of the more exclusive houses and the admiral being suddenly summoned to the phone. Yamamoto came smartly to attention and began speaking softly into the mouthpiece, with courtly deference, before leaving in haste. From the admiral's excessively respectful tone and form of address on the telephone, there was no doubt in the minds of anyone present, Ross recalled, that the voice on the other end of the line had been the emperor's.

On his departure for navy maneuvers, Hirohito still had no government consensus on the exact amount to be earmarked for navy spending. The navy asked for five hundred million yen. Both the finance and prime ministers pleaded with Hirohito to reduce it to three hundred million yen. Finally, Hamaguchi obtained the compromise figure of 374 million yen.

But by this time Hamaguchi himself was a marked man. By agreeing to the arms limitation treaty, and cutting back on the navy's estimates, he had become identified by the lunatic-fringe rightist movements as one of the emperor's "evil advisers" who had to be eliminated as a patriotic duty. Rumors that there was a price on his head reached several people, including Saionji himself, now eighty and feeble, and Saionji's confidential secretary, Harada, passed the word on to Hamaguchi himself. The "old lion," as the fiery politician was nicknamed, dismissed these threats with contempt.

The press never mentioned that the prime minister's life was in danger, but the leading figures in the police and palace establishments knew the threats were real. Hamaguchi continued to receive "routine" protection from his police guards, but the fact that the home minister, Adachi, was a charter member of the Black Dragon Society was hardly reassuring. The news that a gunman was stalking Hamaguchi almost certainly reached the palace: the editor of a Japanese right-wing defense periodical, *Japan and the Japanese,* with close Black Dragon and Cherry Blossom connections, told Prince Konoye in early November 1930 that "things may start to happen from now on." Through his extreme right-wing underworld connections, the same editor had had prior warning of the murder of Japan's earlier prime minister, Hara, nine years previously.

Hirohito, meanwhile, had gone straight from navy to army maneuvers, taking along with him the home minister. Hamaguchi was due to join them. On the morning of November 14, as he was about to board a train, Hamaguchi was shot in the stomach by a near-illiterate rightist, Tomeo Sagoya, who was immediately arrested.

The emperor heard the news in the field, three hundred miles south of Tokyo. He did not find it necessary to return to Tokyo to keep in touch with the situation, but carried on with the exercises. Instead, he appointed Foreign Minister Shidehara as interim premier and conveyed his "regrets" for this "mishap" to Hamaguchi himself, through an aide.

At first the doctors who incompetently fussed over Hamaguchi at the Tokyo Imperial University's infirmary thought he would survive. They operated, gave him blood transfusions, and announced he had a 60 to 70 percent chance of recovery. Hamaguchi, in great pain, was stoical but pessimistic. With extraordinary willpower, he managed to attend to some of his essential duties in later weeks. In excruciating pain he addressed the Diet on navy estimates in an almost inaudible voice. But nine months after the attempt on his life he died of complications following a bungled operation.

Though Hirohito did not interrupt his army inspection, Home Minister Adachi did bow out: he found it necessary, he told the emperor with some embarrassment a few days later, to return to Tokyo forthwith for pressing police business. It was against all protocol rules to leave the emperor's presence when one was his guest, and Hirohito was deeply offended. He knew that Adachi's reason for returning to Tokyo was not to inquire into the Hamaguchi murder attempt, but to start planning his own campaign for the premiership, gathering around him his bullyboys and underworld cronies to discuss their election strategy. It proved to be a fatal mistake. After the Hamaguchi murder, Adachi's political career never lived up to its earlier promise: Hirohito saw to that, excluding him from top office thereafter, whenever his name came up for consideration.

What happened to Hamaguchi's murderer, Sagoya, was equally instructive: he spent the next three years out on bail, before his death sentence on November 6, 1933. Three months later, he was pardoned. Like Hara's assassin, he thereafter lived comfortably on a pension, occasionally taking part in gatherings of extremist nationalists. As late as 1956 he was still active in right-wing circles, staging a mock funeral service for Prime Minister Hatoyama in Tokyo's Shinbashi Station to protest against his "treacherous" decision to conclude a formal peace with the USSR.

This further example of the extraordinary Japanese leniency toward crimes of violence, provided they were politically motivated, baffled even some of the members of Hirohito's own court. The emperor could certainly have advised against a pardon in Sagoya's case, had he so wished, and been obeyed. The thought that such leniency might raise doubts about the nature of Japanese justice and encourage future politically motivated assassination attempts never even seems to have crossed his mind. The virtually unpunished Hamaguchi murder marked the end of Hirohito's "liberal" first few years: the age of innocence was over. That of the assassins was soon to begin.

CHAPTER SIX

The police, without the benefit of a prolonged investigation of Hamaguchi's murderer's links with the far right, hastily concluded that the killer had acted alone. But, as the stricken prime minister lingered on (finally dying in August 1931) a series of conspiracies, all invoking the emperor's name, were being hatched. The first, the 1931 March Plot, made nonsense of Marx's aphorism that history repeats itself, first as tragedy, then as farce, for this event, at least, had distinctly comic overtones.

What happened was that some key staff officers, including Colonel Kingoro Hashimoto, the leading light of the Cherry Blossom Society (and the new Russian Affairs desk officer at Staff HQ after a spell in Turkey, where he had become a fervent admirer of Kemal Atatürk) hinted to War Minister Ugaki, early in 1931, that the emperor, tired of dealing with corrupt, bickering politicians, would look with favor on a military "coup" that would restore the integrity of the imperial nation. Ugaki, who had loyally served the emperor as war minister as far back as 1924, presiding over army budget cuts in the teeth of opposition from within the military, was, they hinted, a natural choice as the emperor's chosen instrument, his new military *genro*.

Ugaki was vain enough to express interest, but cautious enough to seek out more proof of the emperor's tacit involvement. He was subsequently wined and dined by several senior palace officials, but the more he was entertained, in their homes and in expensive geisha houses, the more suspicious he became.

The scenario outlined to him was that of a typical Latin American putsch: a large mob would surround the Minseito and Seiyukai party buildings and the prime minister's house while a handpicked army unit cordoned off Ministry buildings, the radio station and the Diet. A high-ranking officer would persuade members of the Diet to vote in favor of military rule, the abolition of political parties and its own voluntary dissolution. The trouble was that when approached by General Ugaki directly, the commander of the 1st Guards Division (the unit earmarked for the putsch) denied any knowledge of it, saying he would certainly not take part in anything illegal without written instructions from the emperor himself, orders that never came. And such was the aura of divinity surrounding the emperor that Ugaki could not even bring himself to ask for a private audience with Hirohito. In any case, the conspirators told him, it was imperative that His Majesty in no way appear involved.

Some of the preparations, however, were real enough: in order to make the crowds besieging the Diet more threatening, they were to be equipped with grenades. Dr. Okawa, the former director of studies of the University Lodging House, was party to the conspiracy; he was to provide the mobs and the arms. Crates of training grenades, each capable of simulating the blast of four artillery shells and sending clouds of smoke into the air, materialized. Colonel Hashimoto, the Cherry Blossom Society activist, who supplied them, said they had been provided by the Chiba Infantry School. Okawa had them stored first in his home, then in his mistress's house. They were never used.

On March 2 there was a token demonstration, masterminded by Dr. Okawa and the Black Dragon society, but there was no march on the Diet, and the army did not move. The conspirators carried on as if the real plot were still to come, and Ugaki was again lavishly entertained in the company of Okawa and various emissaries linked with palace officials. By this time, however, the general suspected he was being manipulated, and announced he would have nothing more to do with such a crackpot scheme.

This, perhaps, was what Dr. Okawa was waiting for. Moving the incriminating training grenades to a "safe house," he demanded money from the conspirators to pay off the Black Dragon bullyboys who had staged the demonstration. Whether he actually blackmailed them into parting with large sums by threatening to reveal the army's complicity is not clear to this day, despite subsequent lengthy investigations conducted by U.S. prosecutors preparing for the postwar Tokyo Trials. He was certainly able to pay off his bills in geisha houses and settle other costs related to the plot, with something to spare. All the while he continued to draw a sizable salary from the South Manchurian Railway Company, as a "consultant," and even after his involvement in the plot was confirmed, his stipend continued to be paid.

If the purpose of the March Plot was solely to discredit General Ugaki, however, it failed. Shortly afterward, Hirohito packed him off to Korea as governor-general: it was a largely honorific post but certainly not a disgraceful end to a long army career. Nor was this his swan song: later, Ugaki would play a key role as a member of the "peace party" urging Hirohito to end World War II. His opposition to military diehards indeed was such that, in retrospect, the whole March Plot could well have been an elaborate hoax to discredit one of the few senior officers who might have opposed the army's more irresponsible, jingoistic representatives.

What was Hirohito's role, if any? The activists who invoked the emperor's name never produced any evidence that Hirohito was involved. So strangely did the plot unfold that Ugaki ended up more a victim than a protagonist. One theory is that both the Minseito party (including the *genro*, Prince Saionji) and some members of the emperor's entourage had become wary of General Ugaki's influence and integrity, and wished to discredit him. Another is that the plot was seen as a necessary preliminary to any direct army intervention in Manchuria. Most Machiavellian of all is the notion that the whole preposterous intrigue represented a test of Ugaki's personal loyalty by Hirohito himself—to see how far he and other senior army officers would rise to the bait.

At the time, very little information filtered down to foreign observers. It was only after World War II that U.S. investigators preparing the IMTFE prosecution's case uncovered some of its odder details. What is certain is that, as Marquis Kido was later to write, it "came out of darkness" to "return to darkness." No one was hurt, or seriously compromised, and that stormy petrel of Japanese right-wing politics Dr. Okawa made a lot of money, which was almost certainly one of his chief objectives. The fact remains that it is unlikely that Hirohito was completely unaware of the March Plot's broad outline: both Marquis Kido, confidential secretary (in 1931) to Hirohito's Lord Privy Seal, and Count Makino himself took part in the manipulation of the unfortunate general, and they could not have kept the intrigue from the emperor without forfeiting his trust. Kido, already establishing himself within the palace hierarchy as a discreet, indispensable staff officer, influential far beyond his junior position, and singled out for high office by Hirohito himself, was clearly not about to sacrifice a coveted career as the emperor's right-hand man in favor of a crackpot conspiracy. In the light of his later, key role as Lord Privy Seal (1940–45) and as the emperor's principal aide and adviser, to have remained silent would have been completely out of character. The enigma will remain: though Kido kept lengthy diary accounts of his activities, he refers to the March Plot as though he had been a disinterested spectator.

While the March Plot was amateurish farce, the plot to gain control of Manchuria, triggered six months later, was superbly planned and executed. Here again the degree, and the nature, of Hirohito's involvement is still a controversial issue. Three officers with considerable Chinese experience—Colonels Doihara, Itagaki and Ishihara—played leading parts, Ishihara as theoretician and overall planner, Itagaki as staff coordinator, and Doihara as political liaison officer with the Manchurian Chinese. But this plot was on such a huge scale, mobilizing such resources and requiring such split-second timing, that it could not have occurred without the tacit consent, and indeed the active support, of most of the Japanese General Staff. Again, it is unlikely, given Hirohito's industriousness and curiosity where army matters were concerned, that he should have remained completely unaware of the plot. He certainly had a broad knowledge of its preparations, for he did finally take halfhearted steps to caution the Kwangtung Army against precipitate action. But, throughout, he was extremely duplicitous in his dealings not only with his generals but with his cabinet as a whole.

One is reminded of General de Gaulle's attitude, during and after the May 13, 1958, army putsch in Algiers: De Gaulle, we now know, was in close touch with the Algiers-based plotters and, while ostensibly disclaiming any links with them, was privately hinting that he approved their intentions, and was only waiting for them to step in and put an end to the despised Fourth Republic. In the same way, Hirohito, while indirectly distancing himself from the plotters, did nothing to deter them.

The question—one that is seldom asked—is why, if really opposed to the Mukden Incident, Hirohito failed to use his discretionary powers, or even to voice his unequivocal disapproval while there was still time to do so. As Richard Storry noted, it was probable that an imperial proclamation "restraining the army in Manchuria, or, later, in China, would have been obeyed by the great majority of officers."* But the emperor preferred to remain completely in the background, using his aides as a "front": the word was duly spread during the Manchurian army takeover that he was "highly displeased," that the movement of troops from Korea to Manchuria was in "disregard of imperial orders"; and Saionji was to say repeatedly that the army's attitude was "unreasonable."† But further than that Hirohito did not go. On later occasions, in particular during the February 26, 1936, putsch (Japanese refer to this later traumatic event simply as 2/26) he was to show impressive qualities of determination and leadership, conspicuously lacking in 1931.

The inference is that, over Manchuria, Hirohito prevaricated, either deliberately or because of indecision. And the behavior of some of those generals closely involved in preparing and masterminding the complicated operation known as the Mukden Incident makes sense only if one assumes that their inner conviction was that, for all the emperor's and the cabinet's public refutations, they did in fact have Hirohito's tacit consent throughout—though the responsibility had to appear to be theirs alone, especially if anything went wrong.

The Mukden Incident was based on Colonel Ishihara's blueprint prepared several years previously, implemented with the assistance of several members of the Cherry Blossom Society. It was remarkable for several reasons. In the first place, it was relatively inexpensive—Ishiwara knew that thrift was, in Hirohito's eyes, a major virtue. The plan was to take over southern Manchuria from the inside, relying almost exclusively on the Kwangtung Army and Japanese railway guards already permanently stationed there in accordance with long-

---

*Richard Storry, *A History of Modern Japan* (New York: Pelican, 1960).
†*The Brocade Banner.*

standing agreements with China. Though troops in Japanese-run
Korea could later be called on as reinforcements, Ishihara saw the
initial move as a short, sharp blitzkrieg using only those Japanese
troops already legally stationed in southern Manchuria.

The plan's other advantage was that it was conceived not just as a
military operation but as part of a relatively bloodless "revolution"
setting up a puppet administration sympathetic and subordinate to
Japan. A Chinese fifth column had to be on hand to take over the overt
running of the country, with real power resting at all times, of course,
with the Japanese military. Two months before the actual Mukden
Incident (September 18, 1931), Doihara and his staff were at work,
cultivating potential allies among Manchuria's more venal officials and
businessmen. It was fertile ground: there were diehard supporters of
the dispossessed Manchu Ching dynasty who had never considered
themselves fully Chinese in the first place, as well as local landlords
and minor noblemen who felt they had a better future under Japan
than under Chiang Kai-shek. And in the Japanese-run part of Tientsin's International Concession was Henry Pu-yi, the last emperor of
China, already being assiduously courted by Japanese officers and who
was to prove the most prominent Manchu quisling of all.

The risk, however, was great, for Chang Tso-lin's son, the Young
Marshal, was a popular and effective warlord. His army outnumbered
the Japanese garrison twenty to one. But, when the coup came, the
Young Marshal and the bulk of his experienced troops were all south
of the Great Wall, fighting the Communists, and most of the Chinese
soldiers left in southern Manchuria were raw recruits.

Two military objectives in Mukden—the Chinese gendarmerie and
the Young Marshal's tiny air force—had to be neutralized if Ishiwara's
plan was to succeed. Months before the September coup, Kwangtung
Army engineers started building an officers' swimming pool conveniently close to both the gendarmerie barracks and the airfield. Chinese laborers were brought in to work on its foundations, then the
army took over. The site became strictly out of bounds not just to the
Chinese but to most Japanese troops as well; access was restricted to
a handpicked squad. The concrete "swimming pool," surrounded by
a vast wooden enclosure, with gates large enough for trucks to enter,
was in fact a gun emplacement, and in due course two 9.5-inch guns
were smuggled into the city from the army base in Port Arthur and
secretly installed in the "swimming pool" bunker. Elite Japanese artil-

lerymen practiced training the concealed guns on the gendarmerie barracks and the airfield.

In June 1931 a Japanese spy, masquerading as an "agricultural expert," was caught by the Chinese in eastern Mongolia and shot. This incident, unforeseen by Ishihara but not unwelcome, fueled the anti-Chinese anger of the Kwangtung Army. Finally, Ishihara took advantage of a fight between Korean immigrants and Chinese farmers (who had been digging ditches on the Koreans' land—perhaps paid to do so by Ishihara's men) and had troops sent to the Korean-Manchurian border. The stage was set. All that was needed was a detonator. Ishihara had thought of that too, but by this time so many high-ranking officers knew about the Manchurian plot that the government, now headed by Reijiro Wakatsuki, a political kinsman of the murdered Hamaguchi, began to get wind of it. On August 4 General Jiro Minami, the new war minister, briefing divisional commanders after a staff exercise in Japan, warned them of a "grave situation" in Manchuria and Mongolia. This was no "passing phase," he said, but was due to "a decline in Japan's prestige and China's mania for recovery of its rights." The speech, noted at the time by A. Morgan Young,* was itself a clear indication that the Japanese army expected to be involved in war in Manchuria. Rumors spread throughout Tokyo that something big was about to occur there.

Inevitably, the news reached the emperor himself. Hirohito saw Minami, and warned him that the Kwangtung Army in Manchuria "must proceed with prudence and caution." Saionji advised Wakatsuki to send a trusted officer to Manchuria to find out exactly what was going on, and to deliver a letter from the prime minister to the commander of the Kwangtung Army telling him to cancel any plans he might have for military action.

The prime minister's choice was an odd one. The man he selected for the task, Major General Yoshiji Tatekawa, was a hard-liner, already compromised in the March 31 plot, who had written a much publicized article advocating Japanese military intervention in Manchuria.† In addition, he was himself one of the key plotters on the

---

*A. Morgan Young, *Imperial Japan* (New York: William Morrow, 1938).
†Yoshiji Tatekawa, "General Principles Concerning the Solution of the Mongolian Problem."

Tokyo end of the Mukden Incident operation. The plotters were immediately advised of the imminent arrival of the letter-bearing Tatekawa by their Tokyo-based co-conspirator, Colonel Hashimoto, who urged them to go ahead without delay. Instead of flying immediately to Port Arthur, Tatekawa took a leisurely route, by train via Korea, and on arrival in Mukden on September 18, three days later, allowed himself to be spirited away to a geisha house without delivering the crucial letter. The new Kwangtung Army commander, General Honjo, was in any case out of town.

That night, while Tatekawa was "resting," Ishihara pulled the trigger: a Japanese army officer laid some small quantities of dynamite along the embankment of the South Manchuria Railway track north of Mukden, designed to explode with the maximum of noise and the minimum of damage. The detonation took place around 10:20 P.M. Later, the Japanese government was to claim that this had been a "warlike act" on the part of Chinese troops, removing parts of the track and seriously disrupting traffic. It was at a loss to explain how, a few minutes *after* the explosion, a trainload of passengers bound for Mukden passed over that same track without mishap, indeed without anyone aboard realizing anything was amiss.

The explosion was, however, heard by a Chinese patrol, which attempted to investigate, and immediately came under Japanese fire. The "incident" was under way: Colonel Itagaki gave the order to attack. The guns from the "swimming pool" went into action, with devastating effect, and all over southern Manchuria Japanese troops, who had been on alert for days, began their surprise attack on Chinese garrisons. In a few hours it was all over and Mukden was under Japanese control, with the initial loss of only a few Japanese lives (Chinese casualties numbered four hundred).

That night Colonel Doihara had been on another kind of mission: at a banquet attended by prominent Chinese, already sympathetic to the Japanese, he asked their views on the new administration. They agreed Doihara should be Mukden's new mayor, but the decision was never implemented.

From the start, the decisions in Manchuria had been made not by generals but by colonels, principally by Doihara, Ishigawa and Itagaki, but the commander of the Kwangtung Army, General Honjo, who had assumed command only in August, agreed to take overall responsibility for military operations that had been initiated without his prior approval. He too was an "old China hand," in favor of direct military intervention in Manchuria, and was identified, in fact, with the most authoritarian clique in the army, the Kodo-ha (Imperial Way) faction, composed of generals like Sadao Araki, Mazaki and Iwane Matsui who were anathema to Japanese liberals. He knew, and liked, the trio of colonels: Itagaki had been his deputy during his spell as military attaché in Peking in 1924, and he had worked with Doihara in China as far back as 1918. "Honjo's actions when the crisis finally broke appear to confirm assumptions that he was in sympathy with his subordinates but short on facts about their specific plans," says Mark R. Peatie, a leading historian of modern Japan, who quotes Itagaki as saying, during the fateful September 18 night, "Never mind Honjo, it's Ishihara's war."*

The Japanese consul in Mukden came to see Itagaki; when he suggested the conflict be settled through diplomatic negotiations with the Chinese and cast doubt on the Japanese army's version of what had happened earlier that night, Itagaki rudely reminded him that the military command had precedence over civilians, and, after he refused to go, one of Itagaki's staff officers threatened him with a drawn sword. Soon afterward, Japanese correspondents were taken to the site of the "damaged" railway track; a length of the track and three Chinese army corps were exhibited as evidence. How the track itself had been so speedily repaired was not explained. Needless to say, the army's version of events was headlined, without question, in all important Japanese newspapers.

Japanese forces took over Changchun, north of Mukden, on September 19, and Kirin on September 21. Incredibly (or was the delay cynically calculated?), it was only late on September 19 that Major General Tatekawa handed over the prime minister's letter to General Honjo, by which time it was, of course, too late: except for mopping-up actions, the Japanese military operation was as good as over. The generals continued to act on their own initiative: Korean-based Japanese planes were used from September 19 to bomb pockets of Chinese troops, and on September 22 a Japanese brigade based in Korea moved into southern Manchuria—all of this without orders from the

---

*Mark R. Peatie, *Ishihara Kanji and Japan's Confrontation with the West* (Princeton, N.J.: Princeton University Press, 1957).

Japanese government. The intervention of Japanese planes from Korea and Tatekawa's ready acceptance of geisha hospitality on arrival, together with General Honjo's elusiveness in the first few hours of the Mukden Incident, all give credibility to the notion that they considered the prime minister's missive, inspired by Hirohito's cautionary remarks, to be a huge private joke.

Back in Tokyo, the Japanese government, faced with a fait accompli, was powerless, and Hirohito did nothing to provide his ministers with a clear mandate. The prime minister, Tatekawa, reported to the emperor that he had ordered the Kwangtung Army to return to its bases, and to "localize" the conflict. Hirohito replied that the government's action was "perfectly appropriate." At the League of Nations headquarters in Geneva, Japanese diplomats informed their colleagues that the "unfortunate incident" had been the work of "Chinese provocateurs," but that Japanese troops would soon be returning to barracks. In a typical hand-wringing exercise, the League of Nations Council urged the Chinese and Japanese governments "to refrain from action that might aggravate the situation."

The prime minister told his war minister, Minami, that the Japanese government's watchword was "nonaggravation of the incident," but Minami informed his subordinates that "nonaggravation did not necessarily mean nonenlargement," and on September 30, a mere twelve days after the Japanese attack, a Japanese emissary from the Kwangtung Army arrived in Tientsin with a highly important message for Henry Pu-yi: if he was prepared to come to Manchuria, Japan was prepared to restore the Manchu dynasty there.

This, more than anything else, suggests that Emperor Hirohito was not as removed from the Mukden Incident as is sometimes claimed, for even the most swashbuckling, activist general would think twice before proposing a throne to a puppet emperor—policy that required Hirohito's consent. Indeed, the Japanese government, and Hirohito himself, were soon to view the new state of affairs in Manchuria with surprising equanimity. The northern half of Manchuria passed under Japanese military control in November, and soon afterward a leading official body, the Economic National Policy Investigation Society, acknowledged that "even though Manchuria may take on the structure of an independent country, she will be no more than a small, weak nation whose fate is controlled absolutely by an advanced nation. Furthermore, she will not be easily granted an opportunity to get out of this situation. Manchuria . . . would become a territory with no international significance in the same manner as Korea."

And less than three months after the Manchurian takeover, Colonel Itagaki himself came to the Imperial Palace in Tokyo to report on progress in Manchuria. Marquis Kido, who mentioned Itagaki's visit in his diaries (the entry is dated January 11, 1932), recorded that he "and persons close to the Emperor" (which, in court jargon, almost certainly meant the emperor himself was present unofficially) heard Itagaki outline Manchuria's new status, with the imminent arrival of the new puppet ruler, Pu-yi, the formal Japanese commitment to "defend Manchuria from its enemies," and the simple but ingenious means of controlling the new puppet administration without contravening international law: "Japanese officials would assume Manchurian nationality."*

Nor is it possible that Hirohito was unaware of the details of the establishment of the new Japanese-controlled puppet state. Kido, in a rare direct critical outburst, deplored, two days later, on January 14, the emperor's excessive involvement in detail. "I am afraid," the diary entry read, "that the Emperor seems too nervous. . . . His Majesty attends to small matters. It is desirable that the Emperor should sit 'as a large mountain.' "

Hirohito's reactions to the behavior of his war minister and his generals were in marked contrast to the decisiveness he was to show later in the wake of the collapse of the 2/26 putsch. Then he would insist on a clean sweep of senior generals, and would replace almost his entire imperial "cabinet" (chief ADC, Lord Privy Seal and Imperial Household minister).

There is no doubt that the disobedience shown by Honjo, Tatekawa, and the commander of Japanese troops in Korea could have cost them their careers. Had Hirohito felt strongly about their behavior, he had the discretionary power to act, either then or later, as he was to act against those who he considered had let him down during the 1936 putsch, by ordering forcible retirements, withholding promotions or suggesting postings to unimportant jobs. But nothing hap-

---

*IMTFE Prosecution Documents.

pened that might imply that the emperor was displeased. On the contrary: Hirohito gave Honjo the strongest possible proof of his esteem, accepting him as his chief ADC (and hence one of the most powerful officers in the imperial army) in 1933. Colonel Itagaki was promoted to general, and became Hirohito's war minister in 1939. The commander of the Japanese troops in Korea, General Senjuro Hayashi, later became first war minister, then, briefly, prime minister. Kenji Doihara also rose high in the military hierarchy, becoming the head of Army Aviation and in due course one of Japan's most notorious generals. Only Ishihara, who fell afoul of the mean, vindictive Tojo, ended his wartime army career as a mere major general in charge of the 16th Training Division, forcibly retired by 1942. He boasted after the war: "Tojo didn't have the guts to retire me, so he got the Emperor to do it instead."

The hallmark of the Mukden Incident was deceit, not only of the trio of colonels who masterminded the plot, but of almost all those in positions of responsibility. Prime Minister Tatekawa and his liberal foreign minister were doubtless privately appalled, but tacitly acknowledged the inevitability of the action. As A. Morgan Young put it, "Japan tried to accredit the thesis that in Manchuria, the army had acted without orders. Certainly there had been no orders from the Foreign Ministry but the notion was untenable: the whole procedure for the seizure of Manchuria was timed so beautifully and carried out so perfectly that the Staff orders must have been very perfect indeed." The excuse that the army had acted without orders, he added, was "an old Japanese diplomatic gambit," though in this case "perhaps the officials themselves did not realize how completely the initiative had passed out of civilian control."

Once it was clear that the Japanese occupation of Manchuria was proceeding at an irreversible pace, Japanese diplomats—once "doves"—started using language almost as aggressive as that of the military. Yoshizawa, the same Japanese minister in Peking who had blandly denied any Japanese territorial ambitions over Manchuria a few weeks previously, now defended the army's action, caused, he said, "by deep-rooted anti-Japanese feelings in China . . . which had compelled Japan to act in self-defence." As an example of Chinese "bad faith" he cited the boycott of Japanese goods in China—a measure imposed only *after* Mukden. Once the fighting had subsided in

Manchuria, the war minister, Minami, no longer bothered to conceal his feelings: at a banquet (on October 23) attended by generals and high officials of the South Manchurian Railway Company, he made a bombastic speech asserting that what had just happened in Manchuria "sets a precedent for future relations with China." Neither the prime minister, Tatekawa, nor the foreign minister, Shidehara, made any move to resign—a gesture that might have drawn worldwide attention to the domestic drama being played out in Tokyo.

The official Japanese line remains that the emperor was completely taken in by the behavior of the Kwangtung Army, had insufficient prior knowledge of the Mukden Incident to act in time, and did his best to restrain his officers and "localize" the conflict once it began. It is also the version accepted by most academics and historians. In the light of Hirohito's behavior, then and later—the promotion of Honjo and Itagaki, and his assiduous courting of the puppet Manchukuo "emperor," Pu-yi—it is untenable.

The fact is that a "forward policy" in China and the establishment of a Japanese-controlled puppet state in Manchuria were popular not only with lunatic-fringe army groups but with a wide cross section of Japanese. Businessmen and entrepreneurs of all kinds were very well aware of the opportunities in store, especially if—as was to happen— they were to be allowed to operate without any other competition, squeezing out all other rivals, Western and Chinese, with trade and investment entrusted to new groups, not the older established zai-batsu; the army, needless to say, favored the creation of a Manchurian puppet state, as proof of Japan's might as Asia's number one power; economists, demographers and university academics also saw in long-term Japanese emigration to Manchuria the only answer to the problem of population. In short, except with a small minority of liberals like Prince Saionji, the Mukden Incident and its aftermath were highly popular. In a conversation with Harada, his confidential secretary, shortly after the Mukden Incident (in Harada's memoirs, the date is given as September 1932), Saionji already saw the writing on the wall—he spoke, significantly, in the past tense:

> In the past, when we thought about Japan's future, we never thought in terms of anything so narrow as "Japan, leader of the East" or an "Asian Monroe Doctrine." The problem of

the Far East can be better resolved through cooperation with Britain and America than through the mouthing of "Asianism" or an "Asian Monroe Doctrine."

The only logical explanation of Hirohito's behavior during and after the Mukden Incident was that he faced a dilemma. While tacitly recognizing the overwhelming strength of the coalition of vested interests in favor of this "forward policy," he was reluctant to alienate the more cautious, "liberal" elements in his cabinet, whose members were well aware of the international consequences of Japan's brutal, aggressive action in Manchuria, and of the domestic consequences of allowing the army a free hand in determining policy. Nor did he want to fall into the trap of becoming an overt military emperor-dictator, in essence a prisoner of the military extremists. By choosing the path of ambiguity, he placated those elements in Japan who were wary of the military without alienating the activists themselves, all the while following the precept, in force since the Meiji Restoration, of not appearing to take any day-to-day decisions himself. He also reassured the Tokyo-based diplomatic corps that "his heart was in the right place," allowing the army to shoulder full responsibility for the origins of the new, controversial puppet state of Manchukuo.

At times, efforts to "sanitize" Japan's takeover of Manchuria reached absurd lengths. The League of Nations' Lytton Report effectively proved that the Mukden Incident had been naked Japanese aggression, and the supposed destruction of the railway track that had provoked the intervention in the first place a carefully planned provocation. But even today there are those who—against all evidence—believe the Chinese initiated the Mukden Incident.

General Honjo, who committed suicide in 1945 rather than face the possibility of standing trial as a suspected war criminal, maintained to the last the official Japanese version of the Mukden Incident long after it had been proved to be a pack of lies. In his 1945 suicide note, he insisted the track really had been blown up by Chinese troops and that subsequent Japanese "peace-keeping operations became necessary to protect Japanese and Korean lives."

Such a pattern of deception, on an almost childish scale, was to be repeated: the same imperial prevarications and contradictions would be a feature of events leading up to Pearl Harbor. It would be difficult at times to differentiate between Hirohito's talent for ambiguity and the grosser Japanese predilection, in some quarters, for the "big lie."

General Honjo's suicide note, however, had nothing to do with Eastern versus Western conceptions of the truth: it was simply his ultimate, spectacular way of demonstrating, even in death, his mystical loyalty to his emperor.

CHAPTER SEVEN

The Mukden Incident and its aftermath did not entirely destroy Hirohito's credibility abroad as a peace-loving young moderate—he had played his cards too shrewdly for that—but it did seriously call into question the aims of the Showa era as he had defined them in his 1926 accession "rescript," or imperial proclamation. Then he had boasted that "a new chapter is being opened in the history of human civilization. This nation's settled policy always stands for progress and improvement. Simplicity instead of vain display, originality instead of blind imitation, progress in view of this period of evolution, improvement to keep pace with the advancement of civilization, national harmony in purpose and action, beneficence to all classes of people, and friendship to all the nations of earth: these are the cardinal aims to which our most profound and abiding solicitude is directed."

Admirable, and probably unattainable at the best of times, these pledges became—after the birth of Manchukuo—an ironic reminder of what might have been. "Friendship to all nations" was already, and would increasingly be, friendship on Japan's terms, the friendship of an arrogant master extended to submissive client nations; "beneficence to all classes of people" turned out to mean unprecedented belt-tightening to pay for Japan's mushrooming arms costs; and "national harmony" now floundered in a welter of plots, the conspirators becoming ever bolder in the knowledge that "patriotic motive" was a catchall excuse guaranteeing judicial leniency.

The years 1932 and 1933 were grim ones for Hirohito, now in his early thirties and in the prime of life, for they coincided with a nagging domestic and dynastic problem: after six years of married life, he still had no male heir. The plots that succeeded each other from 1931 onward were linked in part to this failure. Though the issue was far too sensitive to be raised in the Japanese press, the emperor's inability to produce a male heir led to tensions throughout the court and uneasiness in successive governments and in the armed forces. It also explained why some plotters brought Hirohito's younger brother Prince Chichibu into play as a possible alternative. In the past the free-and-easy morals of the imperial court had ensured a permanent supply of potential male heirs, sons of imperial concubines. There was no stigma attached to them; even the great Meiji himself had been technically illegitimate. But Hirohito was finding it difficult to justify his monogamy in the face of discreet but persistent reminders that he was expected to father a son in the interests of dynastic stability.

Before her wedding, Princess Nagako had received, among her many presents, elaborate "pillow books," including one from Hirohito's own mother. These beautifully illustrated, classic works of art contained advice not only on sex techniques but on ways of ensuring a male heir. Hirohito's mother, Empress Sadako, at intervals, gave her son's bride "herbal infusions" which were supposed to guarantee fertility—and male babies.

Nagako had given birth only to girls: Terunomiya (Little Sunshine) in November 1926; another daughter (who died two years later) in 1927; a third daughter in 1929; yet another daughter in 1931. Even such a Western-oriented palace courtier as Prince Saionji was urging Hirohito, by 1930–31, though always in deferential, oblique terms, to consider reviving the time-honored custom of taking a concubine to bed. Nagako would surely understand, he told the emperor. Lists of suitable young women were prepared, and photographs submitted to Hirohito.

His apparent inability to father a male heir was almost certainly a factor in the 1931 October Plot, which implicated, for the first time, Prince Chichibu: the plotters drew up plans for a coup on the lines of the March Plot but with a far grimmer modus operandi, for this time they intended not only to dissolve the Diet and compel Hirohito to accept a military government, but to murder Hirohito's entire cabinet as well. Dr. Okawa, the perennial plotter, was deeply involved, as was the Cherry Blossom Society activist Colonel Kingoro Hashimoto. Both saw themselves as future members of a new "strong-arm" government, Okawa as finance minister and Hashimoto as home minister; they were arrested, and briefly held in custody by the Japanese military police on October 17, but almost immediately released. "There was a rumor," said the postwar *Brocade Banner* study, using archives from Japanese police files, that the civilian police "had prior knowledge of the conspiracy but had felt they could not interfere because they knew Prince Chichibu was involved." The emperor's younger brother had, by this time, shed his earlier, "socialist" views and was increasingly sympathetic to the army nationalists. Another feature of the plot was that its organizers intended bringing the retired Admiral Togo (the Russo-Japanese war hero and subsequently imperial tutor) out of retirement to "persuade" the emperor to countenance it. Police testimony also included reports of the plotters falling out: they quarreled bitterly, accusing Dr. Okawa of tipping off his patron, Count Nobuaki Makino, the Lord Privy Seal, and presumably reaping a cash reward. Reviewing the whole affair, the war minister, Minami, himself an unashamed nationalist, told his civilian cabinet associates that it was imperative that the October Plot be hushed up "forever."

The rest of the government obeyed: none of the plotters was tried. Okawa was held the longest—twenty days in a comfortable cell. General Minami's warning was heeded, for though the plot was widely discussed within the Japanese establishment and by foreign diplomats in Tokyo, nothing at all appeared at the time in the Japanese press. The October Plot even proved useful to Hirohito, for the League of Nations postponed its expected condemnation of Japan for her behavior in Manchuria on the grounds that the League did not want to irritate the military firebrands while they were already embarrassing the emperor.

The takeover of Manchuria and the March and October plots had destroyed the cabinet's prestige. The loss of face was compounded by the treachery of the home minister, Adachi, who refused to attend cabinet meetings, urging a coalition government with the rival Seiyukai party, with himself as its head. Hirohito dismissed this out of hand.

Instead, on Saionji's advice, he summoned the seventy-five-year-old Seiyukai leader, Tsuyoshi Inukai, and made him premier in 1932. Inukai was an old friend of Chiang Kai-shek, and here was an opportunity to heal the rift brought about by the Mukden Incident. Hirohito gave Inukai a formal mandate to establish lasting peace with China and curb the powers of the military. In their first meeting the emperor castigated the army: its interference in domestic and foreign policies, he told Inukai, "and its willfulness, constitute a state of affairs which, for the good of the nation, we must view with apprehension."

These words are often quoted to prove that Hirohito genuinely meant to crush the army activists and normalize relations with China, and Inukai took them at their face value. He was wrong, and within a year he paid for the mistake with his life. For not only did pro-army informers within his own ministry invariably tip off the militarists, but Hirohito himself ensured that any peace plan with China would fail, and that the pendulum swing toward moderation would be "corrected" by a move in the opposite direction.

The man he chose as the new army chief of staff was a leading prince, a close relative of Empress Nagako and Hirohito's own influential, intimate friend. Prince Haruhito Kanin, trained at the French military academy, Saint-Cyr, was a grand-uncle, a scion of the Fushimi family whose aristocratic credentials were second only to Hirohito's. Since Kanin was "family," he could have worked hand in hand with Hirohito to curb the already dangerous power of certain army hotheads, had the emperor given any kind of lead. But Hirohito instituted no such sweeping reforms: the Cherry Blossom Society activists were left free to plot. Worse still, any chance of a lasting deal with China collapsed with the Japanese-engineered Shanghai Incident of March 1932.

The Shanghai affair had the same pattern as the Mukden Incident, a deliberate provocation of the Chinese engineered by Japanese civilians and sailors in Shanghai, and designed to lead to Japanese military intervention. For several weeks, Japanese sailors and marines fought the Kuomintang armies in the Shanghai suburbs. Japanese planes bombed Chinese civilians, causing several thousand deaths. Earlier, on January 8, 1932, a Korean separatist had tossed a bomb under what he thought was the emperor's carriage while Hirohito was on his way to attend a military review. Some Chinese newspapers wrote that "unfortunately the Korean attacked the wrong carriage." Hirohito himself joked with his palace officials about the clumsy Korean's mistake, but wherever there were Japanese enclaves in China Japanese troops went berserk, venting their rage on Chinese civilians. And while Chinese and Japanese forces were still embattled in Shanghai, Japan was rocked by another plot that was to have catastrophic repercussions abroad.

The secret society known as Ketsumeidan (Blood Brotherhood) was so preposterously fanatical that it made Dr. Okawa's bullyboys and the Cherry Blossom Society activists look like innocent Rotarians. Its founder, Nissho Inoue, a former Japanese spy in China who had become a "born-again" Shinto priest, believed that all Japan's ills could be solved if only she turned her back on the twentieth century and reverted to a rural economy under her "divine" Emperor, who would be in direct touch with his people. Inoue was against the bureaucracy, the zaibatsu, parliament, and anything that smacked of Western modernism or culture; his mystical idealism went hand in hand with a bloodthirsty reliance on selective assassination to bring about his aims. All the members of his tiny sect swore secret blood oaths to murder whomever the mad priest designated. They met regularly in a house in the Tokyo suburbs for prayer, meditation and rites of Inoue's own devising.

Crazy Inoue may have been, but he was also singularly well connected: his brother Fumio was a senior test pilot–instructor in the Japanese naval air service, on first-name terms with Prince Higashikuni (whom he had taught to fly) and Marquis Kido. Through this brother, a small number of naval officers attached to the ultrasecret Misty Lagoon naval air base became converts to the brotherhood, as did some impressionable cadets at the military academy. Dr. Okawa, always on the fringe of any extremist movement, supplied Inoue with pistols and ammunition. The family of the Black Dragon Society leader, Toyama, also took him under its wing. All in all, the Blood Brotherhood acquired considerable support, including army and naval officers advocating the "Showa restoration"—in other words, a military dictatorship under the supreme command of Hirohito himself. Inoue's hit list included Japan's top establishment figures, in banking, government and even within the palace itself.

On February 7, 1932, the Blood Brotherhood struck for the first time: one of its members, a student, gunned down Hirohito's finance minister, who had made no secret of his opposition to increased arms spending. Following the established practice of political assassins, the murderer did not seek to escape, but surrendered to the police. A week later Inoue took refuge in a house belonging to Hidezo Toyama, a son of the Black Dragon leader. Hirohito was shocked by the murder, but regarded it as an isolated phenomenon.

Next to die, almost a month later (on March 5), was Baron Takuma Dan, an elderly U.S.-educated banker and prominent supporter of the League of Nations, shot outside his office in downtown Tokyo. This murder was a personal blow for Hirohito, an appalling "loss of face," for it coincided with the arrival, in Tokyo, of the League of Nations committee, headed by Lord Lytton, which was investigating the circumstances of the Mukden Incident. Baron Dan had given a dinner for the visitors the night before his murder. It was known that Prime Minister Inukai had chosen him to present the Japanese case over Manchuria to influential Americans. Again, the murderer made no attempt to escape.

This assassination led to the first serious crackdown on terrorism: most of the Blood Brotherhood members were rounded up, and their targets given protection. But police action came too late, and failed to prevent another, even more calamitous outbreak of terrorism, which put an end to party government and left the military in an impregnable position: on May 15, 1932, Hirohito's own prime minister, Inukai, was murdered by members of another "back-to-the-land" terrorist brotherhood calling itself Aikyo Juku (the Love of Native Village Academy). The background to the May 15 incident was disturbing: there is a strong case for deducing that high palace officials, and perhaps even Hirohito himself, were aware of Inukai's impending fate. Light was thrown on the affair only during the postwar occupation, but even then it was only partial: the *Brocade Banner* investigators were themselves inhibited by understandable police reluctance to go on record and openly implicate members of Hirohito's court.

The circumstances of the May 15 incident were these: shortly before, Dr. Okawa, free once more (and busy setting up yet another extremist club, the Jimmu Society), accompanied a group of officer-cadets, specially selected for their good marks, to Manchuria, ostensibly to see for themselves the benefits of Japanese colonization. With the cadets went the commandant of the military academy. The group received a pep talk from the Kwangtung Army commandant, General Honjo, who also had private discussions with Okawa. On his return, the doctor met the five leading May 15 plotters in a country inn; one of them was a cadet who had gone on the Manchuria trip.

On May 15, 1932, four groups, all belonging to the Aikyo Juku, struck, in downtown Tokyo. Three of them bungled their assignments, only slightly damaging a power station and failing to occupy banks and ministries as planned. But the fourth squad, composed of civilians, naval officers and military cadets—after first taking a solemn oath before the altar of the Yasukuni shrine, the famous Shinto monument to Japan's war dead—bundled into taxis and went to the prime minister's residence. A bodyguard tried to warn Inukai, and was gunned down. Brandishing revolvers, the terrorists swept through the house, and on the floor above came upon the diminutive Inukai, wearing a kimono and chatting with his doctor and daughter-in-law. With extraordinary composure, Inukai suggested that the intruders, whatever their intentions, first follow Japanese custom and remove their shoes. One of the cadets excitedly called on Inukai to explain how checks and confidential notes from him to the Chinese Young Marshal had been found in the warlord's mansion in Mukden—a fact he could only have learned from the cadets' recent visit to Manchukuo. "I can explain," said Inukai calmly. He was not given time. A naval officer shouted, "No more talking," and shot him in the face. Immediately afterward, the killers surrendered to the Japanese military police.

Inukai did not die for some hours. Hirohito, who immediately learned of the outrage, told aides to contact Prince Saionji to prepare for a successor, and appointed the finance minister as interim premier. Saionji angrily replied that Inukai "wasn't dead yet." He knew that long before Inukai's assassination the topic of his replacement had become palace gossip. Many years later, the unimpeachable *Brocade Banner* report contained the ominous remark that there was "no doubt in the public mind that the [May 15] conspiring was by no means limited to the little men who fired the guns." It named an influential army colonel, Chiaki Shigeto (never officially implicated or brought to trial), as one of the main conspirators, and, more ominously still, noted that among papers removed from Dr. Okawa's home by the police after Inukai's murder were "compromising documents" belonging to Hirohito's Lord Privy Seal, Count Makino, and to the former war minister, General Kazushige Ugaki. This, said *Brocade Banner,* "was why there was such pressure put on the court, during the later trial, to save Okawa's neck." In Manchuria, General Honjo wrote cryptically in his diary that "military men of action *under the gaze of their ruler* [author's italics] today defied authority in a negative deed of daring."

The protracted court case that followed turned into farce: the accused were allowed unlimited opportunities for incendiary speeches; judges and prosecutors permitted them to turn the courtroom into an activist forum, with ample time for speeches and full press coverage. The verdicts, in 1934, were staggeringly lenient: all the killers were free by 1940, and Dr. Okawa's fifteen-year sentence, reduced on appeal to five years, led to his almost immediate release—he and all but six of the fifty-four sentenced were out of jail by 1935.

The May 15 incident marked the end of Japan's attempt at party government: from then on, prime ministers would all be nonparty men, and this meant in practice that Hirohito appointed them from the ranks of the army or the navy. Inukai's immediate successor was a retired admiral, the eighty-one-year-old Makoto Saito, but this time Hirohito's injunctions to Saionji had a hollow ring: "His Majesty desires that the *genro* select as the next premier one who has no fascist leanings and about whom there has been no unsavoury rumour, who is moderate in thought and who is not militaristic." Irreparable harm had already been done. With proper backing for Inukai, and with Prince Kanin's cooperation, Hirohito might well have brought the military into line, had he been determined to do so. The inference is that he either refused to see the military as a genuine threat or else was too preoccupied by his domestic problems to make a stand while there was still time.

There is also the possibility that he was genuinely intimidated by the weight of the militarist movement and its embarrassing ramifications. He cannot have been unaware of his brother's intrigues. Chichibu was Hirohito's opposite in many respects; his beautiful wife and he were frequent guests at diplomatic gatherings (he loved going to American embassy parties best of all, because they were invariably followed by private showings of the latest Hollywood films). But Chichibu's cosmopolitanism implied no commitment to democratic principles, and did not prevent him from flirting with fellow officers who were activists and devotees of a "Showa restoration."

The plots followed thick and fast: in August 1932 police nipped in the bud a conspiracy to murder the new prime minister, Admiral

Saito. The chief instigator, a close friend of Dr. Okawa's, got off with a suspended sentence. In September police uncovered a plot to kill the former premier Reijiro Wakatsuki; in November they discovered a plot to kill Count Makino, though this may well have been designed to draw attention away from his links with Dr. Okawa. In July 1933 came an aborted repetition of the May 15 incident: forty-four terrorists from two little-known secret societies, the Love Country Labor Party and the Great Japan Production Society, were rounded up as they prepared to wipe out the cabinet, politicians and "villains of the Imperial entourage." All were acquitted on the grounds that their intentions had been "patriotically motivated," but what probably inhibited judicial action even more was official police recognition (again revealed in the postwar *Brocade Banner* report) that the army group behind the plotters intended placing Chichibu on the throne, with Prince Higashikuni as his prime minister. Whether Chichibu actually knew his name was being invoked is not known.

The army's effrontery became boundless, as illustrated by the absurd "stop-go" controversy of June 1933. An off-duty soldier was rebuked by a policeman for crossing the street against a traffic light. He then proceeded to defy the policeman by crossing and recrossing the road no less than seven times against the light, until he was arrested. In the ensuing cause célèbre, his Osaka district commander demanded that the charge be dropped and the policeman punished, on the grounds that "no police has the right to check the advance made by a soldier of the Supreme Being." But police officials countered, "Are we not His Majesty's police too?"

The "stop-go crisis" was finally resolved by Hirohito, who, Solomon-like, ordered the Osaka military commander to pay the soldier's fine and the local police chief to apologize in writing to the commander. The army's arrogance was displayed more ominously in the Chinese "occupied territories," where all Chinese were now compelled to bow to Japanese uniforms, and swaggering Japanese soldiers treated the Chinese like serfs.

After the Lytton Report's unequivocal condemnation of the Japanese putsch in Manchuria, Japan left the League of Nations in March 1933, despite Hirohito's halfhearted reservations. As Kido noted in his diaries, the emperor instructed his government to note that despite her enforced but unavoidable, "very regrettable" withdrawal, Japan would "continue its policy of cooperation and intimate international relations with other powers." Hirohito also appears to have believed that limited, calculated gestures might prove sufficient to avert isolation. Japanese troops had by this time advanced close to China's Great Wall, occupying Jehol Province, and then retreated. Hirohito asked Kido in confidence whether "the need to withdraw from the League still held in view of the favorable settlement of the Jehol problem." Cosmetic concessions in return for major diplomatic gains were to be a later feature of Hirohito's diplomacy too. Kido replied it was too late for Japan to appear to be changing her mind. Shortly after Japan's departure at Geneva, her troops overran Jehol Province.

By the end of 1933 Japan's isolation was complete, and there was a grim contrast between Hirohito's blueprint for Japan at the start of the Showa era and reality—so much so that the emperor even hinted to Kido, in 1933, that he was thinking of abdicating. But nine months later he was in a far better mood—and never mentioned the possibility again—for, in December 1933, Empress Nagako finally gave birth to a male heir. Hirohito's grand chamberlain rushed to the emperor's study to bring him the news. "It's a boy," he said. "I saw the honorable signs of manhood myself." Hirohito ordered champagne to be served to all his staff and any visitors. As Marquis Kido wrote that day in his diary: "Now, at last, the biggest problem has been solved."

CHAPTER EIGHT

In 1932, around the time of Inukai's murder, Joseph C. Grew arrived in Tokyo to take up his new post as United States ambassador, at a time when Japanese-U.S. relations were deteriorating but were not yet on a fatal collision course. Shrewd, experienced, and something of a snob, with close family ties with the "old Japan" (his wife was a granddaughter of Commodore Perry) Grew was at first, as his diary shows, highly sympathetic toward Hirohito and Japan generally. He saw more of Hirohito, and of his imperial court, than any other ambassador. As time went on he was to become increasingly shaken by the contrast between the cordial attitude shown toward him personally by most influential Japanese and the growing hostility and double-dealing encountered on policy matters. He analyzed this contradiction dispassionately and—to the last—with equability and balance, reluctantly coming to the conclusion that Japanese "mental processes are different. A Westerner believes that because a Japanese has adopted Western dress, language and customs, he must think like a Westerner. No greater error can ever be made." It was because of this difference that "treaty commitments between East and West will always be open to misinterpretation and subject to controversy. . . . When obligations run counter to [Japanese] interests he will interpret the obligation to suit himself."* Though he refrained from criticizing Hirohito personally, he may have had him in mind when he contrasted the emperor's privately conveyed comments about the need to face up to Japanese chauvinism and the growing evidence of rampant nationalism in all walks of life. He noted, for instance, that for all Hirohito's reassuring remarks, maps of the Far East in Japanese primary schools, as early as 1933, showed French Cochin China (South Vietnam), Thailand, the Straits Settlements, the Philippines and the Dutch East Indies (now Indonesia) all under the Japanese flag.

Grew was very deaf, and while this affliction didn't affect his work in general, it did lead to one embarrassing moment: after the new ambassador presented his credentials to the emperor at the Imperial Palace, Hirohito made a short welcoming speech. Grew had no idea what he was talking about, for the interpreter was not allowed to raise his voice in the imperial presence.

Hirohito, Grew wrote, "has a small moustache and glasses and smiles pleasantly while talking." The empress "looks more like a charming Japanese doll than any of the other women. She is not so pretty as the really lovely-looking Princess Chichibu but she has a nice expression and she does smile delightfully." Attending an imperial banquet Hirohito gave to celebrate the birth of his son, Grew noted that the overornate palace dining room had "too much rather unattractive woodwork and heavy draperies." But he was enchanted by the gold screens, the stunted pine trees, the artistic flower arrangements—and the friendly reception. During the dinner party "the Empress extracted nearly the whole story of our lives." Early on in his assignment, Grew noted how strange it was "to live in a country where individually everyone is thoroughly friendly but where collectively one is constantly aware of distrust and animosity against one's own nation."

It was clear to Grew that even top-level Japanese had a distorted view of the world. An American League of Nations official reported to him that Prince Chichibu had asked, in 1933: "Tell me, is it true that the United States is actively preparing for war against Japan?" The Chichibus were Grew's frequent guests, and with some palace

---

*Joseph C. Grew, *Ten Years in Japan* (London: Hammond, 1945).

officials and veteran politicians the ambassador developed a relationship of mutual trust and real friendship. They and other privileged
sources in contact with the palace never failed to stress that Hirohito
disapproved of his country's move toward extreme, expansionist nationalism. "The Emperor," Grew wrote in 1933, "is a man of mild
and peaceful character. . . . there is no reason to believe he approved
of the Manchurian venture, for the matter did not lie in his decision."
Later, his references to Hirohito become fewer and fewer: the impression is that, having been charmed by him at first, he later regretted
falling under his spell.

Despite his remoteness, Hirohito was, when it suited him, capable
of masterly public relations touches, at least where foreigners were
concerned: early in Grew's ambassadorship, his dog, Sambo, fell into
the palace moat, and its rescue was featured in all the Tokyo papers.
At the banquet held to celebrate the birth of Crown Prince Akihito,
Hirohito's first words to Grew were "How's Sambo?"

With inside information about the palace at a premium, friendly
ambassadors regularly exchanged information, and Grew was quick to
pounce on any visiting journalist who managed to get close to a senior
Hirohito adviser. The *Le Temps* editor Dubosc told Grew (after a
session with the Lord Privy Seal, Makino) that he was wrong to infer
that "Japan was going through dangerous times." "Cut out the word
'danger,'" Makino had told him. "We have a unique safeguard,
namely, the Imperial Household. There will never be 'danger' from
military fascism or communism or from any other kind of 'ism,'
simply because the Emperor is supreme and will *always* have the last
word." The impression Hirohito gave to resident journalists was
somewhat different. The *New York Times* correspondent Hugh Byas
wrote, around this time, that the emperor was "a divine person, a
symbol of the eternity of the State; he is an automaton who accepts
advice without demur when it is offered by the right person; he is a
high priest, but he is not a king ruling a country." The whole issue
of Hirohito's role in the Japanese body politic would soon come out
into the open—a controversy over the nature and origins of
Hirohito's powers that would divide Japan almost as dramatically as
the Dreyfus case had divided France. It broke shortly after Grew
settled down to report on Japan's troubled, plot-ridden state.

The crisis had been brewing since Grew's arrival, but got almost no
mention in the Japanese press until 1934. That year an ultraconserva-

tive intellectual agitator, Koki Minoda, made a virulent attack on Dr. Tatsukichi Minobe, Japan's best-known, most distinguished constitutional law expert, who held the Chair of Constitutional Law at Tokyo Imperial University and whose academic distinction had won him a seat in the House of Peers. Minobe had been writing and teaching since 1903, and his courses had been attended by the elite of Japan's civil servants, diplomats and politicians at the most exclusive university in the land.

In a pamphlet entitled *Dr. Minobe the Anarchist,* which also attacked other distinguished professors from Tokyo and Kyoto imperial universities for their interpretation of Japanese constitutional law, Minoda, the fanatical rightist, described their work as a "violation of the Imperial constitution and a danger to the nation," and criticized the home minister for not banning their books. The response was immediate: Hirohito's cabinet dismissed one of the law professors, Yukitoki Takigawa, after the president of Kyoto University refused to do so. Hirohito's education minister, an arrant fundamentalist, responded with contempt to students' and teachers' protests at Takigawa's dismissal. "Let all the professors resign if that is how they feel," he said. "We do not mind closing the universities altogether."

In February 1935, a politician with strong right-wing connections, Major General Genkuro Eto, resumed the attack, actually in the Diet, and another right-winger, Baron Kikuchi, followed up with a further speech in the House of Peers, in Minobe's presence. A second target of Kikuchi's was the president of the Privy Council (and former Imperial Household minister) Kitokuro Ikki, whom the speaker identified as a "follower" of Minobe.

Minobe's crime was that in books, articles and lecture notes he had defined the emperor's place in relation to the Japanese state as a whole, arguing that Hirohito, like his forebears, was "an organ of the state." The passage in one of Minobe's law books that had particularly infuriated the rightists ran as follows:

> There is an idea current that the Imperial prerogative is sacred and inviolable, that because it is executed by Imperial Will there can be no discussion of it, nor can anyone debate its merits in any particular instance of its exercise. . . . This is a gross error contrary to the spirit of the constitution.

Minobe's first reference to the emperor as "an organ of the state" dated back thirty-one years but had never aroused this kind of controversy in the past. The professor was certainly no radical, criticizing again and again the "inadmissible error" of those constitutional experts who claimed "the Emperor is the subject of government power." In his view, "the state alone is the subject of government power, and the monarch is an organ of the state. . . . in present-day legal terms, Japan's national unity does not differ in pattern from the constitutional monarchies of Europe" and the emperor was "like a brain in the human body."

In fact, as Saionji's biographer, Lesley Connors,* has pointed out, the real instigators of the "organ" controversy—and the behind-the-scenes powers manipulating rightists like Koki Minoda, Major General Eto, Baron Kikuchi and others—were the military: Minobe was the best-known university academic opposed to an extension of their powers, and he had gathered support among a glittering cross section of Japan's academic community. "It was," Connors wrote, "Minobe's untiring academic support of the liberal group's efforts to restrict the role of the military in politics by means of constitutional interpretation which ensured military support for any move to undermine his position."

The Japanese liberals had good grounds for fearing the growing encroachment of the army in areas that were not strictly its concern—as did Ambassador Grew, who regularly reported to Washington on the army's "positive" involvement in government. Everyone in the Japanese establishment, in fact, realized that the "organ" issue transcended arguments over the interpretation of Japan's constitutional law. The challenge to Minobe, and to Ikki, was but the latest example of pressure being exerted by the nationalists to undermine the position of those "moderates"—in politics and in the palace—who opposed Japan's aggressive policies in Asia and her excessive arms spending.

The attack on Minobe was, in its way, the intellectual equivalent of the October and May 15 plots, and it came at a time when Japan's "will to power" was suddenly revealed as a real threat to stability and peace

---

*Lesley Connors: *The Emperor's Adviser, Kimmochi Saionji* (Croom Helm and Nissan Institute for Japanese Studies, 1987).

in Asia. In Manchuria, in September 1934, for example, a reorganization of the local administration, approved by Hirohito without a murmur, put Manchukuo under the overall supervision of the brutal Japanese military police. Shortly afterward, a document widely distributed by the military, and entitled "The True Meaning of National Strength and Proposals for Building It" (it began with the Mussolinian premise that "war is the father of creation and the mother of culture"), advocated "national defense for total war," the wholesale regimentation of the Japanese people and an end to "Western individualism." In December 1934 Hirohito approved a policy declaration on China that represented a final break with Chiang Kai-shek, stating that "for the time being it is desirable to reduce to a minimum the influence of the Nanking (i.e., Kuomintang) government." Finally, just before the 1935 New Year, after protracted discussions with American and British admirals and officials in London, Japan abrogated the naval arms limitation treaty.

Early in 1935 Minobe rose in the House of Peers to refute allegations of treason, using irony as his weapon: "For a Japanese," he said, to considerable applause,

> there is nothing more shameful than to be called treasonous.
> . . . We may question whether the dignity of this House has
> not been violated. . . . If an academician trained in law as I am
> should meddle in a military school and criticize the sayings and
> writings of military specialists, it could only be a laughing
> matter.

While the "organ controversy" was raging, Hirohito greeted Henry Pu-yi, on his state visit to Japan in April 1935—the puppet emperor's reward for four years of docile behavior as the loyal collaborator of Japan in Manchukuo, a country run by Japan but enjoying a fictitious existence as an "independent" state. Prince Chichibu had been Hirohito's representative at Pu-yi's coronation the previous year in Changchun, the railway town selected by the Japanese as Manchukuo's new capital.

Advance arrangements for Pu-yi's visit revealed the extraordinarily ritualistic nature of the Japanese army's emperor worship. While the details of the Pu-yi visit and related ceremonies were being discussed, the War Ministry made the unusual request that Hirohito not attend the military review organized in Pu-yi's honor. As chief ADC Honjo, acting as go-between, noted, "The army authorities explained that the Army's reverence for the Japanese Emperor makes it incapable of saluting a foreign Emperor and not the Japanese Emperor when he is also present."

Hirohito's Imperial Household minister, after consulting the emperor, rejected this demand out of hand, as both a violation of protocol and an "unfriendly gesture" toward the emperor's distinguished foreign guest—himself an emperor, albeit a puppet one. The army and the palace then worked out a compromise: Hirohito would attend but would get a special salute from the army on his arrival and departure; Pu-yi would not.

The crisis seemed over, but the army now requested, through Honjo, that regimental colors should not be dipped on this occasion. Honjo agreed with his army colleagues that this was an occasion honoring a foreigner, and that colors were not to be dipped to foreigners. Hirohito was irritated by such insistence on protocol but decided to think the matter over. Two days later his mind was made up. He intended to stand firm. As Honjo noted in his diaries, the emperor "pointed out that he returns the salute of even a single soldier. If the regimental flags are not to be dipped in honor of the person that I am honoring, does it mean that the regimental flags are held in higher esteem than me?"

Honjo, carefully briefed by his army friends, replied that for the emperor to return a soldier's salute was "a voluntary act based on his magnanimity and benevolence," but the regimental colors were to be dipped for Hirohito alone. "They are not used to return the salutations of even the Empress or the Empress Dowager. . . . I implored His Majesty not to permit any action that might in the least diminish the men's faith in the regimental flags. His Majesty accepted my explanation." Hirohito gave in. The dipping of the flags would not occur after all.

The army authorities then came up with a new demand: it had been agreed that Hirohito would meet Pu-yi at Tokyo railway station. As Honjo put it, the army "contended that it would demean His Majesty's dignity when in exchanging positions His Majesty were to proceed behind the Manchurian Emperor while the troops were in formation in front of them." Hirohito rejected this as "an unreasonable request," but Honjo privately told the guard commander to see to it that "this particular operation be conducted in an inconspicuous manner."

The overall impression is of protocol-obsessed generals testing the ground to see how far they could go. In the event, Pu-yi, who had been appallingly seasick aboard the obsolete Japanese warship that brought him to Yokohama, was unaware that he had been at the center of any such controversy, and the series of official receptions in his honor was poorly attended by foreign missions. Neither Grew nor any of the ambassadors of the major European powers, with the exception of the Italian and German ambassadors, took part in the ceremonies, for only the Axis countries, the Vatican and a few pro-German Latin American countries had recognized Manchukuo diplomatically.

The absurd quarrel over precedence and military rites gives an insight not only into the army's state of mind at this time but also into Hirohito's ability to face the growing jingoism. For it was not just Hirohito's ceremonial presence that was being debated, or the propriety of his playing second fiddle to a state guest. What had been at stake was a minor, but symbolic, battle of wills, and when the chips were down, Hirohito shied away from a head-on clash with the army over a simple, straightforward issue. It was the kind of ambiguity already displayed over Manchuria, and it would be manifest, again and again, on the road to Pearl Harbor. Admittedly, the haggling over where the emperor should stand at the station in Tokyo may have seemed petty enough, but the army's behavior was all part of the same campaign by extremists to erode what remained of Japanese liberalism.

At the time of the emperor-organ controversy, Hirohito revealed the same indecision and spirit of compromise that marked his climb-down over the ceremonial parade. His intentions were clearly honorable: in Honjo's first mention of the affair, he records in his diary (March 11, 1935) that Hirohito told him that "although there might be a difference in status between the two of us, he did not believe that physically there was any difference whatsoever. In light of this the Emperor found it highly upsetting both mentally and physically that in order to attack the organ theory he was being turned into an entity without any freedom whatsoever. I responded that this was not the case at all. His remarks filled me with deep sorrow."

Proof of Hirohito's concern came later in the day. Honjo was again summoned, and told that the emperor was aware that the attack on the organ theory was in fact an attack on his former Imperial Household

minister, Ikki Ichiki, who had written in the same vein as Minobe on
the emperor's role in state affairs. "Ichiki," said Hirohito, "is a loyal
subject and there is no justification whatever for the kind of public
criticisms being directed against him." As for Minobe, the emperor
said, "I think Minobe could never be disloyal. Is there anyone in Japan
his equal today? Minobe may have gone too far in some respects but
I can never think ill of him."

The emperor-organ debate continued in the Supreme War Council,
an advisory body of senior generals and admirals, and once more
Honjo, the go-between, behaved more like an activist spokesman than
a palace official. To Hirohito's remark that in international relations,
labor agreements, loans, etc., "it seems that the organ theory is more
important," Honjo replied that "the military worships His Majesty as
divinity incarnate, and if His Majesty were to be treated just like any
other person, it would create grave difficulties in the areas of military
education and the supreme command."

The whole issue was clearly causing Hirohito considerable irritation. He summoned Honjo later that same day (March 29, 1935) to
point out that Article 4 of Japan's constitution "states that the Emperor
is head of the state. This shows that the constitution is based on the
organ theory, so if the organ theory is revised, the constitution also
will have to be revised." That same day the cabinet met to discuss the
organ issue, with the war, education, justice and home ministers demanding that the organ theory be "rectified."

Later, Hirohito returned to the attack. "If the Emperor is viewed
as the head controlling the entire life of the state," he told Honjo,
"then, if a disaster strikes the Emperor, the state would lose its life
also. . . . To hold that sovereignty resides not in the state but in the
monarch is to court charges of despotism. And difficulties would arise
in concluding treaties and borrowing money from foreign nations."
With disarming candor, he continued, "I, too, would gladly accept the
theory of imperial sovereignty if it did not lead to the bane of despotism, the disapproval of foreign nations and if it did not conflict with
our national polity and history. Unfortunately, I have yet to encounter
an explanation of this theory that is worthy of respect."

Ever the loyal subject and unquestioning believer in Hirohito's
"divine" right, Honjo replied that the military "were not concerned
with academic theories" but with principles of religious faith. Distort-
ing Minobe's theories in a way that showed that this blunt, bluff

soldier, ill at ease in the field of academic abstractions, had nevertheless been well briefed by his army colleagues, he added that "theories
holding that the Diet is the core of the government, that imperial
edicts may be criticized, and that Diet members may not heed the
Emperor's commands, are totally incompatible with the army's faith
and convictions." Needless to say, Minobe had never gone that far.

Given Hirohito's powers, and the role the army wished him to play
as a "divine" sovereign, it would have been relatively easy for the
emperor to turn the tables on the critics of the organ theory by
proclaiming, in some oblique form, his support of Minobe and his
contempt for the professor's critics. An imperial proclamation was out
of the question, but he could have reduced the militarists to silence
merely by summoning Minobe to the palace for an informal audience—or even allowing his court "cabinet" to divulge, to the press
and to the public generally, the views he expressed in private to
Honjo.

Hirohito's passivity, and his tendency to test the pros and cons of
his every move, allowed the emperor-organ issue to grow into a major
crisis: the powerful Military Reserve Association entered the fray, as
did the Army Officers' Association, which published a pamphlet stating that "state sovereignty" was nothing more than "democracy"—a
hated, despised ideology in the eyes of Japanese jingoists.

Honjo finally wearied of his role as go-between: in talks with the
war minister and the fire-eating inspector general of education, Jin-
saburo Mazaki, one of the most vocal opponents of Minobe, Honjo
told them to deal direct with Hirohito if they wanted to debate the
matter further. They replied that they were "not interested in debating its merits as academic theory. Their main objective was denuncia-
tion of the organ theory as an ideology."

Hirohito took the Army Officers' Association pamphlet seriously
enough to study it at length. To Honjo, he delivered a point-by-point
rebuttal two days later (April 27). State sovereignty, he said, was *not*
identical with democracy; it was untrue to say that individualism was
at the root of all Western institutions. How could one explain American Prohibition, or the fact that many members of the English aristocracy sacrificed their lives for their country in World War I? It was
wrong to assume that unlike Japanese emperors, "European monarchs
are only concerned with political matters. In fact, the King of England
devotes much time and energy to cultural affairs."

Hirohito's preoccupation with the organ theory also caused him to spell out, to Honjo, his own intimate convictions and beliefs concerning the nature of government and the lessons drawn from recent history. When Honjo argued that the Allies, in World War I, had used "anti-Statist propaganda" to bring down Germany, and that this proved the need for the "divine right" theory (which presumably would have given the Kaiser sufficient nationwide support to continue the war), Hirohito displayed his superior knowledge of European history. Germany, he said, had not been defeated by propaganda alone. There had been multiple reasons, among them the fact that none of the German states, except Prussia, had any confidence in the Kaiser, the disunity between the army and the civilians, and the Kaiser's misguided flight to Holland. In the same way, he added, the Russian revolution succeeded because, "like the *ancien regime* in France, there were only two classes in Russia: the aristocracy and the lower class. It did not have a moderate, stable middle class"—implying that he saw the growing Japanese middle class precisely as a factor of stability.

As the emperor-organ debate increasingly turned into an army onslaught on "moderates" in general, Hirohito did strike back, but in a limited way: he dismissed his chief naval ADC for taking an arrant "anti-organ" stand, and also replaced General Mazaki, not only because of his support of right-wing movements attacking the organ theory, but because the powerful inspector general of military education had repeatedly encouraged junior officers to plot the violent removal of the cabinet. But the extremists had the last word: Keisuke Okada's lackluster government (the prime minister was another retired admiral, who had succeeded Makoto Saito in 1935) eventually decided to "stamp out the organ theory" and pay more attention to the ideological contents of works written by university professors.

Minobe, who steadfastly refused to resign from Tokyo Imperial University, continued to be hounded by his detractors. He finally gave in to the inevitable, resigning his seat in the House of Peers in September 1935 in order to avoid prosecution in the courts for lèse-majesté, his reputation as a scholar destroyed. Few if any of Japan's establishment, among those who deplored the drift toward totalitarianism, had the courage to stand by him, or even acknowledge his existence. He was repeatedly called upon to commit suicide. Despite Hirohito's regard for the soundness of Minobe's theories, and his anger at the right-wing exploitation of the organ theory, the emperor never conveyed these feelings to the Minobe family. Professor Minobe himself was given police protection, which he supplemented with bodyguards hired at his own expense, but there were two attempts on his life. On February 20, 1936, he was badly wounded, shot through both knees by a right-wing terrorist who immediately became a hero, while he had to be hidden in the children's ward of a Tokyo hospital to ensure that there would be no further attack.*

The emperor's ongoing dialogue with Honjo, recorded at length in the general's diary, also had the merit of defining the extent and the limits of Hirohito's "liberalism." If, on the organ issue, he held moderate views, substantially similar to Minobe's own, on social issues he emerges not so much a conservative as someone hopelessly insulated from the facts of life and the plight of many of his countrymen. Because the army's rank and file (and, increasingly, its officers) were drawn mainly from families of impoverished farmers and the "new poor" generally, a few generals, Honjo among them, attempted to draw Hirohito's attention to the social unrest that fanned the flames of extremism of the secret brotherhood kind.

General Sadao Araki, a former war minister, discussing the May 15 plot with the emperor, remarked that "capitalists could perhaps be criticized for building grand mansions to gratify their expensive tastes." Hirohito replied it was "too harsh" to say that capitalists lived like that simply for pleasure. "It is said that Louis XVI of France, despite the fact that he had the splendid palace of Versailles, built in addition a small palace which he loved and used as his residence. It is not necessarily true that people are inclined towards grand, luxurious things. I myself would prefer to live in a simpler place rather than in a huge palace like this where many people are employed. But . . . my place of residence is determined by the fact that this palace was built by my ancestor as well as by other traditions and customs. I have no way of knowing how other people feel, but I believe there

---

*Minobe's son, a prominent Japanese liberal and postwar governor of Tokyo, was until his recent death one of Japan's leading campaigners against the postwar trend, in schools and politics, toward nationalism and emperor worship.

must be others who feel as I do and prefer to live a simpler life but because of various circumstances are compelled to live in spacious dwellings built by their ancestors."

When the subject arose again a few days later, Hirohito took a tougher stand. "It was inevitable," he said, that officers, and particularly NCOs and soldiers who had close ties with the agrarian life, "would sympathize with and worry about the villagers who are in such dire straits, but if they were to become excessively interested in such problems simply to indulge their own fancy, they would cause harm instead." When Honjo replied that such concern was only natural, Hirohito remarked, "It is, of course, necessary to sympathize with the dire plight of the peasants, but peasants in their own way lead happy lives. One cannot say that members of the aristocracy are always happy. I enjoyed my freedom when I went on a tour of Europe. The only time I feel happy is when I am able to experience a similar feeling of freedom. . . . So, peasants should think about the pleasures of nature that are there for them to enjoy and not dwell merely on the unpleasant aspects of their lives. In other words, in guiding the peasants, one should not rely only on legalistic principles but should emphasize moral principles."

This comment was made at a time when famine was ravaging northern Japan, and farming families, to ward off starvation, were selling their daughters as factory hands, apprentice geishas and prostitutes at a rate unprecedented in the twentieth century; it showed an extraordinary lack of sensitivity to the problems facing his less privileged subjects.

There was a growing belief, among superstitious Japanese, that the arrival of 1936, an inauspicious year, would herald some vastly calamitous event. In the army, rumor was rife that it would mark the start of the expected war against the Soviet Union—to such an extent that the War Ministry found it necessary to ban any references, in the press and army publications, to the "crisis of 1936." It was indeed to be a disastrous year, but it was callousness toward the farmers' plight, and growing anger among young army officers at the ostentatious wealth of the Japanese industrialists and other nouveaux riches, that were to provide Hirohito with his most serious challenge—and leave a permanent mark on prewar Japan.

CHAPTER NINE

On the eve of February 26, 1936, which was to be the worst day in his life until Japan's surrender to the Allies eight years and six months later, Hirohito had several reasons to worry about the state of Japan, but he did have one overriding cause for optimism.

This was the strong family bond between himself, Empress Nagako and their five children. Hirohito was a loving father, and though he doted most on his elder son, Akihito, whose third birthday he celebrated with pomp, dressing him up in a red suit to mark his move away from babyhood and white clothes, he was almost equally affectionate toward the three girls. If ever anything were to happen to the crown prince, he now also had a second son (Masahito, born in 1935), so the dynasty was secure, and no plotter, army or otherwise, could possibly use the succession issue as a pretext for replacing him with the dashing Prince Chichibu, who, ironically, remained childless.

There were, however, serious—indeed intractable—problems. The emperor-organ affair had stirred up a huge controversy, goading every fundamentalist association and secret society into a concerted attack on "red judges and scarlet professors." Beyond these avowed targets, the fundamentalists' and army hotheads' rage was directed at moderate opinion in general, and at the "moderates" in Hirohito's own court cabinet and in the government in particular. Secret police informers reported a continuing spate of assassination plots, and the general outlook seemed grim, but the results of the Diet elections held on February 20, 1936, proved that, for all the bombast and stridency of the ultranationalists, Japanese voters were still remarkably clearheaded and unaffected by jingoistic propaganda. The elections were a particular success for the small left-wing groups and for the more moderate of the two main parties: 205 Minseito party MPs (out of 296 candidates) were elected, while the more right-wing Seiyukai suffered a sizable defeat, with only 174 members elected out of 336 candidates. Even so, Hirohito was aware that the discrepancy between nationalistic fervor and the lukewarm mood of Japan toward foreign adventurism was likely to lead to further plots and further bloodshed.

In the armed forces and among their rightist sympathizers the mood was best reflected in a popular song, written by Takashi Mikami, a navy lieutenant, entitled "The Song of Young Japan," which was a clear call to action. Part of it ran:

> Those in power are swollen with pride,
> but have no concern for the nation;
> the wealthy flaunt their riches,
> yet care nothing for the welfare of society.
>
> Brave warriors united in justice
> in spirit a match for a million
> ready like the myriad cherry blossoms to scatter
> in the spring sky of the Showa restoration.
>
> But let us leave these lamentations
> Gone is the time for idle grieving!
> The day has come when our swords
> shall gleam with the blood of purification!

The consequences of one particularly dramatic political murder were front-page news. Lieutenant Colonel Saburo Aizawa, a former fencing instructor, was standing trial for an especially gory killing in the War Ministry building, and February 25 had been marked by a dramatic court hearing. Aizawa, known personally to Prince Higashikuni, was a fanatical right-wing fundamentalist and fervent disciple of the recently ousted director of military education, General Mazaki. Aizawa, incensed at the dismissal of his hero, had called on General Tetsuzan Nagata, the head of the Military Affairs Bureau, who was rightly seen by fanatical junior officers as Hirohito's éminence grise in the War Ministry, at his home, and urged him to reinstate Mazaki. Nagata's reaction had been prompt: he had immediately ordered the impetuous Aizawa to be posted to Taiwan.

But Aizawa—perhaps thinking that violent action would be condoned by powerful army elements, including even Prince Higashikuni himself—two days later stormed into Nagata's office just outside the Imperial Palace, drew his sword and, after slashing him across the face and chest, ran him through.

Either hoping to provide evidence of insanity or else convinced he was assured of immunity, Aizawa went immediately to the army infirmary to have a cut finger tended to. He mentioned he was in a hurry and needed to buy a new cap to replace the one he had left behind in the struggle in Nagata's office. He also had to pack, he said, because he would be leaving soon for Taiwan. Arrested shortly after leaving the building, he hired two nationalist firebrands as defense lawyers, and they succeeded in turning his trial into a festival of jingoistic "greater Japan" expansionism. On February 25 the courtroom had been packed with off-duty army sympathizers and reporters, for General Mazaki had been summoned to appear as a defense witness. He disappointingly refused to answer any questions, invoking "official secrecy" unless given a personal waiver by the emperor himself, but the defense had had a field day nevertheless. "If the court fails to understand the spirit that guided the accused," said one lawyer, "a second Aizawa and even a third will appear."

These were prophetic words, for in two army barracks across the moat from the palace a score of junior officers were preparing to stage a putsch, which, they believed, would rally the entire Japanese officer corps and lead to the much heralded "Showa restoration," the establishment of authoritarian army rule under Emperor Hirohito that would also trigger widespread social reforms and the end of capitalist, zaibatsu-dominated politics. An artillery officer, Captain Ichitaro Yamaguchi, who also happened to be General Honjo's son-in-law, was party to the conspiracy, and on February 25 had distributed some two hundred city road maps to the rebels to ensure they would not lose their way.

At the palace there was no inkling of an imminent crisis. On the

evening of February 25, two of Hirohito's closest advisers, the grand
chamberlain, Kantaro Suzuki, and the new Lord Privy Seal, the former premier Saito, attended an informal dinner party at the United
States Embassy residence. Grew had planned the evening with care:
after dinner, there was an MGM movie—*Naughty Marietta,* with Jea-
nette MacDonald and Nelson Eddy. The guests came with their wives,
and though it was known that Suzuki liked to retire to bed early, he
stayed on with every sign of enjoying the sentimental love story.
Among the Japanese women guests, Grew noted, there was not a dry
eye in the house. There was a brief interval to change reels during
which refreshments were served. Suzuki could have left then but did
not do so. As the palace officials drove away into the cold midnight
air (it was snowing heavily) Grew could congratulate himself on a
particularly successful evening, for both the chief guests were immensely sought after by Tokyo's diplomatic corps because of their
intimate, daily contacts with Hirohito.

Only a couple of hours later, at 2:00 A.M., within earshot of the
palace, buglers sounded reveille in both the 1st Division and the
Imperial Guards barracks, and the coup was under way. As the sleepy
soldiers stood to, fully expecting yet another night exercise, the officers involved in the plot assembled their men and began briefing them
about the operation they were about to launch.

Both units had been told two months previously that they would
shortly be posted to Manchuria on active service, and while the news
should have been welcomed (neither elite unit had seen any action
since the Russo-Japanese War), it was greeted instead as an unforgiv-
able slur on their integrity. The officers, knowing that the secret police
and the top military hierarchy considered both the Guards and the 1st
Division to be hotbeds of political activism, were convinced that the
order to send them to Manchuria had been a deliberate decision taken
at the highest level to get them out of harm's way as fast as possible
in the wake of Aizawa's trial and amid rumors of further army plotting. It was no coincidence that the men leading the 2/26 uprising
were on close terms with several former army officers dismissed for
their involvement in previous plots and for their uncompromisingly
hostile views toward the military and political hierarchy. One, Captain
Kiyosada Koda, later sentenced to death and executed, under interrogation analyzed his motivation in detail, revealing his resentment at

prevalent social injustice and the huge gulf between rich and poor as well as the irresistible impact of crude, simplistic nationalism.

Introduced into a conspiratorial circle of like-minded officers, Koda helped draft a document called *The Great Purpose,* setting out their aims and grievances. "With due reverence," it read, "we consider that the basis of the divinity of our country lies in the fact that the nation is destined to expand under Imperial Rule until it embraces all the world. . . . It is now time to expand and develop in all directions." The officers blamed "self-seeking, refractory men" who had "encroached on the Imperial prerogative, obstructing the true growth of the people, who have been driven to the utmost depths of misery, making our country an object of contempt. Words fail to express our anger at such wickedness." The sacrifices of the "blood brotherhood martyrs" and "Colonel Aizawa's flashing sword" had had no effect on such evil imperial advisers. "Even after so much bloodshed knaves continue not only to live in ease and selfishness but show no signs of repentance."

> Meanwhile, it is clearer than light that our country is on the verge of war with Russia, Britain and America, who wish to crush our ancestral land. Unless we now rise and annihilate the unrighteous and disloyal creatures who surround the Imperial Throne and obstruct the course of true reform, the Imperial Prestige will fall to the ground. . . . We are persuaded that it is our duty to remove the villains who surround the Throne.

This was the kind of talk the twenty-four insurgent officers gave their men in the freezing cold as they prepared to muster the different units that would venture forth to kill prominent Japanese and occupy strategic points in central Tokyo. The rank and file of the 1st and 3rd infantry regiments of the 1st Division, called on to take part in the plot, dared not refuse. The men of the Imperial Guards Division, however, were not told of its real nature. Significantly, though several officers in both divisions felt that the insurgents were embarking on a mad, doomed adventure, few opposed their colleagues outright or attempted to alert their superiors. The huge majority of the senior officers of both divisions clearly sympathized with the insurgents, who numbered 1,200 men in all, and procrastinated for as long as they could, until it was clear the coup would fail. The insurgents had organized themselves into nine squads, fanning out into the snow-covered streets to occupy their objectives and to set up barricades and roadblocks in front of the buildings they were to move into.

Group number one occupied the official residence of the war minister, General Yoshiyuki Kawashima, with surprising ease. There were no casualties. Kawashima, a nondescript figure whose only claim to fame is as adoptive father of the famous spy Eastern Jewel, the Manchu princess who operated in China for the Japanese secret service, behaved with ignominious indecision. When the insurgent officers asked to see him, he begged to be forgiven. He was ill with a bad cold, he told them. They insisted, finally bursting into his bedroom and reading him their "Great Purpose" memorandum. He showed no indignation and clearly succeeded in staying on the insurgents' right side, for they made no attempt on his life, and—even more surprisingly—allowed senior War Ministry and General Staff officers to come and go freely throughout the next three days, to confer without any constraints.

Group number two stormed the Metropolitan Police Station opposite the Imperial Palace, encountering no resistance either. After setting up roadblocks and leaving a token force, the insurgents joined the group that had occupied the war minister's residence.

Group number three burst into the home of Admiral Kantaro Suzuki, Hirohito's grand chamberlain, who was fast asleep, recovering from the late-night party at the American embassy residence, but was roused by the noise. He rushed to seize his ceremonial sword, but was too late. One of the soldiers asked him, "Are you His Excellency?" Suzuki said, "You must have some reason for doing this. Tell me what it is." There was no reply. An NCO shouted, "No time. We're going to shoot." "Go ahead and shoot," said Suzuki. Three officers fired at him with their pistols, wounding him in the head, lung, shoulder and groin. The insurgents wanted to make sure Suzuki was dead, and one of them put his pistol to the admiral's head. *"Todome* [coup de grace]," he said. Suzuki's wife, who had witnessed the shooting, struggled with her captors. "Don't do it, I'll do it," she screamed. Acceding to her demand, Captain Teruzo Ando ordered his men to leave without firing the fatal shot. But first, in an incongruous homage comprehensible only in the context of Japan's *bushido* culture, they knelt in front of the admiral's body, then saluted him. Ando turned to Mrs. Suzuki. "I am particularly sorry about this," he said, "but our views differ from His Excellency's, so it had to come to this." Miraculously, however, Suzuki survived.

Group number four, three hundred strong, surrounded Premier Okada's official residence, killing four policemen at the gate. "They've finally come," said Okada. The prime minister's brother-in-law and aide, a retired colonel called Denzo Matsuo, looked for a hiding place. With the help of a loyal policeman, both men (Okada still in his nightgown) were bundled into a disused storeroom. Matsuo then left to get further help. The policeman, mounting guard over the storeroom door, shouted to Okada to stay where he was. Okada's private secretary, Hisatsune Sakomizu, who was also his son-in-law, called the Metropolitan Police Station for help. "The situation is out of control," a policeman replied. "What can we do?" Another voice said, "This is the insurgent unit," and hung up.

Matsuo bravely attempted to escape from the house, but was caught by insurgent troops in the courtyard outside. He was pushed against the wall; the soldiers took aim. There was a brief moment's hesitation, until one of the insurgent officers shouted: "What's the matter? You'll be fighting in Manchuria soon! Can't you kill a man or two?" As they fired, Matsuo shouted, "Long live the Emperor!" An officer gave him the coup de grace. Another insurgent, who had taken a framed photograph of the prime minister from the bedroom, compared it with the dead man's face. "Okada," he said. They took the body indoors and left it in a vacant room near Okada's own hiding place.

Moments later the real Okada crept out, stumbled over the corpses of more dead and dying policemen, found some clothes, and then caught sight of his dead brother-in-law. He burst into tears, and wandered off. One of the rebel soldiers caught sight of the old man and told his companions: "I've just seen a ghost." Two maids grabbed Okada and hid him in a cupboard, covering him with a pile of laundry.

Group number five—insurgents from the Imperial Guards Division—arrived at the house of Finance Minister Korekiyo Takahashi. A rebel lieutenant ripped off his bedclothes and shouted: *Tenchu!* [punishment from heaven!]" "Idiot!" Takahashi shouted back. "I gave it to him three times with my revolver," the lieutenant said later, "Someone else slashed him in the side and belly with a sword, and he died instantly." As the insurgents left, their leader told hysterical servants: "Excuse me for the annoyance I have caused."

Group number six took part in an even bloodier killing. About two hundred soldiers from the 3rd Infantry Regiment broke into the house of the ex-premier and newly appointed Lord Privy Seal, Admiral Saito, who had also been at the American embassy party the night before. As the squad's leader later said, "When I approached the bedroom Viscountess Saito opened the door but quickly slammed it shut. She faced us with raised hands and said, 'Please wait.' Saito emerged in his nightgown." The insurgents opened fire, he fell, "but his wife covered him with her body, begging us to shoot her if we had to shoot someone. We had to shove her off, and fired again and again until we were sure there was no more life in the old man. When a soldier entered and asked to be allowed to fire too, we let him have several shots. We wanted to cut Saito's throat, but we gave up the idea because the woman refused to leave the body. Afterwards, we gathered at the front gate and gave three banzai for the Emperor." Saito's body was later found to have forty-seven bullet holes. His wife was treated for multiple sword cuts.

Another group attacked the residence of General Jotaro Watanabe, who had taken over as inspector general of military training from General Mazaki. They fired at the lock on the front door, burst in and made for the bedroom. The general's wife calmly asked them which regiment they were from, and was brushed aside. Watanabe was gunned down, and his throat slit.

More insurgents occupied the *Asahi Shimbun* building, while yet another group, which had set out in cars from Tokyo at midnight, drove to Yugawara, near Atami, where the former Lord Privy Seal, Makino, was on holiday with his twenty-year-old granddaughter, Kazuko. They killed a policeman, and burned down the hotel, but, thanks to Kazuko's courage and presence of mind, failed to kill Makino. She led him up a hill, pursued by soldiers. The accepted story is that she stepped in front of the old man, covering him with her body, daring them to shoot, and that they turned back. In an interview in Tokyo recently, the still-indomitable Kazuko, now Mrs. Aso, insists things were not quite as dramatic. "Our bodyguard managed to kill their ringleader before being gunned down," she told me. "We hid. They lost heart and didn't search the hill too thoroughly." After hiding all night, they took refuge in a farmhouse. A friend collected them in a car the following day, "and we remained in hiding in Tokyo until it was all over."

Yet another group, which should have left Tokyo during the night to seek out the *genro,* Saionji, in his country home, failed to do so. After a mysterious telephone call that warned Saionji that he risked being killed that day, he wisely took refuge in the local police superintendent's house while his country home was guarded by sixty armed policemen.

On that dawn of February 26 Hirohito was still asleep, unaware of the mutiny, the carnage, the roadblocks a mere stone's throw from the main gate to the Imperial Palace grounds, and of the fact that some of the coup ringleaders had turned the Sanno Hotel into a command post. One of the first outsiders to find out about the situation was General Honjo. "While I was still asleep," he wrote, "a Second Lieutenant Ito arrived in a state of agitation, claiming to be a messenger from my son-in-law, Captain Ichitaro Yamaguchi, who was on duty at the 1st Infantry Regiment. Wondering what had happened, I agreed to see him. The lieutenant handed me a hastily written message stating that about five hundred officers and men of the regiment, unable to restrain themselves any longer, have decided to take direct action. It was expected there would be continued reinforcements. An extraordinary message!"

Honjo ordered the officer to tell his son-in-law to prevent any such action from being taken. The troops had already moved out, Ito said, but Honjo "instructed the Lieutenant to tell Yamaguchi in no uncertain terms that the projected action cannot be permitted to take place in the imperial capital. He must do everything possible to stop it." Honjo could not know that his son-in-law, far from discouraging the rebels, was in the conspiracy up to the hilt, being one of its chief logistical planners, in charge of the hit squads' transport (he was later sentenced to life imprisonment, but was released in 1940).

Honjo then telephoned the head of the military police and the palace ADC on night duty, and ordered a car to take him to the palace. On the way he passed some insurgent troops from the Imperial Guards Division. Arriving at the palace at 6:00 A.M., he found the Imperial Household minister and the lord steward already waiting to be summoned by the Emperor. He heard the news of Okada's, Takahashi's and Watanabe's deaths—news that Hirohito, too, had just received. Honjo was ushered into his presence. Hirohito, in army uniform, glowered. "His Majesty was extremely upset and said the incident must be quashed as quickly as possible and a way must be found to turn the disaster into a blessing," Honjo noted. "He also recalled I had expressed fears about such an incident breaking out."

By early morning on February 26, Hirohito had a reasonable idea of the extent of the rebellion. In his methodical, schoolmasterly way he assessed the damage and the consequences of a possible extension, to the country as a whole, of a mass army revolt. So far, it did not appear to have spread beyond Tokyo.

He reacted with calm, but, as Honjo shows in his diary, with growing irritation as the generals and the cabinet, in separate rooms, began their futile discussions. The 2/26 incident was a watershed in Hirohito's life: it was the first time he had been confronted with a truly major, national calamity. The Mukden Incident, in comparison, had been a sideshow; at the time of the 1923 earthquake he had been crown prince and regent but still very dependent on the traditional, protocol-bound palace officials and absurdly deferential cabinet. This time he realized that his entire future was at stake, and, perhaps, his life. The days of compromise and scheming to keep rival groups at bay and in play were over. He ordered his navy minister to mobilize the fleet: if necessary, the navy would have to be used to crush the army, though Hirohito was aware that there were navy diehards, too, who might spread the mutiny to the senior service.

He behaved not just as the commander in chief of a mutinous army but also as clan leader, summoning his family to rally round the throne. The least trustworthy member of the royal family, Prince Chichibu, was ordered to come to the palace forthwith. Hirohito had a special reason for summoning his brother: as a student at the military academy, Chichibu had been friendly with four of the officers now identified as the coup's ringleaders. What was more, he had been, for several years, an officer in the very same mutinous 3rd Regiment, even though, as the emperor's brother, his duties had been light and his leaves of absence frequent. Hirohito knew, from police reports, that Chichibu had met the radical agitator Ikki Kita several times, and that the two men had got on well; it was because of Chichibu's embarrassing friendships and associations that he had been posted away from Tokyo to a different unit (he now commanded a battalion of the 8th Regiment in Hirosaki, where, the emperor knew, activist officers were few and far between). If the coup succeeded, there was the likelihood that the insurgents would turn to Chichibu as the savior of Japan. The younger brother had to be kept out of harm's way, if only for his own good.

That first morning Hirohito's most important visitor was the war minister, Kawashima, who drove straight from the rebel-held Ministry residence and was immediately ushered into the imperial presence. He had never been a favorite of the Emperor's, and his sorry performance, that morning and on subsequent days, was to put an end to his undistinguished career. For, instead of proposing immediate military action against the insurgents unless they surrendered immediately, which Hirohito viewed as the only possible solution, he insisted on reading, in a quavering voice, as he had promised them he would, the rebels' verbose manifesto.

From the moment he first heard the news of the uprising, Hirohito realized that to negotiate with the rebels would lead irrevocably to a fatal loss of face. He knew the rebellion must soon be front-page news all over the world. Most major embassies were close to the square mile of central Tokyo occupied by the insurgents, and Japanese-speaking diplomats were already out in the streets, wading through the thick snow to talk to the rebels, prior to cabling back the news and an assessment of the crisis to their respective governments. The French and German embassies were so close to the rebel army barricades that they were in the firing line, should firefighting start between mutineers and loyalists. Several correspondents had obtained copies of the rebels' *Great Purpose* manifesto, distributed in pamphlet form in downtown Tokyo by sympathizers, despite attempts by the police to seize them all. Buses had to make considerable detours to avoid the rebel-held area, and soon the whole of Tokyo was aware of the army mutiny, even though radio newscasts referred to it in oblique, almost incomprehensible terms.

Inside the Okada residence, the insurgents were still unaware that the man they had killed was not the prime minister. Sakomizu, his son-in-law, with commendable courage, reentered the house with the rebels' permission and, guided by loyal maids, whispered a message of encouragement to the demoralized premier, still hidden under the pile of laundry. A rebel officer told Sakomizu to pick up the telephone. Someone from the palace wanted to talk to him.

It was a message from the Imperial Household minister, Kurahei Yuasa. The emperor, he said, wanted to convey his regrets to Okada's family for what had happened. Should he send a palace messenger to the official or to the family residence?

It occurred to Sakomizu that the telephone call might have an ulterior motive: Hirohito might be trying, in this roundabout way, to find out what was happening. Here was a chance to tell the whole story of the rebels' mistaken-identity murder, but he cut himself short. He might be overheard by one of the officers and, besides, the telephone might be tapped. He gave a vague reply, suggesting that the palace defer sending a messenger for the time being. He was aware that at the other end of the line there was considerable uneasiness, and he even had a nagging suspicion that the official he was talking to was wondering whether he too had not rallied to the rebels' cause. He needed to convey to the palace without delay the news that the prime minister was still alive.

Much time was lost in the endeavor. In the first place, protocol dictated that any civilian official entering the palace and seeking audience with a member of the emperor's court staff had to be properly dressed. This meant Sakomizu's returning to his own home, and donning court dress—morning coat, striped trousers and top hat. Taking a taxi to the palace gate, he had to talk his way past a rebel checkpoint. They eventually let him through.

By the time he arrived at the palace, however, an unforeseen event had taken place, complicating things still further: Hirohito had just appointed his home minister, Fumio Goto, interim prime minister—a move he was to regret almost immediately. So by the time Sakomizu finally reached the Imperial Household Ministry office, Hirohito actually had two prime ministers.

Protocol also required that inside the palace everything must proceed at a quiet, leisurely pace. Yuasa did something no Imperial Household minister had ever done before: as soon as he learned that the prime minister was alive, he actually ran to Hirohito's quarters to break the news, charging in unannounced. Flushed and almost incoherent, he was back, still at a run, a few minutes later. "His Majesty is most pleased," he told Sakomizu. "He said, 'That is excellent,' and he wants Okada brought to safety with all possible speed." It was the first piece of good news Hirohito had received since the start of the mutiny, for he still had no reliable reports on the state of the army in the rest of the country.

Out of earshot of the cabinet ministers and the generals, Sakomizu

quickly conferred with Yuasa. He suggested that perhaps the commander of the 1st Division might be ordered to escort the prime
minister from the rebel-held residence. Yuasa rejected this out of
hand. Clearly, he felt that none of the generals, at this point, could be
trusted. Some of Yuasa's misgivings infected Sakomizu in turn. Cabinet ministers, waiting for their new interim premier to appear,
crowded around him, asking for details of Okada's murder. Sakomizu
fended them off. There was one member of the cabinet, however, he
felt he *could* tell, Okada's old friend the navy minister, a fellow admiral. Surely *he* could be trusted. Sakomizu asked him for a navy detachment to bring the prime minister away from the residence. Out of the
question, the minister said. It would only lead to further bloodshed.
In a whisper, Sakomizu then told the navy minister that he had vital
news to impart. If he could not help, he would like him to forget he
had ever spoken. He then informed him that Okada was still alive.
The navy minister said, "I haven't heard a thing," and promptly left
the room.

Hirohito now waited for the cabinet and the army commanders to
devise a plan to end the mutiny. Every half hour he sent for his ADC,
Honjo, who by this time was considerably demoralized by the news
of his son-in-law's key role in events. "What's going on?" the emperor
kept asking. "What are they doing?"

Not much, it seemed—and none of it to Hirohito's liking. For
hours, the generals failed to agree on any course of action, or even
on the terms of any address to the rebels. Finally, at 3:00 P.M., they
issued an absurdly mild "Admonition" and announced that Tokyo
had been placed "under the jurisdiction of the First Division." It was
a grotesque attempt to conceal the gravity of the situation from the
Japanese public, a risible, face-saving pretense that the barricades and
checkpoints were officially sanctioned—by the emperor, no less. This
subterfuge fooled no one, for by this time city dwellers and rebel
soldiers were huddled together, discussing the situation, the more
politically conscious officers justifying their action in the grandilo-
quent rhetoric of the *Great Purpose* manifesto.

The "Admonition" was also an admission of tensions within the
high military establishment. All that the senior commanders could
finally agree on was a statement telling the rebels that their purpose
had "reached the Emperor's ears. We recognize that your spirit and
true motives are based on a sincere desire to clarify the national

polity." It added that the generals were "unbearably awed." Hirohito, through Honjo, expressed his displeasure with both decisions, and was further infuriated when, through a slip of the pen that was almost certainly deliberate, the word meaning "spirit and true motives" *(shin-i)* was altered to read "actions" *(kodo)*—implying that the murder of high-ranking palace dignitaries and ministers had official approbation. This doctored version of the statement was the one issued to the media, and it naturally convinced the insurgents that Hirohito was on the verge of surrendering to their demands. Honjo wrote later that he had never seen the emperor so angry, for his orders to Kawashima had been "End this incident as quickly as possible"—meaning, by force of arms.

By the end of the day, the cabinet, in permanent session inside the palace, finally established a consensus on two points: in a meeting with the emperor, the new interim prime minister announced that martial law would be declared forthwith. The second decision was that, in shame at what had happened, the cabinet had decided to resign. Hirohito welcomed the imposition of martial law but told the ministers they should remain in office for the time being. His tone was so cold, however, that their days were clearly numbered. Throughout the night they drafted their letters of resignation, experimenting with different verbal forms of contrition and abasement. It was a measure of his distrust and contempt for the entire group that Hirohito had told none of his ministers or generals—not even Honjo—that Okada was alive and well. After summoning Honjo one last time, around 2:00 A.M., for an up-to-date report on the situation, Hirohito went to bed. By this time, he knew, ships were converging on Tokyo Bay, and loyal units, including tanks, were being prepared for a possible confrontation. That night, for the first time since he had had it installed, Hirohito, still in his army uniform, slept on a camp bed in his office.

That night, too, one more person came to know that the prime minister was alive. A military police sergeant, removing the bodies of dead policemen, stumbled across him and told a minor official in Okada's service. The official was a close and trusted friend of the premier's son-in-law Sakomizu. After making sure the sergeant was to be trusted, the three of them got together to plan Okada's escape.

The following morning, February 27, having smuggled Western clothes into Okada's hiding place, dressed him and put a surgical mask on his face, they ushered him into the presence of his dead brother-in-law, along with a group of mourners allowed in by the rebels to pay their respects. Half pushing him, half carrying him, they guided him through the crowd and into a waiting car, which whisked him away to the temporary safety of a Buddhist temple. Okada was so shocked by his experience that he was clearly unfit to resume his duties for some time.

Now there was another problem—making sure the mutineers remained unaware that the body inside the prime minister's residence was not Okada's. Sakomizu made sure the coffin ordered by the family was a closed one, and, when it was delivered in late afternoon, personally wrapped the corpse in a blanket and closed the lid himself. The rebels saluted as the funeral carriage set off for Okada's private house, where another mourning ceremony was being prepared, complete with visitors' book and black-framed photograph of Okada.

The indefatigable Sakomizu took a taxi back to the Imperial Palace, broke the news to the cabinet that Okada was alive and unhurt and said that Hirohito wanted to see Okada as soon as possible. A fresh obstacle now arose: Goto, the acting prime minister, soon to be relegated to oblivion, claimed in a farcical attempt to prolong his own tenure of office that Okada, by allowing the mutiny to occur, had forfeited his job, and should no longer be treated as prime minister. Sakomizu appealed to the generals, and was ignored. Should the rebels discover their error, he was told, they might well in a rage attack the palace. Once more Sakomizu returned to Okada's private house, to ensure that the funeral ceremonies went ahead in Okada's name after all. He had by this time told the family the truth about the prime minister's survival and Okada's brother-in-law's heroic death. "I am glad," said the latter's widow, "that my husband could be of service." They all agreed to keep up the deception. Sakomizu also telephoned the Buddhist monastery and told his military police sergeant accomplice to keep Okada there for the time being.

While Sakomizu was scurrying back and forth between the palace and Okada's official and private residences, a palace escort waited at Tokyo station for Prince Chichibu's arrival from northern Honshu. In his diary, Honjo wrongly claims that the emperor's youngest brother, Prince Takamatsu, was part of the welcoming group. Hirohito had so decreed, but Takamatsu preferred to remain within the palace walls. Chichibu was taken directly to see Hirohito because, as Honjo euphemistically put it, "the court attendance feared that if Prince Chichibu returned to his residence first, some people might contact him in order to make use of him." Hirohito wanted to find out whether Chichibu was in league with the mutineers (he claimed he was not) and extract from him some pledge of loyalty. Chichibu was being less than candid; one of the mutineers who was later court-martialed assured his family that Chichibu had encouraged them. In a farewell letter after being sentenced to death, one of the ringleaders wrote that "Prince Chichibu told me that when the coup comes, I want you to head a company and invite me to see you off as you leave the barracks."

News did finally leak of Okada's survival. The military police commander, an ailing general so crippled with arthritis he could barely walk, heard from one of his informers, and told the palace. But the news was still not made public.

Hirohito's impatience was increasing: he summoned Honjo every half hour to be briefed on developments. There were none. Hirohito called in the commander newly appointed to administer martial law in Tokyo and ordered him to disarm the rebels "by force if necessary," without, however, setting a mandatory deadline. During his frequent meetings with Hirohito, Honjo did not hesitate to put forth the army's point of view. Of course the "activists" (he carefully avoided derogatory terms like "rebels" or "insurgents") could not be entirely forgiven, "but from the standpoint of the spirit that moved them to action, because they were thinking of the good of the nation, they should not necessarily be condemned."

Hirohito refuted this view in unusually harsh terms. "How can we not condemn even the spirit of these criminally brutal officers who killed my aged subjects who were my hands and feet?" he asked. "To kill these aged and venerable men whom I trusted the most is akin to gently strangling me with floss-silk."

"In response to this," Honjo wrote, "I reiterated that, needless to say, maiming and killing the aged subjects are most horrible. But even if they were misguided in their motives these officers did so in the belief that this was the best way to serve the state." Hirohito replied that their only excuse was that they had "not acted for selfish reasons." Clearly, in his mind, this was not sufficient to warrant any leniency. Invariably, Hirohito used "rebels," not the milder word "activists." The vocabulary of the War Ministry communiqués, throughout the four days of 2/26, was highly revealing. In the first news bulletin the ministry had referred to the rebels as "a party which rose to uphold and clarify the national constitution." It was not until two days later, when it was clear there had been no sympathetic upsurge elsewhere in Japan, that they were called "rioters." The term "insurgent army" did not appear until the last day, when its use was almost certainly at Hirohito's own instigation.

As the hours dragged by, Hirohito again expressed his rage at his generals' inability to act against the insurgents, at their "excessive caution and unnecessary procrastination." If they didn't act soon against the mutineers, he told Honjo, "I will personally lead the Imperial Guard Division and subdue them."

Hirohito, by now, had read the letters of resignation submitted by his cabinet, and ironically noted that their language was identical. "When the Toranomon incident [the assassination attempt on his life in 1923] occurred, and the entire Cabinet resigned, the minister most responsible, the Interior Minister, wrote a statement of resignation completely different from the others," he told Honjo. "He expressed his profoundest sense of agony. When we refused his resignation, he resubmitted it, explaining in highly emotional terms that he was unable to continue in office." In contrast, he said, the war minister's letter was "odd." It was Hirohito's way of conveying—through Honjo—not only his extreme displeasure, but his suspicion that the war minister was in league with the plotters. Late that afternoon, the rebel officers requested a meeting with General Mazaki, whose ousting had sparked the mutiny. The general had been in and out of the War Ministry residence several times already. The meeting took place. It was inconclusive.

Another meeting occurred behind closed doors inside Hirohito's own office. In the presence of his two brothers, and of several close relatives, Hirohito demanded, and extracted, from all those present an oath of loyalty and allegiance. The assembled imperial family also decided that, for the oath to be absolutely watertight, Prince Kanin (bedridden in his house in the country), however ill, had to come to the palace and make a similar pledge. Hirohito told them to make sure Kanin was there without fail the following day. For the second night running he slept on his office camp bed.

On the third day of the crisis, February 28, Hirohito had had enough: he issued a dawn edict ordering the rebels to "speedily withdraw" from the occupied zones and return to their units. If they had not done so within twenty-four hours, they would be fired upon. Police began drawing up plans for the evacuation of some key downtown areas, to avoid unnecessary civilian casualties. Foreign embassy personnel in the sensitive zone next to the barricades were warned to stay indoors.

Two princes who had been absent from the earlier clan meeting appeared: the army chief of staff, Prince Kanin, who swore his absence had been due to illness, and, to prove his claim, immediately took to his bed; and the elderly Prince Nashimoto, a retired field marshal, who emotionally pledged his allegiance and begged Hirohito's forgiveness for the army's "crime." Chichibu, who had convinced Hirohito of his loyalty, was allowed to go home, and talk some of the rebel officers whom he knew into surrendering. General Mazaki, ever the troublemaker, while convincing the war minister that he was negotiating with the rebels on the emperor's behalf, was in fact urging them to stand firm, even arguing with other generals that what was needed was a communiqué approving their aims. But some of the rank and file among the rebels were wavering, and started drifting back to their barracks. Confusion was such that after one of the many meetings between General Mazaki and the insurgents, some of the latter also tried to enter the palace to talk to Hirohito in person. They were turned back.

That afternoon Honjo received a call from his son-in-law: the rebel officers in the War Ministry residence were contemplating suicide as a way out, but would only follow this course of action if an emissary from the emperor was dispatched to witness their ritual deaths. In any case, he added, the 1st Division commander had told him that he would never allow the "loyalists" under his control to fire on the rebels. Honjo dared not relay the second message to Hirohito, but he did broach the theme of collective suicide to take place in the presence of a palace official.

He was brutally rebuffed. "If they wish to commit suicide, let them do so as they please," Hirohito told him. "It is out of the question to dispatch a messenger to such men."

"I have never seen His Majesty display such anger," Honjo wrote. "He ordered me to dispatch strict orders that the troops must be subjugated at once."

Honjo received a second call from his son-in-law and told him the suicide offer had been rejected. At his next meeting that day with Hirohito, Honjo burst into tears. Hirohito left the room, but did not remain silent for long. "He summoned me again and said that I wept while complaining about the slanders against the army, but unless the incident is resolved, there will be serious consequences."

Fearing that Okada, in a terrible state, might himself commit *seppuku,* his son-in-law smuggled him into the palace at dusk, against the advice of all the cabinet. Palace officials goggled at the old man as they would at a ghost. The prime minister, tearful and demoralized, begged to be allowed to resign for causing the emperor such grief. Hirohito refused permission. "I am very pleased," he said, trying to put some resolve into the old man, handling him with gentle firmness, as one would a hysterical child. Okada was given a room in the palace, but—clearly on the verge of a nervous breakdown—never again functioned as premier. The circumstances of his survival were uniquely humiliating in the *bushido* context. He had allowed a less distinguished member of his family to make the supreme sacrifice, one he would never be able to repay. He owed his life to humble men, who had saved him only by making him attend his own funeral ceremony—a farcical trick, something that would have made a perfect scene in a comic interlude at a Noh performance. No wonder, after the event, many Japanese were of the opinion that Okada should indeed have committed *seppuku.*

Hirohito woke on February 29 in better spirits, for the army commanders were at last determined to act: when the ultimatum ran out, at 8:00 A.M., the martial law commander called on the rebels through a loudspeaker to surrender. Tanks rumbled through the streets, and planes flew low over downtown Tokyo, dropping leaflets reading: "Return to your units. It is not yet too late. All who resist are rebels. We will shoot them. Your families weep to see you becoming traitors."

The drift back to barracks by noncoms and private soldiers became a rout. The ultimatum was repeated, again and again, on Tokyo radio. One captain among the ringleaders attempted suicide but failed; another blew his brains out. But all the remaining mutineers surrendered quietly, and were immediately taken to an army jail. They hoped that long-drawn-out trials would afford them endless opportunities for speechmaking, and that the judiciary would be as lenient in their case as it had been on previous similar occasions. It was a major miscalculation on their part, for Hirohito, acknowledging this "indelible black mark on the history of the sacred Showa reign," was determined to make an example of them. Neither Hirohito nor Japan would ever forget 2/26, nor would prewar Japan ever be the same again.

CHAPTER TEN

It was only after the collapse of the 2/26 mutiny that Emperor Hirohito realized how far the rot had spread within the army. "Why did nobody know what was being prepared?" he complained to his chief ADC. Because of his son-in-law's role in the mutiny, and the army's lack of resolve in dealing with the mutineers, Honjo knew his days as chief ADC were numbered. Characteristically, Hirohito played a cat-and-mouse game with him. The first inkling he had of the emperor's determination to replace him was when Hirohito asked Honjo if the army would take kindly to the idea of the next chief ADC coming from the navy.

Honjo alone was scarcely to blame, and, as Hirohito acknowledged, had at least told the emperor that trouble had been brewing. In fact, 2/26, in one form or another, had been the talk of Japan's establishment for months if not years. Secret police archives (brought to light and examined during the postwar U.S. occupation) showed that Prince Chichibu, Prince Higashikuni and even Marquis Kido had all been aware of certain aspects of the conspiracy, though they had not known that it was planned for February 26.

Other senior officers with prior knowledge of 2/26 were General Mazaki, Colonel Ishiwara of Manchurian fame (though he disapproved and played a leading role in suppressing it) and the retired General Araki. Important names found in the notebook of Captain Itobe, one of the 2/26 ringleaders, included those of Yoshiyuki Kawashima, the war minister, and of Honjo himself.

Hirohito, so decisive in his handling of the mutiny, might have reversed the trend toward militarism in the months that immediately followed its collapse. His princely relatives now looked up to him with new respect as their uncontested, determined leader; the hotheaded army extremists had been cowed, for the time being at least, and his military commanders whipped into obedient submission. With Hirohito's knowledge and encouragement, a vast "purge" of unreliable officers began, affecting several thousands.

The scene was set for reform, and the public mood was not yet frenziedly pro-army and pro-war. Yet, less than eighteen months later, and with Hirohito's approval, Japan was locked in an all-out war against China, and well on the way to becoming a full-fledged totalitarian state. In the words of Sir Robert Craigie, the new British ambassador in Tokyo, Japan was "embarked on a policy of aggression no less calculated and methodical than was Hitler's course in Europe after the occupation of the Rhineland." Joseph Grew, the U.S. ambassador, came to the reluctant conclusion that "thwarted in attempts to seize power at home, military extremists committed Japan to a large-scale war in China." Both assessments were correct, though the two diplomats were overinclined to give Hirohito the benefit of the doubt at every twist and turn, blaming his war-hungry advisers instead.

The China war was the decisive step on the road to Pearl Harbor. To further her war effort, Japan needed more raw materials than she could produce domestically or extract from captive Korea and Manchuria; in particular she needed oil for her huge navy. In an attempt to force Japan into a more conciliatory mood, the United States, followed by Britain and Holland, would impose embargoes on oil and severely restrict other raw material exports to Japan. It was these embargoes that finally convinced Japan's military leaders that unless they overran the whole of Southeast Asia to obtain what they needed, Japan would be economically strangled, her huge army and navy reduced to complete impotence. In the long run, Hirohito was to acquiesce in this assessment and give his blessing to Pearl Harbor.

The events that were to lead to Pearl Harbor were set in motion almost immediately after the end of the mutiny—when Hirohito decided that rather than face the likelihood of continuing plots and army unrest at home, he preferred to allow military adventures abroad. So, for all his pugnacious attitude toward the mutineers, Hirohito allowed his hands to be tied by the army as securely as if he had given in to them in the first place.

In a talk with Honjo just after the rebels' surrender, Hirohito recognized "the need to accommodate to the urgent demands of the military to some extent to avoid a repetition of the tragedy." In another indication of the lessons he had drawn from 2/26, he told Honjo, shortly before "letting him go," "that since we fear a repetition of this kind of incident if we do not accede [to the army's demands] we want to take their views into consideration." "Forming the new Government will be difficult," Hirohito informed Marquis Kido. "The Cabinet that will be welcome in military circles will give rise to anxieties among economic circles. However, we can't consider only the interests of the economic circles."

One imperial concession that was to have immediate repercussions was the revival of the old custom whereby all army and navy ministers were drawn from the ranks of serving officers. This gave the army hierarchy a de facto veto over all future governments: whenever the army chief of staff and his acolytes took a dislike to the program or the personality of the prime minister–elect, or to his choice of ministers, they simply refused to allow any serving general to accept the post of war or navy minister. The premier-elect was then forced to report back that he was unable to form a government, and another candidate, more acceptable to the armed forces, was chosen.

The new prime minister (May 1936–January 1937) was Koki Hirota, a former foreign minister. He was, exceptionally, no aristocrat, but a stonemason's son, who—thanks to academic brilliance and hard work, and the help of the Black Dragon leader, Toyama, whose enthusiastic supporter he had been in adolescence—had managed to pass the difficult Foreign Ministry entrance exams and worked his way up as a career diplomat. For all his youthful enthusiasm for extreme Black Dragon nationalism, Hirota as a diplomat had acquired a reputation for liberalism, so much so that Ambassador Grew, welcoming his appointment, believed Hirota was "a strong, safe man and that while he will have to play ball with the Army to some extent I think he will handle foreign affairs as wisely as they can be handled given the domestic elements he will have to conciliate." All in all, he noted, "I would probably have chosen him myself."

Hirota took on the job reluctantly, convinced he would eventually be murdered by army hotheads. He had not been Saionji's first choice: the latter had wanted his protégé and the emperor's close friend and kinsman Fumimaro Konoye. But Konoye, who was to become prime minister from 1937 onward, refused, on grounds of health. He was probably the only man in the whole of Japan able to refuse an emperor's request.

The new war minister, and the most powerful man by far in Hirota's cabinet, was General Hisaichi Terauchi, a hard-liner, who drafted a new imperial defense policy, setting out Japan's long-term foreign policy goals. Terauchi started with the premise that Japan's overriding aim was to "establish the Japanese Empire's leadership in East Asia" while maintaining "friendly relations with foreign powers," and compelling the Soviet Union to give up her "positive aspirations" in the Far East. At the same time, the plan was to "dissuade China from depending on European and United States aid," and to "persuade" China to assume a "friendly [i.e., subservient] attitude." For the first time, Britain, because of her influence and enclaves in China, was included on the list of "foremost enemies of the nation."

For all his professed friendship and admiration for the British royal family, Hirohito accepted and endorsed this document, which also included a blueprint for huge new army and navy expenditures. This could only mean one thing: the military were determined, despite 2/26, to flex their muscles in Asia.

Hirohito summoned his new prime minister to the palace and ordered him to have the huge army and navy appropriations approved by the Diet as quickly as possible. "I speak," he told Hirota, who dared not even look at the emperor but kept his eyes fixed on the low table between them, "in my capacity as Supreme Commander of the Armed Forces." It was Hirota's second major surprise since taking office. His first, on the very day he was appointed prime minister, came with the emperor's summons and his advice to respect the constitution, exercise restraint in foreign affairs, avoid anything that would create an upheaval in the business world and *see that the position of the nobility was not endangered* [author's italics]. Hirota pondered the last injunction for weeks. Did this mean the emperor felt that a plebeian premier could not be trusted to do his job impartially? Or did it represent a new attitude on Hirohito's part, a determination, after 2/26, to place members of his imperial family increasingly in key posts? This would certainly happen, in the very near future.

Hirota very soon realized that General Terauchi had the upper hand, and that there was little a civilian prime minister could do to make his presence felt. He resigned, to become foreign minister, remaining a loyal servant of the emperor but fearful of the army's growing role.

As a final attempt to thwart the army's rising influence, Prince Saionji now put forward the name of General Ugaki, the man banished to Korea as governor-general in 1931 after a plot in his name for which he had had little or no responsibility. In the intervening years Ugaki had become extremely wary of the army's expansionist ideology.

Hirohito accepted Saionji's choice, out of respect for the old man, but did nothing to help Ugaki when, as expected, he encountered army blackmail tactics. When Ugaki was on his way into Tokyo to see Hirohito, his car was stopped by the military police, the dreaded *kempei.* Their commander, General Kesago Nakajima, entered Ugaki's car and advised him not to accept the emperor's offer to form a cabinet. When this threat failed, the army simply refused to provide a war minister to serve under him. Ugaki, in desperation, asked Hirohito to command the army to endorse the war minister of his choice or else order a reservist of Ugaki's choice back onto active duty, to fill the post. Hirohito turned down the request, and Ugaki gave up his attempt to form a government.

The next prime minister was a former war minister, General Senjuro Hayashi, far more acceptable to the army than Ugaki. But his government lasted only a few months, resigning after a massive row in parliament, caused by General Terauchi's bullying tactics toward Diet members. This time, Prince Konoye, yielding to both Hirohito's and Saionji's pressure, agreed to become prime minister.

Prince Fumimaro Konoye was, in 1937, well known to the Japanese public, and one of the few truly popular politicians, because of his frequent writings in the press and his unusual (for Japan) sense of public relations. Indolent, opinionated, passionate and unpredictable, Konoye was the only man in Japan who dispensed with protocol when addressing the emperor. His predecessor Hirota had been amazed to see Konoye, ten years older than Hirohito, sit in the emperor's presence, even casually crossing his legs. He treated the emperor like a younger brother, indulging in gossip and banter. Such behavior baffled Hirohito, who was not used to informality of any kind: the humorless emperor could not distinguish between private conversation and official business.

Konoye was a member of the Fujiwara clan, which had married into the imperial family since the seventh century, and he regarded himself as the emperor's equal in lineage and his superior in intellect. His loyalty, as he was to demonstrate, tragically, in 1945, was beyond reproach. Hirohito liked and admired him. His casual elegance and life-style reminded him of that of the Prince of the Wales.

Konoye owed his political career to Prince Saionji, whom he had accompanied to the Versailles Peace Treaty conference as a junior aide. This did not mean that he shared the prince's patrician, liberal approach. Like Saionji, he despised the run-of-the-mill Japanese politicians, but, unlike him, he was, in his youth and up to 1941, when he dramatically altered his views, both a nationalist and a radical. In a famous essay, written when he was a young man just before setting out for Versailles in 1918, he had attacked the League of Nations, then under discussion, as a convenient instrument for British and American domination of the poorer Asian powers. Japan should only join the League, he argued, if the Western powers showed they were prepared to do away with "economic imperialism" and the discriminatory treatment of Asians by Caucasians.

These youthful radical views, and a flirtation with "tatami socialism," went hand in hand with a strong sense of personal privilege and awareness of his princely superiority. His childhood had been a traumatic one: he had experienced sudden poverty after his father's early death, and terrifying perplexity brought about by the knowledge that the woman he worshiped as his mother was in fact his aunt, for his father had secretly married his wife's sister after the former's early death. Though he refused the traditional "arranged marriage" (his was a love match), he almost immediately afterward took up with a concubine. His active sex life was the topic of constant gossip in aristocratic clubs, and there were persistent rumors of bisexuality. Physically, he was tall, good-looking in a 1930s film-star way, and strong, though he claimed to be plagued by ill-health and was a notorious hypochondriac.

Barely a month after Konoye's investiture as prime minister, Japanese troops, legally garrisoned in northern China as part of the limited occupation forces there, deliberately contrived to clash with Chinese troops just north of Peking on July 7, 1937, in what became known as the Marco Polo Bridge Incident. What began as a limited exchange of gunfire, on a pattern that had occurred on several earlier occasions, quickly escalated into a full-scale war. As with the Mukden Incident, it had been carefully rehearsed and planned. With Hirohito's consent, Japanese troops immediately poured into northern China to reinforce the Kwangtung Army, quickly occupied Peking and moved south on Shanghai; amphibious landings on the coast were supported by massive Japanese navy shelling. Konoye, at this stage of his career, at least, fully approved of the incident: his goal was the overthrow of Chiang Kai-shek and his replacement by more docile, pro-Japanese puppets. Hirohito's uncles, Prince Higashikuni and Prince Yasuhiko Asaka, were to become senior commanders in this fateful China war. By the end of 1937 Higashikuni commanded Japan's air force in China, while Prince Asaka was in charge of ground troops fighting their way past Shanghai.

From the start, the British, French and U.S. governments viewed this latest example of Japanese belligerence as proof that the military had virtually taken over the running of Japan, and that this had happened under a reluctant, and powerless, Hirohito. This assessment ignored two factors: the Marco Polo Bridge Incident occurred only two days after the Kuomintang–Chinese Communist pact whereby these two rivals decided to shelve their differences and regard Japan as their main enemy; and on July 17, only ten days after the outbreak of war in China, nineteen rebel officers sentenced after 2/26 were executed by firing squads. Because Japanese newspaper headlines, by this time, were exclusively devoted to the China war, these executions went virtually unnoticed, except among the families concerned. The Kuomintang–Chinese Communist pact had revived Hirohito's visceral anti-Communist fears; and the Marco Polo Bridge Incident neatly consigned the executions to obscurity. Hirohito had worried greatly about the impact of the sentences: the inference is that he was pleased by the way they were handled.

Because he was kept informed of all troop movements and service promotions, the further inference is that Hirohito must have had full advance knowledge of what his commanders were planning in China before the Marco Polo Bridge Incident took place. He had audiences with all senior generals before they left with their units for China. His outward behavior, shortly before the incident, reveals, however, a considerable capacity for deception: Hirohito had had an unusually friendly chat with Chiang Kai-shek's ambassador in Tokyo, and no opportunity was lost to emphasize Hirohito's personal links with the United States and Britain. On his way to America, President Manuel Quezon of the Philippines, accompanied by General MacArthur, was received in audience by Hirohito and stayed to lunch. Hirohito oozed cordiality. "I have seldom seen the Emperor so affable," Ambassador Grew noted. Two months after the outbreak of war in China, presenting his credentials to Hirohito on September 11, 1937, Sir Robert Craigie recorded that in spite of the strain on Anglo-Japanese relations occasioned by the war, "the Emperor was particularly gracious and showed an interest in everything that concerned the members of our Royal Family and the British people generally." Craigie added that his first impression of Hirohito was "of an impassive figure going rather stiffly through the motions of an accustomed ceremonial. But this impression quickly changed when, after a few moments' conversation, His Majesty became interested in the topic and his face assumed an eager, almost anxious expression, indicative of his deep concern with current events. Here was no automaton, but rather a man who felt things deeply and, under the control imposed by a stark military tradition, was genuinely anxious to play a useful and beneficent role in world affairs. Despite a nervous manner, his bearing was dignified and he conveyed an impression of great sincerity." The empress, he noted, "displayed a good knowledge of affairs and events in England. . . . I was told afterwards that both the Emperor and Empress had prolonged their conversation with us beyond the normal time-limit."

Craigie also called on the dowager empress, "a little lady of forceful personality, extremely well informed about everything and everyone." When Chichibu returned from England, where he had attended George VI's coronation, Craigie was at Yokohama to witness the scene. What struck him most was the distance at which the crowd was kept from his special train. Soon after, Prince Arthur of Connaught, who had twice visited Japan, died, and the Chichibus, as well as senior cabinet figures, attended a memorial service at Tokyo's Anglican St. Andrew's Church. Clearly, despite Britain's inclusion on the list of major enemies of the Japanese nation, the world was to be kept in ignorance of Japan's real intentions.

Gestures like these, perhaps the result of Hirohito's fondly remembered trip to Britain, did much to foster a personal element of goodwill between Craigie and the palace. While diplomats invariably believe they possess the skills to charm and influence others, they are usually less able to detect instances when they themselves are being manipulated: in the case of Grew and Craigie, both were very susceptible indeed to the "aura" of royalty. They were, in very different ways, snobs, with an intrinsic respect for the institution of monarchy. What was more, either through privileged contacts with members of the Imperial Household, or subtly influenced by a brilliant Japanese exercise in public relations, they were convinced that, for all the tough, pro-Axis talk of the Japanese military, the emperor not only meant what he said when he referred to his trip to Europe as the happiest time of his life, but implied that it still conditioned his whole attitude toward the West. The notion was firmly established that—for all his failings or constraints—his "heart was in the right place." But was it?

In Hitler's Germany, those who were anti-Nazi and were prepared to risk their lives to bring down totalitarianism were a tiny, isolated minority. Among them was an Asian scholar from one of Germany's best-established army families, Ernst von Reichenau, a Catholic who, from the start, saw Hitlerism as an affront to civilization and was determined to fight it. As early as 1929, while Hitler's Nazi party was still on the road to power, Von Reichenau took the crucial step of contacting the French army intelligence organization, the Deuxième Bureau, to warn the French of the dangerous rise of Nazi feeling in Germany. He continued to feed the French with information right up to the outbreak of World War II, and also established a good working relationship with British intelligence, a logical step in view of his Asian connections and frequent trips to Hong Kong and Canton. Ernst's brother Walter happened to be one of Hitler's favorite officers and a rabid Nazi, and for this reason the brothers were no longer on speaking terms. Ernst von Reichenau's British "control" in Hong Kong advised him to patch things up with his brother in order to gain access to any confidential information Walter might then pass on. The advice was taken, and Ernst, now professing pro-Nazi views, staged a formal reconciliation with his brother.

On an arms-sales promotion tour to both China and Japan in 1937, Marshal Walter von Reichenau gave his brother Ernst the following detailed account of his meeting with Hirohito (which Ernst von Reichenau later passed on to British intelligence):

> For China it was easy to sell anything in the way of antiquated arms and equipment. It was difficult to sell Japan anything but the best of up-to-date inventions. It must also be recalled that China was merely a customer, but Japan was handled most carefully as a future contemplated and already approached partner of the Axis. The mission of Marshal Walter von Reichenau to the Mikado was to represent as strongly as possible how formidable a future German-Japan pact would figure in the Japanese domination of the Far East. At this time the German-Japan axis was not yet formed. But at this time the idea was presented to the Emperor by one of Hitler's most prominent favourites, my brother.
>
> My brother described in detail the happenings at the audience with the Emperor, which climaxed in his approaching the Emperor privately in order to tell him solemnly:
>
> "Your Majesty, my Fuehrer looks forward—beyond economies—to a greater union between Your Majesty's country and his."
>
> My brother said that the Emperor bade his interpreter go away and when they were alone the Emperor stared straight into my brother's eyes and answered:
>
> "I have heard and I am pleased." Then the Emperor turned and left the room while my brother stood to attention with the Hitler salute.

What happened between the end of 2/26 and the start of Japan's full-scale China war has been difficult for Hirohito's apologists to explain away. The Reichenau episode, had they known about it, would have baffled them still further. For, unlike the circumstances of the Mukden Incident, it was impossible to claim that key decisions were taken behind his back by army commanders facing him with a fait accompli—with the exception of two incidents in Mongolia and on the Soviet Union border, when his troops overstepped their orders and were promptly ordered back. His stance during the 2/26 mutiny proved that he could act with the utmost toughness when he so willed.

Hirohito's most articulate apologist, the late Leonard Mosley, skirts over this period with some embarrassment. Dedicated to the proposition that the emperor either knew nothing of events that took place or did his best to stop the drift to totalitarianism and in the last resort lacked the powers to avert it, Mosley puts all the blame on two of Hirohito's "post-2/26" premiers, Hirota and Prince Konoye, claiming that Hirohito was kept "in total isolation." Lord Privy Seal Yuasa, he says, was "a fusspot with no feelings other than protocol"; Kido "was no longer there" to give the emperor good advice; Baron Matsudaira, the new Imperial Household minister, "had failed to establish friendly relations with the Emperor," and Prince Chichibu, his son-in-law, who "could have bridged the gap between them" [a doubtful proposition] was away in Hokkaido with his regiment. Prince Saionji was old, infirm and dispirited, and Prince Konoye "was (no doubt) asleep."

This picture does not bear scrutiny. Yuasa, as Imperial Household minister, had, almost alone among top palace officials, shown complete loyalty to Hirohito and a healthy distrust of all army commanders during 2/26. For all his change in status, Kido retained his palace links as director of the Peerage and Heraldry Bureau, saw Hirohito (as his diaries prove) almost as frequently as before, and in any case—before returning to the palace as Lord Privy Seal—was to remain in close touch with the emperor since he became first his education and propaganda, and then his welfare, minister. Brought into the government at the emperor's request precisely so that he might remain his "eyes and ears," he was in closer touch with the emperor than any education minister before or since. The notion that Hirohito would ever trust Chichibu (in view of his volatile past) with any sensitive mission involving either the army or the palace is too ludicrous to dwell on; Prince Saionji, as an authoritative biography later showed, was more saddened by Hirohito's response to events taking place around him than affected by his physical infirmities and the onset of senility.

Mosley attributed Hirohito's new failure of will to isolation, depression, helpless frustration and "the lack of anyone to galvanize him in

this direction. . . . he had always been a character who needed a push."
But the thesis that Hirohito was cut off from all those who tried to
draw his attention to the dangers of a "positive" China policy does not
stand up either. Of course Hirohito received disastrously wrong advice from many of those around him, but the notion that he was
completely sealed off from any contact with those who held opposite
views is simply not true. As the Kido diaries show, there was an
unending stream of visitors to the palace, not all of them committed
to aggression in China. One example comes to mind: on August 30,
1939, at a time when war against China was in full swing, General
Kanji Ishihara, the mastermind behind the Mukden Incident who, by
this time, had become a resolute opponent of war with China, found
himself in the same train compartment with a close friend of Admiral
Yamamoto—a Navy Ministry official called Eiichi Sorimachi. The two
men knew each other. Sorimachi asked him where he was going. To
the palace, Ishihara replied, for an audience with Hirohito before
taking up his new post as commander of the 6th Training Division.
"I intend to advise him," said Ishihara, "that the present war with
China should not be allowed to continue. I also intend to tell Princes
Chichibu and Takamatsu this. I know the train's loaded with military
police in plainclothes and with political police, but it won't stop me
saying that this business will ruin Japan if we go on with it."

Hirohito's behavior at the time of the outbreak of the China war,
or China Incident, as it was euphemistically referred to, differed completely from his aloofness and shilly-shallying at the time of the Mukden Incident. Reinforcements were sent to the new theater of
operations with his full consent. Hirohito's apologists have been quick
to point out that he became an increasingly vocal critic of the China
war, but have failed to point out that most of his repeated criticism
of his generals had to do with the fact *that they were not winning the war
fast enough,* and that it was becoming an increasingly futile proposition, especially after 1940, when Japan's military resources were
needed elsewhere; Hirohito again and again reminded the generals
that they had promised it would all be over in a matter of months. It
was the recognition that Japanese troops became bogged down in an
interminable conflict in China that infuriated Hirohito—rather than
the war itself.

Why, after crushing the 2/26 rebels so thoroughly, did Hirohito
allow the China Incident to escalate into full-scale war, leading, in

time, to Pearl Harbor and "the great Asian war"? There were two reasons: the first is that, for all his show of strength during 2/26, Hirohito believed that the only way of ensuring that there would be no further insurgencies at home was to allow the army to have its fling abroad. The other is that despite his eagerness to establish a lasting neutral relationship with the Soviet Union, Hirohito was motivated by a rigidly obsessive anti-Communism, and saw the Communist threat not in terms of a hostile USSR (which could be contained) but of a threatening, increasingly Communist-dominated China.

What makes Emperor Hirohito's views during this crucial period so difficult to pinpoint is their very ambiguity. It would be wrong to assume that they were solidly entrenched, immutable and guided by rigid principle. As the "organ" controversy shows, the emperor could privately support a view that he failed to defend outright. His powers of dissimulation were, however, considerable, and there is evidence that, as the military consolidated its power, his own foreign policy attitudes oscillated wildly, one day favoring the United States and his British connections, the next flirting with Hitler.

The major, tragic casualty of the policy inaugurated as a result of the Marco Polo Bridge Incident was Prince Saionji, the *genro*. He had become a sad, isolated and increasingly irrelevant figure. The uncontested leader of Japan's small liberal intellectual elite, he was witnessing the destruction of all his cherished ideals, the shattering of all his dreams for a modern, internationally minded Japan. He had been an enthusiastic proponent of Japan's wholehearted involvement in the League of Nations—and Japan had withdrawn from the League in the wake of the Mukden Incident. He had condemned Japan's arms race—and watched the Hirota government earmark an unprecedentedly large sum for new divisions, planes and battleships. He had advocated friendship with Chiang Kai-shek, only to see the emperor accede to the army's demands for a full-scale war with China and the determination to remove Chiang Kai-shek from the political scene altogether. He had staked his reputation on Japan's need to maintain close relations with Britain and the United States, only to witness Japan's growing links with Fascist Italy and Nazi Germany. He saw as well the triumph of personal enemies like the right-wing nationalist Baron Kiichiro Hiranuma, who in 1936, in the wake of 2/26, achieved his lifelong goal when he succeeded Prince Konoye to become president of the Privy Council, over Saionji's objections. One

of the bitterest pills to swallow, for Saionji, was the emperor's endorsement of the anti-Comintern pact, which Japan signed in 1936,
incontrovertible proof that Nazi Germany and nationalist Japan were
moving closer to each other. By this time old age (Saionji was eighty-
eight), illness and a liberal, patrician hatred for the "ultras" who now
had the emperor's ear brought about a melancholic, lethargic passivity. On hearing of Baron Hiranuma's promotion, Saionji told his
confidential secretary, Harada: "It comes as no surprise. . . . that is the
trend of the times and there is nothing to be done. . . . It is a great
pity for the Emperor's sake."

Saionji's greatest sorrow was not just that he had lived long enough
to witness the shattering of his dreams; what hurt him at least as much
was the emperor's involvement in an adventure that Saionji felt could
only end in tragedy, as well as Hirohito's contempt for the old man's
vision of a liberal, open Japan. Without criticizing the emperor
openly, Saionji—with great dignity—told Harada, again and again,
that he felt utterly baffled by the disturbing course taken by Japan, not
least by the emperor's refusal to follow his advice; though Hirohito
still went through the motions of consulting Saionji from time to time,
he neither listened to nor acted along the lines Saionji advocated. The
genro's comments became ever more bitter and disillusioned. "What
can we do tied to Italy or Germany?" he asked Harada. "It is ridiculous and I am deeply suspicious. To think of Japan with the United
States to the east and Britain to the west—that is meaningful. But an
alliance with Germany and Italy . . . what possible meaning could that
have?"

He was also distressed by Hirohito's increasing aloofness: he deplored the stringent security precautions surrounding the emperor.
"He must go out a little more openly," he told Harada. "If this does
not happen, the people will become distant from the throne."

A year before his death (in November 1940, long after he had
ceased playing any role at court) Saionji refused point-blank to advise
the palace any further on the choice of premier. "If I felt that one
would be better than another, I would say so. . . . On three occasions
I have received a message from the Emperor saying, 'Please advise me
on affairs of state.' If I had anything to say which I considered necessary, I would say it *even if the Emperor told me not to speak* [author's
italics]. But at present I have nothing to say. . . . ultimately, there is
nothing to be done but to hold one's tongue and watch. If I were a

little better physically and had a little more energy, I would like to see the Emperor and talk to him about a number of issues, but the way things are, that too is unthinkable.''

The implicit rebuke to the emperor remained unanswered. There would be much to watch, from 1940 onward. Mercifully, Saionji would not be alive to see his fears of Japan's apocalypse confirmed.

CHAPTER ELEVEN

The July 1937 Marco Polo Bridge Incident, which was rapidly leading to full-scale war, did not prevent Hirohito from spending part of the summer, as usual, in the seaside resort of Hayama, fishing for specimens every day. An American neighbor and author, Willard Price, has left a decidedly idyllic account of what it was like to live in close proximity to the emperor in the late 1930s.

In this fishing village thirty miles from Tokyo, Price noted that Hirohito "has a horseman's balance and a swimmer's suppleness. One would never dream this to see him rigid and unresponsive in his limousine as crowds look on. Then the mantle of divinity rests heavily on him. At home he can forget his Godhood."

His appearance, fishing or wandering along the seashore, said Price, reflected aspirations of "gentle dreams and intellectual delights."

Price must have been taken on at least one tour of the "summer palace" in the emperor's absence, for he describes it in detail. "The outer boards of the house are unpainted wood weathered a dull grey. There is lots of dust in the rooms." He noticed there were neither telephones, refrigerators, electric stoves, heating plants, cooling systems nor electric washing machines in evidence, but there were plenty of mosquitoes. "The plainness of the place was a surprise. It was almost shabby. I was ashamed to go back to the luxury of our own home."

Often, Price was wakened by Hirohito, wearing "a three dollar chrome Japanese watch," chopping wood in the garden at dawn. On fishing and specimen-gathering expeditions, Hirohito did not entirely escape from the protocol that was a constant feature of his court. "He handles the spear and the net himself," Price noted, but his "every move is scheduled by the Court, watched by attendants, recorded by scribes. . . . fully-clothed attendants and courtiers in morning coats march hip-deep into the water, on either side of his fishing-boat, to bow and then pull it in."

One day Hirohito left a copy of Aesop's *Fables* (in Japanese) on the seashore. Price came across the book "but a guard snatched it up and conveyed it reverently away." As Price records, ordinary Japanese residents living in the same area were not banned from the beach, "but they never gape." Price may have underestimated the security precautions in force in Hayama and along the coast wherever the emperor decided to fish for specimens, for other eyewitnesses tell of whole fishing villages temporarily evacuated before his arrival. The awe Hirohito inspired was extraordinary: according to Price, a Japanese subject who named his son Hirohito "later killed both the son and himself for his presumption."

The 1937 summer over, Hirohito returned to Tokyo. Inside his palace War Room, he could follow the progress of his troops in China in minute detail. Civilian Chinese casualties in Shanghai were severe: for the first time, large-scale bombing of civilian urban targets took place in the Shanghai suburbs. Western correspondents followed the progress of the war from the relative security of the international concession, which was barred to Japanese troops. All reported the huge troop buildup and the impressive Japanese navy presence. Some were even invited to board the Japanese flagship, and were briefed by Japanese admirals.

The thrust southward from Shanghai to Nanking that took place in November–December 1937 culminated with the "rape of Nanking," the massacre of over one hundred thousand Chinese army prisoners of war and civilians, the rape of twenty thousand Chinese women and the wholesale looting of the town, a stain on Japan's reputation for which the diminutive General Iwane Matsui, the overall commander of ground forces on the Nanking front, eventually paid with his life at the conclusion of the Tokyo Trials. It is one of the grim ironies of history that the International Military Tribunal handed out the death sentence to the one Japanese general who was appalled by the Nanking atrocities and did his best to prevent them.

As is not the case in Japan, where the subject remains taboo in school history books, or else is dismissed in a few lines, the Nanking massacres have been well documented by Chinese, American, British, American and German observers, but two questions remain: why did the rape of Nanking occur in the first place, and did the emperor know? Some of the veterans of the Nanking massacre, filled with guilt for their past behavior (and determined to atone as good Buddhists before their own deaths), have spoken up about their participation in it. One of them is Shiro Azuma, who beheaded ten Chinese soldiers, and returned to China in 1987 to apologize to the Chinese people. He, like his fellow soldiers, who impaled babies on bayonets, buried prisoners alive and then ran over them in tanks, gang-raped women aged from twelve to eighty and executed them when they were beyond satisfying their sexual needs, did not do so in a sudden fit of uncontrolled, undisciplined rage: all acted on orders handed down from on high. This is the message several veteran Japanese ex-servicemen have courageously and stubbornly imparted recently to tiny audiences of concerned Japanese citizens—mostly peace groups and antinuclear lobbies.

The rationale for the savagery was that news of the rape of Nanking would put the fear of God into all Chinese, and compel them to accept Japanese occupation of their land as a more viable alternative to more Nankings. The corollary was that the atrocities would also spell Chiang Kai-shek's doom, for surely the Chinese would begin questioning his leadership after such an appalling debacle? On both counts, the brutal arguments were wrong: the Chinese will to resist the Japanese increased, and Chiang Kai-shek, though he fled first to Hankow, then to Chungking, did not fall.

Japan's "positive" Chinese policy, inaugurated at Nanking on an unprecedented scale, had a name, used in inner cabinet and military conclaves but never in the Japanese press—China's "war of punishment." This catchphrase has a far more brutal connotation in Japanese than it does in translation, and it made nonsense of the professed policy of friendship and of the extended hand—the officially promulgated view that if only the Chinese would get rid of Chiang Kai-shek and fall in with Japanese wishes insofar as trade, recognition of Manchukuo and general Japanese hegemony over China were concerned, all would be sweetness and light. One of the hypocritical aspects of Japan's professed "policy of friendship" with China was that—as, the opium committee report of December 12, 1938, was to prove—Japan had no overriding reason to stop the war because its expense was largely met by officially sanctioned drug trading, almost all of it in the hands of the army or gendarmerie or licensed by them.

To what extent was Hirohito aware of the various aspects of this "war of punishment"? There is no doubt that he was familiar with its terminology, for it was mentioned in his presence time and time again. But what of the policy itself? Leonard Mosley claims, citing palace sources, that Hirohito had no inkling of it, only learning about the details of the rape of Nanking, to his intense grief, years later, after the war. He also argues that there is nothing, either, in the Kido diaries, about the events taking place in Nanking. But the *Kido Nikki* (Diaries), invaluable as they are, are personal entries reflecting Marquis Kido's own activities—in no respect are they daily news bulletins: there is no entry, for example, on the start of the China war provoked by the Marco Polo Bridge Incident, the only reference to it being a somewhat cryptic sentence noting that Prince Konoye failed to come to a dinner party given by Kido because of "events in China."

So it is instructive to turn to Hirota's biographer, Saburo Shiroyama,* for a detailed account of the Nanking massacre, as seen from Tokyo, and its impact on Japan's ruling circles.

As Shiroyama describes it, "the occupation of Nanking provided Hirota with another troublesome and, in the long run, fatal problem." A distinguished Japanese diplomat, Shunrokuro Hidaka, who would become Japanese consul general in Nanking, had entered the city in the wake of the troops and cabled back to his Foreign Ministry a vivid, horror-stricken report of what he had witnessed there. A copy of his report was sent to the War Ministry. "When Hirota heard the reports he was violently angry," wrote Shiroyama. He went to see War Minister Hajime Sugiyama to protest and to ask him to take immediate steps to tighten up the discipline in the army. At the same time, Counselor

---

War Criminal, the Life and Death of Hirota Koki (Tokyo: Kodansha, 1974).

Hidaka and others in Nanking visited local army leaders in order to urge them to do something. General Iwane Matsui, commander in chief, admitted that those under him seemed to have behaved outrageously. When Hidaka asked him whether perhaps the ordinary troops had not heard their superiors' orders, he muttered darkly that it seemed the superiors themselves were sometimes to blame.

Matsui's orders had been flagrantly disobeyed: he had wanted only a few handpicked units to enter the city, and in a special message reminded them that their conduct was to be irreproachable. But several divisions entered Nanking. The most infamous were troops of the 16th Division, under the sadistic Major General Nakajima, the former *kempei* commander who had boarded General Ugaki's car to warn him not to take up the premiership. But behaving almost as barbarously were infantry divisions under two other commanders: Major General Heisuke Yanagawa, an old rival of Matsui's, and Prince Asaka, Hirohito's uncle by marriage (to one of Emperor Meiji's daughters), a lieutenant general who had only recently arrived from Japan and taken over command a mere ten days before the rape of Nanking.

Hidaka, the upright diplomat, also called on Prince Asaka to express his indignation and ask him to discipline his men. Though nothing had appeared in the Japanese press about the troops' behavior (nor would it), Hidaka knew how damaging the reports of the large foreign community in Nanking would be. Ironically, many Chinese soldiers tortured or executed out of hand by bullet or bayonet had given themselves up after taking refuge in Nanking's International Concession, where the foreign community leaders had assured them that the Japanese would treat them "honorably" and urged them to surrender. Understandably, the leaders of Nanking's foreign community felt searing guilt at subsequent events.

Hidaka's report was the talk not only of the Foreign Ministry (where not all its staff were, as yet, the willing tools of totalitarian Japan) but also of the War Ministry and General Staff. A senior staff officer, Lieutenant General Masaharu Homma, was sent to Nanking from Tokyo to investigate, and two months later eighty staff officers who had been with the Japanese forces in Nanking at the time were discreetly recalled to Japan. Among them was Prince Asaka, who called on the prime minister, Hirota, at his office "especially to apologize to him, in the presence of Foreign Under-secretary Horinouchi, for all the trouble that he had caused him."

It is difficult to believe that this—one of the most appalling events of the China war—came and went without Emperor Hirohito becoming aware of it. Even if the General Staff, the War Ministry and the Foreign Ministry did make a concerted effort to conceal the atrocities from him—and there is no proof that they did—it is inconceivable that he should have neither read any of the reports on the Nanking atrocity nor wondered why Prince Asaka, whom he had seen just before his departure for China to take up his command, should have returned so soon. Only a few days before the drive toward Nanking, in November 1937, Hirohito had established his Grand Imperial Headquarters inside the palace, an elaborate war room complex from which he was to follow all major subsequent battles, and from which politicians, even the prime minister, were rigidly excluded. No major piece of military news failed to reach the emperor through this, his latest plaything, and the uproar caused by the Nanking atrocities was the main topic among Japanese diplomats and staff officers throughout January and February 1938. Within a week of his abject apology to Hirota, Prince Asaka resumed his regular game of golf with his kinsman Hirohito. What did they talk about, one wonders—the weather?

The China war was also one of the first theaters of operations where chemical and bacteriological weapons were used on a vast scale, and in time the Japanese were to become the world's most advanced practitioners of this form of warfare. Buried in the hugely expensive 1936 blueprint for military expenditure, which Emperor Hirohito had commanded Hirota to get through the Diet as fast as possible, had been allocations for an obscure "epidemic prevention and water purification supply unit," established that year by a formal order bearing the imperial seal. This unit had in fact existed, on a very small scale, since 1933, but only with the China war—and an epidemic of cholera among the invading Japanese troops—did it become a full-fledged "imperial" unit, with sections eventually posted to all Japan's army divisions serving overseas. Veterans of this organization, otherwise known as Unit 731, are inordinately proud of their "imperial" origins, pointing out that theirs is the only army unit ever set up by "imperial decree." Needless to say, the Diet was never aware of the detailed use of the considerable sums earmarked for Unit 731 (three million yen for personnel, two hundred thousand to three hundred thousand yen per autonomous unit and six million yen for experimentation and research in the first year of its existence).

The story of Unit 731 is probably the darkest single chapter in Japan's immediate prewar history—and, as we shall see later, it is an equally dark chapter in American history too, an indelible stain on MacArthur's reputation, adding to the farce of the Tokyo Trials. For Unit 731 had a double function: its teams, attached to every single division in the field, did indeed man water-purification plants and provide Japanese soldiers with drinking water, but that was only a tiny part of its activities. The more important, secret role of Unit 731 was to develop and put into practice biological warfare techniques, which, some senior military strategists argued, would probably tilt the war—any war—in Japan's favor. In order to perfect these techniques, detailed scientific data had to be amassed, and this meant experimenting not just on crops and animals but on human beings too. In time, Unit 731 was to have laboratories and experimental stations as far afield as Singapore, Nanking and even Rangoon, and its huge staff would include most of Japan's brightest civilian scientists, either invited to participate as experts or else, if they refused, drafted and posted to Unit 731 as conscripts from 1936 onward.

Unit 731 was the brainchild of General Shiro Ishii, a gifted scientist whose brilliantly simple mobile water-purification plant was exhibited to the emperor himself during one of his many inspection tours of army units in the immediate prewar period. Shocked palace officials saw General Ishii literally turn urine into drinking water in front of a fascinated Hirohito, even inviting him to drink the "perfectly safe" end product (the emperor refused, but watched as Ishii quaffed a glass). Ishii had other, more sinister scientific goals. As one veteran Unit 731 member told a British television team at work on an exceptionally disturbing documentary entitled *Did the Emperor Know?* in 1985, "I had the impression Ishii saw this [bacteriological warfare] as a means whereby Japan could conquer the world." In the prewar, pre–atom bomb era, the impact of bacteriological warfare on the battlefield and on civilian populations was a fraught subject. General Ishii firmly believed that Japan, a nonsignatory to the 1925 League of Nations protocol outlawing germ warfare, should have that capability.

As early as 1931 Ishii, then only a colonel, had set up a small research laboratory in Tokyo's Army Medical College, without much official encouragement and with only token funds. Then, in 1935, something happened that totally transformed the attitude of Japan's army General Staff: a serious cholera epidemic broke out in Manchuria, killing six thousand men of the Kwangtung Army there. Japanese security officers claimed this had been no ordinary epidemic, but had been provoked by Chinese spies deliberately spreading it through polluted water. They also claimed to have captured Chinese saboteurs with flea-infested rats bearing typhus, anthrax and smallpox germs. Overnight, Ishii was given a large budget, and told to establish Japan's own bacteriological warfare capacity on a huge scale.

Ishii was made a two-star general, and based himself at Ping Fan, forty miles south of Harbin, in northern Manchuria. By 1939, according to veteran members of Unit 731, Ping Fan was a closely guarded, sprawling cluster of laboratories, living quarters and barracks, with a garrison of three thousand scientists, laboratory technicians and security guards, out of bounds to all Japanese troops save those with the requisite clearance. Huge vats contained bacteria of typhus, tetanus, anthrax, smallpox and salmonella.

General Ishii's attitude to his work was strangely ambivalent: to his army colleagues and superiors he boasted about the contribution he was making to Japan's defense capability and the interest taken in his work in the highest circles; among his subordinates he instilled the notion of secrecy, making them swear they would never divulge what they saw at Ping Fan. To make sure of secrecy, he packed his headquarters, and his laboratories, with recruits and volunteers from a small village near Tokyo called Kamo, where he happened to be the biggest landowner.

For his work to have scientific value, Ishii needed live human beings to experiment on. Under the brutal *kempei*-run regime of puppet Manchukuo he had no difficulty in obtaining them.

Even the most hardened war criminals prefer to depersonalize their victims. In the case of Unit 731, the guinea pigs—convicts, vagrants, suspected spies or saboteurs, Communists, White Russian "stateless" persons with no rights whatever under the Manchukuo puppet regime of Henry Pu-yi, and, later, after the start of the China war and then the Great Asia War, Chinese, and possibly British, Australian and U.S. prisoners of war as well—were known as *maruta* (wooden logs). There were several "holding camps" for them. One of them, in the early years, was the basement of the Japanese consulate in Harbin. The guinea pigs were transferred to Ping Fan in the dead of night, and their special entrance was through a tunnel.

Several of Unit 731's former members, now old men racked with guilt, have spoken about their activities. One of them, Naionji Ozono, responsible for the printing and restricted circulation of the unit's top-secret documents, estimates the total number of guinea pigs experimented on and killed in various ways at three thousand. Other Japanese experts on Unit 731, including Masaki Shimosato, an experienced reporter on the staff of *Akahata,* Japan's Communist daily newspaper, believe the total figure is more likely ten thousand. Ozono described how the *maruta,* who were allocated numbers on entry to further depersonalize them, were experimented on in various ways: some were infected with dysentery or injected with tetanus; others (some wearing gas masks) were staked out in the open and "bombarded" with cyanide gas; still others were exposed to a temperature of minus 50 degrees centigrade in "cold rooms," and frozen to death. Since many senior staff officers, in 1936, believed that war with the Soviet Union was only a matter of time, it was important to Japan's army planners to know what were the human limits to warfare in an excessively cold climate, or in high-altitude flying. One Unit 731 veteran described how he had seen two Caucasians—White Russians—freezing to death behind glass, hugging each other for warmth, entirely naked except for tubes attached to their bodies monitoring their hearts, lungs and pulse rate. Other experiments were even more frightful: to monitor the limits of human endurance, prisoners were made to carry heavy army packs and march round and round in the cold winter climate of Manchuria, with only minute quantities of food and water, until they died of exhaustion.

There were no survivors among the *maruta*: the only way out, says Shimosato, "was up in smoke through the cremation chimney," but, again according to Ozono, General Ishii maintained a large collection of pickled specimens, including whole bodies, for scientific study. Some experiments, said Ozono, including dissections of live *maruta,* were of doubtful scientific value, and in one "prisoners' revolt" all the *maruta* being held in two cell blocks inside the center were "put down" with poison gas.

General Ishii's greatest problem was not the manufacture of bacteria on a huge scale or the paucity of guinea pigs, but lack of efficient delivery systems: when the time came to experiment on "offensive delivery methods," it was found that low-altitude bombs would—on explosion—destroy the very bacteria they were supposed to spray over the enemy. Eventually, Ishii found a safer, and cheaper, way of diffusion: plague-carrying rats. During the course of Japan's China war, beginning in 1936, such infected-rat "air raids" became common, and were the subject of reports sent to Roosevelt and successive British cabinets by Chiang Kai-shek. They were not always believed. Japan's General Staff knew otherwise: during one such "rat raid," the germ strike got out of hand and spread to Japanese troops in the field, killing sixteen hundred of them.

To what extent was Hirohito aware of all this? Even some of Japan's most outspoken experts on Unit 731, about which there is now, in Japan itself, a considerable body of work, shy away from even asking this question. On the one hand is the undoubted fact that he apposed his seal on the order setting it up in the first place (and, as a member of the imperial family told me, "the Emperor read everything he put his seal to—he would never use his seal like a stamp machine"). There is also the matter of Unit 731's cost: the emperor always kept a tight rein on expenditure, whether it concerned his own household or that of the military, and Unit 731 was expensive—one of its administrators even described it as "a bottomless pit" (by 1941 the initial yearly three-million-yen grant for research had increased tenfold). Another survivor says that the "imperial origins" of Unit 731 meant that its budget was virtually unlimited. Furthermore, Hirohito himself was a scientist of no mean stature, even though his own field was far removed from that of General Ishii, whom he knew, of whose meteoric rise in the military hierarchy he was aware, as he was of Ishii's Order of the Rising Sun promotions. There is also his overall legal responsibility to be considered: because he was commander in chief, everything done by Japan's imperial army was in his name. Finally, it is a fact that where his beloved armed forces' research and development were concerned, the emperor's standing orders were that he was to be fully briefed about every scientific experiment: toward the close of the war, for instance, he was kept constantly abreast of Japanese aeronautical engineers' efforts to develop a high-flying experimental plane able to destroy U.S. B-29 bombers in the air.

"Guilt by association" is an unacceptable concept in the West, but the involvement in Unit 731 of immediate members of the imperial family cannot be ignored. A Unit 731 photographer recalls taking a group photograph at Ping Fan of the officers there, with Hirohito's youngest brother, Prince Mikasa, in the place of honor, during an inspection tour. The photographer, Yamashita, was not allowed to accompany Prince Mikasa and his party inside the out-of-bounds laboratory sections, so he cannot tell whether the prince "saw everything" or not. He remembers the occasion well, however, because he received a severe dressing-down from General Ishii: reflection from the sun on the prince's spectacles marred the picture, obscuring Mikasa's eyes. Later, in his memoirs, Prince Mikasa mentioned Unit 731— without citing its actual name, noting that he had watched a film about it and talked to a senior medical officer who had given him details of prisoners deliberately infected with cholera.

Prince Chichibu did not visit Ping Fan, but (on February 9, 1939) attended a secret lecture given by Ishii at the War Ministry, and was "awestruck" by the general's findings.

But far and away the most knowledgeable of Hirohito's relatives was a first cousin, Prince Tsunenori Takeda, who became, within the Kwangtung Army's HQ, its chief financial officer. Takeda, whose wartime alias was Colonel Suneyochi Miata, acknowledged in an interview granted in 1983 to the London *Observer*'s Peter McGill (but never published) that he had visited Unit 731 in the course of his army duties. Though reluctant to talk about Unit 731, Prince Takeda told McGill that he felt no qualms about the principle of biological warfare as such ("I believe we needed to study all means of waging war") and also boasted that Japan had had the wherewithal to develop an A-bomb "earlier than the United States." "Japan could have come first," he said.

It is, of course, common knowledge that Hirohito became progressively isolated from his brothers and cousins as the Great Asian War continued, deliberately restricting his contacts with them on the grounds that since they had no official policy-making role in the actual running of the war, he did not want them to meddle in affairs that were not their concern. But in the immediate prewar period such constraints did not apply.

One of the aging veterans of Unit 731 has said that "the Emperor must have known because the budget was very large and the people involved were top-level." A former Unit 731 scientist adds that the "reports would have been circulated to all involved in important research. The intermediate termination of the flow is inconceivable," he said. "I believe it's ridiculous to believe that such information was not circulated to the Emperor." The activities of Unit 731 were known to many doctors working in the large military hospital at

Shinjuku, in Tokyo, where hundreds of pickled human specimens were kept (and destroyed in the month following Japan's surrender, before the U.S. occupation forces became organized).

Paradoxically, Shimosato believes that Hirohito, though he may have been aware of the "broad lines" of Unit 731 work, was ignorant of its human experiments. "All information was distributed on a need-to-know basis," he says, "and there's no recorded document that shows the Emperor was aware of all that went on." The best-selling novelist Seichi Morimura, who has written several books on Unit 731 (leading to death threats from right-wingers), says that Hirohito "might have had a very rough idea of what it was all about." One argument advanced by Morimura is that the army may have deliberately kept the more gruesome details away from the emperor, "on the grounds that he was a humanist and might have ordered its dissolution had he been fully aware of what was going on." But all such arguments are based on nothing more than the premise that the emperor was at all times "humane," "peace-loving" and "fundamentally anti-war"; both Shimosato and Morimura prefer to speculate on who, among Hirohito's entourage, "must have known." Tojo certainly, Konoye and Kido probably, and of course all the senior generals, including successive war ministers and army chiefs of staff. How such a secret could have been kept for so long from a sovereign as hard-working and as inquisitive as the Emperor is never explained. But dwarfing all such speculation, including that concerning Hirohito's knowledge (or ignorance) of Unit 731's experiments, is the monstrous fact that neither General Ishii, nor any members of his senior staff, some of whom later went on to hold senior hospital, laboratory and university appointments in postwar Japan, were ever prosecuted for what they did—nor is there more than a cursory mention of Unit 731 in the thirty thousand files of IMTFE.

CHAPTER TWELVE

On December 11, 1937, at the height of the siege of Nanking (the massacres were only a few days away), Japanese naval planes bombed the U.S. warship *Panay* on the Yangtze River, near Shanghai, and Japanese artillery sank the British frigate *Ladybird*. Both ships routinely patrolled the Yangtze River to protect foreign shipping and reassure Shanghai's international community by "showing the flag," and their sinking, with several fatal casualties, caused a major diplomatic incident. That it did not lead to war, or to a break in diplomatic relations, was largely the result of the deft handling of the situation by Hirohito's vice navy minister, Admiral Isoroku Yamamoto. Rejecting his subordinates' attempts at a cover-up, the frank Navy Ministry communiqué approved by Yamamoto read:

A naval air unit mistakenly bombed three steamboats of the Standard Company, striking the vessels in question together with an American warship which happened to be in the vicinity. This incident, involving as it does the United States Navy, is extremely regrettable.

Yamamoto personally apologized to Ambassador Grew, saying, "The Navy can only hang its head," and promptly sacked the rear admiral responsible. Yamamoto's fury at the *Panay* incident was genuine. Earlier, he had railed against the imperial Japanese army's behavior in China ("It makes me so mad I'm quitting smoking till it's all over") but what infuriated him even more was that the army failed to discipline the officer responsible for the shelling of the *Ladybird*. He was Colonel Kingoro Hashimoto, a reservist on a spell of duty in China, the same Hashimoto who had been active in plotting right-wing army coups in the thirties as the leading light of the Cherry Blossom Society.

It was this kind of army behavior that gradually led Yamamoto to believe that Japan would never achieve a balanced form of government unless a crackdown on the "rightists" occurred—a move that might lead to a brief confrontation on a far larger scale than 2/26 but would rid Japan of its army hotheads for good. As late as 1937 Yamamoto was convinced that in such a confrontation the navy would rally around the emperor along with most of his army. People like Colonel Hashimoto, he told a friend, deserved to be shot.

This was the same Admiral Yamamoto who was to become the mastermind behind the attack on Pearl Harbor and the man singled out, as a result, by the American press as the incarnation of everything hateful about Japanese militarism. Ironically, Yamamoto could be claimed as one of the very few authentic Japanese heroes in this troubled period. From the start of the China war up to Pearl Harbor, he was in fact not only pro-American, and perfectly aware of the emperor's huge error of judgment in allowing Japan to enter the war, but also deeply distrustful of most of his colleagues; he himself was mistrusted by the jingoists who increasingly called the tune in army and navy circles, and would have murdered him had they been given the slightest chance.

This tiny (he was five foot three, and weighed 120 pounds) but imposing man, with a head like a billiard ball and a wickedly irreverent brand of repartee, had been singled out since his training at the naval academy as a "high flier" and had enjoyed his two spells in the United States—once as a junior attaché seconded to Harvard as a student, the second time as a full-fledged naval attaché, getting on splendidly with his American colleagues, who found him entertainingly different from all other Japanese they had ever met. During a leave of absence in the 1920s, he had traveled to Mexico to study her oil industry and report back to his superiors (such semiclandestine behavior was routine for all ambitious staff officers posted abroad) and had been picked up by the Mexican police, who informed the FBI that "a man claiming to be Isoroku Yamamato, a Japanese naval commander, is travelling around the country inspecting the oil wells. He stays in the meanest attics of third-rate hotels, and never eats hotel food, subsisting entirely on bread, water and bananas. Please confirm his identity."

Even judged by the standards of the times, Yamamoto's family life was odd. After playing host to Hirohito aboard his flagship, the *Nagato,* during a naval review, he decided, for once, to sleep at home, which was such an unusual occurrence that he had to climb over the garden wall and break in as if he were a burglar. His love life was tumultuous: he inspired strong passions in three women of the "water trade," one of whom was only twelve, an apprentice geisha, when they first met. He behaved outrageously at times, openly entertaining his women friends aboard the *Nagato,* and making no secret of his relationships with "ladies of the night." A talented calligrapher, he decorated the geisha houses of his past and current mistresses, and lived far beyond his means, earning a second income from his phenomenal skill at bridge and poker. A firm believer in the occult, he hired an expert in physiognomy and palmistry to spot outstanding fliers among the recruits to the Japanese navy's air arm, and briefly funded a charlatan who claimed he could turn water into oil.

But this compulsive exhibitionist and gambler—who, for a dare, would do perilous handstands on high balconies and ships' railings, and said, after receiving congratulations for Pearl Harbor, "If they really want to please me, why don't they give me a licence to run a casino in Singapore?"—was also one of the most original military minds of the century. Just as De Gaulle, after 1918, was among the first to understand how the tank would revolutionize modern warfare, so Yamamoto sensed that the naval battles of the future would be fought and won in the air. Unlike De Gaulle, who remained a prophet without honor in his own country until World War II, Yamamoto was given every encouragement to develop a carrier-based air arm striking force without which Japan could not have fought a major war. As head of the imperial navy's aeronautical department, vice minister of the navy, and finally commander in chief of the Combined Fleet,

Yamamoto was indeed the architect of Pearl Harbor, but the irony was that he drew up plans for the strike on Hawaii with extreme reluctance and even foreboding, fully aware that, in the long run, it would spell Japan's doom.

Yamamoto had been head of the aeronautical research department at the time of 2/26, with an office in the Admiralty, and on the second day of the putsch some young naval officers had burst in on him, clamoring to join the rebel army officers. Yamamoto ordered them out of his offices, and such was the sheer force of his personality, they went back to their desks without a murmur. This stand, and his mercilessly mocking comments on the shortcomings of his colleagues and superiors in the government and armed forces, earned him more than his fair share of enemies. As a precautionary measure, during the time when he was vice minister of the navy, he had an armored car blocking the entrance to his office building at all times, and, unlike other senior commanders, refused the protection of security guards from the *kempei*, whom he regarded as spies for the rightists.

Though he was as fanatically devoted to the emperor as any of his navy colleagues, his forthrightness made him something of a maverick. When Prince Takamatsu, Hirohito's younger brother, joined the Navy Ministry in 1937 as a lieutenant commander after graduation from the Navy Staff College, Yamamoto's chief aide drew up plans for an elaborate greeting ceremony, with the entire Ministry staff parading outside the building to receive him. Yamamoto angrily canceled the ceremony, reminding his colleagues that Takamatsu—inside the Navy Ministry, at least—was not a prince but a junior staff officer, and should be treated as such.

Later, in 1940, during the elaborate ceremonies that were to mark the twenty-six hundred years since Jimmu, Hirohito's ancestor, had supposedly acceded to the throne, Yamamoto did not attend the rites staged in front of the palace. He explained his absence as follows: "Japan is at war with China, and if I were Chiang Kai-shek, I would have used all the planes at my disposal to wipe out the Imperial Family and Japan's entire leadership at one fell swoop. So I declined the Imperial invitation and spent two days at sea instead, keeping an eye on the skies." Yamamoto, says his biographer, Hiroyoki Agawa, may have used this unlikely eventuality as an excuse for staying away, for he disliked the way in which Japan's propagandists were increasingly relying on "divine" myths, "the way of the Gods," to induce in the public's mind the notion of the invincible nature of the Japanese armed forces, discouraging any hardheaded, long-term comparisons between Japanese and U.S. potentials for war.

He made this attitude clear while he was vice navy minister, in a report to the government, which was probably read by Hirohito himself. "A war between Japan and the United States would be a major calamity for the world," he wrote, strongly denouncing moves (finalized in 1940) for a tripartite pact between Japan, Italy and Nazi Germany. In private he was even more forthright: Saionji's confidential secretary, Harada, also a compulsive diarist, recorded a conversation he had over dinner on October 14, 1940, with Yamamoto, during which the admiral described the possibility of war between the United States and Japan as "outrageous . . . However, with the understanding of the Navy Minister and the Chief of Naval Staff, it is also necessary to make preparations for whatever the Navy is to undertake" (Yamamoto had already begun initial plans for the Pearl Harbor raid). "In my opinion," he went on,

> in order to fight the United States, we must fight with the intention of challenging practically the whole world. In short, even if a non-aggression pact is concluded with the Soviets, Russia cannot be entirely relied upon. While we are fighting the U.S., who can guarantee that they will observe the pact and not attack us from the rear? At any rate, as long as matters have come to this point, I shall extend my utmost efforts and will probably die fighting on the battleship *Nagata*. During that time, Tokyo will probably be burnt to the ground. . . .

"Well-informed Japanese might pray for miracles," Harada recalled, "but realistically (in Yamamoto's view) they should be prepared to do and die." Earlier, the admiral had told an aide: "Japanese cities, made mostly of wood and paper, would burn very easily. The Army talks big, but if war came and there were large-scale air raids, there's no telling what would happen. Have you ever seen the sea on fire when a Navy aircraft crashes and the gasoline starts burning on top of the water? It's hell, I can tell you—and that's on *water!*" He was also astonishingly accurate about future war tactics in the Pacific: "As I see it, naval operations of the future will consist of capturing an island, then building an airfield in as short a time as possible—within a week or so—moving up air units, and using them to gain air and surface control over the next stretch of the ocean." These would be MacArthur's very tactics, but Yamamoto realized they could never be Japan's, for, as he put it, "Do you think we have the kind of industrial capacity to do that?"

Admiral Yamamoto's tragic dilemma illustrates the extraordinary capacity for doublethink shown by leading Japanese statesmen—including the emperor—during this period: they were intermittently aware of the folly of the appallingly risky policies to which they had committed themselves, including the fact that they were gearing themselves up for war against an immeasurably superior adversary. But caught up in a thinking process that had its own crazy logic, they became enmeshed, unable to extricate themselves without unacceptable loss of face.

Worse still, they started believing their own propaganda, and their view of the outside world, never profound, became progressively more warped. Even Hirohito, who had read and studied widely, and knew all about the vicissitudes experienced by the Kaiser in the closing stages of World War I, argued at times like an extraterrestrial.

What strikes one most about Japan's slide into war is the short-term nature of the thinking involved, and the gullibility shown toward Fascist Italy and Nazi Germany; neither the emperor, nor his advisers, nor the dogmatic, narrow-minded military leaders seem to have had any real understanding of the forces they unleashed when Pearl Harbor was bombed.

Hirohito himself reflected this curious myopia. He genuinely believed that, even after Pearl Harbor, Japan would quickly be able to negotiate peace terms that would legitimize her hegemony over Asia. There was little realization that the only option open to the Allies would be Japan's total surrender, that her short-term victories were simply not negotiable; and, among the handful of lucid Japanese Cassandras, there was no one brave or powerful enough to say so to the emperor's face. Not all were taken in by the expansionist rhetoric— Admiral Yamamato for one was prophetically eloquent, in carefully chosen company, about the terrible future in store for Japan if she went to war. While most of the men around the emperor lost all sense of reality, he was one of the few who never believed Japan's official propaganda.

There was another, crucial element in Japanese thinking. It is impossible to understand the sequence of events leading up to Pearl Harbor without bearing in mind that Emperor Hirohito—in common with almost all other Japanese decision-makers (with the possible exception of Admiral Yamamato, who was more of a player than a leader despite his reputation after Pearl Harbor)—believed, until the tide of war started going against them, that the late 1930s in Europe, at least, marked the beginning of a "new era" and that Hitler would win the war. Thus, there was no appreciable outcry when in December 1936 Japan signed the anti-Comintern pact with Germany—an agreement stating that Hitler would come to Japan's defense if she was attacked by the Soviet Union—in effect, guaranteeing Japan's freedom from Soviet interference if she were to invade China. Japan's hypocrisy was such that orders went out to her ambassadors abroad that they were to try to persuade other countries to duplicate such a pact with Germany, on the grounds that it was only a defensive measure to prevent the spread of international Communism. Shigeru Yoshida, then ambassador in London, refused point-blank to convey such a notion to the British Foreign Office, knowing full well the ridicule he would experience.

The clash within Japan between "moderates" and "warmongers" from 1937 onward was no longer between a liberal minority (epitomized by Prince Saionji), resolutely opposed to war and determined to maintain Japan's traditional friendly links with America and the great democratic European states, on the one hand, and the partisans of military-based Asian fascism on the other. It was between those who believed in the chances of success of an *immediate* war and those who, like Kido, while approving of war as a long-term goal, believed that Japan should hold off from actual fighting for another few years—when her strength would be even greater. And the situation was further complicated by the fact that some of Japan's leading dramatis personae, including the emperor himself, were prone to change their views with disconcerting suddenness, at one moment sounding like moderates and the next striking out in all directions, tempted into using the sophisticated military machine within their reach; the hubris of Japanese expansionist nationalism could suddenly overwhelm even the most cautious and timid of rulers.

From 1937 until the very end of World War II, Marquis Koichi Kido was Emperor Hirohito's closest adviser and trusted friend. He was an indefatigable diarist, recording the most banal events in his life as well as the most salient ones. The *Kido Nikki* (Kido diaries) became a sort of bible for the post-1945 American prosecution team investigating Japanese war crimes. In the Japanese bureaucratic tradition, diary-keeping fulfilled a very clear purpose, enabling high officials to keep a record of their day-to-day activities, should subsequent inspectors call their work into question. For this reason, they are seldom self-deprecatory, and tend to reflect the diarist's activities in the best possible light. In Kido's case, they proved a godsend not only to IMTFE investigators, but also to Kido himself, who was widely praised by the Americans for voluntarily handing them over. In fact there was considerable debate inside the palace about the advisability of doing so, for while there was much in them that reflected favorably on Emperor Hirohito, there were many entries, also, that showed him in a singularly ambiguous light. Not surprisingly, perhaps, in the light of MacArthur's postwar attitude to Hirohito, it is the "positive" aspect of the Kido diaries concerning Hirohito that has been consistently emphasized.

Kido had been the Lord Privy Seal's confidential secretary at the time of the 2/26 mutiny, earning high praise from Hirohito for his cool-headed zeal and utter loyalty. From October 1937 to August 1939 he was a cabinet minister in several governments, at Hirohito's request. In June 1940, he became Lord Privy Seal, the single most influential figure in the palace, and perhaps in Japan. As his IMTFE assessors noted, Kido "made every office he held more important than it would have been in the hands of other men." He was a born "number two"—loyal, discreet, immensely hardworking. His diaries show that he can have had no private life to speak of, for all his days (and some nights too) were devoted to the emperor's service.

Yet, in a very important sense, his diaries, for all their extraordinary detail, fail to tell us much about the "real" Kido: we are aware of a superbly competent bureaucrat with an analytical mind and an encyclopedic knowledge of Japan's civilian and military ruling elite, but are told little about his own feelings, his likes and dislikes, his moral commitments. As the IMTFE assessors noted, "he was not so concerned about the rights and wrongs of any policy as with the risks accompanying it." There is no trace, in the diaries, of the tub-thumping nationalist propaganda that became the leitmotif of everyday life in Japan from 1937, but neither is there any entry that reveals Kido's distaste for it. "From start to finish," said the IMTFE report on him, "it does not appear that he ever drew Hirohito's attention to the moral aspect either of the initiation of the Pacific War or the manner in which it was conducted. His whole mind was on expediency."

In due course, after the war, Kido would be interrogated at length by U.S. Army Colonel Henry R. Sackett, one of IMTFE's prosecution team. It was the nearest anyone came to questioning Hirohito himself, for the emperor, like all members of his imperial family, had been declared out of bounds by U.S. Chief Prosecutor Joseph Keenan, who was merely relaying General MacArthur's own instructions to that effect.

The lengthy exchanges between Sackett and Kido are a mine of information, since both the investigator and the accused clearly realized that the emperor was safe, and that nothing Kido said in private about him in these preliminary pretrial sessions would be used against him or cited in court. But for all the "Hands off the emperor" warnings issued by Keenan, it is clear from the transcripts that Sackett was curious about the emperor's actual role and responsibility in those years leading up to the war, and could not entirely inhibit questions Keenan would have preferred to remain unasked.

Early in his questioning of Kido, Colonel Sackett asked him whether he had ever cautioned the emperor into "curbing" the militarists. Kido replied with the precision of the trained civil servant. He could remember twelve instances, he said, when he had addressed the emperor on the subject. Of his own accord, he added that he could remember only three instances when the emperor had followed his advice: at the time of the February and May 15, 1932, plots, and during the 1940–41 French Indochina crisis.

The implication was clear: during the crucial period from 1936 onward, Hirohito failed to take steps to curb the military, and it must therefore be assumed that—with the exception of the two occasions when the Japanese army overstepped the mark by attacking Soviet units across the Manchurian border and in Mongolia and were given an immediate dressing-down—Hirohito approved of his army's behavior in China, felt no overriding compunction either to complain about his officers or to discipline them, and was in tune with Japan's increasingly aggressive or, to use the euphemistic Japanese term, "positive" foreign policy.

This was Prince Konoye's policy, too, although, as Japan became increasingly entangled in the China war, he periodically attempted to resign. Cynical, self-deprecating, witty and casually informal, Konoye would have made an admirable minister of information, for his persuasive gifts were enormous and he charmed all those he met, but as prime minister he was a disaster. Intermittently he realized he was leading Japan to her doom. His attitude toward the Army was ambivalent: he despised the generals, but was enough of a nationalist to entertain the dream of an imperial Japan ruling indirectly over a docile China administered by handpicked pro-Japanese puppets. He further reduced the possibility of cutting Japan's losses in China and coming to terms with Chiang Kai-shek by bringing into his government two virulent nationalists. One was Admiral Nobumasa Suetsugu, a fire-eating, fiercely anti-British officer, whom he appointed home minister. The other, even more disastrous appointment at the start of Konoye's second administration, in 1940, was that of Yosuke Matsuoka, a maverick career diplomat who became his foreign minister, to the dismay of all those who still hoped to avoid a major confrontation with the United States.

Konoye's rationale for appointing Suetsugu, whose links with the "ultras" were well known, and who in fact represented only a minority in the navy, and also General Itagaki (the architect of the 1931 Mukden Incident) as war minister, was that these were men who had a considerable following in the services, and would therefore be obeyed. Konoye often boasted of his shrewdness in "fighting fire with fire," but was reluctant to recognize his poor choice in subordinates. When Matsuoka started showing signs of megalomania on a scale that called his sanity into question, Hirohito pointed out to Konoye that since he had personally selected him, he could equally easily replace him—to which Konoye replied that he was responsible for him, and would stick by him, or else resign himself. One of Konoye's most serious flaws was his fundamental indecisiveness: he understood other people's points of view only too well. The army hotheads saw him as one of their own, whereas Prince Saionji, until the mid-1930s, had felt that Konoye's nationalism was less important than his popular persona and his natural influence as a leading aristocrat. Hirohito was certainly aware of his shortcomings, but treated him with extraordinary indulgence, shrugging off his obvious faults. There was, in Konoye's makeup, a self-assured casualness and contempt for the accepted social conventions of the time that Hirohito found irresistible because they illustrated an individual freedom the protocol-bound emperor could never hope to enjoy himself. What Hirohito would have regarded in others as inexcusable dereliction of duty was shrugged off with a smile.

With men like Suetsugu and Itagaki around Konoye, no hope of a compromise solution to the China war was possible, nor does Hirohito appear to have pressed for one, beyond repeating, more and more often as the conflict dragged on, that his generals had let him down by promising an early victory within months. Suetsugu argued that any pullout would lead at home to an ugly situation, which might easily become uncontrollable. Britain and the United States were, of course, increasingly worried by Japan's determination to pursue the war in China. So, ironically, was Hitler: he already looked forward to the time when Germany and Japan would become allies against Britain, France and the United States, and saw the continuation of Japan's war with China as an irritating diversion, weakening Japan and scattering her forces. For this reason, German ambassadors in Tokyo and with Chiang Kai-shek in Hangkow acted as intermediaries in an attempt to bring about a cease-fire acceptable to both sides. But Japan's terms—including as they did nonnegotiable demands that Chiang Kai-shek recognize the puppet regime of Manchukuo, stop collaborating with Chinese Communists, pay war reparations, accept the presence on Chinese soil of Japanese troops for an indefinite period, and virtually agree to China becoming a Japanese vassal—were clearly unacceptable.

Konoye reacted by announcing he would henceforth cease to deal with Chiang Kai-shek, and, before the Diet, boasted that even if Chiang were to sue for peace he would ignore him. With the precedent of Henry Pu-yi, the puppet emperor of Manchukuo, in mind, Japan already had her eye on Wang Ching-wei, one of the leaders of Chiang Kai-shek's Kuomintang, as the possible head of a pro-Japanese government in Japan-occupied northern China. As Kido noted in his diaries (in an entry dated January 14, 1938), "We expect a lot from the new government of China."

Because Britain was determined to maintain her enclaves within China's international concessions, which she regarded as part of her vital international trading strength, British support of Chiang Kai-shek was strong, even if, after Munich, her overwhelming concern was Nazi Germany. Whereas American help to Chiang Kai-shek was mainly financial, British assistance took the form of allowing the transport of essential equipment to "free" China along the Burma Road. As a result, Britain became more unpopular even than the United States in Japanese eyes, and in 1939, just before the outbreak of World War II, Japan demanded that this support route be closed.

The official version of the worsening state of Anglo-Japanese relations is that Emperor Hirohito deplored it because of the traditionally friendly ties between the two countries and his excellent personal relations with the British royal family, and that he regarded the drift toward confrontation with hand-wringing sorrow and dread.

Hirohito may indeed have had qualms at times, but an entry in the Kido diaries, dated July 21, 1940, shows that this was not always the case. That day, Kido called on the emperor at the palace. "He is in his swimming trunks, very relaxed," Kido wrote. They talked about the Burma Road crisis. The emperor (Kido noted) remarked: "I imagine Britain will reject our request to end the support route for Chiang. In this case, we will occupy Hongkong, and eventually we will declare war on Britain."

Taken aback, Kido urged both caution and careful preparation of public opinion. But Hirohito was clearly excited, speculating on the possible need to agree to a compromise with China in order to prepare for a confrontation with the Soviet Union.

As it turned out, the emperor was not put to the test. Because of the outbreak of World War II in September 1939 and Britain's commitments in France, China suddenly seemed infinitely remote. To the disgust of Henry Stimson, the United States secretary of state, Britain, immediately after the Dunkirk debacle, agreed to interrupt supplies of arms, equipment and food to Chiang Kai-shek along the Burma Road for three months, from July 1940. This coincided with the monsoon period, when the road was frequently impassable, but Hirohito must have regarded this concession as further proof of the decline of the West, Hitler's irresistible rise, and the validity of Konoye's Grand Design.

CHAPTER THIRTEEN

After 1937, and for the next seven years at least, it would be difficult for any Japanese to view his country's unfolding history in perspective: everything seemed to vindicate the attitude of the hard-line right-wingers and militarists who believed that the "new order" in Europe was all part of a Grand Design allowing Japan to assume her predestined role as the most advanced, efficient and racially superior nation in Asia, with a "divine right" to assert her will over the lesser breed of Asian nations and colonies. The notion of *hakko ichiu* (eight corners of the world under one roof) was now no longer a mythical Shintoist catchphrase justifying, in the abstract, the emperor's divine right to dominate the world, but a slogan with very real, practical applications, the religious vindication of Japan's new power and influence. Germany's successful and unopposed aggression in Europe (until the invasion of Poland) and Mussolini's transformation of Italy into an efficient, highly centralized state were reported in admiring detail by Japan's ambassadors in Berlin and Rome, both unconditional devotees of fascism, so much so that some wags in the Japanese Foreign Ministry referred to Ambassador Hiroshi Oshima as "Germany's ambassador to Berlin."

Even the unexpected 1939 nonintervention pact between Hitler and Stalin failed to shake the German-Japanese alliance: Baron Hiranuma, who had succeeded Konoye as premier, though only for a few months, did resign, along with his whole cabinet, "for giving the Emperor bad advice," and Ambassador Oshima was recalled, but not for long. Within little more than a year he was back in Berlin, more influential than ever, and a year after the nonintervention pact (on September 27, 1940) the agreement for the Tripartite Alliance, between Italy, Germany and Japan, was signed.

The timing was significant—only a few weeks after Dunkirk, the collapse of France and Italy's entry into the war on Hitler's side—and its purpose clear: Article Two stated that "Germany and Italy shall recognise and respect the leadership of Japan in establishing a New Order in East Asia," and the three signatories pledged themselves to go to war against any nation not yet in conflict with Germany that would dare to attack any of them—a deliberate warning to the United States to remain neutral or face the consequences.

Japan appeared set on an irresistible course: had she not, with impunity, moved troops and aircraft into northern French Indochina in the wake of France's defeat—ostensibly to open a "second front" against Chiang Kai-shek, a pretext no foreign power could take seriously? And had not Britain meekly suspended aid to Chiang along the Burma Road?

By midsummer 1940, as the historian Richard Storry noted, "it argued either staunch pro-British feelings or remarkable prescience in even the wisest Japanese for him to imagine that Germany would lose the war," though a handful of diplomats and statesmen instinctively felt that Japan had backed the wrong horse—among them two ambassadors to London, Shigeru Yoshida and his successor, Mamoru Shigemitsu, who both tried to caution Hirohito against believing too much Nazi propaganda about Britain's decline and imminent collapse, and wise old Prince Saionji, who told his faithful secretary, Harada, a few weeks before his death, "In the end I believe Great Britain will be victorious."

In the armed forces, Admiral Yamamoto was not the only commander to express his private misgivings, but this was now the era of "thought control," of the growing influence of the *kempei,* and any public criticism of the Tripartite Alliance was treasonable: only General Kanji Ishihara openly dared defy the military police, and he was a special case: it would have been embarrassing to arrest one of the heroes of the Mukden Incident.

How did Emperor Hirohito react to these events? Was he, as the official Japanese record would have it, privately appalled by both the rise of Japanese fascism at home and her expansionist policy abroad? Did he have any influence? Was he, as his many apologists claim, a virtual prisoner of the militarists and their allies during this whole period, or did he come to embody Japan's nationalist trend, to the extent of believing in her "divine mission" to rule over half of the world?

It would certainly have required exceptional insight and statesmanship, in his position and in the historical context of the time, to discern the underlying weaknesses of Japan's position; and, from his exalted vantage point, the notion that Japan was riding the crest of a historical wave must surely have been irresistible. It was his trusted kinsman Konoye, after all, who put forward (as early as December 22, 1938), the notion of a "new era" and a "new order in East Asia." It was Konoye, again, in his public radio address "Receiving the Imperial Mandate," who proclaimed that the old order in Europe was collapsing and that Japan must prepare to cope with a radically different world, and who, a few weeks later (August 1, 1940) in his "Outline of a Basic National Policy," called for a strong national "defense state" to face "an unprecedentedly great ordeal." Meanwhile his handpicked new foreign minister, Yosuke Matsuoka, was asking his fellow countrymen to demonstrate "the Imperial way throughout the world" and coined the phrase "Greater East Asia Co-Prosperity Sphere"—to include both French Indochina and the Netherlands East Indies. This was heady stuff.

Had Hirohito conceded his involvement, later, as did his kinsman Prince Konoye, few would have continued to denigrate him. But Hirohito never once admitted anything of the sort: his attitude was always that he consistently opposed the "war party" at every twist and turn of events, fighting a dogged rearguard action against the warmongers. This is what he told MacArthur (who believed him unreservedly) at their first postwar meeting; it was what he told John Foster Dulles in 1952 and what he hammered home ever after, in his yearly, highly formal "press conferences" with a handful of accredited Japanese "court correspondents." Hirohito's version of events has become the officially accepted history of Japan, vouched for internationally by historians and diplomats alike. The facts, as we now know them, tell a very different story.

Until Japan's new postwar constitution stripped Hirohito of his "divine" qualities in 1946, all Japanese were supposed to view the emperor with "awe and trepidation." These, in retrospect, are the key emotions that seem to have swayed Hirohito himself during the heady months leading to the Great Asia War: oscillating between awe at Japan's growing power and trepidation at the possible consequences of her aggressive policies, teetering between elation and doubt, he carefully covered his tracks, making final judgment difficult by encouraging the notion that he was swept into war against his will. That Hirohito restrained his commanders and ministers at times, urging caution and diplomacy, has been amply documented and the record shows that he did indeed, on occasion, deflate their sense of infallibility and saber-rattling self-confidence. But, as the record also shows, Hirohito not only became infected with their hubris but also behaved most of the time, during his many sessions with his commanders, less like a doubter than an instructor, coaxing and guiding his pupils into an acceptable "school solution" through persistent questioning of their aims and tactics.

Japan's war with China is often cited as a conflict over which Hirohito had next to no control, though he did his best to bring it to an end by criticizing his generals to their faces on every possible occasion. But the fact is that Hirohito backed Konoye's hard-line stand in January 1938, withdrawing Japan's recognition of Chiang Kai-shek against the advice of most of his generals, who were then seeking accommodation with China because they felt that the China war was a "bottomless pit" that would fritter away Japan's military resources and prevent her from waging a later, far more essential war against the Soviet Union—something many senior military men felt was inevitable in the long run. As the Kido diaries show, Hirohito prevaricated when Prince Kanin, his army chief of staff, requested a meeting to discuss the possibility of Japanese forces being pulled out. As the emperor told Konoye: "The Chief of Staff wanted to see me before I met you but I suspect they want to cancel what's already been decided [nonrecognition of the Chiang Kai-shek regime] so I said I already had an appointment with the Prime Minister and turned down his request."

When Hirohito did finally agree to meet Kanin, he asked him, "Why does the Chief of Staff want to stop the war with China and get ready for war with Russia? Does this mean Russia is on the move?"

Kanin replied that preparing for conflict with the USSR was a form of contingency planning, "just like the security precautions for the Emperor's travels. We have to be ready for the worst scenario." Hirohito later told Konoye about this conversation, adding, "If this is the case, then we shouldn't have started the war with China in the first place, but since we've started it, we should carry it through to the end."

As Professor Inouye points out,* Hirohito was highly skilled at playing the military off against the government, and the army against the navy, in order to get his way. Far from deploring the escalation of the war after Nanking, the Harada memoirs show that the emperor used his influence to keep it going. Konoye told Harada (January 15, 1938) that "the chiefs of staff strongly wished to finish the war with China to get ready for the war against the Soviet Union," but, Harada added, "the Emperor kept silent." Hirohito clearly sided with the hard-liners who believed that Japan should take no initiative over a China cease-fire, since this would lead Chiang Kai-shek to claim that, despite his military defeats, he had ultimately been victorious. Later still (December 2, 1940), Kido recorded Hirohito's account of his meeting that day with the army chief of staff, General Hajime Sugiyama—who had recently replaced Prince Kanin, because by this time Hirohito realized that Japan might soon be at war and did not want members of the Imperial Family to be in the limelight "in case events turn against them."

At this meeting the emperor asked Sugiyama, "Is there any way to hit Chiang Kai-shek once and for all?" to which Sugiyama replied it would be difficult to "destroy him completely."

Hirohito asked, "Can we scale down operations on the China war front?"

Sugiyama replied it would be impossible to "withdraw our troops without a serious loss of morale because then you give the impression you've lost."

Hirohito told Sugiyama to "drastically review the situation"—not because he believed the "war of punishment" was morally wrong, but

---

*Kyoshi Inouye, *The Emperor's Responsibilities* (Tokyo: Gendai Hyoronsha, 1975).

because, by this time, he had accepted the Strike South option and realized this would be difficult with his troops bogged down in China.

Another issue about which Hirohito is supposed to have had severe qualms was the Tripartite Alliance, and indeed news was carefully leaked to the diplomatic corps in Tokyo that both Hirohito and Konoye disliked the pact intensely and had agreed to it only under pressure. That Hirohito had initial reservations is certain. But as he told Kido, "I believe the signing of the German Military Alliance cannot be helped in the present situation. If there are no other means of dealing with the United States it may be the only solution."

His doubts prompted him to tell Konoye, "We're in this together, you and I, for better and for worse," which can be interpreted in various ways—as an appeal for loyalty, a plea for support, even a veiled threat. In the months that followed, Hirohito was to become a staunch convert to Foreign Minister Matsuoka's thesis that only the tripartite pact would stop the United States from attacking Japan.

As usual, the emperor's statements were leaked so as to present him in the best possible light: as Ambassador Grew wrote, on October 22, 1940:

> I was told today on excellent authority that both the Emperor and Prince Konoye were dead against the Tripartite Alliance but that it was brought to the Emperor's attention that he might not survive a refusal and that he said to Konoye: "Well, you and I will have to stand or fall together." *This came indirectly from a member of the Imperial Family* [author's italics].

The imperial rescript announcing the Tripartite Alliance to his people is, for all the emperor's supposedly strong reservations, an exaggeratedly flamboyant piece of prose, and it is surprising, in the light of Hirohito's supposed opposition to it, that he failed to have it toned down. Beginning with "It has been the great instruction bequeathed by Amaterasu that our grand moral obligation be extended in all directions and the world unified under one roof. This instruction is one we are faithfully observing day and night. . . ." it goes on to praise the agreement as

> . . . a source of great joy . . . We believe that to let all nations seek their proper places and myriad peoples enjoy the piping

times of peace are enterprises of unexampled magnitude.
. . . Our subjects are requested to give clearness and distinction
to the concept of polity and to conquer the situation of great
moment by deliberation and cooperation, thereby guarding
the Imperial Throne coexistive with heaven and earth.

Perhaps tradition required this kind of jargon, perhaps there was
nothing Hirohito could have done to modify it or to hint, as he later
claimed he did, in the rescript declaring war on the United States and
Britain that he was acting reluctantly.

But what, then, is one to make of Kido's September 24, 1940, diary
entry? Summoned by Hirohito, and "recording his words with awe,"
Kido noted that the subject of their conversation that day was

the Tripartite Alliance and the form of rites that should take
place to commemorate it. The Emperor has asked the Imperial
Household Minister to consult past records to find out what
kind of sacred rituals took place at the time of the signing of
the (1904) Anglo-Japanese Friendship Treaty. The Imperial
Household Minister has discovered there had been no Shinto
religious rites.

The Emperor has decided that, dealing with this highly
important occurrence . . . we should have a special ceremony
at the shrine inside the palace, and to ask for the blessing of
the Gods on his Tripartite Pact.

It is impossible to underestimate the significance of this decision.
Hirohito attached enormous importance to precedent, and for him to
have broken with it under any circumstances was exceptional. The
Anglo-Japanese Friendship Treaty was the crowning achievement of
Emperor Meiji, perhaps the single most important treaty of the Meiji
Restoration period, and to put the Tripartite Alliance on a par with
it makes nonsense of the notion that Hirohito accepted it with heartrending reluctance. Indeed, his decision to opt for solemn religious
rites—which had *not* been thought necessary for the Anglo-Japanese
Friendship Treaty and which came as a complete surprise to Kido—
shows that Hirohito placed it *above* the 1904 treaty in his order of
values.

Another example of Hirohito's "positive guidance" was over

French Indochina. Japan was quick to exploit France's reverses and humiliation in the wake of her collapse in June 1940. Two days after Pétain's meeting with Hitler at Montoire, acknowledging the occupation of Paris and France's withdrawal from the war, Japanese inspectors arrived in French Indochina to investigate arms shipments to China, Japanese warships circled Haiphong harbor in a demonstration of gunboat diplomacy, and General Georges Catroux, Indochina's governor-general (who would slip away to join De Gaulle very soon afterward) had no alternative but to agree to demands that all arms shipments to Chiang Kai-shek cease forthwith, and the Hanoi–Yunnan railway link to China be severed.

By then, Japanese military thinking had shifted, in the light of France's defeat, to the need for permanent Japanese military bases throughout French Indochina, and on August 2, 1940, as a first step toward that end, Japan sent the new governor-general of Indochina, Admiral Jean Decoux, an ultimatum demanding transit rights for Japanese troops in northern Indochina and the use of French airfields there. Decoux prevaricated, but his options were extremely limited, and on August 30 Vichy France allowed Japan "military facilities" in northern Indochina (Tonkin) and promised to provide large quantities of badly needed Indochinese rice to Japan in exchange for a pledge, extracted by Decoux, that Japan would continue to recognize French sovereignty over Indochina. Several thousand battle-hardened Japanese troops moved into Tonkin, around Hanoi. The United States retaliated by declaring an embargo on the export of scrap metal to Japan—a measure that many of Roosevelt's advisers felt was an insufficient, as well as tardy, "graduated response" to Japan's growing policy of aggression. Japan, given a clear indication of future probable U.S. measures, promptly began stockpiling oil and mineral reserves, putting pressure on the beleaguered Dutch government of the Netherlands East Indies to sell Japan five times as much oil as in the past for the next five years.

Thailand, who had also taken advantage of France's weakened international position, now demanded the surrender of tracts of Cambodian land she regarded as rightfully hers, and Japan, setting herself up as a highly partial, pro-Thai mediator, saw to it that the disputed territories were returned to Thailand.

But this was not enough for Japan. By this time, Japanese territorial ambitions had grown, the Greater East Asia Co-Prosperity Sphere (with both Indochina and the Netherlands East Indies shown on Japanese maps under the Japanese flag) had become a concrete objective, and Japanese military leaders had openly started discussing their Strike South strategy with the emperor. In their new way of thinking, Indochina was important, but now only as part of their overall strategy, as a stepping-stone to Indonesia, Malaya and the Philippines.

It so happens that we know a great deal about Hirohito's conversations with his military leaders and with Konoye during this period, thanks to the famous *Sugiyama Memorandum,* an almost verbatim transcript summary of top-secret meetings between the army chief of staff and the emperor. Sugiyama burned the original manuscript just before committing *seppuku* in August 1945, but a copy belonging to his chief aide miraculously escaped destruction, and was preserved in the archives of the Japanese Self-defense Forces GHQ, where it remained until a senior archivist there allowed a respectable Tokyo publishing firm, Hara Shobo, to bring it out in a deluxe two-volume edition in 1967.

Though initially it attracted surprisingly little attention, it remains a unique record of top-secret and frank conversations between the emperor and his military commanders, almost as immediately evocative as tape recordings. Since the discussions were often informal, the language used by both the emperor and his commanders is understated and elliptical, a kind of shorthand: all parties are familiar with the events and conceptions they are discussing, so there is no need to refer to them in full—and in any case there has always been a natural Japanese reluctance to call a spade a spade. The envisaged invasion of Malaya, the Philippines and the Dutch East Indies, for instance, is referred to as "doing the South," or "the Southern problem."

By January 1941 the military were not content with their limited bases in Tonkin. With Strike South in mind, they wanted more, and felt that the demoralized French had no alternative but to grant them the run of Cambodia, Laos and southern French Indochina as well.

They wanted bases in Thailand too, but expected to obtain Thai permission for these as a matter of routine. The stationing of Japanese troops in Tonkin and the cutting off of all supplies to Chiang Kai-shek from across the Indochina border were logical steps in Japan's four-year-old struggle against the Chinese leader. The stationing of Japanese troops in southern French Indochina, Cambodia and Thailand, however, could not be explained in terms of Japan's China-war strategy. Such bases would, however, be invaluable if, as was the case, Japan intended to invade Malaya, the Philippines and the Dutch East Indies. They could indeed mean only one thing: preparation for an eventual Strike South, to gain a complete hold over East Asia. Sugiyama said as much to Hirohito in a report dated February 1, 1941, using the usual oblique references to Strike South: Japanese military bases in southern French Indochina, he wrote, were a necessary stepping-stone in dealing with "problems which might arise, if eventually there were problems in the South." In any case, he added, French Indochina was in no condition to resist Japanese armed might.

Hirohito presided over several sessions with his chiefs of staff, sometimes alone with them, sometimes with Premier Konoye sitting in during "liaison conferences." As the *Sugiyama Memorandum* shows, the emperor was fully aware at all times of what his commanders were planning. On January 23, 1941, he asked his chiefs of staff: "Can you keep a military pact with Thailand secret?" Some kind of arrangement was indeed necessary if Japanese troops were to cross Thailand on their way to invade Malaya. The army was in favor of a formal military pact, while Matsuoka, the foreign minister, felt that Thailand, having obtained a satisfactory "readjustment" of frontiers thanks to Japanese "mediation," was sufficiently beholden to Japan already, and should simply agree to Japanese troops moving through her territory as a matter of course. The following day (January 24) Hirohito returned to the subject. He told Sugiyama that "since pro-British influence in Thailand is strong," extreme care was needed to bring about a "military pact" with the Thais, for the British were almost bound to hear of it.

On the question of military plans to move land, air and sea units into southern Indochina, Hirohito reminded his chiefs of staff that same day that negotiations between Japan and Vichy France were currently taking place in Tokyo, so that, if the French acquiesced to Japanese demands, the use of force would be superfluous. Sugiyama readily agreed. A few days later, on February 1, still concerned about world reaction to a large-scale Japanese move into Indochina, Hirohito asked his commanders how Japanese bases in Indochina could be established without "agitating" the United States and British governments. His commanders reassured him that "there was no warlike atmosphere." At the time they were probably bluffing, but in the event they were accurate enough: though U.S. opinion was to harden markedly against Japan after the latter's occupation of southern Indo-china in October 1940, Admiral James O. Richardson, then commander in chief of the Pacific Fleet, quoted Roosevelt as saying, "If the Japanese attacked Thailand, or the Kra peninsula, or the Dutch East Indies we would not enter the war, that even if they attacked the Philippines [I doubt] whether we would enter the war."

Hirohito asked some highly practical questions: "How much naval force will you need? Where do you intend locating the new air and naval bases in Indochina?"

Admiral Osami Nagano, the naval chief of staff, replied that the navy intended to occupy Camranh Bay; Sugiyama said that there would be new army bases in Saigon and Pnom Penh, and air bases in Saigon, Natrang and Tourane (Danang), adding, *"This will be necessary for landing operations, for the Malay peninsula* [author's italics]."

Hirohito accepted this without comment or demur, adding only: "Do you need an air base in Thailand as well?" Sugiyama replied that it was essential to have an air base in Saigon, "but we are not at this stage thinking of one in southern Thailand." Hirohito realized, of course, that the Japanese plan to move into French Indochina on a large scale would not have been conceivable without France's collapse in Europe, and he was human enough to have mixed feelings about this ruthless exploitation of an erstwhile friendly nation's misfortunes. He told Kido it was a bit like a thief looting a burned-out house. "I don't like it," he said. "but I suppose it can't be helped," adding that it was no good being too softhearted. One should not be overcivilized, he went on, or behave like Prince Song, citing the legend of the Chinese prince who was so chivalrous he would never attack an enemy who was unprepared for battle.

The negotiations with Vichy France continued. U.S. and British reactions to Japan's establishment of bases in Tonkin had been strong, but not overwhelming. Trade restrictions were troublesome, but temporary; by stepping up steel production in Manchuria, Korea and Japan herself, the war planners expected to overcome any shortfalls within a year. High-level talks had at last begun between Japan and the United States on a possible solution to the China war. The emperor believed this had been possible only because of the deterrent value of the Tripartite Alliance. As he pointed out to Kido, its usefulness was thus proved. "Patience," he told Kido, "patience, endurance and perseverance are everything." Hirohito eagerly agreed that Matsuoka should undertake a long trip to Europe and talk to Hitler, Mussolini and Stalin. His discussions were to stress the importance of the Japanese "Monroe Doctrine" of Japan's superiority in Asia, and he was ordered to try to reach an understanding with the Soviet Union, possibly to bring that country into some form of association with the Tripartite Alliance signatories.

By this time (March–April 1941) Hitler was already preparing his offensive against the USSR, and, in his megalomania, assumed that he could use Japan like an obedient vassal. His sole concern was to persuade and, if necessary, coerce Japan into seizing Singapore and Malaya, thus bringing Britain to her knees. The argument Ribbentrop and Hitler used on Matsuoka was deliberately crude: Germany had virtually won the war. As the Japanese themselves acknowledged, the old order was crumbling. The tripartite pact would effectively keep the United States neutral, even if Japan did move against Singapore. If Japan wanted to be part of the new order, it must help Germany, or else the Asian spoils of the defeated European nations, including the oil-rich Netherlands East Indies, would pass her by. To Hitler's dismay, Matsuoka talked endlessly, but confusedly, and brought no clear mandate from the emperor to engage in immediate war against Britain in the Far East. As Herbert Feis put it, in his admirable study,* "The invited guest, it had been hoped, would be a man of radiant action; the arrived guest turned out to be a man of excusing talk." On his way home, Matsuoka did conclude a nonintervention agreement with the USSR; he was in blissful ignorance of German preparations for Operation Barbarossa, Hitler's plan to invade the Soviet Union.

On his return to Japan, just in time for the emperor's birthday celebrations (on April 29), Matsuoka proved that the incessant pressure put on him in Berlin had had its effect: almost daily, he bombarded Hirohito with reports or called on him to express his point of view directly. Japan, he told the emperor, must attack Britain in the Far East without delay. He had become a total convert to Hitler's viewpoint, so much so that when—on June 22—Hitler launched his attack on the Soviet Union, Matsuoka, his own neutrality talks with Stalin and Molotov notwithstanding, now urged Hirohito to take on

---

*Herbert Feis, *The Road to Pearl Harbor* (Princeton, N.J.: Princeton University Press, 1965).

the Soviet Union as well. Hirohito could no longer tolerate his foreign minister's volubility, inconsistency and irresponsibility. Matsuoka, he started telling Kido, would have to go. In typical Japanese
fashion, the pressure on him to leave would be exerted indirectly. In
due course, Matsuoka would be forced out of the government not
only because his megalomania and undiplomatic behavior had grown
worse but because the rest of Japan's ruling elite, including the emperor, refused to accept his thesis that it was Japan's duty to hit the
Soviet Union on its easternmost flank in order to help Germany bring
her Russian blitzkrieg to an even speedier culmination.

But, on June 25, 1941, only three days after Hitler's invasion of the
Soviet Union, the conference attended by Hirohito, Konoye and his
chiefs of staff was not concerned with the USSR but with French
Indochina. The now imminent invasion of that country was discussed
in further detail. The military leaders were adamant that there should
be no compromise with the procrastinating French, despite Konoye's
plea that since the French were showing goodwill in the Tokyo talks,
"is it right to force this matter on them?"

Sugiyama said that it was now more important than ever to carry
out the Indochina move as quickly as possible. "The ABCD Powers
(America, Britain, China, Dutch East Indies) have been collaborating
against Japan to suppress us day by day; we need to establish this
sphere as soon as possible. In a very pressing situation like this, with
a total ban on exports to Japan and the strengthening strategic structure of the United States and Britain we have to do this very quickly."

Hirohito expressed no reservations at this stage, showing more
interest in the overall cost of the operation and asking, "Is it enough
to hit French Indochina alone?" Sugiyama replied that for the time
being it would be unwise to move troops into Thailand ("we think
it'll be better to take care of Thailand afterwards"), not least because
to invade both countries simultaneously could reveal Japan's long-
term plans.

Hirohito asked if there was any connection between this plan and
the Russo-German war. Sugiyama replied that the Indochina operation should take place regardless of what was happening on the Russo-
German front or indeed in Washington, where negotiations between
America and Japan were still progressing.

Hirohito again asked for logistical details. How many troops would
be sent to French Indochina, and where would they come from?

Again, his chiefs of staff provided him with a detailed breakdown of units and proposed Indochina bases. Only now did Hirohito express some guarded misgivings. "I worry greatly about the international repercussions," he said. "Our morality could be called into question. But let it pass." In a strong voice, Hirohito added, "That's fine with me." In his account of the day's proceedings, Sugiyama noted that the emperor appeared pleased, and "more cheerful than on previous days."

The diplomatic niceties were preserved, but the instructions that went out by secret code to Japan's diplomats abroad gave an unvarnished version of events. "The Imperial Government," read the cable sent to the Japanese consul general in Tokyo on July 16, 1941, "has decided the Imperial Forces are to invade the southern portion of French Indochina with a view to securing military bases. As far as the Imperial Government is concerned, it makes no difference whether this invasion is carried out peacefully or in force."

Because of the possibility of French armed opposition to the "invasion," and to forestall reprisals, the telegram to Hanoi ordered all Japanese nationals to be evacuated to Taiwan, and in order to give them time to embark, a specially freighted passenger ship was to remain in Haiphong harbor—"so please give out the reason that [its slowness in departing] is due to loading and unloading delays. Please take every precaution not to allow the French authorities to learn of our plans."

The extraordinary veneration shown by his subjects to Hirohito was also illustrated in the cable: a special emissary was to "respectfully carry out the Imperial Portraits and request that on arrival [in Taiwan] they be placed in the custody of the Provincial Office."

Other ambassadors received slightly different versions: to Oshima, in Berlin, the announcement contained a rider pointing out that *"this plan is the first step in Japan's southward advance which Germany has been looking forward to for a long time"* (author's italics), and the cable to Japan's minister to Vichy France added, ominously, that he should point out that "if the French refuse [the occupation], this will have a bad effect not only on Tokyo-Vichy relations but on Berlin-French relations as well"—in other words, that Japan would see to it that Hitler cracked the whip in both occupied and unoccupied France if Pétain's government continued to equivocate.

In the face of such a ruthless exercise of power, Vichy France capitulated. Minor face-saving measures were included in the Franco-Japanese agreement that allowed Japan large numbers of army, navy and air bases throughout Indochina; the fiction was maintained that Japan would continue to "respect French sovereignty and territorial integrity" in Indochina. On July 21, 1941, Admiral Jean Darlan, Vichy France's vice premier and foreign minister, acknowledged that his government had "no choice but to yield" to Japanese demands and agreed to "cooperate with Japan in the defense of French Indochina."

From Hirohito's exchanges with his chiefs of staff, it is clear he knew perfectly well that the Japanese bases in Indochina would be used not against Chiang Kai-shek but for another purpose altogether. The IMTFE prosecutors did not know of the existence of the *Sugiyama Memorandum,* but Colonel Sackett, Kido's interrogator, showed he was well aware of the nature of the emperor's role in the events leading up to Pearl Harbor. On February 26, 1946, the following exchange took place in Sugamo Prison:

SACKETT: The Emperor knew [in July 1941] that the country, through its foreign policy, had become pretty much committed to an expansion into the south, whether by the force of arms or not, and he thought it was an inopportune time to start fighting a war in the north, against the USSR, when you were trying to obtain materials in the south?

KIDO: Yes.

SACKETT: It is a condition precedent to the dispatching of troops to a place like Indochina that the consent of the Emperor must first be obtained?

KIDO: Yes.

SACKETT: In other words, the supreme command would not have despatched troops to French Indochina without first appearing before the Emperor and obtaining his consent?

KIDO: No.

The Japanese planes that sank Britain's warships the *Repulse* and the *Prince of Wales* off the Malayan coast two days after Pearl Harbor came from bases in southern French Indochina.

CHAPTER FOURTEEN

While Japan was busy planning her network of military bases abroad for an eventual Strike South, at home patriotic frenzy reached fever pitch with a growing, officially sponsored emperor cult of awe-inspiring proportions.

The twenty-six hundredth anniversary of the start of the reign of Jimmu, the mythological first emperor, celebrated with pomp and circumstance in 1940 with naval reviews and religious ceremonies, was followed, a year later, by even more spectacular festivities, which reminded the *New York Times* correspondent Otto Tolischus (who arrived in Tokyo in January 1941 after his expulsion from Berlin) of the many Nazi rallies he had so recently attended.

The 2,601st anniversary of the founding of the Japanese empire was marked by more religious ceremonies and a parade of over 120,000 factory workers, schoolchildren, "representatives of national organizations" and members of the Industrial National Service Federation, with flags and brass bands, all marching hour after hour past their emperor, who tirelessly returned their salutes.

The main speaker was Baron Hiranuma, the Japanese home minister, former president of the Privy Council and premier. What made

Japan a uniquely superior country, he told the massed crowds, was that "foreign kings, emperors, presidents are all created by man, but Japan has a sacred throne inherited from the Imperial ancestors. Japan's Imperial Rule is therefore an extension of heaven. Man-made dynasties collapse, but the Heaven-created Throne is beyond the power of mere mortals. . . ."

Ambassador Grew noted that according to custom no Japanese was allowed to "look down" on the emperor: the rooftops facing the palace in the Marunouchi district remained bare. Tolischus remarked that while, in private, foreign residents irreverently referred to Hirohito as "Charlie," Japanese newspapers constantly harped on the emperor's divinity, and Japan's totalitarianism so closely ressembled the Nazi program that he "was intrigued to find out who had learnt from whom."

A few years later, there would be a concerted effort by both Japanese and U.S. occupation authorities to minimize the emperor's prewar role, but in April 1941 the Japanese imperial image-builders were out to prove the opposite: at a conference of senior provincial officials just before the emperor's birthday, the Imperial Household minister told them that "the press of war affairs" on the imperial time was such that Hirohito had had to give up his early-morning horseback riding, and that he was "constantly giving decisions on various state papers concerned with politics and military strategy. . . . He rises very early and retires very late, receiving reports as late as midnight." It was "beyond the average person's imagination," too, "how deeply the Empress is concerned about the war dead and wounded [the casualties of the "China incident"]. . . ."

On the emperor's fortieth birthday—April 29—the *Japan Times and Advertiser,* the English-language paper faithfully reflecting the views of the Foreign Ministry, ran an important editorial on the "new world order" as seen from Tokyo. This curious document, establishing a rigid hierarchy of "strong" powers, with Germany (and Italy as its junior partner) heading the list in Europe, and Japan in Asia, undoubtedly mirrored the views of Prince Konoye at his nationalist worst and of Foreign Minister Matsuoka, who had just returned from a triumphal tour of Berlin and Rome, and had been embraced by Stalin after signing a neutrality pact with the USSR.

The British Empire, the United States and the Soviet Union were afforded a mention in the proposed "new order," which by and large

Hirohito as a young boy.

Crown Prince Hirohito with King George V during his 1921 visit to Britain.

After his European trip, Hirohito became fond of Western dress and customs.

Empress Sadako and
her three sons:
Hirohito, Chichibu and
Takamatsu.

Emperor Hirohito and Empress Nagako during the 1928 enthronement
ceremony.

The royal family in 1936. From left: Crown Prince Akihito, Emperor Hirohito,
Princess Teru, Princess Yori, Prince Yoshi, Empress Nagako and Princess Taka.

March 1945: Hirohito walks through the ruins of Tokyo.

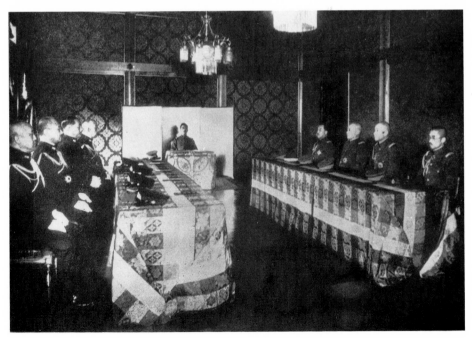

In this Imperial Palace bunker, Hirohito met with his officers and decided to end the war.

After the war, a civilian emperor greets a still-deferential crowd.

Hirohito's first meeting with General MacArthur at the U.S. Embassy
in Tokyo on September 27, 1945.

The emperor and
empress in 1982.

The new emperor and
empress.

could have been drawn up by Hitler himself: it called for the demilitarization of Gibraltar, the eastern Mediterranean, Malta, Aden, the
Red Sea, Singapore, Hong Kong "and all United States Pacific bases,"
the total withdrawal of Britain's Royal Navy from the Mediterranean,
joint British-Axis control of the Suez Canal, joint German-Italian control of certain British African colonies and of North Africa "from
Gibraltar to Somaliland" with continental Europe "organised as one
state under the German Reich."

The editorial also demanded German participation in the Iranian
and Iraqi oil industries, the opening up of the Dutch East Indies to
"Japanese advisers," the demilitarization of Siberia, Japanese immi-
grant access to Australia, Indian self-government and "religious and
political liberty for all." Perhaps its most important aspect was the
arbitrary division of the world into "zones of influence," with Japan
the uncontested leader of Asia. The United States "sphere of influence" was recognized over Canada, Central and South America, New-
foundland and Greenland—provided there was "no U.S. hegemony
in Latin America inamicable to the Axis powers," and no U.S. bases
west of Hawaii.

Although wildly hysterical articles, fanning the flames of Japanese
nationalism, were common enough in 1941, the *Japan Times and
Advertiser* was no fly-by-night rag but a respectable, well-produced
paper, in layout and typography astonishingly similar to the *New York
Times,* and the timing of its publication—the emperor's birthday—was
deliberate.

That same afternoon, as if to underline the importance of the policy
statement, and give it special relevance, the biggest military parade
ever staged in Japan took place: Hirohito, astride his favorite white
charger, Shirayuki, reviewed a march-past of thirty thousand troops
and a hundred tanks, and a flyover of five hundred planes. A month
later, on Navy Day (May 27), an equally impressive display of force
took place, and Japanese spokesmen took this opportunity to announce that Japan had five hundred warships and four thousand navy
planes in combat readiness—more than the United States could muster. On June 18, in a deliberate snub to the Allied countries supporting Chiang Kai-shek, Hirohito attended a state banquet for the
Chinese quisling, head of state Wang Ching-wei, a former Kuomintang leader whose Japan-supported puppet "Nanking government"
included most of coastal central China—an honor never granted to the

puppet Manchukuo emperor, Pu-yi, who (in 1935) had had to be content with a banquet hosted by the prime minister.

Three months after the *Japan Times and Advertiser* editorial, another "philosophical exposé" of Japan's beliefs, goals and policies of much wider import was made compulsory reading in Japan. This was *The Way of the Subjects,* which made considerable use of Hirohito's own rescripts, and was distributed throughout the country to schools, adult groups and associations of all kinds, including, of course, the Imperial Rule Assistance Association (IRAA). This was a one-party-type "vertical" structure, established in 1940 with Konoye's initial blessing, which was in the process of replacing political parties and was organized along compulsory, totalitarian lines in offices and factories, with "street committees" monitoring the behavior of adherents.

The Way of the Subjects deserves close study, if only because it said out loud what Japan's leaders were reluctant to tell foreign diplomats to their faces. It's also important as a statement of totalitarian aims through the use of Hirohito's own proclamations, and as a general reinterpretation of Japan's history along militaristic lines, a posthumous vindication of the ideals of the dead 2/26 rebels. Significantly, this was no polemical pamphlet put out by hotheads in the IRAA, but an official document written by government officials and distributed by the Education Ministry.

It began with a withering condemnation of European and American culture, and its nefarious, debilitating ways. "Individualism, liberalism, utilitarianism and materialism" were the evils that these cultures had brought to Japan. Countries outside Europe, "in their sound sleep," had allowed this to happen, but "now the old order is crumbling," and the Western world's economic and political domination was on the wane.

The Manchurian affair had been "a violent outburst of Japanese national life long suppressed," and Japanese intervention had occurred because China "had started to trample over Japan's position in Manchuria, resulting in heavy sacrifices in Japanese lives, menacing Japan's lifeline." With the Mukden Incident, "world history began its new pages," for Manchukuo "has the Kingly way, as a land of bliss and racial concord . . . and has marked a quick and sound growth year by year, thereby consolidating the foundations of the structure of Japan-Manchukuo oneness." Quoting extensively from Hirohito's rescript at the time of Japan's withdrawal from the League of Nations,

The Way of the Subjects said that Europe and America "felt greatly menaced" by the founding of Manchukuo and had tried to sabotage it through the "so-called Lytton report."

The naval arms limitation talks were also an example of evil foreign intervention, "designed to hamper the advance of Japan as the stabilizing factor in East Asia." As for China, whose "wholehearted rapprochement and coordination are sorely needed for the construction of a new order over the whole of Asia," *The Way of the Subjects* again quoted the imperial rescript on the first anniversary of the China incident ("We believe that unless the evil causes existing for many years are eradicated, the stabilization of East Asia cannot ever be hoped for. . . . The solidification of a Sino-Japanese coalition and realization of their coprosperity will contribute to the establishment of world peace") as well as the rescript celebrating the tripartite treaty—"Japan's mission of world historical significance," it said, was embodied in that text.

But the China affair "would not and should not end with the mere downfall of Chiang Kai-shek. Until the elimination of the evils of European and U.S. influences in East Asia that have led China astray is realized, until Japan's cooperation with China yields satisfactory results, and East Asia and the rest of the world are united as one on the basis of moral principles, Japan's indefatigable efforts are sorely needed," for Japan "has a political mission to help various regions in the East Asian coprosperity scheme so as to rescue them from the control of the colonial powers." Culturally, too, Japan had a mission to "fashion East Asian nations into changing their following of European and American culture and to develop oriental culture to contribute to the creation of a just world."

Japan's concrete objective was now "the perfecting of a highly geared and centralized defence state and the strengthening of a total national war framework." Embodied in *The Way of the Subjects* was the concept of total war: "Military action now means diplomatic and economic thought and scientific warfare blended into one harmonious whole." There was a divine precedent for all this, for "Japan's mission of constructing the world on a moral basis originated in the empire-founding itself." The fundamental character of Japan, the document concluded, "is based on this theocracy: the Emperor rules and reigns his state with a solemn mind of serving the Gods. The Emperor loves his subjects with a paternal heart, and the subjects love the Emperor with a spirit as of bowing to their great father. There is no country of this sort in any other part of the world. . . . Japan's fountain source is the Yamato (Japanese) race, Manchukuo its reservoir, East Asia its paddyfield."

With growing restrictions and shortages, and industry on a centrally planned basis, Tolischus's first impressions were that Tokyo "was already at war" when he first set foot there. However, as Tolischus noted, raw materials required by the China war amounted to only 10 percent of Japan's productive capacity, and the "guns before butter" economy seemed to be working.

Reporting restrictions were phenomenal: the Military Secrets Protection and the National Defense Secrets acts meant that "nearly everything a correspondent did was a crime."* This was compounded by restrictions on cable languages (limited to Japanese, English and German), on international phone calls (limited to Japanese and English) and ("this really screws things up") on domestic phone calls, which could only be made in Japanese so that the police could listen in.

Japan was clearly on the brink of war, and the *Japan Times and Advertiser,* for all its reassuring social reporting, read at times like an English-language verson of a Nazi daily, full of news items about the war written from a strictly Axis point of view and, in its American coverage, giving huge prominence to the isolationist lobby and to its one American hero, Charles Lindbergh. On April 26, 1941, a front-page picture of the devastated City of London illustrated a story headlined "British Capital Feels the Full Force of German Strength."

In such circumstances, negotiations to reduce tensions between the United States and Japan must have seemed futile, but were taken seriously by both sides; in Washington, Roosevelt was guided by Ambassador Grew's belief that it was best to continue talks in the hope that saner counsel would eventually prevail, for was not the emperor a man of peace? The truth is that both sides were playing for time: the United States and Japan wanted to wait and see how the war in Europe would go, especially after Hitler's attack on the Soviet Union on June 22, 1941.

It is necessary to take a brief step backward at this juncture to report

---

*Otto D. Tolischus, *Tokyo Record* (New York: Reynal & Hitchcock, 1943).

on a vitally important imperial conference, or *gozen kaigi,* that took place on July 2, a few days after Hirohito's detailed cross-examination of his chiefs of staff (June 25) and shortly before the Japanese occupation of Saigon, Camranh Bay and Danang. This meeting, a turning point in Hirohito's attitude toward the coming war, showed that the thinking behind *The Way of the Subjects* (then being drafted inside the Education Ministry) was no mere propaganda exercise.

The decisions of a *gozen kaigi,* which took place in the presence of the emperor, key cabinet ministers (premier, war, navy, foreign affairs), the president of the Privy Council, and the two chiefs of staff, were sacred and inviolable. Because of the *gozen kaigi's* vital importance, and because a remarkably concise summary of its resolutions exists, it's worth quoting them in full:

Policy Outline

1: The Imperial Government is determined to follow a policy which will result in the establishment of the Greater East Asia Co-Prosperity Sphere and world peace, no matter what international developments take place.

2: The Imperial Government will continue its efforts to effect a settlement of the China Incident and seek to establish a solid basis for the security and preservation of the nation. This will involve an advance into Southern regions, and, depending on future developments, a settlement of the Soviet question as well.

3: The Imperial Government will carry out all of the above program no matter what obstacles may be encountered.

Implementation

1: Steps will be taken to bring pressure on the Chiang regime from the Southern approaches in order to bring about its surrender. Whenever demanded by future developments the rights of a belligerent will be resorted to against Chungking and hostile concessions taken over.

2: In order to guarantee national security and preservation, the Imperial Government will continue all necessary diplomatic negotiations with reference to the southern regions and also carry out various other plans as may be necessary. In case the diplomatic negotiations break down [my italics throughout], *preparations for a war with England and America will also be carried forward.* First of all, the plans which have been laid with reference to French Indochina and Thailand will be prosecuted, with a view to consolidating our position in the southern territories.

In carrying out the plans outlined in the foregoing article, we will not be deterred by the possibility of being involved in a war with England and America.

3: Our attitude with reference to the German-Soviet war will be based on the spirit of the Tripartite Alliance. However, we will not enter the conflict for some time but will steadily proceed with military preparations against the Soviet and decide our final attitude independently. At the same time, we will continue carefully correlated activities in the diplomatic field. In case the German-Soviet war should develop to our advantage, we will make use of our military strength, settle the Soviet question and guarantee the safety of our Northern borders.

4: *In carrying out the preceding article all plans, especially the use fof armed forces, will be carried out in such a way as to place no serious obstacles in the path of our basic military preparations for a war with England and America.*

5: In case all diplomatic means fail to prevent the entrance of America into the European war, we will proceed in harmony with our obligations under the Tripartite Pact. However, with reference to the time and method of employing our armed forces, we will take independent action.

6: We will immediately turn our attention to placing the nation on a war basis and will take special measures to strengthen the defence of the nation.

7: Concrete plans covering this program will be drawn up separately.

"The Emperor," Sugiyama wrote afterward, "very satisfied, gave his assent to all this at 13:30 immediately after lunch."

Hirohito had several reasons to be pleased. In his report on the state of the war in Europe, Sugiyama told the emperor that it was clear that Germany was winning, and, consequently, it was virtually certain that the United States would not intervene and risk war with both Japan and a victorious Germany by trying to prevent even the forcible establishment of Japanese bases throughout Indochina. Another reason for relief was that War Minister Tojo, who had a reputation for speaking his mind and never concealing awkward facts from the emperor, stated at the *gozen kaigi* that the level of discipline among the officers was satisfactory and that the possibility of a young officers' revolt was nil. Finally, the *gozen kaigi,* by rejecting Matsuoka's demand for an immediate attack on the Soviet Union, put the foreign minister in an impossible position: Hirohito now knew that the unpredictable and increasingly embarrassing Matsuoka would soon be dismissed by Konoye if he did not resign of his own accord.

But the emperor clearly had second thoughts about the meeting, and summoned the chiefs of staff to the palace for more informal talks on July 22. Hirohito wanted to hear more about the chances of successful diplomatic negotiations with the United States and about the attitudes of the chiefs of staff toward such negotiations; he also wanted formal assurances from both chiefs of staff that if war did break out, it would quickly lead to a decisive Japanese victory. What they had to tell him was scarcely reassuring.

In the morning session, General Sugiyama explained that the outbreak of World War II had completely altered Japan's strategic plans. "Before [the outbreak of war in Europe] we could only think about the 'China incident.' After the start of the war and Hitler's attack on Russia, the situation moved toward total world war." Chiang Kai-shek's forces were on the defensive, weak and demoralized, only sustained by United States, British and Soviet aid. For this reason, "the only way of solving the 'China incident,' " he said, "is to defeat Britain and the United States."

In the afternoon, Hirohito asked both chiefs of staff several probing questions. In the light of what they had said in the morning, was armed force the only way? Since they had painted such a bleak picture of the armed forces in China, "can we realize our purpose by using force?"

Sugiyama's reply, taken up by the navy chief of staff, Admiral Osami Nagano, was that the emperor was quite right to point this out, but that "if we let things slide further, Japan will not only be unable to solve the 'China incident' but will get into other difficulties as well—so we have to take action at the right moment."

Hirohito objected: "You say you don't have enough equipment."

Sugiyama said he couldn't speak for the navy, "but the army can manage for about a year."

"You say so," said Hirohito, "but is a year enough to win?"

Sugiyama replied he couldn't guarantee a year would be enough, "but we have to grab the right moment and take measures to expand [the war]. For example, we should carefully watch the Russo-German fighting and pick the right moment and stabilize our Northern border. It is necessary to decide whether we move North or South. For both the army and the navy, the more time we waste the more difficult it will be."

"I wonder if you're right," said Hirohito. "Is there any way to avoid using force? If things are carried out as planned in Indochina, that's fine. However, I've heard that Britain has put some of its troops in Thailand."

Not so, said Sugiyama, who went on to brief Hirohito on British dispositions in Asia: thirty thousand men in Burma and between forty thousand and fifty thousand in Malaya, "but only a quarter of these are British, the rest are locals or natives, mostly dissatisfied with British oppressive rule. . . . They cannot move aggressively," he said, adding that Japanese military attachés in the area "had submitted the same opinion." "However financially or economically dominant [Britain might be], suppressing Britain will be the right judgment." In case British troops entered Thailand "we will make the right judgment on how to cope with that and will seek your approval." Hirohito, still worried about the consequences of the Indochina move, said, "You won't have to use force in French Indochina, will you?" Again, he was reassured that the French would not give Japan any trouble. In a note that Sugiyama insisted should remain top secret, he added that the emperor "seems determined not to use force" and "we must make him change his mind." Hirohito must also, Sugiyama added, make his final decision: did he want to go for a Strike North (war with the Soviet Union on Germany's side) or a Strike South?

On July 30 Hirohito had further talks with his chiefs of staff, and again felt profoundly uneasy at what his naval chief of staff told him. According to the Kido diaries, Hirohito, almost thinking aloud, told Admiral Nagano: "Of course we will be victorious against the United States and Great Britain, but it will surely not be the kind of total victory we scored against Russia in 1905, will it?"

Nagano replied that such a total victory was indeed out of the question. "Indeed, we're not even sure of winning."

This unexpected reply filled Hirohito with gloom.

Talking to Kido about this meeting afterward, Hirohito said that while he wasn't "in principle" against the option of war with the United States and Britain, "one shouldn't make war without foreseeing victory," for this would mean embarking on a 'war of desperation.' "

But the countdown had, in effect, already started: Admiral Yamamoto had handed over his blueprint of Pacific operations (including a rough draft of the Pearl Harbor attack) to the naval chief of staff, and a mock-up of Pearl Harbor was under construction in the Naval Staff College (where Prince Takamatsu, in and out of the Staff College in 1941, must almost certainly have seen it).

Upright War Minister Hideki Tojo reassured the emperor about the state of morale of the armed forces, but he had not been completely frank: the officers were getting restive, demanding the implementation of the measures submitted to the emperor at the July 2 imperial conference without delay, the speedy occupation of Indochina, and an assurance that the ongoing negotiations with the United States would "maintain the orientation already decided on, and not go against the spirit of the Axis powers."

In effect, Hirohito's position at this stage was ambiguous: he was now thoroughly apprehensive about the war option with the United States, not on moral grounds, but because his chiefs of staff had informed him that the odds were longer than he had at first been led to expect; at the same time, he was reluctant either to scale down the Strike South plans, or to make any real concessions to the United States on China.

In retrospect, one's impression of Hirohito during these months is of a sovereign trapped into following an irrevocable course of action through a series of intermediate measures none of which can be annulled, unwilling to accept the consequences of his past decisions, unable to put his war machine into reverse or to lose face by accepting a compromise solution on China. The U.S. response to the occupation of southern Indochina—the total embargo on oil sales to Japan and the freezing of her assets in the United States from July 29 onward—only reinforced the arguments of Nagano and Sugiyama that there was no time to lose, and that the sooner Japan waged war the better.

Colonel Sackett, in his cross-examination of Kido in 1946, was to show an almost intuitive understanding of the emperor's dilemmas—and Kido's answers, for once, were less than bland.

SACKETT: Isn't it true that the Emperor wasn't so much opposed to Japan acquiring bases in French Indochina as he was fearful of the trouble it might cause in the negotiations with the United States?

KIDO: Yes, that was the prime concern.

SACKETT: So we can say that the Emperor wasn't really opposed to the expansion of Japan in the South if it could be accomplished without incurring the illwill and bad feelings of nations like Britain and the United States?

KIDO: Because the military said they would conclude the Chinese Incident and the Emperor naturally wanted this to happen as quickly as possible, he was in a difficult position.

SACKETT: In fact, there wasn't anyone in high office opposed to the expansion of Japanese influence into the South if it could be done without bringing war with the United States and Britain? Is that correct?

KIDO: Yes.

SACKETT: But when it was decided at the Imperial Conference that Japan would not tolerate interference on the part of the United States, it was then known that the United States might well resent the sending of troops to French Indochina and in spite of that fact, it was decided as the foreign policy that Japan would fight the United States, if necessary, to maintain her program of landing the troops?

KIDO: Yes.

SACKETT: On July 26, you make some references to air raid defenses in the Palace grounds. Why was it that the Palace grounds were being armed for the defense of air raids? Who was it that Japan feared might attack the Palace ground by air?

KIDO: With the negotiations between Japan and America becoming critical, the construction of air raid shelters was discussed with the Emperor.

SACKETT: In other words, that was just one of the plans that Japan started to make in anticipation of a possible clash with the United States. is that right?

KIDO: Yes.

[Later, Sackett was to return to the informal July 28 meeting.]

SACKETT: Was the Emperor disappointed in the point of view that Nagano took when he said that the Navy couldn't win a war with the United States and really desired him to express more enthusiasm for really being able to win the war?

KIDO: The Emperor upon hearing the report of the Chief of Staff said that more consideration must be given to this problem. We must not try to overdo [*sic*].

SACKETT: Who did the Emperor side with? The navy group as a whole or with Nagano? Whom did he believe or whom was he inclined to believe?

KIDO: The Emperor in the first place did not want war with the United States. He had to have more assurance of victory before he was willing to place the nation into war.

SACKETT: The Emperor was very much concerned about the fact that the Navy said they could win the war while the Chief of Staff himself said they couldn't. Isn't that correct?

KIDO: Since the positive success of the plan presented by Nagano was so dubious, the Emperor was greatly worried.

SACKETT: In other words, the Emperor wanted the Navy to take a stand one way or another. He didn't want two views as to whether they could win or not?

KIDO: The fact that Nagano presented the plan of which the outcome was victory and professed dubious doubts in his mind regarding that victory, the Emperor was very perplexed.

[Sackett left this line of questioning for a moment and turned to another item in Kido's diaries.]

SACKETT: The Emperor requested you make some investigation as to the amounts of rubber and tin the United States had and sources of supply in Latin America. Why did he want to know this?

KIDO: I believe it was as a result of a newspaper article.

SACKETT: Why? Wasn't it from the standpoint of whether or not Japan was capable of fighting a war with the United States successfully?

KIDO: I don't believe he had such a deep interest as that. Because the Emperor is quite a scientist, he has made such requests on a great number of previous occasions.

SACKETT: The Emperor was trying to get this information in order to make up his mind as to whether Japan could fight the war with the United States, was he not?

KIDO: Perhaps his thought may have some relation to that respect, correlated to the situation.

As both Kido and the *Sugiyama Memorandum* show, Hirohito may have tiptoed into war but he clearly knew what he was getting into. He had detailed blueprints of the Strike South order of battle in his possession for several months before Pearl Harbor, and his questions to his chiefs of staff showed he was fully aware of all operational details. At every stage of its preparations, he was actively concerned with points of detail, and there would be further question-and-answer sessions in September and October, right down to the final count-down. For all Hirohito's reservations, the July 2 *gozen kaigi* text was not rewritten, though it would later become more explicit.

The most surprising aspect of Hirohito's ongoing debate with his chiefs of staff is its cold, dispassionate tone. There are no moral qualms, no mental reservations about casualties and the potential sufferings and sacrifices of the Japanese people. Nor does there seem to have been any awareness of the monstrous scope of the Japanese challenge or of its inevitable consequences: clearly, Hirohito believed that a brief, successful blitzkrieg could lead to early negotiations, with Japan retaining at least part of her gains and preserving her ill-gotten hegemony over Asia. As members of a U.S. bombing evaluation committee were to note with amazement after the war, nobody, in 1941, seemed to have had any clear idea of how it would all end, or seemed to care. And Hirohito's own brief recommendations—that the Vatican should be cultivated as a mediator, that Hitler and Churchill, and Hitler and Stalin, should be prevented at all costs from making a separate peace with each other—reveal an abysmal ignorance, or imperial indifference, about the way of the world outside Japan. Hirohito simply could not grasp that having provoked a war, he would not be able to end it at will.

Nor can it be said that he remained unwarned: for all his deference, Kido could speak his mind to the emperor, and he, perhaps alone among the emperor's advisers, was intuitively aware of the dangers ahead. On the very eve of Pearl Harbor, he noted in his diaries that he intended to tell the emperor that

> Once the final decision is made, it will be truly the last and irrevocably final one. Thus if there should be any doubt in Your Majesty's mind I pray that Your Majesty should be pleased to elucidate the same without the least reserve and take appropriate steps which Your Majesty might not repent of afterwards. . . .

And after seeing the emperor, he noted (November 30, 1941) that

> . . . His Majesty's decision is of such gravity that, once decided, it could not later be retracted. Hence it is felt [by me] that if there is the least uncertainty, every possible precaution should be taken to do that to which His Majesty can give assent.

But Hirohito's mind, by August 1941, was made up: as the events leading to the final countdown show, the cautious emperor was to show, not for the first time, a considerable capacity for ruthlessness and guile.

CHAPTER FIFTEEN

With Emperor Hirohito's approval, Japanese troops and naval air squadrons started moving into their new southern Indochina bases by ship from Hainan island on July 29, 1941. By August 1, both the United States and Britain had retaliated by freezing Japanese assets, declaring an oil embargo and virtually cutting off all trade to Japan. Konoye, who had not expected this, was furious, blaming the military for providing him with inaccurate information about America's reactions. The new restrictions encouraged the more engagé Japanese diehards to step up their cry of "encirclement," and use the total oil embargo as an additional argument for immediate war. Despite all this, diplomatic negotiations between Japan and the United States did not abruptly come to an end, but lingered on for another four months. In retrospect, it is clear that they continued because at this stage both countries, like sumo wrestlers, were still eyeing each other warily and were not yet ready for the final, irrevocable, head-on clash.

There were several unusual aspects to these negotiations. The new Japanese ambassador to Washington, Admiral Kichisaburo Nomura, was inexperienced, and had only reluctantly accepted what he knew would be a thankless task. The talks began as "private" contacts among nongovernmental groups, and this virtually guaranteed that there would be, at some stage or another, charges on both sides of duplicity and bad faith. Finally, for the Americans there was the immense advantage of Magic, as their code-breaking operation was called. During this whole period both Roosevelt and his secretary of state (but only a handful of other top decision-makers in the administration) were uniquely well briefed about Japan's real, as opposed to her publicly proclaimed, intentions, because the United States had broken Japan's top-secret code, and was able to decipher her most confidential cables to her representatives abroad.

The implications of Magic were vast, and would later have a huge impact on the course of the war. In the immediate pre–Pearl Harbor months, Magic meant that United States negotiators were able to contrast Japan's true intentions with her declarations specially concocted for American consumption. In any negotiation, knowledge of one's opponent's fallback position is of the greatest value. Because of Magic, Americans not only had this capability, but were also fully aware that while Japan was talking reassuringly about peace, she was actively preparing for war on the basis of the July 2 *gozen kaigi*.

Some historians and a handful of diplomats have argued that it was the strength of the Washington-based "China lobby" that accounted for U.S. "intransigence" and the final deadlock between Japan and the United States. Sir Robert Craigie, British ambassador in Tokyo from 1937 to December 1941, would later accuse the Americans of ineptitude, and claim that a modus vivendi might well have been worked out had the talks been allowed to continue. But if the American attitude was firm, this was less due to Washington's "China Lobby," powerful though it may have been, than to knowledge provided by the Magic intercepts. On an almost daily basis, the handful of American policy-makers dealing with Japan at the highest level were confronted with the huge gulf between professed Japanese intentions and the stark implications of Japan's unswerving dedication to a new order within the Greater East Asia Co-Prosperity Sphere, and her readiness to use force to bring it about. By early August 1941, for instance, U.S. Secretary of State Cordell Hull, thanks to Magic, knew the gist of the decisions taken at the July 2 *gozen kaigi*. Magic also allowed Americans to know what really lay behind the establishment of Japanese military bases in southern Indochina, for the cables from the Japanese Foreign Ministry to her embassies abroad, whether in Berlin or in Vichy, had also been decrypted.

There was, however, some basis for Japanese charges of American bad faith, though this was mostly due to the behavior of the new Japanese ambassador. Nomura, a bluff, somewhat pompous admiral who was more at ease with American naval officers than with diplomats, spoke little English, and found it extremely difficult to deal with his foreign minister.

He was not alone in this respect. One of Foreign Minister Matsuoka's odder characteristics was his highly idiosyncratic, and highly un-Japanese, tendency to ramble at interminable length about anything that came into his head. He alternated between elation and anger, professing feelings of deep friendship for Americans one day, regarding them as hateful enemies the next. Even long-suffering Ambassador Grew was nonplussed when Matsuoka, after his return from his March–April 1941 trip to see Hitler, Mussolini and Stalin, started ranting at him that the "manly, decent and reasonable" thing for the United States to do would be to declare war on Germany, "since America's attitude to Germany is so provocative," and Hitler "so very patient and generous." "On my taking exception to the Minister's remarks," Grew wrote in his diary, "he withdraws the implication that the United States is guilty of 'unmanly, indecent and unreasonable conduct,' and later writes me that owing to his inadequate knowledge of English he inadvertently used the word 'indecent' whereas he meant 'discreet.' " Later, in a personal letter to Grew, Matsuoka wrote that he was speaking not as foreign minister but as one "indulging in thought in terms of one thousand or two or even three thousand years, and if this strikes you as a sign of insanity, I cannot help it as I am made that way." Shortly afterward, Matsuoka complained to Grew that he should never have reported his "highly personal" remarks to Washington in the first place.

In another age, Matsuoka's mood swings would have been attributable to drugs. As it was, his unpredictability led to charges, among those close to him, that he was mentally unstable, an additional "wild card" in an already highly complicated, explosive situation. Grew himself recognized Matsuoka's intermittent capacity for charm, when his moods were on the upswing, and Matsuoka himself could be inexhaustibly eloquent about his early years as a poor schoolboy in

Washington State, the kindness of a little old American lady who had raised him as her son in Seattle, and how, in 1933, he had had a monument erected on her grave. But the last thing to look for in Matsuoka, professional diplomats knew, was any element of consistency.

Strangers, however, were more easily taken in, as they often are in casual encounters with the mentally unbalanced, and among those charmed by Matsuoka were two American clergymen, Bishop James E. Walsh and Father James M. Drought, both of the Catholic Foreign Mission Society of America in Maryknoll, who returned from a trip to Japan in March 1941 determined to bring about a better relationship between the United States and Japan. They approached a prominent Catholic, Roosevelt's postmaster general, Frank C. Walker, suggesting an attempt at "parallel diplomacy" with selected Japanese contacts, and Roosevelt gave his grudging, distracted approval.

The delighted American priests got in touch with their Japanese contacts, among them a banker close to Konoye called Tadao Ikawa and an army colonel close to Tojo, but professing strong personal feelings of friendship toward America, called Hideo Iwakuro. With the postmaster general's blessing (and funds) they rented room 1802 in Manhattan's Berkshire Hotel as a discreet office.

Shortly afterward, on April 19, this odd group submitted to Cordell Hull its "Proposal Presented to the Department of State Through the Medium of Private American and Japanese Individuals." Whether Roosevelt and Hull between them saw this merely as an exercise to test the depths of Japanese duplicity, or whether they took it seriously, will probably never be known. Both Ikawa and Iwakuro were sufficiently experienced, and wily, to "play it straight." What is beyond doubt is that Colonel Iwakuro's credentials were, to say the least, mixed, since he was also one of the founders of the famous Nakano Spy School, an army establishment that selected highly motivated officers and NCOs for training not just in intelligence and espionage but in "special forces" and survival techniques as well. Iwakuro made several trips to the United States, ostensibly on "draft understanding" business, but this could also have been ideal cover for his intelligence activities.

Though the text of that initial draft was on the whole quite unacceptable to Hull, it did contain two "positive" clauses: one was the assertion that Japan would take only peaceful measures in the Pacific, the other the promise that Japan would enter the war on Germany's side only if it suffered an "aggressive attack" from the United States. Other than that, the draft proposal was a series of familiar Japanese requests: in return for these two somewhat vague pledges, Japan demanded an end to all trade restrictions, U.S. help in making Chiang Kai-shek agree to peace on Japanese terms, and an end to all U.S. aid to China if he refused to either recognize Manchukuo or amalgamate his own Chungking government with that of the Nanking government puppet, Wang Ching-wei. Finally, the United States was to give Japan assistance "for the removal of Hongkong and Singapore as doorways to further political encroachment by Britain on the Far East."

Cordell Hull promptly rewrote the "draft understanding" and asked Nomura whether Japan was prepared to present this amended text as an official Japanese "first draft," which could be the basis of substantive talks. Nomura understood this to mean that the United States regarded this text as an acceptable basis for negotiations, which was a completely false interpretation of the U.S. position.

To make matters worse, Cordell Hull then submitted four points to Japan as "paramount preliminaries," which, he said, Japan had to agree to before any such talks could take place. These "points of principle" begged the question: they ensured that, if accepted, no further negotiations would be needed, since they involved Japan's "respect for the territorial integrity and sovereignty of all nations, support for the principle of non-interference in international affairs, respect for equality of commercial opportunity" and a pledge that there would be "no disturbance in the status quo of any Pacific territory except by peaceful means."

Nomura compounded his initial semantic error by failing even to transmit these "points of principle" to Tokyo for some time. Perhaps, carried away by his own optimism, he felt that what mattered above all was to get official negotiations started, at almost any cost, and realized that if he forwarded these additional demands, the initiative would be aborted then and there. Hirohito was informed, erroneously, that the United States was willing to accept the amended Hull text as a "basis for negotiations," but thought the draft was one elaborated by the State Department itself: he was not told, until later, that it was the outcome of a private initiative in which the State Department had had no role so far.

But in any event, by this time Matsuoka was no longer interested in the private peace initiative he had so airily encouraged a few weeks previously, for his mind was elsewhere: just back from his "victorious" trip to Berlin, Rome and Moscow, and completely subjugated by Hitler, he was now convinced that Japan must enter the war on Germany's side as soon as possible, and his ego was such that he was determined to sabotage an initiative that had been elaborated in detail by others. On May 8 he told Hirohito that this dubious peace initiative, clearly a U.S. plot, would come to nothing. A week later, he requested, much as Cordell Hull had demanded a Japanese "declaration of principle," that the United States, before any negotiations started, sign a "neutrality pact" that would have left Japan free to act in any capacity without any possibility of U.S. retaliation. Cordell Hull countered (on June 21) by requesting that Japan abandon the Tripartite Alliance, declare Indochina a "neutral" zone and pull out all Japanese troops from northern China.

An impasse had been reached even before serious talks began, but Hirohito was alarmed by Matsuoka's eagerness to do Hitler's bidding prematurely, and wanted the negotiations to continue. On June 21 Hull saw Nomura again, and told him that one of the main obstacles to progress was the influence of "some individuals in high places" (by which, of course, he meant Matsuoka) committed to the unwavering support of Nazi Germany. In a written submission, he noted that the continued presence of Japanese troops on Chinese soil irrespective of a peaceful Chinese settlement was unacceptable, and this, again, the overoptimistic Nomura seized on as evidence of progress: could it be, he wondered, that this was the sole American objection to what Japan now saw as a possible "peace package"?

Germany's invasion of the Soviet Union the following day paradoxically gave U.S.-Japanese talks another lease on life. For one thing, it spelled Matsuoka's doom, for even the most tub-thumping militarist was unwilling to commit Japan's admittedly large forces to simultaneous war with the United States, Britain, the Netherlands *and* the Soviet Union, as Matsuoka now advocated; for another, Germany's move provoked a change of attitude in Konoye himself: he had always, admittedly misguidedly, hoped that Stalin might in time become an additional member of the Tripartite Alliance, and now he saw the invasion as "an act of betrayal" on Germany's part. From that moment onward, Konoye began having doubts about Japan's policies in general. He was too shocked, and listless, to speak up when, a few days later, the July 2 *gozen kaigi* set Japan firmly on the course of war, but he was determined to try his best to stave it off if he could—after all, even the *gozen kaigi* had stated that Japan would go to war only if negotiations broke down, and Japan and the United States were still talking. This, he felt, was also Hirohito's view, and as a last, romantic resort, he suggested (in August) a personal "summit meeting" with Roosevelt.

It was a typical Konoye volte-face, even though it was seen in Washington as yet another example of Japanese duplicity. In retrospect, Cordell Hull was possibly wrong to deny it any validity, for there was undoubtedly an element of irrationality in Japan's foreign policy, and Konoye may have been sincere. It's difficult to be certain, however, for in his eagerness to resort to "summit diplomacy" Konoye suddenly became all things to all men: he told Tojo he would be uncompromising, if he faced Roosevelt, about the need for a Greater East Asia Co-Prosperity Sphere. As a result War Minister Tojo, though dubious, agreed not to veto such a "summit" but wrote Konoye that if it failed, he was not to resign but to assume leadership in the war against the United States; in his later memoirs Konoye made no mention of this but said he was ready to pull Japan out of the tripartite pact.

If Roosevelt and he met, and came to an understanding, he intended, he later wrote, to cable the text of their agreement directly to the emperor. Hirohito would then issue an imperial rescript along the lines dictated by Konoye, and the army would then be compelled to respect the imperial order. Whether Konoye intended to put a fait accompli before the emperor, or wait until he was about to depart to broach this plan to him, will never be known.

Apart from this backhanded proof that the emperor's word was law, and that an imperial rescript could indeed determine peace or war, there is no evidence that Konoye actually talked to Hirohito about pulling Japan out of the tripartite pact, or intended making any other substantive concessions that would have made nonsense of the July 2 *gozen kaigi*. But in the last week of July, the emperor was still reeling from the disappointment of learning that the Navy was not convinced that it could win the war against the United States. When Konoye asked Hirohito for permission to meet Roosevelt, the emperor simply replied, "I am in receipt of intelligence from the Navy pertaining to a general oil embargo against Japan by America. In view of this, the meeting with the President should take place as soon as possible."

In any case, the emperor could have no objection to Konoye's summit proposal because it fulfilled the July 2 *gozen kaigi* clauses on "continuing diplomatic negotiations," and even if it ended in failure, it would have been a spectacular propaganda coup.

So now Konoye, the usually indolent patrician, who took to his bed whenever faced with a difficult course of action, threw himself into preparations for a summit meeting with unaccustomed energy, and as a first step proceeded to remove Matsuoka with unusual dexterity— resigning, with his cabinet, on July 26, and becoming prime minister again two days later, with the same cabinet, except for a new foreign minister, the more moderate and certainly saner Admiral Teijiro Toyoda.

For summit diplomacy to work, however, considerable mutual trust is essential, and to Roosevelt and Cordell Hull, Konoye remained a warmonger, the advocate of a single-party system, one of the architects of the new order, the man who had given his blessing to the start of the war with China and done his best to destroy Chiang Kai-shek. Unfamiliar with the Japanese mind, or with Japan's ancient myths, they couldn't adjust to such sudden, born-again changes, although such spectacular conversions among ancient Japan's heroes were part and parcel of Japanese legend and folk history. To Roosevelt, Churchill and Cordell Hull, the sudden Japanese interest in a face-to-face encounter was a sinister reminder of Hitler's meeting with Chamberlain: all that would ensue, they believed, was another Munich. The continuing stream of Magic transcripts only underlined the extent of Japanese equivocation: to Hull, Nomura insisted that the Tripartite Alliance remained a strictly defensive device and that Japan would not automatically go to war against the United States in the event of a clash between the German and American navies in the Atlantic—a possibility that haunted Roosevelt night and day. To General Hiroshi Oshima, Japan's pro-Nazi ambassador, the new foreign minister insisted that Japan would indeed declare war if this happened. No wonder Hull refused to believe anything any Japanese said. As he put it to an aide, "Nothing will stop them except force. . . . The point is how long we can maneuver the situation, until the military matter in Europe is brought to a conclusion. I don't want us to take for granted a single word they say, but appear to do so, to whatever extent it may satisfy our purpose to delay further action by them." In short, if Japan was duplicitous, America should be too.

So both Hull and Roosevelt were prepared to explore the Konoye proposal for a summit meeting, if only to find out, from Magic intercepts, what he really meant by it. Nomura in Washington, in mid-August, met an unusually cordial Roosevelt, and made the by now well-worn point that Japan's decision to move into southern Indochina had been strictly defensive, and that this was as far as Japan would go in Asia. Magic told a different story, and by this time a seriously worried Churchill, warned by his own intelligence sources that Japan was planning the invasion of both Singapore and Thailand, was pressing FDR to agree to a Tripartite Alliance in reverse, with America pledged to go to war against Japan if she attacked British or Dutch possessions in Asia. So Roosevelt, full of sympathy for his British ally, but still fearful of the isolationist lobby and the reluctance of Congress to agree to any such thing, smiled and smiled, and listened with feigned interest as Nomura told him that a specially equipped liner, the *Nitta Maru,* packed with sophisticated radio equipment, was ready to steam from Yokohama to any point of the globe to act as a communications HQ for Konoye for the length of such a summit, and even proposed a venue—Juneau, Alaska. Then, having raised Konoye's hopes, Roosevelt dashed them, as though wanting to inflict on him the same kind of emotions Hull experienced whenever he contrasted Nomura's bland promises with the evidence of Magic.

By September 3, when Roosevelt next met Nomura, he backed off from the summit proposal and said he needed a clearer idea of what was at stake, and what he and Konoye would talk about, and this would have to be resolved by traditional diplomatic means *before* their summit meeting could take place. It was a restatement of the "four principles," and now not only Konoye but the emperor himself realized that Japan was being strung along and duped.

Hull wrote later, in his *Memoirs,* that "Japan's insistence on holding the meeting and leaving 'details' to be worked out later was in itself significant. It seemed to us that Japan was striving to push us into a conference from which general statements would issue—and Japan could then interpret and apply these statements to suit her own purposes, as she had always done in the past. Moreover, she could then say she had the President's endorsement of her actions. . . . Unless the President were willing to agree to vague generalities that would all be to Japan's advantage, there was every likelihood that the meeting would end in failure. In that event Japan's military officials could declare to the Japanese that the United States was responsible for the failure and then proceed to prepare public opinion for war in the Pacific."

Japanese patience was exhausted, and the very day Nomura met with Roosevelt and was given an indirect thumbs-down for a summit meeting, a "liaison conference" of inner cabinet and military leaders took place in Tokyo to prepare for a diplomatic ultimatum, whose failure was a foregone conclusion—and for another, even more "historic" *gozen kaigi* three days later (September 6), committing Japan even more irrevocably to war. The Japanese demands this time were still to be obtained if possible by diplomatic means, but with a cutoff date: after October 31, Japan "would not avoid war with the United States, Britain and the Netherlands." The "minimum" diplomatic demands were as unacceptable as ever: no American or British "meddling" in Japan's dealings with China, an end to all U.S. and British aid to Chiang Kai-shek, a restoration of normal trade with Japan, and British and American "friendly cooperation" in Japan's trade ties with Thailand and the Dutch East Indies. This time the only "positive" element in the hard-line list of demands was a vague pledge that Japan would be ready to evacuate her troops from Indochina "after conclusion of a just peace treaty in the Far East."

On September 5 a demoralized Konoye called on Hirohito to ask him to preside over a *gozen kaigi* the following day. After reading its agenda, Hirohito said he had questions of substance to ask his military commanders. Rather than raise them at the formal meeting, Konoye suggested an immediate meeting with his chiefs of staff. Hirohito agreed. They were summoned, and faced their most stringent cross-examination yet.

Hirohito first of all lectured them on the need to give diplomacy precedence over war. "You mustn't simultaneously prepare for war and for diplomacy," he told them. Then, having got this out of the way, he started off on a series of detailed, practical questions: did the chiefs of staff think that they could "do the South" as outlined in their operational plans?

Sugiyama, whose nickname in the army was "Toilet Door," not because he was stupid but because he had, among his peers, the reputation of a vacillating, easily influenced figurehead, apt to swing this way and that like a toilet door in an army barracks, didn't answer directly, but wasted a lot of time, to Hirohito's ill-concealed irritation, running through the detailed operational plans for the invasion of Malaya and the Philippines instead of answering the emperor's question in a straightforward way.

Hirohito asked him, "Are you sure all this will go according to plan? Nothing ever does, exactly. You say it will all be over in five months. You said you would get rid of Chiang Kai-shek within a year and he's still there. Surely one must make allowances for the unexpected?"

Sugiyama replied that the operational plans "had been studied very closely, and we think it will take place as planned."

Hirohito said, "Do you really think the landing operations will be that easy?"

"I don't know whether they'll be easy, but I think they are possible," said Sugiyama.

Showing considerable detailed knowledge of recent maneuvers, Hirohito pointed out that during the simulated invasion exercise held off Kyushu Island recently, a lot of ships were declared sunk by enemy aircraft. "If the same thing happens in real life, what will you do?"

Sugiyama said that was what maneuvers were for: the fleet had made its move before the air cover was ready. That mistake wouldn't occur again.

Hirohito asked what would happen if the weather was bad.

Sugiyama said that would complicate things, but not fatally.

How could he be so confident? Hirohito asked. "When you were war minister, you said the 'China incident' would be over in five months—and it's not over yet."

Sugiyama blamed "special circumstances" in China. Konoye noted in his diary that Sugiyama told the emperor: "I can't give you an absolute 100 percent guarantee of victory, but I do say there are good chances of winning." What Japan wanted, and must be prepared to gamble for, was a permanent settlement. "Even if we get peace in six months or a year, it would not be satisfactory to face the same difficulties later on. We must look for peace for twenty, fifty years."

This argument struck home. In a strong voice, Hirohito said, "I understand." Admiral Nagano chipped in with an illustration from seventeenth-century Japanese history, making the point that Japan should not agree to delay war if, in so doing, the delay only benefited the enemy. This too, Sugiyama noted, had a strong effect on Hirohito.

The following day Hirohito returned to the issue of diplomacy versus war. In a prearranged question, the president of the Privy Council, Yoshimichi Hara, speaking in Hirohito's name, asked for a firm assurance that the former would take precedence over the latter. The navy minister assured him this would be the case, but the chiefs of staff remained silent. Hirohito intervened directly from the elevated throne at the end of the room. Why had they not said anything? "Hara has spoken well, but you did not answer. Why? This is an extremely serious matter."

Hirohito referred to a scribbled note before him, and read a poem composed by his grandfather, Emperor Meiji:

> *"Throughout the world*
> *Everywhere we are all brothers.*
> *Why then do the winds and waves*
> *Rage so turbulently?"*

He often thought of this poem, he said, in his own effort to uphold his dedication to peace.

Both chiefs of staff protested they had not meant to ignore the emperor's remarks. They simply had nothing to add to the navy minister's apt remarks. The *gozen kaigi,* Konoye noted, broke up in a state of great tension.

This incident, and the Meiji haiku citation, are often quoted as proof of Hirohito's desperate striving for a peaceful solution. But if he felt so strongly, why did his remarks remain so utterly vague? Now, if ever, was the moment for him to give some form of guidance to his government and military commanders that would enable them to meet some U.S. requirements without losing face. Konoye was by now desperately apprehensive, still clinging to the notion of a possible Roosevelt summit. The navy minister and most of his senior officers would have welcomed any statement from Hirohito that would have enabled them to postpone actual war. True, it was impossible, in a formal *gozen kaigi,* for Hirohito to speak his mind informally, but, as the Kido diaries show again and again, whenever the emperor wished to convey his point of view to others, all he had to do was to summon

Kido and use him as a sounding board: Kido would invariably relay
the message, and such was his intuitive understanding of the way
Hirohito's mind worked that he never erred, always faithfully reflecting the emperor's finer shades of meaning.

There is another possible explanation for the Meiji haiku quotation.
As Michael Montgomery points out,* "peace," in the context of the
great Meiji Restoration, did not have quite the same meaning it had
in the rest of the world, being more synonymous with "paradise," that
idyllic state of affairs symbolized by *hakko ichiu* (eight corners of the
world under one roof)—and Meiji himself, who had wanted to lead
his armies into battle in Korea and had destroyed the Russian fleet
without a formal declaration of war, could hardly be regarded as a
paragon of peace. What Hirohito may have been expressing, Montgomery wrote, was frustration rather than apprehension, for the haiku
could also be construed as meaning, Since the world is destined to lie
under the divine protection of Japan, why is it that some other nations
so obstinately refuse to accept this state of affairs, decreed by nature?

In retrospect, Hirohito seems to have behaved as though he was
fully aware of what was about to happen, but was determined to
provide himself with an alibi, to shift the blame for war on others. At
no point, in discussions with any of his advisers, or in hints dropped
to Kido, did the emperor attempt to examine, one by one, the many
irreconcilable differences between Japan's and the United States'
points of view and see where, if at all, Japan could possibly give
ground. He was still, almost obsessively, concerned about obtaining
from his military leaders formal assurances of victory, and had they
been less honest and forthright in their views, the inference is that he
would have raised no objections at all. What Hirohito seems to have
required from them was a miraculous ability to bring the United States
to heel without having to resort to war, and without making any
concessions whatever. For all the drama of the September 6 *gozen
kaigi*, Hirohito did not attempt to postpone what all concerned must
have known was inevitable: after this meeting, war was a virtual
certainty from November 1 onward.

The updated operational blueprints for Strike South were handed
over to Hirohito on September 9. By this time it was clear that

---

*Michael Montgomery, *Imperialist Japan* (London: Christopher Helm, 1988).

Hirohito understood, deep down, that all talk of diplomacy was so much window-dressing, as he asked Sugiyama: "What will you do if there's pressure from the North [i.e., if the Soviets attack] while we are attacking the South?"

Sugiyama said he could cope. "Your answer reassures me," Hirohito replied. The following day mobilization plans were given Hirohito's express consent. A few days later the executive director of the single authorized party, the IRAA, boasted that "heaven did not create superior races only to starve them to death." On September 18, the tenth anniversary of the Mukden Incident was celebrated with great pomp. In the presence of Prince Takamatsu, Tojo called it "the heavensent tocsin signalling at home and abroad the epoch-making dawn of East Asia." And that same September, the Imperial Mint began printing Japanese "military occupation yen" for future use in the Greater East Asia Co-Prosperity Sphere.

CHAPTER SIXTEEN

The September 6 *gozen kaigi* should have convinced Prince Konoye that his chances of preventing war, or of meeting Roosevelt, were now nil. Instead, he redoubled his efforts, a doomed one-man band, caught between his own war-bent establishment and the severe, schoolmasterish Cordell Hull.

That very evening Konoye had a three-hour meeting with Ambassador Grew. They met like conspirators: apart from Konoye and his personal aide, and Grew and *his* personal interpreter, the only people who knew of the meeting were Prince Hirobumi Ito, in whose house they met, and Ito's daughter, who prepared their meal. All servants, by this time, were assumed by diplomats and politicians alike to be unreliable, possible spies bribed or blackmailed into working for the secret or military police, and Ito's staff had been given the evening off. Both Konoye and Grew used vehicles with ordinary Tokyo license plates, instead of their official cars.

For Konoye, knowledge of the latest decisions taken earlier in the day in the emperor's presence must have given him an added sense of urgency. He knew he had less than a month to bring off a summit meeting, and he still couldn't accept that it was forever beyond his grasp. Now he was determined to do everything he could to persuade

Grew of his good faith, even subscribing to the "four principles" Hull had insisted on as a necessary preliminary to all talks, admitting Japan's responsibility for the deteriorating situation, and promising no more "irresponsible" assurances Japan would not be able to keep.

It was not true, he conveyed to Grew, with almost pathetic frankness, and in scarcely veiled terms, that he was isolated and no longer carried any clout, that the military alone had powers of decision. Why, if the "summit" was staged, he would be taking with him a full general designated by Tojo, as well as the vice chiefs of staff. Japan, he implied, had turned over a new leaf, and now wanted a thoroughgoing reconstruction of U.S.-Japan relations. Of course it will take time, he said in essence, of course my track record is a dubious one, but trust me, I am your only chance of avoiding war.

Grew was impressed, convinced of Konoye's sincerity, and in favor of "constructive conciliation." Hull was not. The presence at the proposed summit of generals at Konoye's side, he felt, was simply further proof that the Japanese wanted a "Munich," and the Japanese counterproposals reaching him (on September 6 and 25) didn't help either. Instead of reflecting Konoye's new approach, as reported by Grew, they were a mere restatement of Japan's earlier China demands, couched in admittedly more reassuring language.

On October 2 Hull replied to them in words that effectively put an end to any hopes Konoye might have had of meeting Roosevelt. But Konoye still wouldn't give up. Despite Magic, no one on the American side knew about the countdown, but Konoye for one was aware he had even less than a month left, for by this time the fatal date was no longer October 31 but October 15, the military having arbitrarily decided they needed an extra fortnight to put their plans into practice. Konoye asked Tojo to give him more time to arrange for a summit. Tojo replied that to tamper with the holy decisions of a *gozen kaigi* would be to behave disloyally to the emperor.

On October 12, Konoye's fiftieth birthday, he made one final effort to convince Tojo. He was unusually frank, and pathetically grave. He told Tojo he had been responsible for one conflict—in China—and he could not take the responsibility of leading Japan into another war. The only way was to yield, "temporarily," to some American demands, and accept the withdrawal of some Japanese troops from China. In any case, it was an unwinnable war, as Japan would be forced to recognize sooner or later.

Tojo was adamant. To yield anything would be to tamper with the army's morale, and how, then, could one expect it to fight properly? "I think you are too pessimistic," Tojo said, "probably because you know our weaknesses too well. Doesn't America have weaknesses of its own?" The prim war minister's irritation was palpable, and, from his viewpoint, reasoned: in the none too distant past, Konoye, more than any other civilian, had insisted on Chiang Kai-shek's removal and had been the driving force behind the establishment of the Wang Ching-wei–led puppet Nanking government. Now, in emotional turmoil, he was trying to compel the army to move in a completely different direction and sacrifice the efforts and casualties of the past four years. After this meeting, Konoye realized he had shot his bolt, and that there was nothing further to be done.

A day later Hirohito came to much the same conclusion, but his mood was very different from Konoye's, for the emperor now accepted the inevitability of war with apparent equanimity. "In the present circumstances," he told Kido, "I think U.S.-Japan negotiations have little hope of succeeding." If war broke out, he said, he would have to issue an imperial proclamation, and he set about telling Kido (who would draft it) what it should contain. Unlike Konoye, with his intuitive sense of foreboding about the immediate future, Hirohito was looking ahead, beyond war, to negotiations from strength.

If it came to war with the United States and Britain, he told Kido, the European situation should be well under control. Germany would have to be watched very closely, for any attempts by Hitler to make a separate peace with either Churchill or Stalin would be devastating blows to Japan's war effort, so "we need to have good diplomatic contacts to see to it that Germany maintains her cooperation in Japan's war against the United States." It was also necessary, Hirohito went on, to start thinking, even before war started, of the means of ending it, and to look for a suitable mediator. The Vatican would be ideal, and Japan should begin by establishing top-level diplomatic relations with Pope Pius XII.

On October 14, at a cabinet meeting, the decision was taken to let the countdown take its course, and Konoye decided this would be his last cabinet meeting. That evening he was a guest at a working dinner party organized by some aides to decide on the next president of the

North China Development Company. Konoye arrived at 6:00 P.M. in a kimono and said, "Our discussion is no longer necessary. My cabinet is about to fall." The army minister had refused to delay the count-down, he told his hosts, and the navy minister had refused to go on record and voice in public the navy's reservations about fighting a war with the United States. Konoye smiled wanly, and said, "Tonight I am here only to enjoy your hospitality." After dinner, his hosts recalled, he picked up a brush and drew in bold strokes the ideogram for "dream." "Two thousand six hundred years," he said. "It's been a long dream."

Later still, that same night, a messenger showed up at Konoye's residence with a message from Tojo. Belatedly Tojo had himself discovered what Konoye knew all along: that within the upper eche-lons of the navy, there was serious disagreement about Japan's chances of winning. If the navy was refusing to go to war while refusing at the same time to say so, there must have been grave dereliction of duty somewhere, Tojo's messenger said. The news he had just received called the decisions of the September 6 *gozen kaigi* into question, and this in turn meant that all those who had attended it had failed in their duty to the emperor. There was only one way out: Konoye's entire cabinet should resign, and Prince Higashikuni should take over as premier—only he had the necessary prestige to conduct a policy re-view and bring the two services together.

Konoye got little sleep that night: weighing his few remaining options, he even considered the possibility of secretly leaving Japan on his own authority, making his way unofficially to Washington and forcing a face-to-face meeting on Roosevelt. The following day (October 15) he dismissed this "Rudolf Hess" alternative. It might not work, and it would be a terrible affront to his emperor. Instead, rallying to Tojo's arguments, he called on Hirohito, urging him to appoint Prince Higashikuni as premier. The next day (October 16) he resigned, explaining his reasons in a lengthy note to the Council of Elders, that informal body of ex-premiers, which met only at the emperor's request when grave issues were at stake. Konoye's letter was addressed to them, but it was really meant for the emperor himself.

Professor Inouye sees this letter as Konoye's final ultimatum: a plea to Hirohito to choose between negotiations or war. Had the emperor refused Konoye's resignation, as he had several times in the past, Konoye would then have known that the emperor was on his side, and that there was a glimmering of hope for peace.

But Hirohito did nothing of the kind. And despite Tojo's and Konoye's advice, Hirohito also said no to Higashikuni, a tough, able officer who was known to be less enthusiastically inclined to war than Tojo. Kido, with the interests of the imperial family as usual foremost in mind, argued that if an imperial prince became premier and declared war, this might bring "the wrath of the people" down on the imperial family. So instead of Higashikuni, Kido proposed that Tojo should be made prime minister, and Hirohito enthusiastically endorsed this proposal.

Many years later, in an interview with Yoshio Ando of *Ekonomisuto,* Prince Higashikuni himself threw additional light on what actually happened during those fateful October 16–17 days. "Konoye asked me to form a government," Higashikuni said. "The Emperor agreed and so did Kido. I didn't want to be the next premier. I said to Konoye: 'If Tojo doesn't listen to you, why don't you form the fourth Konoye Government and then sack him? There are some people in the army who want to avoid war.' Konoye said: 'I'll suggest this to the Emperor.' While we were talking along these lines, General Abe [Nobuyuki Abe, briefly premier in August 1939 after Konoye's first government and that of Hiranuma] and Kido were together and they proposed Tojo as premier, and the Emperor accepted. So Konoye [who had left the room to find out what was going on] rushed back to me and said: 'Tojo is going to be the next prime minister and I can't do anything about it any more.' Harada [Saionji's confidential secretary] commented: this is the end of Japan."

Kido's championship of Tojo was, on the face of it, odd, but the ultrasophisticated aristocrat and the puritanical, narrow-minded soldier got on well together, and had more in common than was apparent. Both were highly competent bureaucrats, with a strong practical bent, and both were selflessly devoted to Hirohito. Of all the generals in the limelight, Tojo appeared to be the most reliable. Hirohito liked him, Kido noted later, because he never held anything back. He was also intensely hardworking and impeccably honest. Whereas other military police chiefs in Manchukuo had become rich men, Tojo had remained poor, and still distributed part of his salary to destitute veterans of his former regiment.

There is another possible reason for Kido putting his name forward: the astute Lord Privy Seal, so close to the emperor that he could unfailingly detect his slightest change of mood, must have realized by this time that Hirohito had resigned himself to the inevitability of what he thought would be a short, sharp war with the United States, Britain and the Netherlands, to be followed by a peace treaty that would officially underwrite Japan's hegemony over East Asia for all time.

On October 20, three days later, Hirohito praised Kido's choice. Basking in the emperor's praise, Kido explained that Japan had been in danger of going to war on a preestablished calendar without adequate preparations, but that Tojo, known for his organizational ability, would put this right. Hirohito had clearly recovered from his earlier gloom, caused by Nagano's remarks concerning the navy's doubts about the war, for at the very end of his conversation with Kido, he made an extraordinary remark: "We are now in a very difficult situation, very close to war," he told him. "But you can't capture the baby tiger without going into the mother tiger's lair." ("I was very awed," Kido wrote afterward.)

This is a much stronger Japanese equivalent of "Nothing ventured, nothing gained." Its only possible interpretation, in the context of the rest of Hirohito's talk with Kido that day, and of his remarks three days earlier on the need to keep Germany in the war on Japan's side, is that the emperor, convinced of the imminence of war, and no longer doubting its outcome, regarded Tojo as the best possible premier in a war situation. Significantly, in his new cabinet, Tojo retained the war and home ministry portfolios, the first prime minister to do so. It was a clear indication that war was at hand. Tojo's insistence on becoming home minister was understandable: that way, he controlled both the secret and the military police.

Many years later (in 1958), Konoye's faithful aide, Kanji Tomita, would record his patron's distress during those crucial weeks. Why, Tomita asked Konoye (during the war years), given his unique access to Hirohito, and the family and friendship bonds that united them, hadn't he appealed directly to the emperor, to point out how calamitous Tojo's premiership would be?

Konoye implied sadly that the emperor vacillated during those crucial days, didn't really know his mind and, in any case, by October 16, had already come down on the pro-war partisans' side. He told

Tomita: "When [in the final days of his premiership] I used to tell the Emperor that it would be a bad thing to start the war, he would agree with me, but then he would listen to others and afterwards tell me I shouldn't worry so much. He was slightly in favor of war and later on he became more war-inclined. Eventually, he started believing that I was no expert on strategy or military matters generally. As Prime Minister, I had no authority over the army and there was only one person I could appeal to: the Emperor. But the Emperor became so much under the influence of the military that I couldn't do anything about it."

From the tone of his diary after October 16, it's clear that Kido and Tojo cooperated closely—and that Tojo unburdened himself about the navy's last-minute doubts. In his diary, Kido noted that the top priority was to restore harmony between the two services and reopen discussions on the September 6 *gozen kaigi.* He must have been Tojo's efficient intermediary, for very soon afterward the emperor, through Kido, asked Tojo to bring this about, and also told Tojo that the "automatic countdown" decided on at the September 6 *gozen kaigi* should be reviewed. There should be more thought given to Japan's domestic and foreign policies before an irrevocable decision was made. This, Kido told Tojo, was "an Imperial order." But it was also a highly ambiguous one, for at no time did Hirohito indicate how the "harmonization" should take place. Should the navy swallow its fears, and align itself on the army's bellicose position? Or should the army reflect on the navy's doubts, and consider the implications of the navy's reluctance to fight a war, and its pessimistic projections, on the Strike South operation as a whole? With Tojo as premier, home and war minister, the final realignment could hardly be in doubt, unless the emperor made his preference felt, which he did not. What happened was that the navy agreed to soft-pedal its negative views, and that Admiral Nagano cravenly aligned himself with his fellow chief of staff, Sugiyama, while the navy minister, equally cravenly, continued to voice his doubts privately, but refused to repeat them in policy-making committee meetings.

Between October 23 and November 1, eight top-level meetings took place to amend and refine the decisions taken at the last *gozen kaigi,* and at these meetings eleven separate questions were discussed. Ten of these agenda items dealt with Strike South and the probable course of the war; only one concerned talks with the United States.

By November 1 naval doubts had been dissipated, for the decisions of September 6 were reemphasized, though the calendar was put back and X Day was now brought forward to December—the last possible delay, for the weather was fast deteriorating, and if the December deadline was ignored, everything would have to be rescheduled for March 1942. The navy was now to be fully operational by December. Negotiations with the United States were to continue, but this was sheer window-dressing, for another crucial countdown decision was taken: that military relations with Thailand would be established "just before the start of war" to enable Japanese troops to use Thailand as a base from which to invade northern Malaya with maximum surprise. However, if negotiations with the United States succeeded—i.e., in the unlikely event that the United States, after resisting unacceptable Japanese demands for several years, abruptly caved in and virtually surrendered to Japanese requests that it abandon Chiang Kai-shek, giving Japan an entirely free hand in Asia—then all Strike South plans would be scrapped.

Interestingly, in the light of Hirohito's "tiger's lair" talk with Kido, highly placed palace sources were still providing Ambassador Grew with reassuring "leaks": in a diary entry for October 25, Grew mentions an "anonymous informant" who claimed to have talked with the emperor. As Grew wrote, the emperor "is said to have asked leading members of the Privy Council and the armed forces to enquire if they were prepared to pursue a policy which would guarantee that there would be no war with the United States. When the Emperor failed to get a satisfactory reply, he quoted Meiji and ordered the assembled individuals to obey his wishes." It was a curious amalgam of half-truths, subtly and probably deliberately concocted.

In fact, question-and-answer sessions between Hirohito and his chiefs of staff were now taking on the aspect of an operational checklist. On November 2, Hirohito asked them what was their estimate of initial losses. Their answer was, in retrospect, overpessimistic: one battleship, two heavy cruisers, four light cruisers and eighteen hundred planes. Hirohito told them they should also take ground casualties into consideration. "I hope you are also remembering the damage to [sea] transport," he said. "Is air defence satisfactory? What do you do if the enemy destroys Korean dams?"

Sugiyama reassured him on all counts.

Hirohito then turned to the operational calendar in the China–

Hong Kong zone. "I understand," he said, "that you will 'do' Hong-kong after securing Malaya [this had been decided to enable the attack on Malaya to take place with maximum surprise] "but what about the foreign concessions in China?" At what stage, he asked, would Japan launch her attacks there? If Japan moved too soon, Hirohito warned them, surprise would be lost and "the Malaya attack will fail," so he assumed that this, too, would happen after the initial surprise attacks.

Sugiyama assured him that this was indeed the plan.

Hirohito returned to the possibility of bad weather. The rainy season was fast approaching. How would this affect landing operations?

It was because of fear of prolonged rain over Malaya, Sugiyama replied, that he had finally decided against a massive initial air strike. In the Philippines sector, he added, such weather problems were not expected.

Then, addressing Admiral Nagano, Hirohito made his sole reference to Pearl Harbor, and the cryptic exchange that followed revealed that he must have been thoroughly aware of its details.

Hirohito asked, "What is the Navy's target date?"

Nagano replied, "December 8."

Hirohito said, "Isn't that a Monday?"

Nagano pointed out the time difference between Hawaii and Tokyo (December 8 in Tokyo was December 7 in Hawaii) and reminded the emperor that the Sunday had been chosen "because everyone will be tired after their holiday." For months spies had been at work in Hawaii, and they had early pointed out that weekends were taken seriously by the U.S. Navy, and that merry, bibulous Saturday nights were followed by lethargic Sunday mornings.

The emperor asked whether everything would be planned in such a way as to occur simultaneously. Nagano replied that because of the great distances involved, this would be difficult. As he pointed out, again referring to Pearl Harbor without, however, mentioning the plan in detail: "The outcome of the war depends greatly on the outcome of the first stage, and the outcome of the first stage depends on the outcome of the surprise attack. We must hide our war intentions at all costs." In the context of the talks that day, it was clear that Hirohito understood what was meant by the "surprise attack."

Nagano added that the initial stages of the war would be more hazardous than anything experienced in China because of the presence of enemy planes and submarines, but "once we land successfully, we're quite sure we'll win. We'll try to end the war quickly," Nagano said, "but we must be prepared for a prolonged war." The United States had to be prevented from using Soviet bases.

Still on navy matters, Hirohito asked Nagano to remember the possible threat posed by submarines based in Australian ports and the damage they could do to Japanese oil tankers.

On November 4 Hirohito gave Kido a detailed account of what had taken place. He also gave Kido the specific task of preparing an official brief to be used "when we invade Thailand." Hirohito, in his earlier discussions, had told his chiefs of staff there were two alternatives in dealing with this traditionally friendly, pro-Japanese country. One was to prepare a military treaty in advance, so that Japanese troops transiting through Thailand on their way to Malaya would do so quite legally; the alternative was to invade Thailand, and then get the Thais to sign a document agreeing to the Japanese military right-of-way. Hirohito had finally opted for the latter option because it made military sense, for a pact drawn up shortly before the invasion would have given the game away.

That same day (November 4) a top-ranking Japanese diplomat, Saburo Kurusu, left Tokyo to join Nomura in Washington to "strengthen" Japan's negotiating team in Washington. Kurusu's wife was American, and his new appointment was given exceptional prominence in Japanese newspapers. Kurusu, a former ambassador to Berlin, was aware of the overall operational plans for war, though the secret of Pearl Harbor had been kept from him (Tojo testified as much after the war). Ambassador Nomura knew nothing. Indeed, it was he who had asked for Kurusu to join him in Washington, because, as he put it to his minister in Tokyo, "I cannot tell you how much in the dark I am. I am now, so to speak, a mere skeleton of a dead horse, and I do not want to continue this hypocritical existence, deceiving myself and other people. I am unable to perceive the delicate shades of the policy of the government and am quite at a loss what to do." Kurusu's brief was to keep the Washington negotiations going for as long as possible. As will be seen later, it was all part of a highly sophisticated, orchestrated plan to further lull the United States into believing that, for all the inevitability of an eventual war, it wouldn't happen just yet, or in the form already minutely planned.

Three days later, on November 5, another formal *gozen kaigi* ratified the earlier decisions of November 2. The emperor showed he was familiar with all the points under review, and took the formal decision immediately, Sugiyama reported. Then came some informal questions afterward on the practical aspect of it all. Hirohito asked at what stage field commanders would be finally briefed and sent to join their units. What was the optimum date, given the need to maintain total secrecy?

Sugiyama replied that the detailed briefings would begin on November 7. How long, Hirohito asked, could they be kept secret? Since the scale of the operations was so vast, Sugiyama told him, it was very difficult to say. Once more, Hirohito urged Sugiyama not to fight on too many fronts: "Don't disturb the North," he said. A Soviet "spoiling operation"—an incursion across the Manchurian border in aid of the United States—was clearly feared, and Sugiyama told the emperor it might be necessary to reinforce the units along China's contiguous border with the Soviet Union, though he was unwilling to transfer troops from the Shanghai area. In no uncertain terms, Hirohito told him: "It's best to transfer the soldiers from Senshow [the main Japanese military base on the Yangtze River]."

A minor crisis within army headquarters further revealed Hirohito's overall grasp of Strike South operational plans and his minute attention to detail: it concerned one of the units earmarked for the invasion of Malaya, the 5th Division, recruited from the Hiroshima area. In the original overall Malayan invasion plan, it was to join the Malayan invasion force directly from its Chinese operational base. Because they came from Hiroshima, which was located on the coast, most of its men knew how to swim, and this was regarded, by GHQ, as an advantage for the Malayan theater of operations. Since all troop movements had to be approved by Hirohito, a formal request went to the palace for the 5th Division's transfer from China. To the army's surprise, the emperor failed to acknowledge this troop-movement request. Eventually, as X Day neared, army commanders worried, and a General Staff letter respectfully asked the emperor whether he had any objections to the 5th Division's role.

The emperor replied that he did not believe moving the 5th Division directly from China to Malaya was a good idea. This particular division had been involved in heavy fighting in China, he noted, and the nature of operations in Malaya would be different from that in China. (By this, the emperor meant that he was well aware that the 5th Division troops had killed civilians and committed various atrocities in China, and if they behaved like that in Malaya this could become embarrassing, for the divisions involved in "South" operations had to be on their best behavior at all times.) So, Hirohito went on, he could not agree to a direct shift. Instead, as he ordered, the entire division was given a week's leave in Shanghai, to "decompress," and returned to Japan prior to the Malaya invasion.*

On November 7 Ambassadors Nomura and Kurusu called on Hull for the first time since Tojo took over as premier. Hull immediately took a strong dislike to Kurusu (he looked "deceitful," he wrote later), but continued to discuss the possibility of a U.S.-Japanese settlement. Three days later Ambassador Nomura was received by Roosevelt. On that same day, in Tokyo, Striking Force Operations Order Number One was issued, ordering all Japanese warships to complete preparations for battle by November 20 and for the Pearl Harbor strike force to assemble off the Kuriles.

Still, even though Roosevelt and Hull were certain by now that Kurusu was in Washington merely to deflect attention from battle plans, a last attempt at a compromise now took place. The two Japanese ambassadors laid their final proposals before the American president. These were pale variations of earlier proposals: Japan and the United States were not to move in any areas of Southeast Asia (but Japanese troops were to remain in French Indochina); all Japanese concessions (eventual troop withdrawals from Indochina and from China) were to be predicated on "equitable peace" in the Pacific and in the meantime the United States was to lift its embargo on oil and trade, and "refrain from actions prejudicial to peace between China and Japan."

It was the old story Hull knew so well: in return for vague promises belied by Japan's past behavior, the United States was being asked, in advance of "peace" in China and any troop withdrawals, to consent not only to the lifting of trade and oil embargoes but also to Japan's remaining a member of the Tripartite Alliance, pledged to attack the United States if Germany attacked U.S. shipping in the Atlantic. For Hull, this last series of proposals was as "clearly unacceptable" as previous ones. "The commitments we should have to make were virtually a surrender," he wrote later. On November 22 he met

---

*Private testimony from one of those involved.

Nomura and Kurusu again, hoping they might have last-minute concessions to offer. By this time Magic had decrypted a vital cable to Nomura from Tojo's new foreign minister, Shigenori Togo. No change in any deadline could be considered, it said, "for reasons beyond your ability to guess," but "if you can bring about the signing of the pertinent notes [i.e., a draft agreement on the latest proposals] we will wait until November 29. After that things are automatically going to happen."

It was now Roosevelt's turn to stage his own *gozen kaigi* equivalent with his topmost civilian and military commanders—Hull, Secretary of War Henry Stimson, Navy Secretary Frank Knox, Admiral Harold R. Stark, chief of naval operations, and General George C. Marshall, the army chief of staff. The talk was less about pursuing diplomatic negotiations with Japan than about what to do after Japan began the war. As Stimson wrote, Roosevelt told them that "we were likely to be attacked as early as next Monday [December 1], for the Japanese are notorious for making an attack without warning." From more conventional intelligence sources, Roosevelt now knew that large concentrations of Japanese ships were converging on Shanghai and embarking large numbers of troops. On November 26 Hull completed his final reply to Kurusu and Nomura—a reply he knew would be interpreted as a *fin de non-recevoir.* It proposed a nonaggression pact among all countries in Southeast Asia and Japan's withdrawal from both China and Indochina. Hull knew it would be regarded as an unacceptable ultimatum, but he had had enough. As he told Stimson, "I have washed my hands of it." American troops abroad were put on full alert, and Admiral H. E. Kimmel in Pearl Harbor was given a "war warning." But Roosevelt, and his War Council, at this stage felt that the war would begin with attacks on Malaya and the Dutch East Indies. There seems to have been no inkling that Japan had the capability to conduct a land, sea and air blitzkrieg on several fronts at the same time.

Nomura had been bitterly disappointed by Hull's note, but still urged Tojo to keep the talks open. Tojo refused. On November 29, the day "things automatically began to happen," a council of former prime ministers met with the emperor. Hirohito asked each one of them to speak his mind. The military ex-premiers were all unreservedly for immediate war; others, without openly voicing their opposition to an immediate war, countered by asking questions:

Could Japan withstand a long war? Would the food and supply situation enable Japan to carry on beyond the first few months? Former premier Mitsumasa Yonai, an ex-admiral, was the most forthright: "We must be careful," he told Hirohito, "in trying to avoid poverty, not to become bankrupt." If Hirohito was looking for a clear dissenting voice, he was disappointed: the doubting Thomases were too deferential to speak up.

It was Prince Takamatsu, the career naval officer, who nearly got Hirohito to change his mind at the very last minute: the navy's doubts, Takamatsu told Hirohito on November 30, had been stifled, but not eradicated. "The Navy," he told his older brother, "will be very pleased if a war can be avoided."

Hirohito immediately summoned Kido and asked him for advice. "What's going on?" he said. "Are they hiding something from me?"

Kido replied that if the emperor had the slightest doubt, he should once more seek out his navy minister and naval chief of staff and cross-examine them again.

That afternoon, Hirohito summoned Tojo, then the navy minister, then Nagano. His fears must have been allayed, for he told Tojo to carry on. There was no problem in the navy, the emperor told Kido later. From that day on, Hirohito's relations with Prince Takamatsu cooled considerably.

The following day, December 1, at a final *gozen kaigi,* the decision for war was taken, and December 8 (Tokyo time) confirmed as X Day. Tojo did all the talking. The emperor did not intervene, nor did he ask any questions afterward. Things had "automatically started to happen," including a final, brilliantly executed disinformation campaign.

CHAPTER SEVENTEEN

In Tokyo, diplomats and foreign correspondents alike were aware, after Cordell Hull's last note and its brutal Japanese rejection, that war was now only weeks, and perhaps days, away. President Roosevelt's main preoccupation, in the week beginning December 1, had shifted away from negotiations with Japan to thoughts of countering Japanese armed aggression in Asia, but he felt there was little he could do. He toyed with, and dismissed, the notion of a six-month truce; he also considered giving both Britain and the Netherlands government-in-exile formal assurances that if and when Japan attacked their Asian territories, the United States would enter the war on their side against Japan. But because he could not be sure of massive congressional support for such a decision, even with the United States and Japan so clearly on the brink of war, he held back, despite repeated cables from Churchill urging him to declare publicly that "any further act of aggression by Japan will lead immediately to the gravest consequences."

In this curious lull, during that last week of peace in America, correspondents could not know that the die was already cast. Admiral Yamamoto had received his coded message ("Ascend Mount Nitaka! 1208") meaning he should attack Pearl Harbor at dawn, Tokyo time, on December 8. The Japanese fleet had already left the Kuriles, leaving behind a tiny "smoke screen" of communications vessels simulating the cable traffic of the entire fleet, and was already making full speed ahead, to reach the Hawaiian coast just out of range of American reconnaissance planes, with orders to sink any ship that spotted them on their way, Japanese or foreign. *New York Times* correspondent Otto Tolischus found Ambassador Grew unusually aloof and unhelpful, unwilling to say anything that might lead to a further deterioration in U.S.-Japanese relations. Like his Japanese counterpart, Nomura, the American ambassador felt out of things, conscious that in the decisions being taken elsewhere, his advice no longer counted; as he told his staff, he wondered whether his superiors were still bothering to read his cables.

With war so near, and so inevitable, observers clutched at straws, and the principal straw, for both Tolischus in Tokyo and Matsuo Kato, Domei (Japanese news agency) correspondent in Washington, concerned the *Tatsuta Maru,* Japan's most prestigious passenger liner. For several weeks the *Tatsuta Maru* had been about to sail for the United States, but each sailing date had been postponed, and each postponement was interpreted as a further drop in the barometer of U.S.-Japanese relations. The liner was the pride of Japan's merchant shipping, a fast, ultramodern passenger vessel not nearly as big or as luxurious as the *Normandie* or the *Queen Mary* but a tribute, nevertheless, to Japanese naval architecture and engineering. It made sense for the Japanese authorities to prevent its departure, for if war broke out while it was in American territorial waters or in an American port, it would become an exceptionally valuable war prize, easily convertible into a troopship. So, when the *Japan Times and Advertiser* announced, on December 1, that the *Tatsuta Maru* would leave for Balboa (Panama) and Los Angeles on December 2, correspondents and diplomats alike breathed easier. They reckoned that war would not break out for another two or three weeks at least, time for the *Tatsuta Maru* to get to Los Angeles, pick up its Tokyo-bound passengers there, and start back on its way to Yokohama. In its cable traffic to the Japanese embassy in Washington, the Foreign Ministry advised on those Japanese groups in America to be repatriated on the *Tatsuta Maru.*

On the basis of the liner's schedule, diplomats and correspondents (and, of course, British and American military intelligence specialists as well) calculated that there would probably be no actual declaration of war on Japan's part until December 14 at least, and probably not until after Christmas. Until the very last moment, uncertainty prevailed. Would the *Tatsuta Maru* leave or not? On December 2 it *did* sail, with 151 passengers, including twenty-three American passengers and scores of first-generation Japanese immigrants from the United States, mostly on the West Coast, who had not yet acquired U.S. nationality, but had made the trip to Japan to visit relatives they sensed they would not be seeing again for a long time.

The unfortunate passengers aboard the *Tatsuta Maru,* who also included some British nationals, were to became the passive victims of a brilliant stratagem. For the *Tatsuta Maru* never *did* make it to Los Angeles, but, instead, on leaving Japan, circled the Pacific for thirteen days. On December 14, it returned to its point of departure, Yokohama, where its passengers disembarked and the British and Americans among them headed for internment, surely among America's earliest, and most forgotten, victims of Pearl Harbor.

The *Tatsuta Maru* affair was a minor example of Japanese deception, of interest because of the human element involved and because it revealed the degree of preparation and the large numbers of people involved in X Day. A far more important game, lulling Roosevelt himself into believing that the war would not come for maybe a couple of weeks at least, was played out in Washington itself: the main protagonist was Hidenori Terasaki, a brilliant Japanese diplomat who, at the time of Pearl Harbor, was Ambassador Nomura's personal assistant (and number three in the embassy pecking order, at any rate in salary terms) and has gone down in history as the one Japanese who genuinely tried to save the peace single-handed, at considerable personal risk.

Gwen Terasaki, his American wife, in her book, *A Bridge to the Sun,* has left a moving testimony of this humane, cultured, pro-Western aristocrat (later to become one of Hirohito's postwar interpreters) who entered the Japanese diplomatic service in the twenties, and whose elder brother, a former consul in New York, was head of the Japanese Foreign Ministry's America desk but resigned his post on October 18, 1941, the day after Tojo became premier.

Hers is an eloquent, understated story of an American girl falling head over heels in love with a handsome Japanese diplomat, marrying him in 1930, and devoting the rest of her life to him, overcoming the cultural differences between her own background and that of a traditional upper-class Japanese family and becoming a superbly efficient and "loyal" embassy wife in Shanghai, Havana and, eventually, Washington, without ever forgetting that she was, by birth and culture, American.

As told by Mrs. Terasaki (from her husband's talks with her, then and later), Terasaki approached Ambassador Kurusu, on November 29, and said, "Ambassador, why don't you become a 'national traitor'? Why not go ahead and tell the Americans we will get out of China? We can't remain there for long anyway, and the war party knows that."

Kurusu shrewdly turned the offer around. "How about being one yourself?" he asked. "I think we should approach the President [Roosevelt] through an intermediary, someone who has his ear, and suggest that he send a cable directly to the Emperor appealing for peace. I warn you that I have already cabled Tojo for permission to do this and been refused. Such a cable will have to be sent over Tojo's head directly to the Emperor. Of course, if your part is discovered, it may mean your death and the death of your family too. But you thought I should take such a risk and now it's your turn."

Terasaki agreed to go ahead, and arranged for a secret meeting with Chiang Kai-shek's ambassador in Washington, Dr. Hu Shih, and the man Terasaki hoped to use as intermediary—E. Stanley Jones, a well-known Methodist preacher who was a personal friend of Roosevelt's.

In a private room at the Purple Iris restaurant, they discussed the best approach to take, and decided that Jones should deliver an oral message to the president. He was to say—with the tacit blessing of the Chinese ambassador—that Ambassador Kurusu and Terasaki believed that Roosevelt should send the emperor a personal message, as a last-minute effort to stave off an otherwise inevitable war. As Terasaki told Jones at the restaurant meeting, "If the Emperor interfered, it was known the Japanese would comply, including the military"—another backhanded reminder that, despite his constitutional limitations, the emperor's powers were not quite as diluted as later experts have implied.

Jones wrote Roosevelt, asking for a meeting, and on December 3 went to the White House to see him. Jones spoke of the secret meeting in the Purple Iris restaurant. Roosevelt told Jones he had been thinking of sending such an appeal, "but I've hesitated to do so, for I didn't want to hurt the Japanese here in Washington by going over their heads to the Emperor."

Jones said his demarche came as a direct result of Japanese embassy insistence: "They asked me to ask you to send that cable, but obviously they could not let me write that, for there must be no written record since they are going over the heads of their government to the Emperor."

"That wipes my slate clean," Roosevelt replied. "I can send that cable."

Jones then advised him not to send his message through the Japanese Foreign Ministry. A previous personal cable from FDR to the emperor at the time of the *Panay* incident had never reached the palace. "Send it direct to the Emperor himself," he urged Roosevelt. "I don't know the mechanics of it but that's what they [Kurusu and Terasaki] suggest."

Roosevelt said, "Well, I'm just thinking out loud. I can't go down to the cable office and say I want to send a cable from the President of the United States to the Emperor of Japan—but I could send it to Grew. As Ambassador he has the right of audience with the Head of State and he can give it to the Emperor direct. If I don't hear for twenty-four hours—I have learnt to do some things—I'll give it to the newspapers and force a reply."

Jones asked Roosevelt never to refer to Terasaki as the instigator of the cable.

"You tell that Japanese," said Roosevelt, "that he is a brave man. No one will ever learn of his part in this from me. His secret is safe."

Terasaki's decision to approach Kurusu rather than Nomura with the proposal to get Roosevelt to send Hirohito a personal message could be explained on the grounds that the "special envoy" had more clout than the regular ambassador. It was also understandable that he should tell his wife, for they were very close, and Terasaki, at home, behaved more like an American than a traditional Japanese husband. Gwen Terasaki knew all about the Roosevelt message, and was proud that her husband was risking his career in the cause of peace. That was why, when the sudden news came of the attack on Pearl Harbor, she was bewildered as well as appalled. Her first thoughts were: What had happened to the Roosevelt message? Had the emperor actually received it?

Though she was aware of Terasaki's secret plan, there were certain things concerning her husband she did not know about and is perhaps still unaware of to this day. For instance, there is no mention in her book of Terasaki's active lobbying of the isolationist America First group or of his investigation of pro-American sentiment among Argentina's expatriate community. Nor did Terasaki tell her that he was on the urgent repatriation list cabled to Washington from the Japanese Foreign Ministry on December 5. As her book makes clear, she kept on hoping against hope, right up to December 7, that war would somehow be averted and that she and her husband would stay in Washington. From her portrayal of Hidenori Terasaki, one gets the feeling that he was himself of two minds about returning to Japan in the event of war, that he was almost tempted, at one stage, to become an early dissident, even if this meant facing treason charges.

Her book paints such a sympathetic portrait of this fearless, liberal diplomat torn between his innate patriotism and his love of America that it comes as a considerable shock to learn that Terasaki was not quite what he seemed. Whether his "liberal" sentiments were real, or were a useful cover, only he could tell us from beyond the grave. What is incontrovertible is that, for all his efforts to prevent war between Japan and the United States, he was, in fact, right up to Pearl Harbor, a senior intelligence operative rather than a straightforward diplomat.

After receiving, two days before Pearl Harbor, the list of those embassy staffers required to leave Washington urgently, Kurusu cabled back to Tokyo that he would *"greatly appreciate it if Terasaki, as organiser of our Intelligence setup"* (my italics) remained in Washington, since he was "extremely important in view of the conditions of Japanese-US negotiations."

This secret message, later decoded by Magic, throws a completely new light not just on Terasaki but on the entire Kurusu-Terasaki version of the origins of the Roosevelt message. As "head of our Intelligence setup," Terasaki could well have collaborated with Kurusu in concocting the whole thing for very different reasons. Most State Department experts later concurred that Kurusu was specially dispatched to Washington not so much to assist Nomura in trying to bring about a U.S.-Japanese solution to outstanding problems as to drag things out and mastermind a "spoiling operation," which Nomura, the bluff, honest sailor, was incapable of executing on his own, and would probably have refused to carry out if ordered to do so.

Terasaki may indeed have had genuine doubts about the outcome of a war between the United States and Japan. But he was also a senior, brilliantly effective intelligence operative, and we have only his version of his earlier talks with Kurusu. My personal feeling, after discovering the nature of his intelligence role, is that he could well have persuaded Jones to get Roosevelt to send his message to Hirohito, not to try to prevent the outbreak of war but to lull the United States into thinking (as with the *Tatsuta Maru* trip) that war wasn't quite *that* imminent. As Hirohito had himself emphasized, surprise and secrecy were all-important. In the world of intelligence, every little bit helps: Roosevelt's security threshold, as a result of his sending his message to Hirohito, may not have risen significantly. On the other hand, Japanese intelligence, almost certainly unaware of the lackadaisical conditions prevalent in the United States' defense establishment in the first place, may have seen this whole covert operation, presented as the perilous initiative of a handful of peace-minded diplomats, as an additional, admittedly minor but effective, piece of deception.

Roosevelt sent his personal, elegantly penned message to Hirohito via Grew. "Almost a century ago," it began,

> the President of the United States addressed to the Emperor of Japan a message extending an offer of friendship of the people of the United States to the people of Japan. That offer was accepted, and in the long period of unbroken peace and friendship which has followed, our respective nations, through the virtues of their peoples and the wisdom of their rulers, have prospered and have substantially helped humanity. Only in situations of extraordinary importance to our two countries need I address to Your Majesty messages on matters of state. I feel I should now so address you because of the deep and far-reaching emergency which appears to be in formation.

Developments were occurring, Roosevelt went on, "which threaten to deprive each of our nations and all humanity of the beneficial influence of the long peace between our two countries." Americans had hoped for peace, and watched the negotiations between the United States and Japan closely. They had witnessed the buildup of

Japanese forces in Indochina. Now, Roosevelt made a personal plea to Hirohito to bring about a withdrawal of those forces, to allay the fears of those people in Thailand, the Philippines, the Dutch East Indies and Malaya threatened by war. If this happened, there would be no Western interference in Asia. He ended with the reminder that both he and the emperor "have a sacred duty to restore traditional amity and prevent further death and destruction in the world."

The message, only lightly coded so that it could be dealt with quickly, left Washington at around 6:00 P.M., December 6, Washington time, just as a much longer cable, from the Japanese Foreign Ministry to its Washington embassy, began arriving on the Japanese embassy telex (transmission began around 6:30 A.M., December 6, Tokyo time). This was the text of the fourteen-part memorandum ending with a declaration of war on the United States, originally timed—or so Japanese Foreign Ministry officials later claimed—to arrive in Washington in time to be delivered at least thirty minutes before the actual attack on Pearl Harbor.

As the whole world knows, it was actually delivered *after* the attack on Pearl Harbor (no declaration of war whatever was ever issued to either the British or Netherlands governments), and the Japanese explanation has always been that slow decoding (only a handful of diplomats enjoyed the necessary security clearance to work on it) and shortage of staff competent to type the final English version of the memorandum were exclusively to blame. The emperor, as Kido told IMTFE interrogators later, was "most displeased" at the "sheer idiocy and incompetence" of the Japanese embassy officials in Washington, according to palace insiders quoted by biographer Leonard Mosley.

The testimony of Domei agency correspondent Matsuo Kato invalidates this version of events. In his book *The Lost War* Kato recalls that on December 6 the whole Japanese embassy staff attended a lengthy farewell luncheon party for one of its officials posted to Rio. The party, at the Mayflower Hotel, went on well into the afternoon, but the diplomats, including those with top security clearance, showed no particular urgency to pursue any kind of work that afternoon. By this time the bulk of the memorandum was already on the Japanese embassy telex.

After the party, Kato noted, "A correspondent for *Mainichi* and I began a game of table tennis in the [embassy] basement, while Katsuzo Okumura,* the First Secretary of the Embassy, watched. He was idle for the moment, although [as Kato learned later] he had personally been typing the first portion of the Tokyo reply." The atmosphere in the Japanese embassy was clearly relaxed, and Okumura, who spent most of the afternoon in the basement watching the table tennis, was certainly aware of the minutes ticking by. "We began to discuss whether or not the *Tatsuta Maru* . . . would arrive in America," Kato wrote. "Okumura said, 'I'll bet you a dollar she never gets here.'" Kato took him on. Later, when both were internees, awaiting repatriation to Japan, Okumura admitted he had been one of the few embassy staffers aware in advance of the Pearl Harbor attack, and had bet on a sure thing, since of course he also knew in advance of the *Tatsuta Maru* deception.

Grew did not receive Roosevelt's "triple urgent" message for another twelve hours, but actually learned of the president's move from monitored U.S. radio broadcasts long before receiving the text. Why there was a delay of some ten hours at the Japanese end of transmission has never been satisfactorily explained, except that Japanese officials later blamed "military censors," though how they could profit by censoring a coded cable is not known. The more likely explanation is that, warned by intelligence sources in Washington that Roosevelt had decided to communicate directly with Hirohito, they were determined the cable should reach him too late.

Grew, fuming at the ten-hour delay, immediately called the Foreign Ministry (it was past midnight—0300 hours, December 8, Tokyo time) to try to make an appointment with the emperor. The dapper, mustachioed Shigenori Togo, usually friendly (he had spent nearly four years in the Japanese embassy in Washington and spoke fluent English) was, this time, coldly formal. Grew insisted that the American president's message was so important he "respectfully [requested] the opportunity to deliver it to His Majesty in person at the earliest possible moment." It was out of the question to disturb the emperor so late at night, Togo countered. Besides, the Imperial Household minister would have to be consulted. There was not much likelihood of an early audience. Togo, of course, knew that the attack on Pearl

---

*Okumura would become Hirohito's chief interpreter during the U.S. occupation, and was present at the September 27, 1945, meeting with MacArthur.

Harbor was only a couple of hours away. He was embarrassed, playing for time, yet unwilling to give Grew a point-blank refusal because
this might arouse his suspicions. Grew insisted on reading the message
to him. Togo listened patiently, and fobbed Grew off by telling him
the matter would be presented to the throne at the earliest possible
opportunity.

Grew returned to the American embassy, and to bed, still hoping
against hope he might see Hirohito in person the following day. Togo
immediately drove round to the prime minister's office and found
General Tojo awake. He showed him the text of the Roosevelt message. Both men knew how futile it now was, but that diplomatic
pretenses had to be maintained. The two men decided the note contained nothing new, except, perhaps, a totally insufficient offer of
"neutralization" of Indochina. Together, they drafted a rejection in
the emperor's name, simply referring back to an earlier rejection of
American proposals, and asking Roosevelt to "kindly refer to this
reply." Tojo and Togo between them added a line about "establishment of peace in the Pacific, and consequently in the world," which
"has been the cherished desire of His Majesty." While this quick draft
was being prepared, Japanese planes were revving up on the strike-
force aircraft carriers 120 miles or so from Pearl Harbor and Japanese
submarines were edging toward the harbor.

Togo's night wasn't over: around the very time (2:45 A.M., Tokyo
time) that the air strikes were beginning on the American fleet in Pearl
Harbor, Togo was being greeted at the palace by Kido, readying
himself for an audience with Hirohito. Kido had been warned of the
Roosevelt message, and had motored from his home to the palace in
the middle of the night. In naval uniform, Hirohito received Togo
alone, listened to the text of the Roosevelt message, and approved the
draft reply, which was never delivered. Togo went back to bed for a
couple of hours of badly needed sleep. The emperor withdrew to his
war room. According to some reports, he listened in to radio traffic
with his naval ADCs to hear, from the *Nagato* (Admiral Yamamoto's
flagship commanding operations from its position just off the Hiroshima coastline), the earliest results of the raid.

It was now morning in Washington (December 7), and, ironically,
the top U.S. administration and armed forces officials with Magic
clearance now had most of the fourteen-part Japanese memorandum
on their desks, in advance of notification of war, hours before it was

to come their way officially. The first thirteen parts were simply lengthy recapitulations of past negotiations. The "sting," the actual announcement that a state of war existed between the two countries, had not yet been transmitted, and the decoding process, resumed at 10:00 A.M. inside the Japanese embassy, was still slow, possibly deliberately so. The final, fourteenth part arrived around 10:30 A.M., together with an uncoded cable, in English, telling Nomura and Kurusu to deliver the text at 1300 hours. It was this brief message that finally alerted top U.S. Navy officers, and some of General Marshall's subordinates, that Japan might be gearing up for a surprise strike on American military installations just after that time. Marshall now agreed to send a top priority warning to bases in San Francisco, the Philippines and the Panama Canal to be on the alert. A similar message could not be delivered to Hawaii because of atmospheric conditions.

At 1347 hours Navy Secretary Frank Knox received the first report of the Pearl Harbor attack. Roosevelt was informed almost immediately, and phoned Cordell Hull at 1405 hours. Ambassadors Nomura and Kurusu had at that moment arrived at the State Department and were waiting to see him, clutching their translated fourteen-part memorandum, which, by this time, thanks to Magic, Hull had already read in its entirety. At 1420 hours they were ushered in. Hull ignored their outstretched hands. The ambassadors remained standing.

Ambassador Nomura handed over the memorandum, saying he had been instructed to deliver it at 1300 hours.

"Why should it be handed over at one o'clock?" Hull asked. Nomura said he did not know. Hull scanned it, pretending he had not already learned of its contents, and then told the two envoys he had never read a document "more crowded with infamous falsehoods and distortions." As they left, Hull audibly called them "scoundrels and pissants." After returning to the Japanese embassy on Massachusetts Avenue, Kurusu and Nomura were told, by First Secretary Okamura, that Japanese planes had bombed Pearl Harbor.

Even as the attack was proceeding, elaborate security precautions against the new "enemy aliens" went into effect: the British and American embassies in Tokyo were sealed off at dawn, British and American newsmen were rounded up and taken to police stations, where some of them, including Tolischus, were brutally interrogated

for days. The war was announced to selected Japanese newsmen at
6:00 A.M. at a specially convened War Ministry press conference. At
a later briefing for foreigners, at the Foreign Ministry, Robert Guillain, the French correspondent for Havas, noted the absence of all his
British and American friends. He somewhat cheekily asked the
spokesman why they were not present, and whether the attack had
taken place before or after the declaration of war. He was rebuffed.

Inside the sealed-off U.S. embassy, Robert Fearey, a recently arrived, athletic young attaché who was Grew's personal aide, heard the
news vendors' cries outside, daringly scaled the wall and brought back
several copies of the *Japan Times and Advertiser* announcing war. They
became a collector's item: two hours after the issue went on sale, the
military police impounded all remaining copies—the paper, in its
inside pages, carried lengthy stories on the negotiations leading up to
war, and, in the eyes of the now all-powerful military censors, made
too many references to Prince Konoye's role in trying to avoid the
conflict. Since his resignation, Konoye had become something of a
nonperson.

Aboard the *Nagato,* Admiral Yamamoto asked an aide to check on
the time the declaration of war had been transmitted to the United
States. An honorable man, he had not wanted this additional deception to take place, and had assumed that the notification had come
thirty minutes before the actual attack. The emperor, too, according
to many later palace sources, was "furious" at the delay.

The emperor's wrath could be a terrible thing. The thought inevitably arises: if Hirohito felt such rage at the "idiocy and incompetence"
with which the declaration of war had been handled in Washington,
leaving an indelible stain on Japan's record as a civilized nation, what
reprisals did he order taken against the culprits? Such grave dereliction of duty should, by rights, have cost those involved their careers
at the very least. The dilatory decoders should have been shaking in
their shoes all the while they were in luxurious American detention
and in transit to Japan (ironically, on board the *Tatsuta Maru).* They
don't appear to have worried, and Kato, in his detailed, humorous
account of the months ahead, makes no reference to any apprehension
on their part.

Colonel Sackett questioned Kido on this very point in his pretrial
interrogation.

KIDO: I heard from the Emperor himself that the plans were to transmit the declaration of war first then make the attack.

SACKETT: How was it this was not done?

KIDO: I don't know why there was such a hitch.

SACKETT: Was there any investigation over the hitch? That was most unusual, wasn't it?

KIDO: I haven't heard of any.

In one of the rare IMTFE reports implicating Hirohito by name (document no. 3245, dated November 10, 1947—"Crimes to which document applicable: question of Emperor's knowledge of Pearl Harbor plans") a report submitted by the immediate postwar cabinet of Prince Higashikuni made the following points, all designed to protect Hirohito from court proceedings and minimize his personal responsibility.

The report read, in part:

> 1- We believe that the Empire was compelled to start the Great East Asia war in view of the surrounding circumstances.
> 2- That the Emperor was exceedingly anxious to conclude peacefully the negotiations between Japan and America.
> 3- That the emperor, in following the practice established in the application of the Constitution, did not reject matters decided by the Imperial Headquarters and the Government in regard to decisions for the commencement of hostilities and the carrying out of plans for operations.
> 4- That in order to make every effort to avoid making a surprise attack while negotiations were in progress, efforts were made to communicate the notifications of the discontinuation of negotiations between Japan and America. (NOTE: that since we exercised our right of self-defence in the light of the actual circumstances of the economic pressure, etc., imposed on the Empire, we are of the opinion that the provisions of the Hague Treaty pertaining to the commencement of hostilities can be nullified.)
> 5- That the Imperial Rescript for the declaration of war was of a domestic nature intended chiefly for the people of Japan.

6- That we could not deal with England and other countries separately in view of the relations existing between America and these countries at that time.

In a further outline of Hirohito's position, the document stated that "prior to the attack on Pearl Harbor, although the Emperor had heard of the outline of military operations in the initial stages from both the Army and Navy chiefs of staff, he did not receive any reports concerning the details of the operation. . . . He understood that when the above plan of operations was to be carried out, diplomatic measures would be taken towards the American Government before resorting to arms."

It's interesting, then, to contrast this statement with further pretrial cross-examination of Kido on this point. Colonel Sackett asked him how much Kido himself knew about Pearl Harbor:

KIDO: Generally, the Emperor tells me everything, but on matters of operation, the Emperor is very reserved and would not tell me everything.

SACKETT: In other words, when the War or Navy Chiefs of Staff would discuss operational questions with the Emperor, they were of such a high degree of secrecy, he normally would not tell anyone about them?

KIDO: And perhaps the Emperor thought that if he disclosed these matters to the Lord Privy Seal, I may be encumbered or may be made to regret for it [sic].

SACKETT: The Chiefs of Staff would disclose major operational questions to the Emperor even though you didn't know about them, did they not?

KIDO: There are occasions when he does talk about great problems.

SACKETT: The Emperor, no doubt, knew from the army and navy in their private conferences about this plan to attack Pearl Harbor before it took place, did he not?

KIDO: *I believe he did know about the attack on Pearl Harbor* [my italics].

And later:

SACKETT: The Emperor, no doubt, knew about these operational plans for the attack of Pearl Harbor and the actual plan to attack it long before the attack took place, did he not?

KIDO: I believe that the Emperor was informed previously because the Naval General Staff submitted directly to the Emperor the general outline of the attack.

Sackett tried hard, but without success, to get Kido to give him the earliest probable date of the emperor's knowledge of Pearl Harbor. Kido stalled and stalled; he didn't know, he said. Sackett replied he found this hard to believe.

In fact the Higashikuni document submitted to IMTFE set out to prove far too much: while the lack of advance warning was attributed to happenstance ("due to the unexpected length of time required for deciphering and organising the above telegraphic notification at the Japanese Embassy in America, the notification to the American Government was delayed"), it also advanced the "right of self-defense"—assimilating "economic pressures" (brought about by Japanese aggression in Indochina) to a kind of economic Pearl Harbor in reverse, thereby "nullifying" the terms of the Hague Treaty.

The explanation of the nondeclaration of war on Britain and the Netherlands is the least convincing of all. As a further note explained, "The situation was such that in view of the Anglo-American relations existing at that time, it was expected that the final notice to America and the exercise of military forces would be transmitted immediately from the American Government to the British Government and others."

Why was there no attempt made to communicate with Foreign Secretary Anthony Eden in London through the active Japanese embassy there? An "immediate" notification to the British embassy in Washington by Cordell Hull would still take minutes, and it would have been hours before the British forces in Malaya were informed, via London, of the impending attack, for radio communication was often hampered by atmospheric conditions, and coding and decoding took time. As it happened, of course, the first inkling of the Japanese intention to wage war on Britain came with Japanese landings at Kota

Bharu, in Malaya,* and the land invasion, via Thailand, from the north.

The real reason was, almost certainly, that by attacking Malaya without any prior notification, at roughly the same time that Japanese planes began strafing Pearl Harbor, Japanese commanders were merely implementing the imperial advice on surprise and secrecy that, as Hirohito himself had remarked earlier, were essential if the complicated, multiple-front operation was to succeed.

The question-and-answer sessions transcribed in the *Sugiyama Memorandum* reveal Hirohito's detailed knowledge of the multiple plans of attack, his equally detailed questioning and informed comments on the importance of secrecy, timing and the chronology of events to be followed in Hong Kong, Thailand and the Chinese international concessions. There are also veiled references to Pearl Harbor itself ("Isn't that a Monday?" "It all depends on the initial surprise attack"), Kido's candid admission of Hirohito's prior knowledge of Pearl Harbor and the immunity of embassy staffers in Washington who bungled the transmission of the declaration of war. In the light of all this, the Higashikuni report to IMTFE makes fairly humorous reading.

But in the history-rewriting process a new twist was added: after the war, the Methodist preacher who had been Terasaki's intermediary, E. Stanley Jones, was received in audience by Hirohito. As Gwen Terasaki wrote, Jones told Terasaki afterward that the emperor had said that "if he had received the Roosevelt telegram a day sooner he would have stopped Pearl Harbor." Apart from providing further confirmation that Hirohito was no puppet—since he himself claimed he could have called off Pearl Harbor, and was therefore less than candid with MacArthur in claiming his hands were tied from the very beginning—it was also, given Hirohito's behavior during the lengthy Pearl Harbor countdown, and his perfunctory interest in the Roosevelt text when it did arrive, the most mendacious allegation of all.

---

*Which took place an hour *before* the attack on Pearl Harbor.

CHAPTER EIGHTEEN

The impression conveyed to the outside world by members of the Imperial Household Ministry, successive Japanese governments, leading scholars and opinion makers, and, last but not least, Hirohito himself, in his frequently reiterated postwar statements on the subject, is that the war years were a perpetual nightmare and far and away the worst time of his life.

So they may have been, but only from the moment the tide began turning against Japan, as it did, decisively, from 1943 onward. The image of an anxious, guilt-racked emperor, reluctantly forced into war, deploring from the start the death and destruction wrought on innocents by troops over whom he had no control, is a carefully elaborated fiction, part of a grand design to convince the world at large that Hirohito, from first to last, bore no responsibility for the war.

Kido was to note that Hirohito did increasingly speak of his friendship with the British royal family, of the kindnesses they showed him as crown prince, and of his bitter regret at the state of war between their two nations. With tongue in cheek, perhaps, Kido observed that the worse the state of war for Japan, the more nostalgically the emperor seemed to harp on those blessed days in London and Balmoral. Immediately after promulgating the imperial rescript of the declaration of war, on December 8, 1941, Hirohito did mention to Kido how heartrending it was to have the British king as an enemy, but, after that, recollections of friendship with the royal family do not seem to have been uppermost in his mind as long as Japan was on a winning streak. One sentence in the emperor's imperial proclamation of war, eight hours after Pearl Harbor ("It has been truly unavoidable and far from Our Wishes that Our Empire has now been brought to cross swords with America and Britain") was later cited as proof that he did so reluctantly. But the war rescript also contained other flowery formulas, including the somewhat untenable claim that Japan's invasion and forcible occupation of Malaya, the Philippines, the Dutch East Indies, Hong Kong and the foreign enclaves in China were all in the cause of world peace.

Because he knew that war was a colossal gamble for which, as head of state, he would be held responsible, Hirohito may well have had inner reservations, despite the elaborate operational planning he had monitored so thoroughly. But in the heady early months of the war, as veteran correspondent Robert Guillain wrote, the whole of Japan was in a state of euphoria, celebrating her victories with wild parties and sake toasts.* The occupation of Malaya and the Dutch East Indies resulted, at least for a short while, in more food and consumer goods in the shops, loot in the form of "liberated" automobiles and radio sets from Singapore and Batavia, the Dutch East Indies' capital, along with rice and other badly needed raw materials, and nearly all Japanese were elated, proud and on an almost tangible high. As Kido's diaries show, Hirohito, far from urging caution on his commanders and aides and displaying a Cassandra-like sense of doom, shared in this euphoria, at least at first. One gets the impression, from Kido's day-to-day entries, that he wished the emperor would at times show more restraint and start asking himself questions about Japan's long-term strategy.

In the circumstances, having opted for war and declared it, Hirohito's relief at the success of the surprise attack was understandable, and it was of course his duty, as commander in chief, to congratulate his troops and his navy (which he did at regular intervals) on their major victories in the early weeks of the war.

---

*Robert Guillain, *I Saw Tokyo Burning* (London: John Murray, 1981).

But Hirohito's rejoicing went far beyond such formal responses. It was perhaps normal, in the early flush of the Pearl Harbor report on December 8, for him to tell Kido and Sugiyama: "When I heard the good news of the surprise attack, I felt the goodwill of the Gods." The emperor, Kido noted that day, was "poised and serene, and I detected not the slightest anxiety in his behavior."

When Kido congratulated Hirohito on the fall of Singapore, in mid-February, he found Hirohito in an even more elated mood. "The Emperor," he wrote, was "very cheerful," and lectured him about the excellence of the planning that had made it possible. "My dear Kido," he said, "I know I harp on this all the time, but as I've said before and will say again, it all shows the importance of advance planning. None of this would have been possible without careful preparation."

When Hirohito advised Tojo to draw up possible peace plans, as he did on February 10, 1942, these were conceived more as terms of limited surrender on the part of the Allies: from Japan's point of view, her victories entitled her to negotiate from a position of strength. Having given him these instructions, Hirohito immediately qualified them. "Of course the end of the war does not depend on ourselves alone," Hirohito told Tojo. "It also depends on the United States, Britain and how things turn out on the Eastern Front. One should not give up halfway in order to ensure access to raw materials from the South. You should think about all this and act accordingly." The peace terms Hirohito was urging his commanders to draw up in fact amounted to a virtual Allied recognition of Japan's hegemony in Asia.

The emperor's "humane" qualities do not seem to have been very noticeable at this stage. The end of the war was desirable as soon as possible, Hirohito told Tojo, not, as one might have expected, because the longer it continued, the more loss of life and suffering would ensue, but because, as he put it, "If it goes on for too long the quality of the army will inevitably be lowered"—a professional soldier's view of war, certainly, but a singularly cold-blooded one.

David Bergamini imputes to Hirohito overall responsibility for the wholesale massacre of Chinese in Malaya and Singapore, on the basis of the emperor's allusive conversation with General Sugiyama at a "liaison conference"; but there is no "smoking gun" in the form of a direct order or reported statement in either the *Sugiyama Memorandum* or the Kido diaries that might prove that Hirohito actually encouraged the atrocities that took place in Malaya and during the

Bataan death march. He did, however, follow the campaigns there closely, dispatching aides from the imperial court to both the Singapore and Philippines battlefronts. And while the infamous orders calling for massacres of wounded personnel and nurses as well as the systematic ill-treatment of POWs stemmed from Colonel Masanobu Tsuji, one of General Sugiyama's principal staff officers, who claimed to have the emperor's ear, he, like other Japanese military men, may have used his imperial connections to give orders in the emperor's name without Hirohito's specific authorization. What is certain is that when, in 1943, a detailed account of the horrors of the Bataan death march was released to the world, and was brought to Hirohito's attention by Kido, the emperor changed the subject, and never ordered an investigation into the conduct of those responsible.

Changing the subject or avoiding it altogether was Hirohito's favorite way of indicating his preferences to his generals. On February 23, 1942, he was present at a liaison conference that should have discussed an enormously important issue: the invasion of Australia. One school of thought, among military commanders, was that this was the only step that would enable Japan to win the war in the long run. Admiral Yamamoto held this view, and had also been in favor of a land invasion of Hawaii. Tojo, by nature a cautious and unimaginative general, was against it. As it happened, the subject was not raised by the emperor at all. He preferred to ask questions about the possible occupation of Portuguese-owned Timor and Japanese bank guarantees for the occupation-currency yen. The possibility of an Australian invasion was never raised again in the emperor's presence.

Whether Japanese peace, cease-fire or truce proposals had been made, there was no chance, of course, by this time, of their acceptance by either Roosevelt or Churchill. Hirohito badly underestimated the fighting mood of the United States after the humiliation, and the indignation, caused by Pearl Harbor; as for Churchill, he was preoccupied, first and foremost, with the war in Europe. After the disastrous British defeats in Malaya and in the Pacific, he was resigned, as Australian historian David Day has pointed out,* to see Japan overrun Asia—even Australia—temporarily: Japan, he felt, could be dealt with after Hitler had been crushed.

---

*David Day, *The Great Betrayal* (London: Angus and Robertson, 1988).

On March 9, 1942, three weeks after the fall of Singapore, Kido was summoned into Hirohito's presence and found him "smiling and tearful with joy." "Kido, do you realize Java has surrendered, that our troops have obtained the complete surrender of the Dutch East Indies, that Burma is ours, that Rangoon has fallen! The series of victories are too much, too fast," he exulted. The emperor, Kido wrote, "looked tremendously satisfied. I couldn't find words to congratulate him, I was so moved."

Hirohito's delight extended to his German ally's successes as well. On June 28, 1942, Hirohito told Kido that "the Germans have not only taken Tobruk but are well on the way to Egypt, having captured Sidi Barrani on the way." He wished to send a telegram of congratulation to Hitler on the fall of Tobruk, he said.

Kido said he would talk to the Imperial Household minister about this. No such telegram was sent, but only because Tsuneo Matsudaira, the Imperial Household minister, advised against it, on the grounds that Hirohito had never received a congratulatory telegram from Hitler after *his* Asian victories. It's almost certain that Matsudaira, known for his prewar Anglophilia, deliberately resisted having such a cable sent, for, in the event, he told the emperor an innocent lie: Hitler, King Umberto of Italy, and, inevitably, the craven Pu-yi, the Manchukuo puppet emperor, had all in fact dutifully cabled their fulsome congratulations to Hirohito after Pearl Harbor and the sinking of the *Repulse* and the *Prince of Wales.*

In one respect, Japan emulated her German ally without, however, going all the way. In March 1942, at another liaison conference in the emperor's presence, Japan adopted a series of measures concerning Jews on Japanese soil and in the newly occupied territories that was a pale copy of laws in force in Nazi Germany. Immigration of Jews to China, Manchuria, Japan and all occupied territories was banned; Jews already living in these areas were not arrested, but "due to the special racial characteristics of the Jews, surveillance of their residence and businesses will be intensive. At some time also their pro-enemy activities will be eliminated and suppressed." Jews "who can be useful to the Emperor (including those who can be useful for Axis nations and those not against the national Polity) will be carefully selected and given appropriate treatment." Sugiyama admitted that such actions stemmed directly from Germany's own restrictive measures ("This has forced us to take special regard for our new relationships with third countries in the treatment of Jews") but that they were in any case necessary: "If immediate and appropriate measures are not taken concerning Jews and their racial characteristics, it cannot be excluded that there will be untoward incidents in occupied areas." German Jews "will be regarded as stateless and will be kept under strict surveillance." But Sugiyama added that "to persecute Jews is not our policy and would make propaganda for the United States and Britain." The new legislation affected very few people—mostly refugees from Europe who had emigrated as far as Japan, Dutch Jews in the Dutch East Indies, Jews in the former international concessions. White Russian Jews, nearly all living in Manchuria or northern China, were already subject to appalling discrimination, not as Jews but as stateless White Russians, and potential "wooden logs" to be used in laboratory experiments.

The March 1942 measures are chiefly interesting as an example of Japanese sensitivity to German attitudes. The notion of the "emperor's Jews" probably stemmed from memories of the Russo-Japanese War of 1904–5, during which the American banking firm of Kuhn, Loeb had been Emperor Meiji's chief financial backer.

The wartime rules concerning Jews are a reminder that Japanese anti-Semitism, a phenomenon of the seventies and eighties (illustrated by a series of best-sellers blaming the U.S. "Jewish lobby" for America's alleged anti-Japanese policies) also goes back a fairly long way. Aristocratic Japanese, including Prince Konoye, often displayed the prejudices of their eighteenth-century British counterparts. The anti-Semitism of Konoye, the tolerant aesthete who admired Proust and Oscar Wilde, as his posthumous writings showed, was bound up with his fear of Communism: he saw Marxism as a "Jewish disease."

Not everyone reacted enthusiastically to Japan's victorious advance in Asia. Konoye was despondent, wrote his friend Morisada Hosokawa. "At the Peers Club, everyone around him was revelling in excitement over the success of Pearl Harbor. In a voice filled with dread and sadness, he said: 'It is a terrible thing that has happened. I know that a tragic defeat awaits us in the end. I can feel it. Our luck will not last more than two or three months at best.' "

On New Year's Day, 1942, Konoye, in semidisgrace but in his capacity as close kinsman and ex-premier, called on Hirohito to present his New Year's greetings. He later told his aide, Tomita, that "everybody at the palace was celebrating the success of Pearl Harbor.

Even Admiral Okada [the former premier, left for dead during 2/26, and later a leading "peace party" figure] was carrying on, giving toast after toast. A number of other old fellows who understand nothing at all started singing boisterously with Okada. What an unpleasant spectacle! How vulgar they are! At this rate, they will push us all the way to defeat. . . ." His outspoken antiwar remarks almost got him into serious trouble with the political police and the *kempei*. He was already under a cloud for his past friendship with a former aide, Hotsumi Ozaki, who had been a "closet Communist" for years, and the chief informant of Richard Sorge, the *Frankfurter Zeitung* correspondent in Tokyo and probably the Soviet Union's single most valuable spy.

Another leading figure who refused to join in the jubilation was Admiral Yamamoto himself. Aboard the *Nagato,* just after the attack on Pearl Harbor, there was considerable rejoicing in the messroom. "Yamamoto, alone, apparently, remained sunk in apparent depression." He also replied in subdued, prophetic terms to those fellow officers who sent him their congratulations. To Mineichi Koga, a fellow admiral, he wrote: "The mindless rejoicing at home is really deplorable."*

Dowager Empress Sadako (the late Emperor Taisho's widow) was one of the few senior members of the imperial family to take a resolutely antiwar stand, and her relations with her son Hirohito, in the early months of the war, were seriously strained as a result. She moved out of Tokyo, to Numazu, on the coast, where she had lived with Emperor Taisho during his declining years of illness. On April 17, 1942, she summoned Kido and asked him pointed questions about the events that had led to Pearl Harbor and the "subsequent expression of brute force." When Kido later related this to Hirohito during a rare, relaxed country excursion, the emperor changed the subject and lectured Kido on mushrooms.

Prince Takamatsu, reflecting the fears and unspoken apprehension of many of his fellow naval officers, was, from the start, a dove, and would, in due course, play an important if little-known role in edging Japan toward peace. But Prince Mikasa was, at least at first, a willing "public relations" figurehead, deputizing for Hirohito on morale-boosting visits to the front. On May 8, in Manila, in a ceremony

---

*Hiroyuki Agawa, *The Reluctant Admiral* (New York: Kodansha, 1982).

organized by the victorious Japanese troops, he watched American POWs march through the Manila streets on their way to detention. Empress Nagako—for all the later image-building—was a hawk rather than a dove in the early days of the war. She did not share Hirohito's once-close relationship with the British royal family, and was convinced, even after Hirohito himself had ceased believing in an Axis victory, that Hitler would win the war. One entry in the Kido diaries tells of the former Japanese ambassador in London being brought specially to the palace to lecture the empress on the fortitude of the British people during the battle of Britain and the bombing that followed, in an effort to convince her that the Axis propaganda then at its peak in Japan had to be treated with circumspection.

The first telltale signs that the war would not be the hoped-for quick romp followed by negotiations acceptable to Japan came with the first air raid on Tokyo, Yokohama, Nagoya and Kobe by B-25 bombers led by Lieutenant Colonel James H. Doolittle on April 18, 1942. This hazardous operation was strictly for badly needed American morale-raising purposes, for little damage was done, but the impact on Japan's ruling elite was considerable. The planes, originally lifted by cranes onto the *Hornet,* took off in choppy seas 650 miles from their target. The army fliers had never before operated from an aircraft carrier, and every successful lift-off was a miracle.

After dropping their bombs, some from treetop level, the sixteen planes were due to land in friendly Kuomintang-controlled China, but some, short of fuel, crash-landed in Japanese-occupied China, and one plane landed in Soviet territory, near Vladivostok, where its crew was temporarily interned. Eight crewmen were captured by the enemy, and—to Japan's lasting shame—tried as "terrorists." Though Hirohito commuted five death sentences, he must take responsibility for the three remaining executions; Sugiyama had demanded "severe punishment" and, after a farcical court-martial (preceded by extensive torture), the death penalty for all eight of them. They were not the only captured aircrews to suffer this fate—similar executions occurred throughout 1943 and 1944.

On this occasion, Tojo did his best to get the sentences commuted, and five were. As he was to tell the IMTFE court after the war, he discussed the case of the downed fliers with Hirohito, and asked the emperor to commute the death sentences. The commutation, Tojo told the court, "was the Emperor's because of the fact

that the Emperor is invariably benevolent." At the trial, all defendants, at almost all times, did their utmost to protect the emperor, and
no one was more protective than Tojo, but it was clear, both in his
pretrial cross-examination and at the trial itself, that Tojo had argued
against the execution of any of the downed airmen, and that the
emperor had not shared his views. Had Hirohito been a little more
"benevolent," he could easily have commuted the death sentences
of the remaining three Americans without a murmur from
Sugiyama. The inference is that he did not wish to do so.

American reactions to the downed crewmen's deaths, and to the
news of the Bataan death march and other atrocities that followed the
1941–42 Japanese blitzkrieg, were partly responsible for the ensuing
stream of Allied anti-Hirohito propaganda, identifying him, along
with Hitler and Mussolini, as one of the "three most hated men in the
world." Ironically, among those who resented the decision to execute
the downed American fliers were the Germans, who regarded this as
an embarrassing precedent that might affect the morale of their own
bomber crews.

The Doolittle raid was a bitter personal defeat for Admiral
Yamamoto, but it was also a matter of considerable concern for Tojo
himself, proving that the emperor himself was not immune from
possible retribution from the air. An elaborate military parade was
about to be staged for the emperor's forty-second birthday (April 29,
1942) and many top-level meetings took place to debate whether to
cancel it and what to do if an air raid warning went off while it was
in progress. The generals and court officials argued endlessly; finally,
it was decided that the parade should go ahead as planned ("for if it
is known that the Emperor stays away from the parade because of an
air raid this would be shameful," Kido wrote), but that if an air raid
warning sounded immediately before he was due to appear outside he
was not to leave the palace.

By the fall of Tobruk, in fact, the tides of war had already changed,
for, that same June, Japan lost the battle of Midway, though the
implications of this defeat were not understood for some time. Admiral Yamamoto, who had gambled so successfully on Pearl Harbor,
wanted to strike a further decisive blow against the United States
Navy. This time he lost, partly because his operation was ill conceived,
partly because skilled U.S. cryptanalysts had broken the Japanese

naval code, so that the U.S. Navy knew exactly where his fleet was heading, and in what formations. At the battle of Midway, Japan lost four aircraft carriers, one heavy cruiser and the pride of her naval air pilots, to the American loss of one aircraft carrier and one destroyer. The Japanese did land troops on the islands of Attu and Kiska, and still showed their superiority in the air (U.S. dive-bombers destroyed the enemy aircraft carriers while their planes were on deck being rearmed) but never again would Japanese ships attempt to score a major "classic" sea victory—henceforth their naval war was to be a war of attrition, or, eventually, of kamikaze strikes on a huge scale. Not the least blow to Japan was the loss of one of its famed Zero planes, which crash-landed almost intact on a U.S.-held atoll. U.S. specialists took it apart, and as a result, American pilots were to fly the Hellcat, superior to the Zero, in the later stages of the war. The fears of the cautious minority within the Japanese naval staff were proving correct, but for many months the Japanese public was lulled into believing that Midway had in fact been a victory.

Hirohito was aware of the truth, but probably not of its implications, and he reacted like a warrior king faced with a minor, temporary setback. "It's really regrettable, it's a shame," he told Kido, "but I've given orders to the Chiefs of Staff to be careful not to lose our sense of combativity, not to become passive as far as operations are concerned." Hirohito's behavior on this occasion, Kido noted, was "worthy of that of a great leader . . . I see in His Majesty's reaction the glittering quality of an Emperor and I am overwhelmed by my feeling for the Japanese Empire." Hirohito also showed that he approved the way the Midway defeat was camouflaged for propaganda purposes into a Japanese victory, even asking Kido whether, to give the "official" version more credence, he should not issue an imperial rescript praising the Midway "victors." Kido advised him against it, and Hirohito followed his advice.

The Midway defeat, followed by U.S. combined offensives in the Solomon Islands and at Guadalcanal, had immediate repercussions: army and navy chiefs started squabbling over available resources, especially planes, and Hirohito found himself increasingly forced to arbitrate between the two services. Congratulatory messages to the imperial forces became more restrained, and diminished in number. But as the U.S. counteroffensive gathered strength in the Pacific, and

long after most of the Japanese government and military elite had
tired of Tojo's increasingly high-handed ways, Hirohito continued to
pin his faith on him.

The strains became personal ones: the emperor, as in the crucial
stages of the China war in 1937–38, gave up his weekend visits to his
palace laboratory, his early morning horseback riding, and, as food
shortages increased, his English-style breakfasts, reverting to soups
and coarse rice to set an example to his people. A year after Pearl
Harbor the euphoria was gone. Early in 1943 Buna, in New Guinea,
was lost, partly because of insufficient sea transport for Japanese reinforcements. Hirohito praised the fighting qualities of the troops de-
fending New Guinea and noted that the Buna battle "must be rated
a failure but if this can be the basis for future success it may turn out
to have been a salutary lesson." He showed a considerable grasp of
detail about the fighting there. "I understand the enemy used twelve
or more tanks. Don't we have any tanks in this area?"

By the end of 1943 U.S. forces had reoccupied the Solomon Islands
and Guadalcanal, after long and bloody battles.

In a letter to Kido in 1943, Admiral Yamamoto aptly compared the
war to unequally matched sumo wrestlers. "Instead of waiting for the
usual limbering-up ceremonial exercises, the little chap attacked and
almost pushed the big fellow out of the ring, while the audience
cheered this clean, direct, bold approach." But the heavyweight champion had "staggered back from the brink of disaster, planted his feet
firmly on the ground and slowly come forward again. Now (in 1943)
he faces the small wrestler in mid-ring. From now on we are in a real
power struggle when reactions, training and technique will count for
everything. The perseverance of the last five minutes will decide the
game." Perhaps, knowing Hirohito's passion for sumo wrestling,
Yamamoto was trying, through Kido, to convey the hopelessness of
the situation.

But Yamamoto never did see the end of the game, for shortly
afterward, as he had predicted, he was killed in battle, though not
aboard his beloved *Nagato*. From his land headquarters in Rabaul, he
decided to fly to Bougainville on April 18, 1943, to boost the morale
of young navy fliers there who had been making repeated sorties
against Allied shipping. United States cryptanalysts decoded his flight
plan and detailed itinerary. A sophisticated operation was mounted to

blast him out of the skies. Because U.S. field commanders felt this was tantamount to a cold-blooded assassination, and might also lead the Japanese High Command to suspect its codes had been broken, approval was sought at the highest level. Roosevelt gave it without compunction, and a daring long-range P-38 raid was organized. At dawn on April 18, eighteen Lightnings converged on the admiral's plane, with its nine Zero escorts, shortly after its takeoff, and shot it down. When Yamamoto's body was finally recovered in the depths of the jungle, it was found that he had died instantly from a bullet in the face.

He may have had both a premonition of death and a secret longing for it, for he was known to be saddened beyond belief by the huge losses in his elite corps of naval air arm flyers, all of them handpicked, man for man probably the very best pilots of World War II. Among his personal effects, a poem, in his superb calligraphy, was found, which Kido was later shown and almost certainly handed over to Hirohito. It read:

> *So many are dead.*
> *I cannot face the Emperor.*
> *No words for the families.*
> *But I will drive deep*
> *Into the enemy camp.*
> *Wait, young dead soldiers,*
> *I will fight farewell*
> *And follow you soon.*

His death led to a further drop in navy morale, though his state funeral, on June 5 (on the ninth anniversary, to the day, of that of Admiral Togo, the hero of the 1905 Russo-Japanese War) became yet another occasion for military pageantry (of the kind Yamamoto hated) and a propaganda exercise on the virtues of self-sacrifice, with senior representatives of the emperor, empress and Dowager Empress Sadako in attendance. (Kido attended on the emperor's behalf: protocol banned the imperial family from attending any funeral ceremonies in person, except those of their immediate kith and kin). Yamamoto's real loves, the three geishas with whom he had kept up a detailed correspondence from the start of the war, were excluded from the official ceremony. They regarded themselves, however, as his real family, and their grief was in sharp contrast to the dry-eyed self-control displayed by his stern, poker-faced widow.

The fighting on Attu in the Aleutians, in May 1943, ending in a kamikazelike final sortie of its 2,500-man garrison, all of whom were killed, was parlayed by Japanese military propagandists into a heroic episode illustrating the traditional Japanese virtues of courage and self-sacrifice in the emperor's name. But by now Hirohito was openly blaming his chiefs of staff for their failure to bring about a single clear-cut victory. He warned them to be more conscious of the United States military tendency to cut off Japanese lines of retreat. "You should not forget about this."

Three days after Admiral Yamamoto's funeral (on June 8, 1943), in a postmortem on the fighting at Attu, Hirohito told his chiefs of staff this kind of strategy was "regrettable. I wonder whether the Army and the Navy are really cooperating." He came back to the same subject two days later: "You make all sorts of excuses like thick fog and so on, but this should have been taken into consideration beforehand. I wonder if the Army and the Navy talk to each other at all? . . . We can't win with this kind of lack of cooperation. If we go on fighting like this we will only make China rejoice, confuse neutrals, dismay our allies and weaken the Co-Prosperity Sphere. Isn't there any way, somehow, somewhere, of closing in on a United States force and destroying it?"

Shortly afterward, Tojo visited the Solomon Islands theater of operations, with a personal message from Hirohito to the field commanders. Despite the emperor's understanding of Tojo's difficulties, Hirohito spoke to him harshly: "You keep saying the Imperial Army is invincible, but whenever the enemy lands, you lose the fight. You have never been able to repulse an enemy landing. If we don't stop them somewhere, where, I ask you, will it all end?"

Two months later his impatience reached new levels. "When will you start hitting the enemy on all fronts?" he asked his chiefs of staff. "Can't we at least have one spectacular success against the United States? We can't go on retreating like this." Hirohito also asked Sugiyama detailed questions about the impact on Germany of the Allied landings in Sicily: Did this mean that Italy would pull out of the war, and out of the Tripartite Alliance? Did Germany have sufficient resources to send reinforcements to Italy? How would the loss

of Italy affect German oil supplies from Rumania? On September 8,
1943, the emperor's worst fears about Italy were realized, for it pulled
out of the war. The Tripartite Alliance was now reduced to two
partners, each in parlous shape.

Hirohito was becoming more and more irritated by Sugiyama, and
alarmed by Admiral Nagano's increasing fatalism. But despite his
frequent outbursts, he still trusted Tojo, who was as determined as
ever, and now reassured the emperor that the interservice squabbles
were "small misunderstandings" that wouldn't seriously affect the
outcome of the war. But the problems wouldn't go away: the chiefs
of staff requested 40,000 planes, then upped the figure to 52,000.
After endless arguments, the army agreed to take 27,000 and the navy
25,000, but only after Prince Takamatsu had been specially briefed
by senior navy staff officers to present the navy's needs to the emperor.
In the event, they had to settle for far less, for in the next year (1944)
only 28,000 planes were built.

To use Japanese manpower more effectively in conquered territories, turn passive garrison troops into fighting units on the Pacific and
Burma fronts, and give substance to the Co-Prosperity Sphere, some
of the Asian colonies occupied by Japan had been granted independent status under suitably docile or pro-Japanese politicians. Dr. Ba
Maw became head of state of an independent Burma on August 1,
1943; under José Laurel, the Philippines became an independent
Japanese "client" in October of that same year. On November 5,
1943, a gathering of Co-Prosperity Sphere leaders met in pomp in
Tokyo to discuss further steps toward Asian unity and attend a banquet in Hirohito's presence.

A group photograph of them, with Tojo in the center, is dismal
proof of Japan's growing isolation: Wang Ching-wei, the overweight
Chinese puppet, who was to die of cancer a year later; Pu-yi's representative, Chang Chung-hui, a shady ex-businessman with drug connections; a Thai prince; President Laurel of the Philippines; Burma's
Ba Maw and—as "observer"—the Indian National Army's Subhas
Chandra Bhose completed the group.* None of those present could

---

*The INA was raised by Bhose from Indian POWs captured in Malaya. At its peak,
it was over a hundred thousand strong, but, like the BNA (Burmese National Army),
was dependent on dwindling Japanese weapons and supplies.

help Japan with her growing difficulties, and most of them were dependent on Japanese generosity for their continued existence. The one credible collaborator, Indonesian nationalist leader Sukarno, was uninvited, because Japanese policies toward the Dutch East Indies were as yet unclear: this rich colony was Japan's lifeline for oil and other raw materials, and Tojo was not about to grant the maverick Indonesian nationalist leader independent status, not, at least, at that point.

By January 1944 not only Konoye but a substantial part of the Imperial General Staff, including most of the navy, were aware that Japan had lost the war. U.S. troops landed in the Marshall Islands; a huge air attack on Japan's big naval base in Truk further depleted its fighting capacities. Tojo worked round the clock; the military machine was no longer reacting obediently to his commands, but instead of perceiving the underlying causes for this failure, Tojo's reaction was to try to concentrate more and more power in his own hands.

It was scarcely a new phenomenon: as early as September 1942, when Japan was still in full control of the Pacific, Tojo had advocated the establishment of a Great East Asia Ministry under army control to run the newly occupied territories along standardized military lines. Foreign Minister Togo saw this as a major erosion of his own powers and objected. Because Hirohito felt that Tojo was far more essential to the war effort than Togo, he sided with Tojo in this cabinet crisis, and, using Navy Minister Shigetaro Shimada (a Tojo stooge) as an intermediary, obtained Togo's resignation. Tojo added the Foreign Ministry to his other jobs (he had, in the meantime, given up the Home Ministry), but this was still not enough. As prime minister, war minister and now foreign minister, Tojo was experiencing—from the civilian end—the frustration of dealing with the military, who still saw themselves as a separate entity, their bonds to each other far more important than their loyalties to the government, even a government headed by a lifelong professional soldier.

Tojo's brisk "can do" approach to problems was that of a clean-living workaholic whose philosophy was more suited to simple army life than to complicated diplomatic and political realities. Even when it became clear to others that Japan's war-production economy was hopelessly faltering, he continued to believe that longer working hours, leaner rations and mobilization of women (and later children) would lead to a turnaround; faced with the problem of the unresponsiveness of the military, he took the simplistic line that by assuming the functions of army chief of staff, in addition to his other duties, he would cut through red tape, compel the army to obey, and institute a new pattern of working relations between the cabinet and the services. Long after Konoye, Kido and the emperor's dovish brother Takamatsu were convinced that Prime Minister Tojo's leadership and conduct of the war was disastrous, and military defeat inevitable, Hirohito still had faith in him. He was impressed by Tojo's "unflappable" qualities, his spirit of quiet, dogged determination. Also, unlike most top army and navy commanders, Tojo gave the impression of speaking frankly, of taking the emperor into his confidence. For all these reasons, the emperor was prepared to allow Tojo to break with tradition and assume the additional burden of being army chief of staff. He was by now (January 1944) completely disillusioned with Sugiyama—whose forecasts had turned out so wide of the mark—and anticipated no problems.

Sugiyama, however, proved reluctant to leave. "I've heard His Imperial Majesty has already decided to sanction [this] change," he said. "It's a grave matter affecting not only the military but the entire nation. If His Majesty has decided, I have no more to say, but even so, I wish His Majesty would make clear this is a special case for the present circumstances only and will not become routine."

What finally destroyed Tojo, however, was a combination of military disasters and the emergence of a powerful cabal of former politicians and elder statesmen, working hard behind the scenes to extricate Japan from the appalling mess brought about by the war. Kido, a pivotal power broker, was won round to their cause; by January 1944 they were already looking beyond the end of the war to the new postwar Japan. To some it was inconceivable that Hirohito should remain on the throne, but all were determined, as their top priority, to preserve the "emperor system," with or without him.

CHAPTER NINETEEN

Discreet blueprints to end the war had been in existence ever since Pearl Harbor. Only six days after the battle of Midway, Shigeru Yoshida, the former ambassador to the Court of St. James's (and, in earlier days, the young diplomat who had boarded Hirohito's flagship in 1921 at Gibraltar to bring him details of his British schedule during his extended trip to Europe), had submitted a brief to Kido proposing that he and Konoye discreetly leave for Europe, establish a base in Switzerland, and sound out belligerents and neutrals alike on the chances of a settlement. Kido felt the time was not yet ripe, and did nothing to encourage Yoshida's proposal; there is no record, in his diaries, of his referring it to the emperor.

In February 1943, with the war situation deteriorating rapidly, Konoye, still in semidisgrace, met Kido in the home of the Lord Privy Seal's confidential secretary, Yasumasa Matsudaira, and urged him to get the emperor to end the war as soon as possible, arguing that if it went on for much longer, Japan would fall prey to Communism. The following March Kido saw Yoshida again. The diplomat was still idle, because of his lukewarm sentiments toward the war, and once more Kido and he talked of possible peace scenarios. Once more, there is no evidence that Hirohito was kept informed.

But by 1944, when Japanese naval, air and ground losses started to become horrendous, a hard core of prominent politicians and commanders began trying to shape long-term peace policies. Their motivations were various: some, like Princes Fushimi and Higashikuni, were consumed with hatred for the upstart Tojo, who had dared to break with military tradition and concentrate operational military power as well as cabinet responsibilities into his own hands; others, like Prince Takamatsu, reflected the growing demoralization of the navy, which had no confidence in its mediocre navy minister, Shigetaro Shimada, the Tojo crony who had become Tojo's navy counterpart, cumulating the jobs of navy minister and naval chief of staff.

Others, like the ex-premiers Okada and Hiranuma (the latter once a hard-liner), had long since abandoned thoughts of victory, and hoped for an honorable peace short of unconditional surrender. All, especially the princes, were concerned about the survival of the "emperor system," and realized that with mounting casualties, shortages of all kinds, and the piecemeal loss of all of Japan's conquests, the tide could very well turn against Hirohito himself.

By 1944 the secret police began reporting growing animosity against Tojo, who, having assumed so many positions of responsibility, was being blamed for everything. But they also noted that the emperor was beginning to be blamed as the person who had made him premier and allowed him to take on so many different responsibilities. Even the cautious Kido noted in his diaries that if Hirohito continued to trust him, hatred concentrated on Tojo could well spill over and extend to the emperor as well, and this had to be avoided at all costs. As early as January 1944, Konoye and Higashikuni, both princes with a huge stake in the emperor system, met secretly in Tokyo to discuss how to preserve it in the increasingly likely event of Japan losing the war.

The denouement came with the U.S. attack on Saipan beginning June 15, 1944. Saipan was not like the Gilbert Islands, Tarawa, Kwajalein and Eniwetok, all now occupied by the United States after bitter fighting. It wasn't just another Pacific island conquered by Japanese troops in the wake of Pearl Harbor but the first integral part of Japan to be invaded, a former German colony, part of the territories assigned to Japan after World War I, with over ten thousand Japanese civilians living there in addition to a large Japanese garrison. Tojo insisted that Saipan was impregnable—the killing zone that would compel the United States to reconsider any further plans for confrontation on land—but for Japan's small elite, aware of the disastrous erosion of Japanese ships and planes, and the huge imbalance between dwindling Japanese war production and the enormous American production capacity, there was no doubt that Saipan would eventually be overrun. Thereafter, as Prince Konoye was among the first to note, the war would take on a completely different character, for from Saipan America's B-29 bombers would be within striking distance of most of Japan's major cities, and the round-the-clock bombing of Japan, as Admiral Yamamoto himself had predicted, would almost certainly begin.

Tojo had put his faith in Saipan's 32,000-strong army garrison and interlocking networks of underground bunkers, immune to shells, and the protective screen of what remained of Japan's Combined Fleet. But the U.S. task force included one hundred thousand men, seven battleships, fifteen aircraft carriers, twenty-one cruisers, sixty-nine destroyers and nearly one thousand aircraft. By the time Saipan fell, three and a half weeks later (July 9), Japanese military deaths totaled nearly thirty thousand plus at least ten thousand civilians, all but thirty-five of its 475 combat aircraft had been shot down, and its Combined Fleet largely destroyed.

Seven days after the start of the battle for Saipan, imperial approval was given for the development of the first piloted one-way "flying bomb" prototype design, later the standard vehicle for kamikaze pilots. Orders were also drawn up in the palace to be relayed to the governor of Saipan, promising that all civilians who died there would achieve the same glorious status as soldiers who died in battle. This ambiguous imperial message, which could be—and was—interpreted as a call for self-immolation as an alternative to falling into American hands, was not at first relayed to the Saipan authorities, and, as Tojo told IMTFE interrogators later, he tried to have it stopped. But it *was* sent, on whose responsibility no one knows to this day: the emperor was certainly unaware of its contents, some say. But imperial messages of this kind were not easily faked, or slipped through the highly efficient, fussy court bureaucracy against the emperor's will or even without his knowledge. Whoever was responsible, thousands of civilians—men, women and children—were, as a result, to throw themselves from cliffs into the shark-ridden sea in the closing stages of the

battle rather than surrender. Shocked U.S. marines filmed the unbe-
lievable mass suicide from afar. When I visited Saipan, over twenty
years later, the same sharks, or their offspring, still circled the sea at
the exact point where Japanese civilians had deliberately plunged to
their deaths, waiting for the unlikely recurrence of such a bonanza.

Frightful though they were, casualties on both sides might have
been even higher, for Unit 731's commander, General Ishii, intended, for the first time, to launch his plague-ridden fleas on the
American attackers. The only reason this did not happen was that the
Japanese ship taking the Unit 731 squad and their lethal cargo to
Saipan at the start of the operations was sunk by an American submarine with the loss of nearly all hands.

While the battle for Saipan was raging, a different kind of contest
was taking place in Tokyo, behind Hirohito's back. Prince Higashikuni was the first to get the news: a Tojo emissary came to see him
on June 20 to say that Tojo no longer felt he had the emperor's
confidence and was no longer sure that he could lead Japan to victory—he was thinking of resigning. Two days later (June 22) Konoye
and Higashikuni met secretly in the house of a mutual friend, a prominent businessman, and Higashikuni relayed the news to him. He
added that he had advised Tojo to stay on. The Machiavellian Higashikuni explained: the important issue was not Tojo's future but the
preservation of the emperor system, and how to prevent Hirohito
from becoming responsible for everything that had happened in the
last four years. If Tojo were to stay on, in a worsening war situation,
he would become a convenient scapegoat, "like Hitler," and could be
blamed for everything. If the government were to be reshuffled,
responsibilities would be diluted and those of the imperial family
would be increased.

Konoye may have appreciated Higashikuni's ruthlessness, but made
the point that, sooner or later, a new government would have to
emerge, and that, to steer Japan out of the war, it was essential for it
to be headed by a member of the imperial family. Only a prince
closely related to the emperor would have sufficient authority over the
military and the people. Higashikuni said that if such a time came (as
it did, thirteen months later), he would not shirk such a responsibility.

By this time the views of the cautious Kido were slowly drawing
closer to those of the two princes. Two days later it was Kido's turn
to meet with Konoye, this time in Konoye's house, in the presence

of his wife, to discuss "family matters," including the forthcoming marriage of Kido's son. Interestingly, this was one of the rare occasions when Kido failed to note in his diaries, the details of their conversation, and simply recorded that "family matters" were discussed. A résumé appears only in Konoye's diary, later expanded into a posthumous memoir. The reason is not hard to seek: the substance of their talk was so out of character, and so devious, that Kido could not bring himself to put it down on paper, even in his private diary. In Konoye's version of events, Kido agreed in principle to a "princely" premier but wondered whether such a new government should not be ushered in *before* the end of the war. He also stated that when the end of the war came, it would be necessary for Hirohito to assume full responsibility for everything, to avoid humiliating mutual recriminations and buck-passing between army, navy and government leaders. This view was not, at first, shared by either Konoye or Higashikuni. In the months that followed, they were to change their minds several times, before coming to the conclusion that for the good of the dynasty the emperor must at all costs be protected from the consequences of his actions.

Two days later (June 26, 1944) the plot thickened: Prince Takamatsu, because of his top navy connections, knew just how desperate things were. Now an organic link was established between him and Konoye, again behind Hirohito's back, thanks to a mutual friend and go-between, Morisada Hosokawa, one of Konoye's former aides who also worked as a political contact for Takamatsu. Hosokawa relayed to Konoye, on June 26, an alternative plan for ending the war, which, he said, had Kido's approval: Tojo should remain premier until the next major military calamity, at which point a new government should be appointed that would change course completely, with a princely figure at its head, and this government should negotiate the best possible peace terms.

Two other prominent politicians, the former premiers Okada and Hiranuma, also contacted Konoye during the course of the Saipan fighting, also telling him that Tojo must go.

No longer a pariah, Konoye decided to relay the thoughts of this small group to the emperor, which he did through Kido's private secretary. He also drafted an up-to-date position paper destined for Hirohito himself, which he handed over to Kido. It was an extraordinary document: had Hirohito taken it seriously, the end of the war might have come far earlier, sparing millions of Japanese lives.

Konoye began by stating that the war situation was so hopelessly compromised that some form of surrender was necessary, but that no one in the emperor's circle, or in the army or navy, had the guts to say so. The emperor should extract the truth from his chiefs of staff, Tojo and Shimada, and request answers, in writing, to the following questions: How bad was the war situation generally? How did the chiefs of staff envisage the future conduct of operations? What were their plans?

Cornered in this way, Konoye went on, Tojo would react in one of three ways: he would either resign on the spot, or ask Hirohito to decide for him, or else reply in deliberately vague terms. In the third alternative, he should not be allowed to get away with it, but should be compelled to resign.

Should Tojo resign, Konoye added, the next premier ought to be a member of the imperial family (Takamatsu, he felt, was the most suitable candidate) and this new government should proclaim the end of the war.

There were different ways of rationalizing this decision vis-à-vis the outside world, Konoye then wrote. One was to explain the end of the war on humanitarian grounds; another was to claim that Japan's objectives had been achieved and Western "encirclement" ended; the third alternative was for the emperor to announce the end of the war on the grounds that he could no longer stand idly by witnessing the useless sufferings and sacrifices of his people. Since the first two options were too laughable to be believed, only one credible course of action remained. By proclaiming an end to needless suffering, Konoye wrote, the emperor would reaffirm his links with the people. The earlier this happened the better. Japan should not be forced into unconditional surrender, Konoye added, for the emperor system had to be protected at all costs. It's noteworthy that in Hirohito's historic radio speech announcing the end of the war, recorded on August 14, 1945, some of the language and vocabulary of this part of Konoye's report is incorporated almost verbatim.

On July 4, as the Saipan campaign was nearing its horrendous end, Kido relayed a message to Konoye. He agreed with most but not all of his proposals. On July 8 Kido and Konoye met secretly: Kido told

Konoye that it looked as if the army and navy were determined to carry on with the war regardless of casualties and sacrifices. This made it imperative to get rid of Tojo. The next government could be a transitional one, headed by a reliable general (Kido suggested Hisa-ichi Terauchi), and then a princely government could take over to end the war. Kido favored Higashikuni over Takamatsu, for he was aware of the extent of bad blood between Hirohito and his younger brother.

Kido and Konoye then returned to the question of the emperor's responsibility: as in his earlier "family affairs" meeting, Kido stressed that Hirohito should take full responsibility for everything. This meant it would probably be necessary for him to resign. The crown prince could be proclaimed emperor, with a regent exercising interim control. (Prince Chichibu by this time was seriously ill with tuberculosis, from which he would die in 1953, and was out of the running.) Kido still had second thoughts about the suitability of Takamatsu, aware of the tensions between the two brothers.

During and after the battle for Saipan, prominent princely relatives in the army and navy (among them Higashikuni, Asaka, Mikasa, Fushimi and Prince Kaya) all started meeting and debating the best way of ending the war, and Hirohito eventually became aware of their comings and goings, and their frequent, supposedly secret meetings. Possibly his informant was Prince Mikasa, the youngest brother, who was more hawkish than either Takamatsu or Chichibu, and who had already informed on a group of army officers plotting the assassination of Tojo.

Hirohito was furious. This was intolerable, "irresponsible behavior" on the part of relatives who had no call to meddle in the affairs of state. Hirohito was particularly incensed by the outspoken views of his younger brother Prince Takamatsu. Kaya, a cousin of Hirohito's, reported that Hirohito got "very excited" whenever Takamatsu talked to the emperor frankly, so much so, Kaya said, that he couldn't envisage helping Hirohito if he persisted in this attitude, and threatened to resign his princely status altogether, formally opting out of the imperial family to become a commoner. Only Prince Higashikuni's talent as a peacemaker prevented this from happening.

On July 13, after a stormy meeting with Kido, Tojo was compelled to give up his army chief of staff "hat," and also forced to oust Shimada as both navy minister and naval chief of staff. He agreed to broaden his government to bring in prominent ex-ministers who were known to be in favor of negotiations, but the ministers refused to serve under Tojo.

On July 18, partly as a result of the cabal against him, and his consequent loss of face, and partly because of the Saipan disaster, Tojo resigned the premiership, but attempted to stay on, briefly, as army minister. A meeting of former prime ministers debated the problem of who should succeed him. General Terauchi was their first choice, General Kuniaki Koiso their second, General Shunroku Hata the third. Kido pointed out to Hirohito that Terauchi (the G.O.C. in C., Southern Regions) would need GHQ's permission to return to Tokyo. Hirohito, still apparently under Tojo's spell, even though he was resigned to the general's stepping down as premier, consulted him about the advisability of recalling Terauchi from operational duties on a highly sensitive, major "front," and Tojo said this was out of the question.

Next to be considered was Koiso, a somewhat colorless personality despite his army nickname, "the Tiger of Korea," about whom Konoye now had second thoughts. Why not, Konoye suggested to Kido, have a two-pronged government, with another senior officer, Admiral Mitsumasa Yonai, assuming an important role? Yonai was a dove, and would be useful to the "peace party." Hirohito agreed. But though this new government was more inclined toward peace than Tojo's, it was not able to get peace negotiations going, and the emperor still showed no sign of wanting to initiate the peace proceedings urged on him by Konoye, or indeed to put out feelers of any kind. Hard-liners still had responsible positions; though Tojo was also compelled against his will to resign as war minister, his replacement was none other than the discredited "toilet door" General Sugiyama, the man who, as chief of staff, had promised Hirohito victory within a year, and who had requested the execution of the downed U.S. airmen after the first Doolittle raid. Hirohito still clearly hoped for the dramatic victorious engagement that might be hailed as the turning of the tide. In March, 1944, the likeliest place where this might have happened was Burma. For this reason, all available Japanese war correspondents were sent to the Burma front to report in suitably glowing terms on the expected fall of beleaguered Kohima and Imphal. But the heroism of British and Indian troops as well as decisive British air power and airlift capability denied Japan this consolation. By July the siege was over: the newsmen were withdrawn long before that.

These were grim but not yet desperate summer months for
Hirohito, for the raids over Tokyo did not materialize as fast as
Konoye had expected, and when they did, damage at first was slight.
As Robert Guillain noted, it wasn't until November 1, 1944, that
the B-29s first appeared on a major scale, and then only on photo-
graphic reconnaissance. By this time students and schoolboys, mobi-
lized as civil defense workers, had cut fire lanes through Tokyo's
jumble of wooden houses to prevent fires from spreading. But despite Admiral Yamamoto's earlier, dire warnings, the Japanese authorities seriously underestimated the threat of incendiary bombs.
As Guillain put it, at this time "air raid warnings were obviously still
considered devices for controlling the population and stimulating its
morale. No thought seems to have been given to the danger involved." Schoolchildren and old people were evacuated; young
Prince Akihito would, later, be among those taken to the safety of
the mountains. Those who stayed were ordered to defend their own
homes and dig their own private shallow shelters. Official Japanese
thinking was that Tokyo houses were such tinderboxes that families
had to be on hand to put out the fires immediately; for this reason
construction of public shelters had been discouraged.

Blazing houses were to be a nighttime feature of Tokyo from the
end of November onward. Aesthetically minded Tokyo residents
called such fires "the flowers of Edo," and when Guillain rode a
streetcar the day after the first major raid he discovered that "a Japanese neighborhood could vanish without a trace." A mass exodus
began soon after, for the rumor spread that B-29s would come in their
hundreds on December 8, the third anniversary of Pearl Harbor.

The shelter inside the imperial palace was deep and practically
bombproof, and Hirohito started spending more and more time
there, eventually using it as an office and conference room, and,
finally, sleeping there as well. Though he heard the drone of the
B-29s, and the sounds of the bombing, it was a long time before he
realized the extent of the damage, for by this time he was virtually
confined to the palace for security reasons, and, at least at first, he was
given sanitized accounts of the bombs' impact.

There was no way, however, of concealing the disastrous course of
the Pacific war; in October the U.S. campaign for the liberation of the
Philippines began. Japanese pilot training had been drastically curtailed because of fuel shortages, and Hirohito vented his spleen, and

his frustrations, on the unfortunate Koiso, just as he had bullied Sugiyama when, after the initial victories, the tide had begun to turn against Japan. Koiso had described the battle for Leyte as "decisive," and that battle had been lost. What did he propose to do now, Hirohito asked. Were Luzon, and the Philippines, definitely lost? If so, what did Koiso have in mind? By this time the Allies were advancing on a broad front in France, and the Soviet armies were fast regaining lost territory.

Since August a Supreme War Guidance Council (including the premier, foreign affairs minister, army and navy ministers and the two chiefs of staff) had been meeting inside the palace twice a week, discussing broad strategy. Increasingly, they took to meeting in the stiflingly hot, airless underground conference room.

Hirohito followed the inexorable U.S. advance in the Philippines in detail on "war room" maps, and knew, too, the ever-widening gulf between propaganda and reality: in October he had agreed to the promulgation of an imperial rescript congratulating the Imperial Navy on its great victories, knowing perfectly well that his warships had suffered almost mortal blows, including the loss of the *Yamato,* which had replaced the obsolete *Nagato* as the flagship of the Combined Fleet. Finally, after a stormy meeting with Koiso, Hirohito told Kido that the situation in the Philippines was becoming desperate, and that he was anxious to listen to advice from "people close to me." By this time the B-29 raids had begun in earnest, hitting industrial centers like Nagoya, and even damaging the sacred shrine at Ise.

In early January 1945 Kido noted that Hirohito was now fully aware of the desperate situation on the Philippines front. On January 4, Hirohito told Kido: "Now a decisive battle will have to be fought on Luzon as Leyte has been lost. . . . We will have to conceal this from the people." Two days later, Kido noted, Hirohito said, "It's reported that the U.S. army intends to land at Luzon. The war situation in the Philippines is extremely grave. So I think it may be necessary to listen to the intentions of the jushin [former prime ministers] stemming from the upcoming war situation. What do you think?"

Kido advised him to discuss the overall situation informally, to get the unvarnished truth, then call in key cabinet ministers, "giving your questions as lucidly as possible," and then summon the former premiers for advice. Kido knew that it was no use suggesting that Prince Takamatsu talk to Hirohito, but arranged, in early February, for all the surviving premiers—Hiranuma, Hirota, Wakatsuki, Okada, Konoye and Tojo—to come to the palace and say their piece.

Whatever their private sense of doom, Hiranuma, Hirota, Wakatsuki and Okada were unable to conquer their diffidence and speak their minds. Instead, they hid behind a smoke screen of hazy generalities. Only two people spoke out: Tojo, who advised Hirohito to continue with "total war," on the mainland and to the death if necessary, and Prince Konoye, who advised Hirohito to make peace on almost any terms. But by this time, perhaps out of a sense of personal guilt, or a need to rationalize his past behavior, the prince had become obsessed with the danger of Communism, which he had begun to regard as an even greater threat to Japan than defeat itself. He now believed that the army "reformists," whom he had once courted and admired, had themselves been, consciously or not, the tools of a vast Communist conspiracy. He lectured Hirohito on the evils they had perpetrated (state planning, a centralized economy), and on their shady alliances with maverick, leftist, reform-minded secret societies. His anti-Communist diatribe must have sounded singularly irrelevant to the emperor, and cast doubt on the soundness of the rest of his analysis.

Hirohito's preoccupations were more down-to-earth: Did Konoye believe, as some of the emperor's generals told him, that the United States would massacre the imperial family?

Konoye replied he didn't think this would happen. "I know Grew and other senior Americans," he said. They would never allow such a thing to happen.

Hirohito said he was inclined to agree. "General [Yoshijiro] Umezu [the army chief of staff] says they will massacre my whole family but I don't entirely believe him." Hirohito added that Umezu was in favor of luring a huge American force into fighting a land battle to the finish in Taiwan, which would be so costly in U.S. lives that negotiations might then start with Japan in a position of comparative strength.

Konoye was unable to gather whether Hirohito believed in the Taiwan option or saw it for what it was—an army excuse to prolong the war and bring it to an apocalyptic ending. A shrewd, lucid observer when he was not trying to rationalize Japan's predicament by blaming everything on a Communist conspiracy, Konoye came away downcast from his meeting with Hirohito. He told Hosakawa that if

Hirohito still took the advice of people like General Umezu seriously, "I am very pessimistic [about the chances of peace]."

B-29 raids were now a daily occurrence, were seriously affecting war production, and civilian casualties were mounting. On January 16, 1945, Kido noted the figures communicated to the emperor since the raids began in earnest: 7,600 dead, 5,000 homes destroyed, 55,000 more evacuated and 20 percent of Tokyo's population (including 200,000 schoolchildren) evacuated. At the same time, there was still an air of unreality about court life: two days later (January 18) Kido noted the almost peacetime schedule of Hirohito and Empress Nagako: a lecture on calligraphy by one of Japan's foremost practitioners of the art, followed by a philosophical discussion on the nature of Chinese culture and its emphasis on politeness, followed by a more relevant lecture by an expert on "the deployment of electric wave weapons" (i.e., radar). All this took place on time between visits to the bombproof bunker during raids and diligent morale-boosting work on Nagako's part, such as writing condolences to families of war dead—until they became so numerous, and communications deteriorated so much that it was no longer possible for the empress to do so, she sent notes bearing the imperial seal to the bereaved families, thanking them for their service to the nation.

Meanwhile, Prince Konoye was pursuing his own, increasingly maverick contribution to the end of war and the preservation of the emperor system. On January 26, 1945, he took the train to Kyoto (a city spared by B-29s because of its profusion of sacred buildings) to see Prince Takamatsu, who had moved there, and put before him a breathtaking proposal. Konoye told the prince that Japan was doomed. Because of the emperor's role in events leading up to the war, it was inconceivable that Hirohito should remain on the throne. But resignation was not enough. He must not be subject to arrest, and should devote the rest of his life to prayer for the souls of the departed war heroes who had lost their lives in the emperor's service. There was a tradition, in the distant past, of emperors voluntarily abdicating and entering monasteries. What Konoye proposed was that the emperor, in advance of total defeat, should not only resign, and appoint his small son, Akihito, as emperor and Takamatsu as regent, but then immediately enter the Ninna temple in Kyoto and become its chief abbot.

Konoye's plan had been carefully prepared. He had talked to the incumbent chief abbot, Okamoto, the thirty-ninth in line since the temple's establishment, who had already agreed to step down and allow Hirohito to take over; Konoye and Okamoto had even decided on Hirohito's new priestly name: Yu-nin ho-oh. ("Yu nin" was a different way of pronouncing Hirohito, using the same calligraphy, and "ho-oh" was the term for an emperor entering religious service.) Konoye spent nine hours trying to convince Takamatsu that this was a viable idea, and the only way of preserving the emperor system. "I will join him in the monastery," Konoye said. He added that he had already talked to Admiral Yonai, the navy minister, and ex-premier Okada about this, and that they were in favor of it.

Konoye submitted this plan to the palace the following month, despite the skepticism of both Kido (who had also been brought into the picture) and of Takamatsu himself, who refused to support it. Takamatsu's opposition was commonsensical: how could the Americans and the British, who were Christians, understand the motives of an emperor becoming a Buddhist priest? It was completely outside their frame of reference. Kido, too, was dead set against it: he now no longer believed, as he had a year earlier, that the emperor should resign and appoint a regent. Such an alternative was now too perilous. "If the Emperor abdicates, it will only become more dangerous for him," he told Konoye. The Allies would not see such a move in its proper religious context, but believe, instead, that the emperor regarded himself as a guilty man, and was running away, ostensibly taking refuge in religion.

Diehard army generals were meanwhile devising another scheme to protect the emperor from the rapidly approaching nemesis. At enormous expense, army engineers started building a huge fortified underground complex at Matsushiro, near Mount Fuji, to house the emperor and his family and ensure their safety while the final battle raged on Japanese soil. They even built a special armor-plated caravan to convey the imperial family from the palace to the Matsushiro bunker. It was because Konoye had got wind of the construction of the bunker that he had taken the trip to Kyoto, for he realized that once the emperor had been spirited away by the army, there was no chance of seeing his plan succeed.

The dowager empress, too, was making her views felt. "The Emperor," Kido noted cryptically on January 29, 1945, "told me of the Empress-dowager's feeling re the war." In the light of her earlier antiwar views, it's probable that the gist of her remarks to her son was "I told you so." Less than a month later, on February 25, her house was burned to the ground during an air raid.

By this time Crown Prince Akihito had been sent to the safety of the mountains. A short letter to him from Hirohito exists, dated March 6, 1945; it is no different from the average letter busy fathers might write to their small sons at boarding school: "Thank you for your letter. I'm very pleased to know you enjoy skiing and are in good health. Our war is in a very difficult phase but I want to go through this by my best efforts and divine power and I appreciate your prayers. Don't worry, I'm alright. I had a walk in the garden with your mother and collected items relating to B-29s—shell fragments."

Shortly afterward, on March 9, came the truly horrendous night raid on Tokyo that killed over one hundred thousand people and destroyed most of the city. Three days later a meeting took place inside the palace to determine whether or not Hirohito should tour the damaged areas. Kido told the grand chamberlain: "An imperial trip under heavy guard, as usual, may cause harm. It is all right to do it but this is wartime so use a very simple system so it looks as if the Emperor did it on the spur of the moment." An "informal" tour of the shattered city, with a small retinue, took place on the morning of March 18.

So far, B-29s had been given strict instructions not to aim for the palace grounds in Tokyo, but a debate was taking place in Washington on whether or not to bomb the palace itself, and an OSS (Office of Strategic Services) report—actually not published until July 1945, when the war was almost over but in preparation during the peak of the incendiary bomb raids—outlined the official pros and cons. It's an interesting document for the light it throws, even while war was still raging, on American attitudes toward Hirohito.

The report noted there were a number of cogent arguments in favor of "taking out" the palace: the possibility that rumors of its destruction might cause panic among the people; "elimination of the Emperor from the political scene might be desirable because of his position as the center of the Japanese nationalistic tradition"; "the satisfaction to Americans demanding revenge for the Philippines and Japanese war conduct."

On the other hand, the OSS experts noted, bombing the palace might, on the contrary, "stimulate the offensive spirit" of the Japanese. Moreover, the authors of the report assumed that the emperor's bunker was bombproof, so his death was unlikely, and in any case "his death would not affect the 'Emperor-concept.' " Strategically, there was no point in hitting the palace, since "no vital documents in carrying out the war" were likely to be kept there. But the most telling argument was that "Hirohito might prove a useful influence later." Even the bombing of the army and navy ministries, situated close to the palace, "might be construed as an unsuccessful attack on the Palace" and was therefore to be discouraged. Summing up, the OSS experts felt the "bombing of the Imperial palace is considered disadvantageous to the attainment of U.S. military and political objectives," and that the net effect of such an attack "will be to increase the will of the Japanese people to carry on the war."

While U.S. might was gearing up to landings on Okinawa, and incendiary-bomb air strikes on Japan continued, Prime Minister Koiso was attempting to end Japan's involvement in China on almost any terms. His reasoning was that, in the last resort, Japanese forces dispersed throughout China would be required on the Japanese mainland for the final battle. Secret talks, through intermediaries, began, but when Hirohito heard about them he was angry, and ordered Koiso to put a stop to them. This was the main reason for Koiso's resignation, on April 2, 1945, and his replacement by another retired admiral, Kantaro Suzuki, a lifelong courtier whose wife had been one of Hirohito's teachers when he was a little boy. And when Hirohito finally learned both the army's and Konoye's proposals to spirit him away, the army to a bunker and his kinsman to a monastery, he firmly refused to budge. When Kido timidly proposed that the three sacred Shinto relics—the mirror, the necklace and the sword—should at least be taken to the Matsushiro bunker, he turned that down too. "I will stay with my people whatever happens," he told his grand chamberlain. To Kido he said, "I will share the fate of the sacred relics." He would eventually show the same flashes of determination, and leadership, that had resulted in the collapse of the 2/26 mutiny, but before this happened Japan would go through considerable suffering, and hundreds of thousands of lives would be lost.

CHAPTER TWENTY

After inspecting parts of bomb-damaged Tokyo on March 18, 1945, Hirohito could no longer harbor any illusions about the outcome of the war. The military, however, still thought in terms of a *Götterdämmerung,* a final sacrificial battle on Japan's sacred soil that would inflict such casualties on the U.S. invaders that an "honorable" peace would still be possible. If one in ten able-bodied Japanese managed to kill one invading soldier, their crazy reasoning went, the war might still be won, and even if they failed, the "honorable death of a hundred million" was preferable to surrender.

The military also believed they still had a few cards up their sleeve. Unit 731's weapons would never be tested against the Americans (at the start of the battle for Okinawa, in April, General Ishii once more proposed his services, but was turned down on the grounds that bacteriological warfare "wouldn't make any difference"), but several high-altitude prototype aircraft were under construction to counter the B-29s. Hirohito was kept abreast of their performances—and their failures—and inquired repeatedly about progress in this field.

There was another secret weapon the Japanese hoped to use against the invading U.S. armada as it approached the Japanese mainland: the atom bomb. As with Unit 731, there is no direct evidence that

Hirohito was aware of progress being made in this direction. The only proof of a link between the "father" of the Japanese A-bomb, the distinguished nuclear physicist Yoshio Nishina, and the palace is a still-extant photo of him, taken in his office in the company of Prince Chichibu, probably in May 1940, after the prince's inspection of Japan's first cyclotron, devised and built by Nishina. The scientist would die in 1951, himself a victim of radiation sickness contracted during his heroic attempt to provide a full report on the consequences of the Hiroshima bomb on the city's surviving population, and though he was debriefed by U.S. interrogators immediately after the war, he was evasive about Japanese efforts to construct a bomb, and did his best to conceal the truth from them. It is, however, almost inconceivable that Hirohito, himself a scientist in close touch with Japan's academic community and indefatigably curious about new scientific accomplishments of all kinds, should have been unaware of the desperately urgent work being carried out by the Rikken, Japan's Institute for Physical and Chemical Research, from 1940 onward, or of the existence of the huge nuclear installation in Hungnam (North Korea), later dismantled by the Soviets, who may have gained as much information about nuclear fission from this top-secret Japanese base as they did from the Rosenberg and Fuchs reports.

Japan's race to be first with the atom bomb, obliquely confirmed by Prince Takeda years later in his interview with *Observer* correspondent Peter McGill, has been chronicled in Robert Wilcox's *Japan's Secret War: Japan's Race Against Time to Build Its Own Atom Bomb,* a brilliantly researched piece of sleuthing. It contains a reference to the late David Snell's story of the Japanese engineer's eyewitness account of an experimental A-bomb explosion off the Hungnam coast on August 10, 1945, that could not easily have been made up; it also has the fullest account so far of Japanese efforts to obtain uranium supplies from Germany even in the last days of the war in Europe that explains why, in the final resort, Japanese military leaders hoped to harness at least one atom bomb to a kamikaze plane or submarine and launch it against a massive American target.

Despite the incontrovertible evidence of Japanese nuclear expertise provided by Wilcox, there is no reference to a nuclear program anywhere in any of the diaries of members of Hirohito's entourage. However, given the emperor's close monitoring, right up to the end of the war, of scientific, engineering and technological experiments of all kinds, and of Japanese efforts to introduce new weapons to counter the crushing numerical and industrial advantage of the United States, my personal belief is that he must almost certainly have known about Japan's nuclear war effort.

The facts were these: increasingly, as the war turned in favor of the Allies in the Pacific, Oshima, the Japanese ambassador in Berlin, began pestering the Nazi leaders for technological help. In particular, Oshima told them, Japan was interested in rocket technology (the V-1s and V-2s were beginning to hit Britain) and was in desperate need of uranium. It had some, mainly mined in Korea, but not nearly enough. A few German submarines were large enough to carry up to 240 tons of equipment, and Germany did allow some of her precious advanced weapons to be taken to Japan by U-boat—by 1944–45 there was no other way.

The last German submarine to make the highly dangerous, lengthy run between Germany and Japan was the U-234, a giant 22,000-tonner, whose captain, Johann Heinrich Fehler, though only thirty-five, was one of the most experienced German navy captains still alive, the former commander of the decoy ship *Atlantis*, which had lured countless Allied vessels to their doom. On March 25, 1945, seven days after Hirohito's inspection of martyred Tokyo, the submarine left Kiel, packed with secret devices, badly needed mercury (hidden as ballast), the latest German antiaircraft shells, parts for jet planes and rockets, and bomb fuses. But the most sensitive cargo was not any of this but 1,120 pounds of uranium oxide, packed in ten containers, capable of providing the wherewithal for two A-bombs.

It's surprising that the U-234's odyssey has never been made into a movie, for it had elements of high drama: after sixteen days in the Atlantic, desperately dodging the U.S. and Royal Navy fleets, which by now had total command of the seas, the U-234 was in mid-Atlantic. By now the war in Europe was over, and by May 2 the submarine's signals were no longer being returned. Fehler did not know it, but Germany's naval HQ was in Allied hands. Shortly afterward, Admiral Karl Doenitz transmitted his last order to his remaining U-boats at sea to surrender, and on May 10 this message was picked up by the U-234. At this point, Fehler was practically equidistant from British, Canadian and American ports. Wisely, he decided not to continue his journey, and headed for the United States' east coast.

Aboard the U-234 were two Japanese Imperial Navy officers, one an expert on submarine construction, another a rocket specialist. Rather than surrender, they told Fehler, they would commit suicide. Fehler told them to go ahead. Out of consideration for the crew, they took sleeping pills instead of committing *seppuku* with their swords, which would have been horribly messy aboard a cramped submarine, and on May 11 were buried at sea. On May 14, five hundred miles from the American east coast, the U-234 was boarded by a U.S. Navy crew and shortly afterward newsmen flocked to Portsmouth to inspect it.

Reporters covering the U-234 story sent back graphic descriptions of the U-boat's surrender but concentrated more on the physical appearance of the disembarking crew than on the U-boat's contents. U.S. naval authorities later took the submarine apart, bit by bit, and in this way the mercury was discovered. At the time, of course, the word "uranium" meant little except to specialists. As Wilcox later discovered, at the U.S. Naval Historical Center's Operational Archives in Washington, the inventory of the U-234's cargo published in May 1945 by the U.S. Navy (but not released to the press) included "560 kilos of uranium oxide for the jap army." This information was kept secret at the time of the submarine's surrender; it could only mean that, in some form or another, Japan might be close to making its own nuclear bomb.

Wilcox tried in vain to find out what use was made of this precious information, and, indeed, what happened to the not inconsiderable amount of uranium oxide war booty. But there are some secrets that remain impenetrable even in the most open of societies, and under the most liberal Freedom of Information acts. It may be fanciful to imagine that the uranium oxide captured aboard the U-234 ended up as part of the Hiroshima and Nagasaki A-bombs. It is not stretching things too far, however, to believe not only that President Truman was told of the find aboard the U-234 but that this may have been one of the unspoken additional reasons for his decision to authorize the A-bomb strikes on Hiroshima and Nagasaki. Neither is it fanciful to believe that Hirohito was aware of the U-234 venture, even though his own decision to surrender came before the U-boat could have reached a Japanese port. He was well aware that German U-boat crews had obeyed Admiral Doenitz's order and surrendered to British and American ships at sea.

From April 1945 on, Kido's daily entries in his diaries became shorter and more elliptical. On April 13, he noted, in only a few lines, that his own house had been burned down during a raid. "I can't escape from the feeling of regret," he noted, "but on the other hand I feel somewhat cleansed." On April 29, the emperor's forty-fourth birthday, he noted: "No celebrations," and, the following day, "Air raid cut short my haircut." That April, the "peace party" éminence grise, Shigeru Yoshida, was arrested by the military police and kept under arrest for a month. Konoye cynically, but with considerable foresight, noted that "this would serve him in good stead in due course."

On May 25, eleven days after the U-234 was brought into Portsmouth, New Hampshire, the palace was badly damaged during an incendiary-bomb night raid. The B-29 raiders had not transgressed the order forbidding them from bombing the palace, nor had bombs landed in the palace compound by error: a strong wind swept burning fragments over the walls and into the palace grounds, and in the ensuing fires twenty-eight members of the Imperial Household, including a dozen firemen, were killed. In that same raid, eighteen square miles of Tokyo were burned to the ground, and the palaces of Crown Prince Akihito, Prince Kanin, Prince Chichibu and Prince Mikasa were destroyed, as were the more modest mansions of Prince Hashimoto, Prince Riken and Prince Rigu, parts of the Navy and War ministries and the official homes of several cabinet ministers.

The emperor's home, most of the time, was now his sweltering air raid shelter, immediately below the imperial library, consisting of bedrooms, bathrooms, a kitchen, a telephone switchboard and conference room. Crown Prince Akihito had been sent to the safety of the mountains, but both Prince Mikasa and Prince Takamatsu spent some nights there, after May 25, and the tensions must have been considerable, for Hirohito had never forgiven Takamatsu for "plotting" the end of the war and relations between the two brothers were still strained.

On June 11 Kido noted in his diary: "Four kempei came to guard me." Whether they were for Kido's physical protection, or whether he, too, was close to arrest for his behind-the-scenes peace ventures is unclear. Perhaps the military police feared demonstrations against the man who had been Hirohito's éminence grise for so long. Two days later (June 13) Kido noted that one of the empress's stewards called on him to discuss "the honorable movement of the Emperor's palanquin" and the "headquarters in the Alps." The army was again urging the emperor and his family to move to their secret bunker built at immense cost in the mountains, and the inference is that the empress may have been more inclined to flight than Hirohito himself.

Still there was no move on Premier Suzuki's part to end the war. It was an absurd situation. By May, Hitler was dead, and the entire resources of the Allies would soon be free to concentrate on Japan. The Soviet Union had formally announced that its nonaggression treaty with Japan would not be renewed. Okinawa was about to fall, and the Allied invasion of Japan was only a matter of time. Despite the romantic death-wish theories of the military, defeat was inevitable, for Japan was running out of food, fuel, planes and raw materials of all kinds. Her major cities were in ruins, millions of her people homeless and starving. Tentatively, the Supreme War Guidance Council began discussing options, not for surrender but for an "honorable" end to the war. It was a measure of Japan's insulation from reality that the Council, Hirohito included, believed that the Soviet Union might intercede between Japan and the Allies, acting as mediator in an "honorable" settlement of the war.

Absurd though this notion might be, and proof of Japan's desperation, it was not even followed through with any consistency, for the initial meetings of the War Guidance Council discussing possible Soviet mediation (May 11 to 14) were followed by diehard, fight-to-the-death assurances by Prime Minister Suzuki that made nonsense of the earlier peace-feeler debates.

The concept of surrender was so alien to anyone steeped in the Japanese military tradition (and Suzuki was a career naval officer, though he had spent many years at court) that the seventy-seven-year-old admiral, confused, exhausted and deaf, simply could not bring himself to adjust to this eventuality for any length of time. Every time Kido expected Suzuki to speak out in favor of peace, the premier made the kind of bloodcurdling, no-surrender speech (to the Diet and to the other members of the Supreme War Guidance Council) that had become the standard conditioned response throughout the armed forces and the country.

So pervasive was the official "no surrender" line that barely three weeks after broaching the subject of Soviet mediation, the War Guidance Council actually passed a resolution, in Hirohito's presence, on June 8, calling for "supreme self-sacrifice" and "the honorable death

of a hundred million" rather than surrender. The official document—
entitled "Fundamental Policy on the Conduct of the War"—endorsed
that day by Hirohito had the sacred, irreversible finality of a formal
gozen kaigi decision. Mesmerized by the climate of romantic self-
sacrifice prevalent during those heady, doom-laden days, none of the
participants at the meeting, least of all the emperor, said anything to
prevent it from becoming official policy. There was not even a reminder, on the part of Foreign Minister Togo, a dove, of the Soviet
mediation option.

Immediately after this latest act of folly, Kido sat down and drafted
his own report ("Measures for Managing the Situation") urging
Hirohito to cease hostilities immediately. This required considerable
moral courage, and the following day he spoke out in person to the
emperor. Finally, thirteen days later, on June 21, the day after the fall
of Okinawa, Hirohito was at last galvanized into action, and told
Suzuki that he should not be bound by the June 8 *gozen kaigi* decision,
but should base his policies instead on the Kido report and examine
the situation "concretely and speedily." By this time, in addition to
military casualties on Okinawa, some 120,000 civilians had died there
too, and tens of thousands more in Japan itself, as a result of the
bombings.

Hirohito had known Suzuki since he was four years old. "To him,"
Hirohito told Kido, "I could pour out my heart." The many barriers
between emperor and subject could never be entirely removed, but
Suzuki, along with Kido and Konoye, was one of the few people with
whom he could have frank and informal discussions. To have waited
so long, and done nothing, while the bombings continued at home
and carnage continued abroad (Rangoon fell in June, and Japanese
troops were mowed down at sea as they fled in makeshift craft) was
an aberration that can only be explained in terms of prolonged catatonic shock, brought about by the unrelenting series of disasters,
compounded by the bombing and the shattering of the Showa dream,
paralyzing Hirohito's will. The prospect of surrender on the part of
an emperor who was also a "living God," the heir to a twenty-six-
hundred-year-old dynasty, that had never been defeated by a foreign
power, was daunting enough. But his generals had deliberately made
things worse, encouraging him to believe that the Americans intended
to destroy the emperor system altogether, exile or try him, deport his
family, maybe even take his small son hostage and keep him in lifelong

bondage in America. These rumors had spread throughout the armed forces: they would soon lead to one of the most absurdly romantic plots in modern Japanese history. Because he felt there was no alternative, and despite the evidence to the contrary, Hirohito still clung to the belief that Soviet Union mediation was the only way of avoiding unconditional surrender. Foreign Minister Togo dropped in on the Soviet ambassador, Jakob Malik, hinted that the USSR would be suitably rewarded if it agreed to cooperate, and was treated with indifferent contempt.

Now, as in earlier times, Hirohito turned to Konoye once more, as the man uniquely suited to argue Japan's case with Molotov, the commissar for foreign affairs, and asked him to go to Moscow to argue Japan's case.

Had Hirohito been aware of what was then taking place in Washington he might have acted sooner, and more decisively, and thus saved the lives of the Hiroshima and Nagasaki victims, for ten days after Kido's plucky, commonsensical report on the need to bring the war to an end with all possible speed, Truman met with his chief aides to prepare for the Potsdam Conference to be held the following month. Despite angry poll results showing how determined Americans were to punish the emperor (30 percent wanted him executed, 37 percent felt he should be tried and imprisoned for life, and only 7 percent believed he should be immune from prosecution or used as a puppet), an influential "Tokyo lobby" headed by Grew and Assistant Secretary of War John J. McCloy argued that Hirohito should remain on the throne as a constitutional monarch, provided Japan renounced militarism. Truman came away from a meeting with his top aides convinced that McCloy's suggestion that the U.S. president should send a personal message to Hirohito outlining such an offer was worth consideration, and that only if it was refused or ignored should the A-bombs be dropped.

Konoye agreed to go to Moscow. Privately, he had no illusions about his mission, "but," as he told his secretary, Tomita, "I could say nothing when I saw the Emperor. He had come out of his air raid shelter to the temporary audience-room, with his usually neatly combed hair unkempt, looking pale and terribly haggard." Konoye hoped to revive the plan he had initially devised for the aborted 1941 Roosevelt meeting. To prevent army obstruction, he suggested the emperor should issue an imperial order drafted by Konoye from

Moscow, endorsing the peace terms Konoye hoped to work out with Molotov. That way, the military would be faced with a fait accompli. Again, as in 1941, this proposal demonstrated Konoye's faith in the sacred nature of the emperor's decisions, and in his unquestioned ultimate authority.

The Soviets stalled and stalled. Naotake Sato, Japan's ambassador in Moscow, found Molotov "too busy" to see him. By this time the victorious Allies were working out the agenda for the Potsdam Conference. Hirohito had no way of knowing that Stalin had no intention of acting as mediator to obtain favorable peace terms for Japan, for one very good reason: seven months previously, at Yalta, he had been urged, by Churchill and Roosevelt, to enter the war against Japan as soon as possible after Germany's defeat. At the Potsdam Conference (in the company of Churchill and Truman) he knew he would be urged to open a second front against Japan—and he was prepared to do so, though as late as he possibly could.

The Allied leaders converged on Potsdam, and on the eve of the first working session (July 16) Truman received the news that a nuclear bomb had been successfully detonated in New Mexico. He told Churchill, whose immediate reaction was that if Truman did order the A-bombs dropped on Japan (and Churchill was convinced that he should), "then we should not need the Russians." Truman decided not to tell Stalin about the A-bomb as such, but did mention casually that America had a powerful new bomb, which it intended using on Japan. Stalin expressed only polite interest. But he did bring up the Konoye proposal, which Truman already knew about, thanks to Magic interceptions. Stalin then told Truman his armies would launch their attack on Japanese-occupied Manchuria in early August, and what should he do about the Konoye peace proposal? Truman replied he should act as he thought best. Stalin said he would keep stalling. So Molotov's deputy finally saw Sato, but only to tell him that Konoye's peace mission was too vague to warrant a visit.

On the final night of the Potsdam Conference a prodigious number of toasts were exchanged, and Churchill, himself unaware he would remain prime minister for only another few hours (Attlee defeated him in the first general elections held after the end of the war in Europe, on June 26) raised his glass and boomed: "Here's to our next meeting in Tokyo."

The joint U.S.-U.K.-China ultimatum to Japan, known as the Potsdam Declaration, should by rights have enabled Hirohito to reply immediately and positively, enabling Truman to reconsider his decision to launch A-bomb raids on Hiroshima and Nagasaki. Without outlining any specific concessions, it fell short of the earlier (Cairo summit) request for Japan's unconditional surrender, calling instead for "the unconditional surrender of all Japanese armed forces," which was a very different proposition. It pledged that, after being disarmed, Japanese troops would be "permitted to return to their homes with the opportunity to lead peaceful and productive lives." It did not mention the emperor at all, and even, between the lines, implied that the emperor system, purged of militaristic influences, might be retained. The influence of Grew and McCloy on the final text was considerable. "We do not intend that the Japanese shall be enslaved as a race or destroyed as a nation," it said, "but stern justice shall be meted out to war criminals, including those who have visited cruelties upon our prisoners. The Japanese Government shall remove all obstacles to the revival and strengthening of democratic tendencies among the Japanese people. Freedom of speech, of religion, and of thought, as well as respect for the fundamental human rights shall be established."

On July 27 the Supreme War Guidance Council met to examine this text. Foreign Minister Togo felt it would be highly unwise to reject it. But the council, and the cabinet in a separate meeting that afternoon, disagreed on ways of presenting the declaration to the Japanese people—and to the armed forces. The emerging consensus, that an expurgated version of the Potsdam Declaration be released to the press without comment, and that Japan take a "wait and see" attitude while still hoping for a positive Soviet response to the Konoye trip proposal, in itself virtually guaranteed that an impatient Truman, interpreting such a reaction as sheer stalling, would press the button and order the first A-bomb strike. But worse was to come. For Premier Suzuki, in a rare press conference on July 28, summed up the government's majority view as a mandate to *mokusatsu* the declaration, that is, to "kill it with silence." The word could also be translated as "treating it with silent contempt." On government orders the *Asahi Shimbun* called the Potsdam Declaration "a thing of no great value." Neither the Supreme War Guidance Council, nor the cabinet, nor the emperor, could know that the fate of the Hiroshima and Nagasaki victims was to be sealed by the use of that unfortunate word, and by the fact that—as Washington was quick to discover—the key phrase in the Potsdam Declaration ("We do not intend that the Japanese shall be enslaved as a race or destroyed as a nation") had been censored in the Japanese version released to the press.

Again, the catatonic shock that had paralyzed the emperor's will earlier now spread to the government as a whole. Hirohito may have believed that a Soviet response was worth waiting for, but very few others did; they may, however, have felt they were gaining time, and that more explicit terms, including reassuring statements on the future of the emperor and the emperor system, might be forthcoming. Truman waited for just over a week. Then, when nothing more seemed likely to emerge from Tokyo, on August 6, at 0815 hours, the *Enola Gay* overflew Hiroshima and dropped its parachute-assisted atom bomb on inhabitants so used to B-29 flights that observing only two planes in the sky and assuming they were on a reconnaissance raid, they did not even bother to head for the shelters.

Not till afternoon did detailed reports on Hiroshima reach Tokyo, but the Japanese army HQ knew straightaway what had happened: Japanese efforts in this field were sufficiently advanced for the army's knowledge to be sophisticated and immediate. And Truman, in a statement of questionable taste, confirmed their suspicions. "The source from which the sun draws its power," he proclaimed, "can now totally eclipse the land of the rising sun, on whose throne sits a direct descendant of Amaterasu O-Mikami, the Goddess of the Sun." Hirohito was informed of the nature of the bomb by Togo, and by the army. Shock, and failure of will, once more engulfed not only Hirohito but the government as a whole, for a whole day went by, and no move to end the war was made.

Only forty-eight hours later, after Togo had met with Hirohito in his bunker, urging him to accept the terms of the Potsdam Declaration with all possible speed, did the emperor react. In a talk with Kido, he said his own personal safety was unimportant. What mattered was the immediate termination of the war. But so cumbersome and slow was government machinery that more precious time was lost. A Supreme War Guidance Council meeting was held only on August 9. On that day Soviet troops crossed the border and poured into Manchuria, and on that same morning, the second atom bomb was dropped on Nagasaki. Now there was a very real possibility, in the minds of Japan's ruling elite, that a third bomb would drop on Tokyo itself, annihilating the imperial family as well as most of the city's population. When the Supreme War Council met that afternoon, in the stifling palace bunker, Suzuki announced at last that there was no alternative: Japan had to accept the terms of the Potsdam Declaration.

Incredibly, three of the military members of the council—General Korechika Anami, the war minister, and the army and navy chiefs of staff—still believed they could impose their own terms on the Allies. As the authors of the admirable chronicle of surrender, *Japan's Longest Day,* noted, these three were still psychologically unable to accept the *idea* of defeat or surrender, and their proposals were in fact a subliminal denial of the *fact* of defeat or surrender. Even now, Anami argued, Japan should insist on a minimal occupation force, trial of war criminals by Japanese courts, and demobilization carried out without foreign interference. "We cannot pretend to claim that victory is certain, but it is far too early to say the war has been lost," he said. General Umezu agreed with him. The Supreme War Council was hopelessly divided—three in favor of accepting the Potsdam Declaration in its entirety, and three against.

Now, dispelling his inhibitions, Hirohito decided to act: he summoned Kainan Shimomura, the former head of NHK, the national broadcasting company, who was now director of the Information Bureau, and remained closeted with him in the bunker for two hours. That evening Shimomura told an aide: "The Emperor has agreed to make a broadcast telling the nation whether we're to have peace or war." Later, Hirohito talked late into the night with Kido. His mind was made up: he would use his imperial prerogatives at last.

Later still, that same night, the most dramatic *gozen kaigi* of the Showa era took place, in the stifling, airless conference room. All those present were drenched in perspiration, especially the civilians, compelled by protocol to wear their obligatory court dress—heavy black morning coats, starched shirts and striped trousers—but by the time it ended, tears as well as sweat poured down their faces. The Potsdam Declaration was read. Suzuki formally apologized to Hirohito for requesting his presence before a divided assembly. He then called on those present to speak. Togo urgently recommended, as he had from the start, that it be accepted. Navy Minister Yonai briefly agreed. Anami, as he had the day before, but with more desperate eloquence, urged that guarantees be obtained for the preservation of the emperor system, and that Japan be allowed to conduct its own war trials, disarm its own soldiers, and limit the numbers of the occupation forces. Umezu agreed. Hiranuma, as president of the Privy Council an ex officio member of the *gozen kaigi,* cross-examined the army and navy members present on the chances of an orderly surrender, and obliquely appeared to side with the three diehards. Toyoda then added his voice to those of Umezu and Anami.

Suzuki then rose. Using the habitual ceremonial, circumlocutory forms of speech that were de rigueur in the emperor's presence on such a solemn occasion, he humbly asked Hirohito to decide for them. The imperial command was known as the Voice of the Crane, for its cry could be heard for miles though it was seldom seen. Now the Voice of the Crane was to decide whether Japan was to survive as a nation or continue the war to the bitter, sacrificial end, the "honorable death of a hundred million."

Hirohito spoke quietly. Continuation of the war could only lead to the annihilation of his people and more suffering for all humanity. It was clear to him that Japan could no longer wage war, nor defend its shores. "That it is unbearable for me to see my loyal troops disarmed goes without saying, but the time has come to bear the unbearable. I give my sanction to the proposal to accept the Potsdam declaration on the basis outlined by the Foreign Minister." As he spoke he seemed to be addressing one person in the room—Anami. Though no full record exists of the proceedings that day, it was later revealed that whereas the emperor referred to the other ministers and generals by their titles, as protocol required, he referred to Anami by name, appealing to him personally, almost as though they were brothers. Hirohito knew that it was Anami's acceptance of the imperial decision that mattered. He was the one who had to be convinced, for he in turn had to persuade the army to obey the emperor's decision. It so happened the two men knew each other well: in the twenties, Anami had been one of Hirohito's ADCs, and Hirohito liked him. Often, he had entrusted him with private errands that had nothing to do with army matters, such as gathering rare butterfly specimens from Taiwan for the emperor's collection. Without waiting for an answer from the eleven men, Hirohito rose and left the conference room.

Suzuki said, "His Majesty's decision should be made the decision of this conference as well." All eyes were on Anami, who remained silent. Silence implied tacit approval by all, and the meeting adjourned, but not for long.

Constitutionally, it was the cabinet that had to take the formal steps
to sue for peace, and now the ministers who had already taken part
in the *gozen kaigi* were joined at Suzuki's official residence by the rest
of the cabinet. A communiqué was hammered out, accepting the terms
of the Potsdam Declaration, which each minister signed. All eyes
were on Anami when the time came for him to add his name to the
document. Even at this stage he could have nullified the proceedings
by withholding his signature, for the cabinet decision had to be unanimous. But the emperor had spoken, and Anami was bound to obey,
even if, as he knew, this would cost him his life. There was an almost
audible sigh of relief when he did so.

Three hours later the following cable was sent to the Japanese
embassies in Bern and Stockholm, for onward transmission to Washington, London, Moscow and Chungking:

> The Japanese government are ready to accept the terms enu-
> merated in the joint declaration issued at Potsdam on July 26,
> 1945, by the heads of the Governments of the United States,
> Great Britain, and China, and later subscribed to by the Soviet
> Government, *with the understanding that the said declaration does
> not comprise any demand which prejudices the prerogatives of His
> Majesty as a Sovereign Ruler"* [author's italics].

This had been the one condition the military diehards had insisted on
to the very end. But all those consulted, including Premier Suzuki and
Kido, agreed to its inclusion: it provided Anami with a strong argument in case his own officers refused to lay down their arms, for if the
Allies explicitly rejected it, he had extracted from Suzuki the pledge
that Japan would continue the war. But it was also the first step in the
long, selfless postwar battle on the part of his courtiers to save
Hirohito from the consequences of the war, and ensure that even if
the other members of that last *gozen kaigi* were to be arraigned as war
criminals, the emperor himself would be immune from prosecution.

CHAPTER TWENTY-ONE

It was now up to the Allies to determine whether Japan's acceptance of their surrender terms was satisfactory, and after much transatlantic debate, they decided it was, but that the part about the "prerogatives of the sovereign ruler" required additional clarification. Their cabled reaction was that "from the moment of surrender the authority of the Emperor and the Japanese Government to rule the state shall be subject to the Supreme Commander of the Allied Powers [General MacArthur] who will take such steps as he deems proper to effectuate the surrender terms." In addition, Truman wanted it put on record that Hirohito in person should take part in the surrender ceremony, but the new British government, with Churchill's assent, felt this was going too far and suggested instead that "the Emperor shall authorize and ensure the signature by the Government of Japan and the Japanese General Headquarters of the surrender terms." Truman agreed to the new formula, as did Chiang Kai-shek.

Incredibly, within Japan itself, none of this, not even the initial Japanese decision to surrender, was yet public knowledge, for no way had been found to announce the government's decision to its people, and the situation was further confused by two completely contradic-

tory communiqués. One, issued by the War Ministry in General
Anami's name on August 10 but without his specific authorization (it
was drafted by a group of diehard junior staff officers) announced
there was only one choice: "We must fight on until we win the war
to preserve our sacred polity . . . even if we have to chew grass and
live in fields." The other, approved by the cabinet, was substantially
different, but equally uninformative, only hinting at an epochal decision to come: "The government will do all it can to defend the
homeland and preserve the honor of the country," it read, "but it
expects that Japan's hundred million will also rise to the occasion,
overcoming whatever obstacles may lie in the path of the preservation
of our national polity." For foreign consumption only, the Domei
news agency was allowed to broadcast, in Morse code, the actual text
of the government's response sent to Bern and Stockholm. Debate
also raged, among Hirohito's aides, on the meaning of the Allied
reply; all, including those most anxious to stop the war, knew it would
be difficult for the army to accept it.

The atmosphere inside the War Ministry resembled that of the
heady days of the 2/26 mutiny: excited officers gathered in small
groups in crowded back rooms; diehard colonels and captains lobbied
Anami and the Privy Council president, Baron Hiranuma, and others
even tried to enlist the support of Prince Mikasa in favor of a continued, sacrificial struggle. Plans for a coup, in the pure tradition of
2/26, using the Imperial Guards Division and elements of the Eastern
Army Command, were in fact already under way, masterminded by
Major Kenji Hatanaka, of the War Ministry's own Military Affairs
Bureau, with help from Lieutenant Colonel Masahiko Takeshita, General Anami's brother-in-law, ex-Premier Tojo's son-in-law and several
other influential middle-ranking officers. The generals suspected that
plotting was going on. Approached by some junior staff officers, General Yoshijiro Umezu, the army chief of staff, made it clear he would
not join in the conspiracy. Neither would Anami: to do so would
mean breaking his word to the emperor—an even more heinous crime
than surrender. Under constant pressure, however, over the next
forty-eight hours, from increasingly hysterical officers whose opinions
he shared, Anami wavered; and egged on by groups of junior staff
officers, the army and navy chiefs of staff met with Togo, and begged
him to change his mind about the surrender terms.

Along with bombs, B-29s were now dropping leaflets in Japanese with the text of the latest Allied reply. With the army in turmoil, the effect could be catastrophic unless the country was told what was actually happening. Kido convinced Hirohito that the only way to prevent an army coup was to stage yet another *gozen kaigi* to bring the wavering generals and admirals to heel.

This took place in the underground conference room on the morning of August 14. After listening to Admiral Toyoda and General Anami's renewed appeals to carry on with the war, Hirohito, in army uniform and streaming with perspiration, wiped his face with a white handkerchief. Gaunt, underweight, exhausted, dizzy with insomnia and rightly apprehensive about his own fate, he nevertheless performed with truly regal restraint, quiet eloquence and authority. It was, undoubtedly, his finest hour.

"I have listened carefully," he said, "to all the arguments. My own opinion has not changed. I shall now restate it." Continuation of the war would bring nothing but further destruction. The Allied reply was "an acknowledgement of our position. In short, I consider it acceptable. Although some of you are apprehensive about the preservation of the national structure, I believe that the Allied reply is evidence of the good intention of the enemy. . . . That is why I favor acceptance of the reply. I fully understand how difficult it will be for the officers and men of the Army and Navy to submit to being disarmed and to see their country occupied. . . . I am not concerned with what may happen to me. I want to preserve the lives of my people. I do not want them subjected to further destruction. It is indeed hard for me to see my loyal soldiers disarmed and my faithful ministers punished as war criminals."

But to continue the war would be to destroy Japan, and, "as things stand now, the nation still has a chance to recover. . . . As the people of Japan are unaware of the present situation, I know they will be deeply shocked when they hear of our decision. If it is thought appropriate that I explain the matter to them personally, I am willing to go on the air. . . . I am willing to go wherever necessary to explain our action. I desire the Cabinet to prepare as soon as possible an Imperial Rescript announcing the termination of the war." Without waiting for their comments, he left the conference room. Some of the ministers were on their knees, kowtowing. All were in tears and their sobs were audible.

There was nothing more to say. Perhaps the most composed person at this, the last wartime *gozen kaigi*, was the emperor himself, who calmly told Kido, shortly afterward, that he had meant what he said: he was willing to go to both the army and navy ministries and speak to the rebellious officers in person, if it would serve a purpose. He also told Kido to get in touch with Kainan Shimomura, the director of information, and tell him he would be ready to broadcast later in the day.

It was unthinkable that the emperor should broadcast live, so a scratch team was assembled at NHK, the Japanese Broadcasting Company, which would cut the record of the emperor's speech that would later be broadcast. Because of the urgency of the situation, they were told, they would not be required to wear frock coats and striped trousers. The baggy civilians' wartime "austerity" uniform (called *kokuminfuku*) worn by almost all Japanese would do.

After the emperor's last *gozen kaigi*, one of the coup leaders, Lieutenant Colonel Takeshita, caught up with his brother-in-law, General Anami, in the prime minister's office and made one last attempt to get him to change his mind and lead a coup to neutralize the "traitors" around the emperor and carry on the war. They talked just before the cabinet meeting that would give official approval to an imperial rescript ending the war.

Anami refused. "The Emperor has made his decision," he said. "There is nothing I can do. As a Japanese soldier, I must obey my Emperor." Takeshita then asked Anami, as one last favor, to resign. Since the cabinet decision to issue the surrender rescript had to be unanimous, this would prevent the meeting from taking place, and delay proceedings—probably indefinitely—until a new war minister could be found. "The war will end even if I resign," Anami replied. "And if I resign, I would not see the Emperor again." After the cabinet meeting—again all eyes were on Anami, for some of the ministers felt it would have been in character for him to resign in the middle of it, and there was widespread relief when it ended without his having uttered a word—the war minister returned to his own office. He, like his naval counterpart, had pledged that the emperor's orders were to be obeyed. He drafted a short statement: "The Imperial Forces will act strictly in accordance with the decision of His Imperial Majesty the Emperor," and had all senior officers and officials at the Ministry sign it. He then addressed his staff, explaining the emperor's decision. "You officers must realize that death cannot absolve you of your duty," he said. "Your duty is to stay alive and to do your best to help your country along the path to recovery—even if it means chewing grass and eating earth and sleeping in the fields." He was asking them not to take the *bushido* path of *seppuku,* but he had said "you officers" instead of "we officers," and this meant, some of those present felt, that for Anami at least there was to be no life after surrender.

One of the members of the NHK team ordered to record the emperor's voice was Shizuto Haruna, then twenty-three, who remembers the day well. A palace car came to fetch him and the rest of the six-man crew at 2:00 P.M., and they set to work in two rooms of the Imperial Household Ministry, a somewhat unattractive neo-Georgian building near the Sakashita Gate. In the room where the emperor would speak, they erected a large stand-up microphone; in the adjoining room, they set up their heavy record-cutting machines. A playback machine was brought over so that the emperor could listen to his own broadcast. "We waited and waited," he recalled. At 6:00 P.M. a meal was served, on Imperial Palace crockery with the chrysanthemum emblem, and then an air raid warning sounded and the lights were dimmed. The all clear sounded, and still the emperor did not show up. There had been a last-minute hitch: General Anami was to blame.

At the prime minister's office, the team of aides and ministers preparing the emperor's broadcast text were arguing endlessly over one sentence. Initially it read: "The war situation grows more unfavorable to us every day." Anami said he could not put his name to this, for it was tantamount to admitting that all the past War Ministry communiqués had been lies. "We have still not lost the war," he insisted. He seemed to have no inkling of the urgency of the situation, and even appeared to be quietly enjoying the irritation he was causing. After hours of discussion, and one intermission, the drafting committee agreed to change the phrase to "The war situation has not developed to Japan's advantage."

At the palace, Hirohito was getting impatient: he asked his chamberlains several times whether the text was on its way. Kido found time to brief Princes Takamatsu and Mikasa on the day's events, and also received Konoye, who called on him to warn him he had heard rumors of a coup. "I don't like it," he told Kido. "I don't like the rumors I've heard about the Imperial Guards Division." The First Imperial Guards Division, whose headquarters was at the back of the palace, near the Inui Gate, was under the command of Lieutenant General Takeshi Mori, known as "the monk" for his devotion to duty and his shaven skull. It was responsible for the emperor's personal safety, and one of its battalions guarded the palace at all times. Kido assured Konoye that Anami had the army under control. But he did pass on the rumor to Hirohito's chief ADC, who promptly sought out Mori and was told the men were "troubled," but that Mori knew of no impending coup. Konoye was right, and Mori was misinformed: several Imperial Guards officers *had* joined Major Hatanaka's conspiracy: they included two men in sensitive posts, Major Hidemasa Koga (who commanded a battalion and happened to be Tojo's son-in-law) and Major Ishihara, a staff officer.

Waiting to broadcast, Hirohito went for his usual evening walk in the palace gardens. Returning to the library, he found Prime Minister Suzuki waiting for him, but only to apologize for the delay in preparing the rescript. It was still not quite ready, he said.

Finally, around 7:30 P.M., the surrender broadcast text was completed to everyone's satisfaction, but the copy brought to the palace was scribbled over with insertions, and would need to be copied on special paper in impeccable calligraphy. This would take more time. It was clear the actual broadcast would not take place that day, and a new time was set. Foreign Minister Togo wanted it to go out as soon as possible, and suggested 7:00 A.M. the following day. Anami objected: he wanted a twenty-four-hour delay so that all Japanese troops overseas would have time to receive it, along with the War Ministry's comments and explanations. As a compromise measure, they decided that noon, August 15, would be the best possible time. In that pre-transistor age, this would also provide the necessary time for electric power to be restored temporarily all over Japan, and for appropriate warning to be given in advance on the radio.

The fair copy of the text to be broadcast was now shown to Hirohito, who read it carefully in the library, and, in his meticulous, schoolmasterish way, proceeded to fiddle with it. In all he made five corrections, changing once more the phrase that had held up the proceedings to "The war situation has developed, not necessarily to Japan's advantage." In the process of final revision, a chamberlain noted a serious grammatical error in the sentence referring to the Hiroshima bomb. Exceptionally, because of the urgent circumstances, it was decided not to rewrite the parchment entirely, but to paste over bits of it.

Now the amended text went back to the prime minister, who made a face when he saw that it was not a perfectly clean copy, and returned it to the emperor, who affixed his imperial seal on it. Then a second copy of the amended text was taken back to the prime minister's office: all the cabinet ministers had to sign it. Anami did so without even bothering to read it, and then went straight to his War Ministry office. Only now did he write his own letter of resignation, and began clearing his desk.

The rescript was now official, and Foreign Ministry officials could draft the cable that would announce Japan's surrender to the outside world:

> His Majesty the Emperor has issued an Imperial Rescript regarding Japan's acceptance of the provisions of the Potsdam declaration. His Majesty the Emperor is prepared to authorize and ensure the signature by his government and the Imperial General Headquarters of the necessary terms for carrying out the provisions of the Potsdam declaration. His Majesty is also prepared to issue his commands to all the military, naval and air authorities of Japan and all the forces under their control, wherever located, to cease active operations, to surrender arms and to issue such other orders as may be required by the Supreme Commander of the Allied Forces for the execution of the above-mentioned terms.

Like the earlier acceptance, it was sent to the Japanese embassies in Bern and Stockholm for onward transmission to the governments of the United States, China, Britain and the USSR.

All over Tokyo, fires began. These were not the "flowers of Edo" caused by incendiary bombs, but huge bonfires, inside the palace, in ministry and military HQ courtyards all over Japan: all confidential documents and files were being destroyed.

It was now past 10:00 P.M., and the NHK team was still waiting. Hirohito was ready to make the recording, but his aides suggested that he stay in the library, ready to move down to the shelter, in case B-29s staged one of their almost nightly raids. If no air raid warning sounded in the next few hours, he could then safely proceed to the nearby Imperial Household Ministry building.

At the prime minister's office, Suzuki had called for one last meeting, to get letters of resignation from his cabinet to pave the way for a new, postwar government. Afterward Anami apologized to Suzuki for causing him so many problems. "My chief aim has always been the preservation of our national polity," he said.

Suzuki attempted to reassure him. "The Imperial House will be preserved," he told Anami. "The Emperor is safe. He will soon be praying to the spirits of his ancestors."

"I trust he will be safe," Anami said.

"I am not unduly pessimistic about the future of Japan," said Suzuki. "If the Emperor and the people are together, Japan will recover."

Anami then handed over a paper-wrapped box of Sumatran cigars, a present from a fellow general in the Dutch East Indies. "I don't smoke," he said. "The Prime Minister should have them." He saluted and left the premier's office. Suzuki told an aide: "I think the War minister came to say goodbye."

It was nearly midnight when chamberlains, senior NHK officials and the director of the Information Bureau headed for the improvised studio set up on the second floor of the Imperial Household Ministry. The emperor was not introduced to any of the NHK staffers; he said, in a businesslike voice, "How should I speak?" Shimomura said an ordinary conversational tone would be fine.

The cumbersome record-cutting process began: first the senior engineer started the machine running, and signaled to the palace official standing in the doorway that proceedings could begin. The palace official bowed to Shimomura, who bowed to Hirohito, who held the text in his hand. The chamberlain made a short voice test in the emperor's stead, to make sure everything was in working order, and the emperor began reading his text.

"Nobody had ever heard the Emperor's voice," said Haruna. "In the past we had been told that if we ever accidentally recorded his voice at an official function, there would be hell to pay. Because I was very nervous, I didn't listen to the meaning of his words closely. I had earphones on, and I was more concerned with the level of the voice than its content, but I caught the gist of it. He spoke for about three minutes, and we were cutting two records at a time. We had plenty of blank records—about sixty in all."

After the first record had been cut, Hirohito asked, in a matter-of-fact, casual tone of voice, "Shall I do it again?" "We would never have asked him ourselves," Haruna said, "and in fact the first attempt was fine." Shimomura bowed in assent, and Hirohito started reading his speech again. The second recording was not as good as the first, Haruna recalls. It was too high-pitched, and the emperor fluffed a word. After he had finished, Hirohito said, "I am perfectly prepared to do it again." The two versions were played to him. It was decided that the first one would be used.

Hirohito left immediately afterward, by car, for the short drive back to the library. A palace official told the NHK crew they could sleep in the Imperial Household Ministry dormitory if they wished, but all were eager to get home. In any case, their work was not yet over: the recording gear had to be dismantled and repacked in heavy containers. As they were completing their task the siren wail began: the last B-29 raid over Tokyo was about to begin, and Hirohito prepared for another uneasy, uncomfortable night in his airless shelter. The four records were put into metal cases, then into two cotton bags. A junior chamberlain, Yoshihiro Tokugawa, a descendant of the famous Tokugawa shogun clan that had once exercised more power than Hirohito's forebears, locked them in a small safe in one of the palace offices rather than take the risk of sending them over to the NHK building in the middle of an air raid.

The text of the emperor's broadcast was released to Domei, and to all major newspapers, with instructions that it not be published until after the actual broadcast had taken place the following day.

While the NHK team was packing up, and Director of Information Shimomura was enjoying a late cup of green tea with one of the palace chamberlains, the coup leaders made their last desperate move: Major Hatanaka and his chief aide, Captain Shigetaro Uehara, of the Air Academy, called on General Mori at the Imperial Guards Headquarters. With the single-minded faith of religious fanatics, they believed they could win him over to their side. Mori was in his office, talking to his brother-in-law, Lieutenant Colonel Michinori Shiraishi. When Mori angrily refused to be part of the coup, Hatanaka shot him with his pistol; Uehara beheaded Shiraishi with his sword. Then, with the help of a Guards officer who was part of the conspiracy, they put the general's seal on a divisional order, already prepared, calling on it to surround the palace, seal it off from the outside world, and also seal off the NHK broadcasting office. The highly disciplined regimental commanders, with no inkling of what had really happened, and assuming they were obeying Mori's orders, immediately got their men together. Some of the senior NHK staff, who had not waited for the technical crew to finish work, were rounded up by Imperial Guardsmen as they left the palace grounds and taken to the division's guardrooms. There were soldiers all over the place, for Major Koga's battalion had already entered the palace grounds without official orders, and, as Haruna and the rest of the NHK recording crew emerged from the Imperial Household Ministry, they too were arrested and taken to the same guardroom to join the senior NHK officials there. As in the 2/26 mutiny, the palace was isolated from the outside world.

Hatanaka knew the emperor had already recorded his surrender speech; he also knew, from questioning the NHK staff as they emerged from the Imperial Household Ministry, that the records must still be inside the palace, but where? His aim, at this stage, was to prevent the speech from going on the air. That was the first step, for there were also plans, already worked out with friends in the Army Air Force, the Naval Air Service, and other army units, including the Yokohama Guards, for a last-ditch resistance appeal, and, as in 2/26, for the murder of the "traitors" who had given the emperor "bad advice." Top assassination targets were Kido and Prime Minister Suzuki.

The rebel officers cut the palace telephone lines and began searching for the records. Imperial Guards officers and NCOs started ransacking the palace, terrorizing the palace staff. Kido and Imperial Household minister Ishiwatari, who knew they must be on the army's hit list, hid in the palace "bank vault," a strong room at least as secure as that of a large bank. Chamberlain Tokugawa was badly beaten by a Guards officer for showing him "disrespect." But the rebel soldiers failed to find the records, and, throughout the early hours of the morning, while all this was taking place, the emperor slept on undisturbed and unaware that the Imperial Guards were swarming all over the palace grounds. His chamberlains gathered at the entrance to the imperial air raid shelter and debated whether to wake him and tell him what was going on. They decided to let him sleep. As it turned out, the emperor, insomniac as usual during these final months of the war, had been awake when they started whispering to each other about the coup, heard their murmured conversation and wondered what was going on.

While the Imperial Guards were searching the palace, General Anami was making final preparations for his own, elaborate *seppuku*. His brother-in-law, Lieutenant Colonel Takeshita, had been sent to Anami's home to make one last attempt to get him to join the rebels. He found Anami drinking sake, preparing for his death like a true samurai. Anami seemed in no hurry to die, and talked dispassionately of the past. By now Takeshita himself knew the crazy coup would fail. Rather than return to Hatanaka's side, he preferred to stay with Anami, and assist him in the *seppuku* rites if asked. For someone about to kill himself painfully, Anami seemed in great spirits; he joked with Takeshita about having had a vitamin injection that day—"I could hardly say I didn't want it because I was going to die, could I now?"

It was customary for someone committing *seppuku* to leave a posthumous message behind. Anami had given this considerable thought: first he wrote a poem, in his elegant hand:

> *After tasting the profound benevolence of the Emperor,*
> *I have no words to speak.*

On another piece of parchment, he wrote:

> *For my supreme crime, I beg forgiveness through this*
> *act of death.*

On the back of this he added, as an afterthought: "I believe in Japan's sacred indestructability."

He dated both pieces of paper August 14, though it was now dawn, August 15. "The Emperor's broadcast will take place at noon," he told Takeshita. "I couldn't bear to hear it." His "supreme crime," Takeshita grasped, was losing the war.

The Imperial Guards officers' coup had so far gone without a hitch, but now one of its regimental commanders, ordered to bring out his men and surround the palace, found this such an unusual order that instead of obeying he decided to check with the Eastern Army Command Headquarters first. He didn't have far to go: it was housed in the Dai Ichi building across the road from the palace. Its chief of staff, Major General Tatsuhiko Takashima, quickly determined that something was wrong. He called his boss, General Shizuichi Tanaka, a much feared martinet, and sent his own trusted officers out on a reconnaissance; he also put the military police, the *kempei,* on alert. By this time some of the rebel Guards officers wondered whether Major Hatanaka was telling them the truth: he had insisted that General Anami had given the coup his blessing, but there was no proof of this. And when two Eastern Army Command staff officers demanded to see General Mori, and found his body, they knew the coup had gone wrong. Minutes later, General Tanaka, the Eastern Army commander, ordered all the Imperial Guards out of the palace. Mori, Tanaka told his troops, had been killed by insubordinate officers. From now on, all the Imperial Guards were to obey the Eastern Army commander and no one else.

In General Anami's house, Takeshita finally blurted out that Mori had been killed in an attempted coup to stop the emperor's broadcast. "One last thing to apologize for," Anami said quietly.

Those palace chamberlains on duty in the library above the Emperor's bunker were now convinced that it was only a matter of time before rebel officers tried to break in; they closed the shutters and barricaded themselves inside.

Now, at around 4:00 A.M., the Eastern Army Command's bureaucratic machinery slowly but inexorably went into action: as a first step, General Takashima phoned the Imperial Guards HQ and demanded to talk to coup leader Hatanaka. "Your situation is hopeless," he told him. "You must obey the Emperor."

Hatanaka wouldn't give up. Now all he asked for was ten minutes of NHK radio time before the emperor's broadcast went on the air "to talk to the people and explain our position." Takashima hung up on him. The ghastly implications of the plot—foisted on the Imperial Guards under false pretenses—made Hatanaka an unwelcome guest, and he left, as he had arrived, by motorcycle.

But part of Hatanaka's plot was being implemented elsewhere: a squad of Yokohama Guards, along with some youthful civilians, had arrived in front of Prime Minister Suzuki's official residence and opened fire on the house with machine guns. When they found out that Suzuki was not there, the insurgents in their rage tried to burn it to the ground. They then moved on to Suzuki's private home; the prime minister, forewarned, had time to flee, but his house was gutted.

Hatanaka now drove as fast as he could to the NHK building and demanded admittance. The Imperial Guards on duty outside, recognizing him, allowed him in. Hatanaka announced to frightened NHK staff that he was going on the air. He was nonplussed when the radio announcer on duty, Morio Tateno, told him this would not be possible: "No broadcasts during an alert," he said. In any case, he added, advance warning had to be given for nationwide broadcasts. "It's a technical matter." Tateno was a well-known radio anchorman who had announced the start of the war on December 8, 1941. Coolly assuming that Hatanaka was part of an army plot to stop the emperor's broadcast, Tateno was determined not to let this happen. If Hatanaka insisted on speaking into the microphone, he would cut off the power switch, he thought to himself. But Hatanaka did not try to use physical force: so authoritative was Tateno's manner that he clearly believed him, and, instead of pushing Tateno out of his chair, simply stayed in the studio, waiting for the air raid to end.

It was now shortly after 5:00 A.M., and outside the Imperial Palace a small cortege of army cars came to a halt. General Tanaka, the Eastern Army commander, got out, surrounded by handpicked *kempei* bodyguards. He arrested one of the Imperial Guards ringleader officers and had him marched away by the *kempei*. He then entered the Inui Gate; his aim was to order the Imperial Guards regimental commanders to get their men together, march out of the palace and release all prisoners. His other urgent duty was to apologize to the emperor for this tragic, undignified, last-minute coup attempt.

It was around this time that Anami, very drunk on sake by now, but with an unerring hand, stabbed himself with a razor-sharp dagger and drew it sharply across his stomach. Blood spurted, smearing his parchment letters. Anami, kneeling, didn't keel over, but watched himself bleed. Transferring the dagger to his left hand, he reached for his carotid artery on the right side of his neck, and made a sudden, deep incision. Blood flowed all over him.

The two chamberlains guarding the entrance to the bunker below the imperial library decided they couldn't delay their grim task anymore: they decided to wake the emperor and break the news to him that he was a virtual prisoner.

Hirohito showed no emotion. "Is it a coup?" he asked. "Tell me what has actually happened." When they had finished, he proposed that he address the assembled Imperial Guards and explain his decision once more. He asked the chamberlains to find his chief ADC, but this officer was confined to the Imperial Household Ministry building, with a screen of rebellious Imperial Guards in between.

General Tanaka, having talked sharply to the Imperial Guards officers, was on his way to the imperial library. He passed a chamberlain trying to slip through into the Ministry to find the ADC. "Is the grand chamberlain in the library?" Tanaka asked.

Not knowing whether the general was on the rebels' side or not, the chamberlain wouldn't tell him. "Stop trembling," General Tanaka said. "The revolt's over." He introduced himself. "I deeply regret," he said, "that so much inconvenience has been caused."

The rebellion was now practically confined to Major Hatanaka and a few officers and men, all in and around the NHK building. Brandishing his revolver, Hatanaka was still insisting on broadcasting, especially now that the all clear had sounded. Morio Tateno, on one pretext or another, was still refusing to let him do so, and soon the Imperial Guards outside the NHK building were withdrawn.

As sound engineer Shizuto Haruna, who had returned to the NHK building after his release from the guardroom, remembers it, a chamberlain, "wearing shabby clothes, looking almost like a beggar," showed up later on that morning with the precious record. He had deliberately assumed this disguise so that rebellious troops would not think he was from the palace and search him. Out of sight of Major Hatanaka, preparations for the emperor's broadcast now began.

Morio Tateno remembers that one final telephone call came through—for Major Hatanaka. It must have been from Eastern Army Command, perhaps from General Tanaka himself, for Hatanaka straightened up, said "Yes, sir" several times, and, hanging up, muttered to himself, "It's all over." He then left the building, with his faithful sidekick, Lieutenant Colonel Jiro Shiizaki. Outside, in a fit of rage, Shiizaki drew his sword, and took wild aim at a pine tree. Around this time, General Anami finally died, and the Yokohama Guards, on their rampage still, set fire to Baron Hiranuma's house before returning to Yokohama.

Hatanaka pushing his motorcycle, Lieutenant Colonel Shiizaki holding his horse, were finally apprehended distributing leaflets outside the Imperial Palace. These read: "Our intention is to protect the Emperor and to preserve the national polity despite the designs of the enemy. . . . We pray that the Japanese people and the members of the Armed Forces will appreciate the significance of our action and join with us to fight for the preservation of our country and the elimination of the traitors around the Emperor, thus confounding the enemy's schemes." The rare passersby glanced at the leaflets, but showed no interest in reading them.

After their arrest, in a final act of defiance, Hatanaka shot himself, while Shiizaki committed *seppuku* with his sword. On Hatanaka's body the *kempei* found a poem he had written: "I have nothing to regret now that the dark clouds have disappeared from the reign of the Emperor." A wake for the two men would be held that night, attended by most of the staff officers from the War Ministry.

Now, at regular intervals, all over Japan, radio announcements warned that the emperor would be speaking at noon and everyone was to listen. In factories, offices, hospitals and village squares, radio sets were readied, and street committees spread the word that the entire population was to be marshaled for this unprecedented, epochal event. In the NHK studio, a brief row flared as Haruna tested the quality of the record by playing a few seconds of the speech in advance. "I had to do this," he said, "to get the overlapping right." The Imperial Household minister objected; "He looked disapproving and uptight," Haruna recalls. Another palace chamberlain with him said, "It's wrong to test the Emperor's voice." At the time, of course, the emperor was still a living God, and "one shouldn't test a God. I said: 'Just let me do it my way,' and the NHK Director, who was standing by, told the Imperial Household minister: 'Do let this young man get on with his job.'

"A broadcast of the highest importance is about to be made," said an NHK voice a few seconds before noon. "All listeners please rise."

There was a brief pause, and the national anthem, "Kimigayo," was played. "His Majesty the Emperor," said the NHK voice, "will now read his Imperial Rescript to the people of Japan. We respectfully transmit his voice."

Hirohito listened, in the safety of his bunker. In the whole of Japan, he was probably the only able-bodied Japanese to do so sitting down.

CHAPTER TWENTY-TWO

Those who listened to the emperor's broadcast speech at noon on August 15, 1945—and they must have numbered upward of fifty million at least, out of a total population of seventy-five million—never forgot the impact of "the Voice of the Crane," or the circumstances under which they heard it.*

Akira Kurosawa, the world-famous film director, then a young, up-and-coming filmmaker compelled to make propaganda films and beset by censorship problems, had been ordered to report to his studio, along with all the other film workers, to hear Hirohito speak. "I'll never forget the scenes as I walked the streets that day,"† he wrote later. "On the way from Soshigaya to the studio in Kinuta, the shopping street looked fully prepared for the Honorable Death of the Hundred Million. The atmosphere was tense, panicked. There were even shopkeepers who had taken their Japanese swords from their sheaths and sat staring at the bare blades."

---

*See the Appendix for the text of the emperor's speech.
†Akira Kurosawa, *Something Like an Autobiography* (New York: Knopf, 1982).

Robert Guillain, by this time interned with other "hostile aliens" in the comparative safety of a mountain village,

> saw people in my corner of the village gather around radio sets, not in each house, but in groups in their *tonarigumi* [civil defense] leaders' houses. No one in these groups of pantalooned housewives and runty elders clustered around the blue-and-white pennants of their civil-defense sections knew what the sovereign was going to say. . . . People clustered in the doorways because the houses were too small to hold them all. . . . Silence. And then that voice never heard before. A little hoarse, slow, too controlled, the voice of someone reading a speech. Surprise! for all practical purposes, no one understood a word of it! The sovereign was speaking the learned and solemn language reserved to the Son of Heaven alone: an antique, almost Chinese, language that had little in common with the language the people spoke and was made even more unintelligible by the fact that while the people may sometimes have read Imperial proclamations, they had never before heard one spoken by the Emperor himself. As soon as he finished speaking, an official commentator had to come on with a vernacular translation of what the Emperor had said. Only then was his speech really understood.*

After it was over, Domei reporter Matsuo Kato recalls,† "people huddled together in the ruins [of Tokyo]. . . . There was no leadership that could have overcome the mass inertia." Kato remembers the "dull, vacant stares" of the people but also their "sense of relief. In a way, it was like a miraculous and unexpected cure after a long illness." Newspaper editors and staff behaved "like a canary released from its cage."

Kurosawa witnessed similar signs of relief: "When I walked the same route back to my home [afterward], the scene was entirely different. The people in the shopping street were bustling about with

---

*Guillain, *I Saw Tokyo Burning.*
†Kato, *The Lost War.*

cheerful faces as if preparing for a festival the next day." Reflecting on the alternative, the "Honorable Death of a Hundred Million" that many Japanese expected the emperor to announce, Kurosawa wrote that if the emperor had made such a call, "those people . . . probably would have done as they were told and died. And probably I would have done likewise. The Japanese see self-assertion as immoral and self-sacrifice as the sensible course to take in life. We were accustomed to this teaching and had never thought to question it. . . . In wartime we were all like deaf-mutes."

Guillain remembers the shock—and relief—caused by the emperor's high-pitched, incantatory broadcast: "When the announcer came on to explain the Emperor's speech, the people remained stiff and silent for a few moments more in the intensity of concentration. Then it was over. They had understood, and the sobbing broke out. . . . Something huge had just cracked: the proud dream of Greater Japan. They scattered and hid to weep in the seclusion of their wooden houses. Absolute silence prevailed in the village. As you walked down the street, all you saw through the doors left open in the August heat was an occasional tear-stained face that turned quickly away as you passed." All over Japan, civilians remained in their homes for several days, weeping continuously.

General Anami was not the only one to prefer death to surrender: among the notable suicides were General Sugiyama and his wife; Admiral Takijiro Onishi, the "father" of the kamikaze idea (he could do no less without losing intolerable face); General Honjo, Hirohito's former chief ADC; General Tanaka, the Eastern Army commander who had nipped the Imperial Guards' conspiracy in the bud; and several other high-ranking officers. Other, lesser-known army and navy officers also killed themselves, some within yards of the Imperial Palace walls and gates, deliberately facing in the emperor's direction. But on the whole there were far fewer such deaths than expected. There were, however, continuing signs of rage: the navy's "special attack corps" overflew Tokyo several times that day, dropping leaflets saying, "Don't surrender, don't believe the Imperial Rescript, it was a false document," and there were brief mutinies at the midget submarine base at Yokosuka, close to Tokyo, and at the nearby Military Cadets School. Very quickly, *kempei* and navy police removed the propellers from still-serviceable planes, to prevent kamikaze attempts on the expected U.S. occupation force advance guard.

It was only later that the ambiguity of the emperor's speech became apparent. As Guillain noted: "How odd the proclamation was, and how Japanese in spirit! How prudently it dealt with the future, how careful it was not to tarnish the book of Japanese history with the forbidden word 'surrender.' . . . Not once was the word 'defeat' mentioned. Should the military, in the future, have occasion to rewrite history to their liking, they will be able to cite the proclamation as witness that Japan had ended the war only because of the inhumanity of her enemies and that, even though his armies were intact, her Emperor had agreed to end the carnage because he wished to be not only the savior of Japan but the defender of human civilisation." This view is shared by Russell Braddon, himself a former prisoner of war and the biographer of Shoichi Yokoi, the Japanese soldier who hid in the Guam jungles for twenty-two years rather than surrender: "The Emperor didn't mention unconditional surrender, only that he had decided to put an end to the war and that fighting must stop," he wrote. "So little like surrender did the rescript sound to our captors that, then and there, they told us, all men go home. Instead of beating us, they bowed. Instead of killing us off, they began to feed us up."

The final tragedy, Guillain noted, "reserved one more surprise for us. Seventy-five million people were supposed to have died to the last man. Even the poorest of them swore, and doubtless believed, that they would commit harakiri rather than surrender. And when, after averting its face to weep, Japan looked up again—it entered tranquilly into its defeat. There seemed a disconcerting facility in that acceptance; the page was turned with seeming effortlessness. And on Japan's new face was a glimmer of something that had not been seen in a very long time: the special Japanese smile." The police "who had so long made us feel the weight of their hate and petty persecution" visited each foreigner, bowing endlessly and offering their amiable services; the civil defense leaders smiled, and handed out sake and new clothes to the foreigners; so did Foreign Ministry officials, obsequiously calling on neutral embassy diplomats and urging them to visit prisoner-of-war camps, whose inspection they had constantly refused in the past. There were even smiles from the man in the street. Traveling back to Tokyo, Guillain noted that "as though the courtesy and hospitality of a long-vanished Japan had been reborn, amiable volunteers kindly offered their assistance. 'Can I help you carry your luggage? Can you find your way? Everything has changed so, hasn't it?' And my unpaid guide gestured toward the ruined station, toward the ravaged plain that was once Tokyo, and he laughed that Japanese laugh. . . . Even the press smiled. With a single twist, all the newspapers turned their coats at once. In only a week, the famous *Nippon Times* (formerly the *Tokyo Times and Advertiser*), fascistic and militaristic before, became a champion of democracy, parliamentary government and the people's rights; having shouted itself hoarse about 'American bestiality,' here it was informing its readers of the impatiently awaited invaders' generosity of soul and protesting that only rude and stupid Japanese provincials could imagine that an American soldier was a gangster in uniform."

There now took place one of the strangest conspiracies not just of the Showa era, but of Japan's twenty-six-hundred-year-old dynasty—a tragicomic episode of the kind Japanese filmmakers like Kurosawa have drawn on to make their epic movies: though seldom referred to, it was certainly discussed within the privacy of the palace, for Prince Takamatsu himself had a small part in it. Whether Hirohito, too, looked on it with approval, or detached amusement, or hostility, will in all probability never be known, for the subject of this plot has never been publicly raised in his presence, though it was later officially acknowledged. Most likely, he approved of what took place, as a means of preserving the emperor system should the Americans have been sufficiently foolish, or bold, to dissolve the imperial dynasty and proclaim a Japanese republic, as many Japanese, at war's end, felt they might.

It all began on a naval air base on Kyushu, Japan's southernmost island, shortly after the emperor's surrender speech. Navy Captain Minoru Genda, Admiral Yamamoto's onetime chief aide, a close friend of Prince Takamatsu (and, according to many military experts, the real brains behind the Pearl Harbor planning), convened one last parade of all the officers and men of his beloved 343rd Squadron. He told them that he, like many officers, had believed at first that the emperor had been tricked into proclaiming the end of the war by "evil advisers." But after flying to Tokyo to consult with senior Navy Ministry officials, Genda told them, he was now convinced that the emperor had indeed decided to end the war. "If we were to continue fighting," he said, "this would be against the Emperor's will." He ended his harangue emotionally ("I will never see you again, farewell"), hinting rather broadly that rather than witness the occupation of Japan he was going to commit *seppuku*. He then asked the officers and NCOs (about two hundred in all) to stay behind. He wanted to take them into his confidence, he said. At 8:00 P.M. he, Genda, would commit suicide. Did anyone wish to join him in this act? About twenty people raised their hands.

"Don't make an emotional, spur-of-the-moment decision," Genda urged them. "Think about it. There's nothing dishonorable about changing your minds."

Eventually some twenty-three officers and NCOs showed up at 8:00 P.M. Genda told them they should first write farewell letters to their families. They did so. Ritual cups of sake were drunk, and fellow officers exchanged toasts. The mood was grim, and some of those present may have wondered why it was taking so long. Genda then explained his real motive in bringing this desperate band together. "I apologize for putting you through this kind of test," he told them, "but there was no alternative. What I have to propose is a mission far more important than death. It begins right now."

On his lightning visit to Tokyo just after the emperor's speech, Genda told them, he had been entrusted with an epoch-making secret: the Imperial Navy intended to kidnap a small child of royal blood, hide him in a remote place where the occupation forces would never find him, bring him up as the rightful heir and wait until the time was ripe to restore him to the throne. It was a plan straight out of Japan's rich, romantic tapestry of medieval legends, but it also had some real-life historical precedents, and had been devised by some of the Navy Ministry's brightest officials and staff officers, with what was left of the ministry's secret-fund "treasure chest."

Genda, together with a small, dedicated group under his command, would become the chosen instrument to preserve Japan's imperial dynasty. From the start (the scheme was first discussed a few weeks before the actual surrender) Prince Takamatsu had been aware of it, had approved it and suggested that Genda was the right man for the job. The officer entrusted with the overall planning was Rear Admiral Tomiyoka, who had briefed Genda on the broad lines of the scheme, earmarked the necessary funds, and told him to get a team together.

In the context of August 1945 the plan, for all its romantic overtones, made practical sense: almost all senior military men were convinced that, at best, Hirohito would be compelled to abdicate; at worst, the entire imperial family might be punished, dispersed and exiled. But this, Tomiyoka argued, was but a temporary crisis, for America and the Soviet Union were bound to fall out soon and eventually fight a war, and then Japan would have a chance of being restored to greatness once more. The important thing was to maintain, in hiding, a member of the exalted Meiji family who would continue to be steeped in the age-old Japanese imperial traditions, and so would be ready to assume the role of emperor once more favorable conditions prevailed. Given the state of the world, Genda told his men, this might not take long, but they should assume it might be a lifelong mission. From now on this small group was to be an elite secret society, and the lives of all its members had to be subordinate to the task of hiding, raising, educating and maintaining in suitable comfort the small boy who would later become the new emperor. They might marry, take jobs, achieve prominent positions in the new Japan, but their ultimate loyalty, in all circumstances, would be to the secret heir to the throne, and they had to be prepared to sacrifice their fortunes, their well-being and if necessary their lives to this new ideal.

As a first step, Genda went on, a suitable hiding place had to be found, and a suitable family would have to be let in on the secret. This selection was all-important, for this family had to be able to impart to the young prince not only Japan's traditional *bushido* values but the Shintoist precepts and rites they all wished to keep alive. The chosen elite of the 343rd Squadron should see the project as a full-fledged military operation, and start looking for a secure hiding place with plenty of food and a suitable climate. There and then, the navy plotters dispersed, with secret funds, trucks, gasoline, blankets and food. They established a secure communications link, with Genda masterminding the operation as a whole.

Eleven days after Hirohito's surrender speech, they had found a possible hiding place—a remote hilltop village on Kyushu called Gokanosho. But Genda was not happy with the local population. He doubted whether they could be trusted, and he could find no reliable locals to assume the role of "parents." Reluctantly, Gokanosho was dropped, and eventually Genda settled on another location, a remote spot on the sparsely populated coast. Here, he decided, a house would be built. There was ample cultivable land for a vegetable garden, and plenty of fish in the sea, so the future emperor would not starve.

What Genda did not know was that an army group had not only had the same idea but had made far more advanced preparations, for this group had already chosen its future emperor and obtained permission at the highest level to go ahead with their scheme.

The mastermind behind this parallel conspiracy was a senior War Ministry official, Hirose, who, long before the actual surrender, had also worked out a plan to preserve the imperial dynasty by hiding a member of the Meiji family from the Americans until the time was ripe for him to reclaim the throne. His candidate was the seven-year-old Prince Kitashirakawa, the grandson of another Prince Kitashirakawa, a daredevil pilot who had died in France in a car crash in 1923 in mysterious circumstances, at a time when Prince Higashikuni had still been "studying" in Paris. Both he and Kitashirakawa had married daughters of Emperor Meiji. His son—the selected boy's father, Nagahisa Kitashirakawa—had also died in unusual circumstances: at a prewar air display, a plane, whose pilot had lost control, had crashed into the spectators' stand, killing him. The accident-prone heredity of the Kitashirakawa family had not deterred Hirose, however. At the time of the surrender, Emperor Meiji's great-grandson was living with his grandmother, mother and a small retinue of servants and ladies-in-waiting in a large house near Mount Fuji, which belonged to a prominent entrepreneur called Tanaka who had business connections with the imperial family. The family had taken refuge there to escape from the bombing, which had destroyed all of the Kitashirakawa family's valuable Tokyo real estate.

The army plotters had not only found the boy, but also enlisted the help of the young prince's grandmother, Princess Fusako, the second of Emperor Meiji's four daughters. Her younger sister Nobuko had married Prince Asaka of "rape of Nanking" fame, and her youngest sister was married to Prince Higashikuni, who was about to become Japan's first postwar prime minister. Princess Fusako had even provided the plotters with a letter confirming her knowledge and approbation of the scheme.

The rank and file of the small secret group entrusted with young Prince Kitashirakawa's secret hiding place were handpicked members of the Nakano Spy School. One of its graduates, Colonel Ichiro Kubota, became the executive officer responsible for the whole scheme, and he devised a plan reflecting his own background in the secret world of espionage.

It so happened that Kubota knew a wealthy ham manufacturer called Takuzo Imanari who was himself a staunch patriot. He decided to bring Imanari into the plot, and hide the young prince in Imanari's village, Rokkamachi, some four hundred kilometers northwest of Tokyo. At least, Kubota argued, the young prince would never be short of food in Rokkamachi.

But when Kubota got to Rokkamachi, he found a somewhat shifty Imanari, who appeared to have second thoughts about the whole thing. No mean interrogator himself, Kubota grilled Imanari on his apparent reticence, and what he discovered made him angry. Imanari admitted that he was already hiding one VIP in his village since the surrender, at the request of the Japanese Foreign Ministry: the Burmese nationalist leader U Ba Maw, wanted by the British as a prominent Japanese collaborator.

The plotters mulled this over, and finally came to the conclusion they had no choice but to stick with Imanari. But another Nakano Spy School veteran, Inomata, decided the risks of hiding two VIPs in the same place were far too great. Inomata had, in the immediate prewar period, been a full-fledged Japanese intelligence agent in Germany and the USSR, under the alias of Joji Imura. Now, after raising funds from former Nakano Spy School veterans (who thought he was making plans to hide the son of one of the topmost Japanese war criminals), Inomata set out for Hiroshima, determined to talk local municipal officials there into providing him genuine identity papers for a seven-year-old boy. He picked the place deliberately because its archives had been entirely destroyed.

Getting papers proved to be more difficult than he anticipated, for he ran into one of those indomitable Japanese bureaucrats who fussed over details and were determined to go by the book, despite the calamity that had recently struck. Under his Imura alias, Inomata said he was a distant relative of a family, the Kimuras, that had been wiped out in the bombing—all but their small son, Michio, who was lying seriously wounded in hospital. He needed new ID papers.

The bureaucrat was either extremely obtuse or very suspicious, perhaps both. It was most unusual for ID papers to disappear without a trace. Was he quite certain the parents were dead? How could he be sure? Inomata said their house had been at the very epicenter of the explosion. Then how come the boy is alive? the bureaucrat asked.

He eventually allowed Inomata to fill out a form, but when he handed it in, the bureaucrat asked him for *his* ID papers.

"I don't have any," Inomata said. "They were destroyed in one of the Tokyo raids."

"Without papers," the bureaucrat said, "I can't do a thing."

How could he be so heartless? Inomata asked. The boy was badly burned and would probably die. Did the clerk want him cremated anonymously, like an animal? Hadn't his family suffered enough?

Eventually the clerk relented, and made out papers for Michio Kimura, born March 31, 1938, of a military arsenal worker who had married and fathered a son in Okinawa (another place, Inomata knew, where no one was likely to check the records).

The real prince, a lively seven-year-old with a beautiful younger sister called Hatsuko, was still living with the Tanaka family in the country under fairly enviable circumstances. Because of Princess Fusako's close connections with Hirohito (she was, in fact, his aunt) the Tanaka house was guarded by the police and by a company of Japanese infantry. Additional rations were provided by the Japanese Foreign Ministry, from its allocation for foreign diplomats. In all, Princess Fusako's retinue consisted of about thirty people, but the U.S. occupation soon put a stop to their various privileges: the soldiers were demobilized, the police transferred to other duties. The ladies-in-waiting drifted away, and a few weeks after the end of the war Princess Fusako returned to Tokyo. But her house was tiny, and the small prince remained in the country. Inomata and Kubota (who had finally rallied to Inomata's plan) decided there was no harm in his remaining there for the time being. When they set about finding a suitable house, and suitable companions and environment for him, they ran into the same difficulties as Genda's group. Just before the War Ministry's operations came under close U.S. occupation scrutiny, before the final demobilization and disbandment of the Japanese imperial army, Hirose obtained five hundred thousand yen from its secret funds for that purpose.

While the plot to keep an emperor "replacement" unfurled, Japanese representatives signed the surrender terms aboard the *Missouri* in Tokyo Bay on September 2, and on September 8 General MacArthur, the "Supremo," arrived in Tokyo, establishing his headquarters in the Dai Ichi building recently vacated by the Eastern Corps Commander. He moved into the U.S. embassy residence, furnishing it, Faubion Bowers, his aide, recalled, with "rather hideous wicker furniture from the Philippines." The general came to Japan with the advance guard of a force that, at its peak, numbered over a million men (by mid-1946 it had been reduced to four hundred thousand, half in Korea, half in Japan); his headquarters staff alone numbered five thousand, and in the early occupation days, several hundred U.S. officers took over local government and administrative duties.

As time passed, and as the U.S. occupation became an accepted state of affairs, plans for the boy prince's survival as an "alternate" emperor failed to get under way: the occupation turned out to be very different from the brutally repressive regime the plotters had anticipated, and some of them got caught up in new, civilian interests. To acquire sufficient funds to maintain the young prince in requisite luxury, Kubota used the money to start a small toy factory, and Inomata invested in a plumbing business. They, too, had taken an oath to dedicate their lives to perpetuating the Meiji dynasty, and saw this as a first step in providing the boy prince with a steady income. They were better plotters than businessmen, however, and far from generating new income for the young prince's upkeep, both their ventures went bankrupt. Worse still, British intelligence, with the help of the newly arrived U.S. Counter-Intelligence Corps (CIC), began actively looking for U Ba Maw.

At the start of the U.S. occupation of Japan, the CIC was almost obsessively concerned with the continued underground existence of extremist Japanese military groups, plotting the assassination of high-ranking U.S. officers and guerrilla warfare against the occupation forces. Though CIC officers did uncover large numbers of arms caches, such anti-American underground activity was largely a figment of their imagination. Colonel Kubota, because of his Nakano Spy School antecedents, did attract their attention, however: informers told CIC agents that his toy-manufacturing activities seemed to be a front for something else. The CIC put Kubota under surveillance, and shortly afterward arrested him.

Faced with the prospect of holding out, and risking discovery of the prince's future hiding place, Kubota didn't hesitate: he betrayed U Ba Maw. On the pretext of finding him a safe, clandestine passage to North Korea, Kubota lured the Burmese ex–head of state to Tokyo. Kubota staged a banquet for him. At its conclusion, a squad led by the

British military attaché arrested him.* So anxious was Kubota to conceal all traces of the restoration plot that he ordered his wife to burn Princess Fusako's precious letter.

But in any case, even a short while after the start of the U.S. occupation, things were not turning out quite as the plotters had expected: it was becoming increasingly difficult to imagine that Japan would ever require a new emperor. Some of the army and navy plotters dropped out. Young Prince Kitashirakawa grew up, first under the Allied occupation, then in the "new" Japan, without ever realizing he had almost been spirited away, and only learned of the Genda and Kubota conspiracies years later. Now a commoner, and a senior Toshiba executive, he retains close links with the imperial family. His beautiful niece, daughter of his good-looking younger sister, is today one of the young women whose name frequently comes up when the marriage of Prince Naruhito, Hirohito's grandson, is discussed by palace insiders.

Even the sequel to the U Ba Maw story has a happy ending, for in the long run—with both India and Burma about to become full-fledged sovereign states—the British were compelled to release him, and he went on to become, briefly, the "father" of Burmese independence. He never forgave the Japanese, though, for delivering him into the hands of the British.

Kubota, Inomata and many of the other plotters simply faded away, but Minoru Genda, the brilliant ex-navy pilot, planner of Pearl Harbor and would-be kamikaze, went on to become the chief of staff of Japan's postwar self-defense air force, and after retirement, a prominent backbencher in the ruling Liberal Democratic party. He too had studied the imperial family tree assiduously, and by an odd coincidence had also selected young Prince Kitashirakawa as the best possible candidate. But Genda, too, was overcome by events, and never got around to approaching the boy's family.

In 1981, at the Togo temple in Harajuku, retired Air Marshal Genda staged a "dissolution celebration" for all those plotters who had once helped him on his romantic quest to prepare a young Meiji descendant to assume the Japanese throne. The survivors of the

---

*In his later memoirs, U Ba Maw claimed he surrendered "voluntarily."

twenty-three officers and NCOs who had sworn a suicide oath with Genda that fateful night in August 1945 were a cross section of the new, prosperous postwar Japan: they included an airline pilot, a businessman, the owner of a bookshop, and several former self-defense air force officers. In a short speech, Genda told them: "Our greatest success was in holding back and not kidnapping the prince. Our mission has been accomplished."

Asked about Genda's romantic plot, many years after the war, Prince Takamatsu merely said that "something like it might well have proved necessary." That must have been Hirohito's view too. In the event, it was the U.S. occupation policy toward the emperor and the U.S. belief in the emperor system as an essential factor of stability in Japanese society that eventually made the Genda and the Nakano Spy School conspiracies redundant.

Immediately after his surrender speech, Hirohito had no means of knowing this, nor had the victorious Allies quite made up their minds about him. There were so many other problems: Japan's towns were flattened, her people starving; her economy was in ruins. How to nurse Japan back to normalcy without, at the same time, reviving her aggressive, military tendencies, how to get Japan to accept defeat without provoking a desperate "werewolf" backlash were far more major preoccupations. Soviet entry into Japanese-controlled Manchuria, in the last six days of the war, further complicated matters; after Potsdam, the Allies knew they were on a collision course with the Soviet Union.

It so happened that in this new equation, Hirohito's role would become paramount: he quickly realized this, and rode out the storm with consummate skill. His talent for self-preservation astonished those who had assumed that catastrophic defeat necessarily brought in its wake the resignation of the emperor. In the astonishing occupation years, marked from the start by unexpectedly cordial U.S.-Japanese collaboration, the biggest collaborator was Hirohito himself.

CHAPTER TWENTY-THREE

As hundreds of thousands of American, Australian, British and New Zealand soldiers poured into Japan, and as MacArthur's huge headquarters began governing the country, some of the earlier, secret plans for maintaining the emperor system in a defeated Japan discussed and elaborated by Kido and Konoye from 1944 onward now became reality. Two days after the surrender, Higashikuni himself, Hirohito's uncle (by marriage to Toshiko, Emperor Meiji's youngest daughter), whose name had been so frequently mentioned, became Japan's first postwar prime minister, as Kido and he had secretly determined he would. An early Supreme Command, Allied Power (SCAP) confidential report on him noted that he had been removed from his China command after the Nanking atrocities, had pioneered the growth of Japanese air power, was "militaristic and nationalistic, a daredevil who drives his car alone in the Tokyo streets," and was known as a "tough disciplinarian, self-willed, stubborn, somewhat erratic, admired in the army for his strength of character and independence and directness of speech."

Higashikuni chose Prince Konoye as deputy premier, minister without portfolio, and real power behind the scenes. The presence of a "royal" and a "near royal" to head the government was dictated by the need to impress on the Japanese people that the emperor system still functioned, even in these abysmally difficult, humiliating times. Significantly, other members of the imperial family were sent to army commands throughout Japan to explain the meaning of the emperor's speech and directives.

In the short space of time between Hirohito's surrender speech, the arrival of the occupation-forces advance guard and the signing of the Japanese capitulation aboard the *Missouri* on September 2, Hirohito was in limbo: like all Tokyo residents, he must have felt immense relief that the bombing had stopped, but for him this didn't mean that the worst was over. B-29s continued to fly over Tokyo, an ominous reminder of an unendurably humiliating occupation to come. On August 30, Empress Nagako mentioned them in a letter to Crown Prince Akihito, still in his mountain hideout:

> Here every day B-29 bombers and fighters fly over noisily from morning till evening. To my regret, the B-29 is a great aircraft. I'm writing this in the library, and as I look up, lots of them are flying over us as I write.
>
> How are you doing? I'm very pleased you're fit and fine in this heat. We've not seen each other for a long time but you must have heard the voice of His Majesty. Your father was worried so much every day but Japan was saved for ever. A lot of people come to the Palace every day with thanks and apologies.
>
> You also should think over what the Emperor said in a great Rescript. Study hard and endure the unendurable, without making any mistakes. Train your body: we have to establish a great nation, to turn bad luck into good.

In the almost unreal first few days of peace, Hirohito was chiefly concerned about his own immediate future: Should he resign now or later? Would the Allies insist on his departure, and, perhaps, on his indictment as a war criminal? Furthermore, in a country where "custom compels senior leaders to take responsibility for serious mishaps involving their organizations" (to quote the *Washington Post*'s story about the resignation of Japan's defense minister following a collision between a Japanese submarine and a fishing vessel in 1988) it was unthinkable to many Japanese, including those closest to him, that he should remain on the throne after what had happened to Japan, and indeed Professor Ikuhito Hata, a leading historian and specialist of this period, describes Hirohito's survival as nothing short of miraculous. But his emperor status also compelled him to think hard about the probable fate of his closest subordinates. Having accepted the terms of the Potsdam Declaration, he knew the Allies intended to punish Japanese war criminals severely. Trials of captured Japanese military commanders had already begun in the Philippines before the actual war had even ended. At first he could hardly bear to talk about it. On August 29 he told Kido: "It is so painful and unbearable to leave all the war criminals in the hands of the allies. Is there any way I can take the whole responsibility by retiring from the throne?"

Kido replied that although "this sacred consideration" was "very moving," "the allies won't be content with this. Foreigners," Kido added, "could have a different approach to things." Besides, to retire risked "abasing the Emperor-system and as a result it could provoke the idea of republicanism and democracy. So we have to be very careful and see what the allies will do." Even before August 15, Kido had correctly concluded that the emperor was safer from prosecution if he remained on the throne, and that to resign would be regarded as an admission of guilt. It's clear, from his subsequent behavior, that Hirohito very quickly realized this too.

At first, however, the war-criminal issue began to assume even more importance in Hirohito's mind than his own uncertain fate. With Higashikuni, his new prime minister, in early September, Hirohito again returned to the subject of war criminals. Some advisers were urging that Hirohito should insist that war criminals be tried and sentenced by Japanese courts, but Hirohito wouldn't even consider this option. "The so-called war criminals," he told Higashikuni, "especially those in positions of responsibility, are only being loyal to the nation, so it is unbearable to execute them in the name of the Emperor. Is there no way of reconsidering this?" On September 13 Higashikuni replied there was no alternative. In any case, he told Hirohito, "MacArthur wants a Nuremberg-style court."

Konoye had no such misgivings. Shortly before the end of the war (in June 1945) he had told his former aide Tomita: "I would like revenge; I would like to make a sweeping roundup of all the intriguers who have brought Japan to this defeat and the selfish profit-seekers who have accused us as traitors. I am better qualified than you to perform such a cruel job. Maybe I should be Home Minister."

At this stage, with Australia, New Zealand, the Soviet Union, the Netherlands and China firmly in favor of Hirohito's trial as a war criminal, France undecided, and the British Foreign Office largely following the views of America's pro-emperor "Tokyo lobby" headed by Grew and Stimson, his future was in Truman's hands, and the die was by no means cast. Hirohito's responsible behavior, in the closing stages of the war, gave additional strength to the already dominant Tokyo lobby determined to keep him on the throne, but both congressmen and senators, responding to public opinion and the wishes of their constituents, lobbied for his arrest, and passed a joint resolution demanding that he be tried as a war criminal.

In Britain's House of Commons, a newly elected labor MP, James Callaghan, later to become prime minister, devoted his maiden speech to a reasoned appeal to "get rid of him." Chiang Kai-shek felt the same way. Australia, closer to the war than the rest of the Allies (it was the only non-Asian country that had actually been bombed by Japan), was extremely irritated by Britain's pro-Hirohito stand. In the list of sixty-four major war criminals established by the Australian Foreign Ministry, Hirohito was number seven, but only because the names were listed in alphabetical order. Even before the end of the war, the Australian government had insisted that Hirohito be made to sign the surrender document aboard the *Missouri*. "There is undoubtedly a small but influential school of thought in some Allied countries which is prepared to save the face of the Emperor," a government memorandum read. "To this we are resolutely opposed." Another External Affairs Ministry report, forwarded to SCAP, which turned it over to the IMTFE prosecution, read: "Attempts have been made to absolve Hirohito from responsibility for the actions of Japan in entering the recent conflict on the ground that he was forced into declaring war by the militarist faction. The fact is that he was not at any time forced under duress to give written approval. He could have refused and supported his protests by abdication or hara-kiri. It is being suggested now that he will abdicate. How much more to the point it would have been if he had taken a forceful stand against those of his ministers who were intent on making war. He could have notified them that in the event of Japan entering the war he would publicly show his disapproval in either of the above-mentioned ways. It may be true that Hirohito never believed in war, but is his crime not greater because he approved of something in which he did not believe?''

The hara-kiri suggestion was naive, displaying an abysmal ignorance of Japanese ways: an emperor did not commit hara-kiri, for the spilling of royal blood would have been a sacrilegious act.

Some Washington analysts were against Hirohito's prosecution not because they felt he was innocent, but because they argued that to do so would lead, paradoxically, to many major war criminals going scot-free. If the emperor *did* assume full responsibility for everyone and everything, and was punished, how could the brutal POW camp commandants and the instigators of the Bataan death march be made accountable for their actions?

The U.S. State Department cast its net wide in its search for an answer: among the experts, Columbia University professor Homer H. Dubs, an authority on Japan, urged in a report to Grew that Hirohito be dethroned. "It makes no difference whether he was inclined towards peace or war," he wrote. "It is the office, not the individual, that is important in Japanese eyes: the essential matter is to remove from the minds of the Japanese people their belief in the sanctity of the Emperor. That cannot be done unless the Allies prove to them that they are able to uproot even their divine rulers.''

Somewhat presciently (his report is dated August 13, 1945) Dubs noted that "the present U.S. practice of refraining from criticizing or blaming or touching the Emperor in any way plays into the hands of the nationalistic Japanese. They can declare to their people that even Americans respect and are awed by the inviolable mikado.'' Dubs's radical view was that, since the permanence of the dynasty was more important than any of the lives of the individuals who made it up, "it is important that Hirohito be prevented from being given imperial honors by a descendant who is himself an Emperor.'' One unusual— and by Japanese standards, at least, highly blasphemous—suggestion was that the three sacred objects handed down through the ages by the sun-goddess Amaterasu—the mirror, sword and necklace—be "desacralized" by public exhibition, under American sponsorship, in major museums all over the world, and shown to be "mere artifacts.''

Hirohito's fate was also a matter of immediate concern to his younger brothers: Prince Chichibu heard the emperor's broadcast in his country home, and immediately returned to Tokyo, despite his worsening tuberculosis. On August 30, Prince Takamatsu, the third brother, called on Kido and "asked about the future of the Imperial Family." Professor Hata feels that both Chichibu and Takamatsu may have been responding to a call that never came, and were readying themselves for a possible role as regents. There were—as Empress Nagako wrote to her son—touching demonstrations of loyalty in the vicinity of the palace in those immediate postsurrender days. But there were also anti-Hirohito demonstrations, unthinkable in the pre–August 15 era, now watched by unarmed Tokyo police (who had replaced the Imperial Guards) and their U.S. military police colleagues. For the first time, there was a spate of anti-Hirohito editorials in the new, postwar Japanese press, some (but not all) translated from the American press.

Higashikuni himself had earlier believed that it would be impossible for Hirohito to remain on the throne. He accepted the premiership, he was to tell an *Ekonomisuto* reporter in 1965, because Kido had told him "Only you can do it" and because the emperor, "who looked so tired, and had lost so much weight" had asked him "gloomily: will you be the next prime minister? I finally couldn't resist." But Higashikuni imposed one condition, immediately accepted by the emperor: he would not go aboard the *Missouri* and sign the armistice. "I said: 'I won't go,' " Higashikuni told the *Ekonomisuto's* Yoshio Ando. "If I'm compelled to go I'll resign. I don't mean to bow there and sign documents." No imperial family member was to be directly involved in this humiliating episode of Japanese history.

In his 1965 interview, Higashikuni also revealed one important detail: whereas it's the accepted view that Hirohito himself decided to visit MacArthur, Higashikuni clearly stated the initiative was his. "I wanted the idea to appear to come from the Emperor," Higashikuni said, "as his idea, not mine. The Emperor behaved very modestly in front of MacArthur and MacArthur was pleased and flattered."

While the substance of that first dialogue between the two men is by now established, no complete version exists. Then, as later, there was an understanding on both sides to keep the talks secret. MacArthur kept his part of the bargain with a vengeance, not even bothering to brief his president or the State Department. In subsequent meetings the Japanese Foreign Ministry carefully debriefed the emperor's interpreter, and records of their conversations exist, but have never been accessible for perusal. (One later, deliberate "leak" to the Japanese press led to the interpreter being removed at MacArthur's request.) It's highly likely, Professor Hata believes, that during this first meeting MacArthur persuaded the emperor not to abdicate. If Hirohito *did* toy with the notion of abdication in those first three weeks of peace, there was precious little talk of this *after* his September 27 meeting with MacArthur. And it's from that date onward, as the *New York Times'* Hanson Baldwin, then a young reporter in Tokyo, put it, that there evolved "a tacit agreement on the Emperor's part to be MacArthur's junior partner in the surrender and occupation." The victim of this new imperial policy was to be Prince Konoye, the very man who saw himself as the stern justiciar of Japanese war criminals.

Before July 12, 1945, because of his "suspect" antiwar views, Konoye had been kept at arm's length from the palace, and, except for one meeting, in February 1945, had not seen Hirohito directly for three years. As deputy prime minister, Konoye was now charged with drafting a new, democratic constitution, and he set about his new task with considerable energy and purpose. But as a loyal kinsman whose links with the imperial family went back several centuries, he was also determined to protect the emperor, however much he may have disapproved of his immediate prewar conduct. The way he embarked on this defense virtually guaranteed his own downfall.

Unlike Hirohito, Prince Konoye did not behave modestly in MacArthur's presence, or "bow deeply like a servant." He tended to think, at this stage, that he and MacArthur were on the same side, and he assumed that MacArthur knew all about his attempts to prevent Japan from going to war on December 7, 1941.

MacArthur *did* know about Konoye, but his knowledge, culled from aides' reports, was highly selective: to SCAP, Konoye was the man who had thrown Japanese troops into China in 1937, had "invented" the "Greater East Asia Co-Prosperity Sphere" and established fascistic, one-party rule in Japan. SCAP staffers were unaware of Konoye's role in trying to persuade Hirohito, and Tojo, not to go to war with the United States, and they remained highly suspicious of his "summit" initiative with Roosevelt, proposed just before Pearl Harbor.

Konoye's first meeting with MacArthur was brief and formal. When he requested a second audience (granted on October 4, 1945), he was deliberately kept waiting for twenty minutes, and at first an aide announced that MacArthur was "too busy" to see him. Only when Konoye threatened to walk out rather than talk to a subordinate did MacArthur's schedule miraculously become less encumbered. But what Konoye had to say only confirmed SCAP in its prejudices against him, for Konoye's defense of Hirohito took an unacceptable form: all responsibility for the war, Konoye told MacArthur bluntly, lay with the militarists and the ultranationalists. Had he stopped there, it would have been an unexceptionable, though hardly original, argument. But Konoye went on to defend the zaibatsu, the large industrial conglomerates MacArthur was determined to break up. These, Konoye said, along with the feudal nature of the imperial institution, "had always acted as a brake on the militarists." It was the "leftist element in the Imperial Japanese army, exploiting the military clique, that drove Japan to war." They were the sole culprits.

He then embarked on the same speech he had made to Hirohito in February 1945—warning MacArthur of the specter of Japanese Communism. If the court institutions and the zaibatsu were liquidated along with the military clique and the ultranationalists, Japan would be Communism's easy prey. This was particularly unwelcome: many of SCAP's staff were New Deal liberals, and to them Konoye sounded like an unreconstructed, hard-line reactionary. Not knowing enough about his past, or about his dramatic change of heart in 1941, they saw his warning, coming as it did in advance of the cold war, as a deliberate attempt to pull wool over their eyes.

MacArthur listened politely, but spoke gruffly, in a clipped, soldierly tone, when Konoye started asking pointed questions about the composition of the future Diet and the organization of government, and made it clear that these were issues to be decided by SCAP. Here again, Konoye misunderstood the nature of his role, assuming that he, Konoye, Japan's most blue-blooded aristocrat barring the emperor himself, was to have a major part in reshaping postwar Japan, with MacArthur as a partner, not as *genro.* MacArthur was prepared to defer to an emperor, but not to someone like Konoye, an ideal scapegoat, who could so easily be blamed for Japan's entry into the war with China—the crucial decision that had led, in the long run, to Pearl Harbor.

Konoye told MacArthur that he was "ready to serve the nation to the best of his ability," unaware that the meeting had only reinforced the Supremo in his belief that Konoye was not to be trusted, and should be got rid of as quickly as possible. Reflecting SCAP's anti-Konoye views, a spate of articles almost immediately appeared in the U.S. press. The *New York Times,* in an editorial reprinted in Tokyo's papers, wrote that if Konoye was given a role to play in postwar Japan, this was tantamount to "making Quisling president of Norway, Laval president of France and Goering chief of the Allied Powers in Europe."

Far from being Japan's postwar justiciar, Konoye now became the target of U.S. investigators determined to bring war criminals to book. With little inside knowledge of the inner crises around the throne in 1941, the SCAP specialists focused on those whose names had surfaced, again and again, in the events leading up to Pearl Harbor. Konoye's name was high on the list, since he had been prime minister three times, had ushered in the Greater East Asia Co-Prosperity Sphere and had been in charge of the government at the time of the Marco Polo Bridge Incident leading to full-scale war with China. (Another prominent prewar figure in SCAP's sights was Koki Hirota, another former prime minister—also, ironically, a spirited opponent of war with America from 1941 onward).

A day later Konoye's fate was sealed. Higashikuni had scored several points in his brief dealings with SCAP. He had successfully argued against the introduction of U.S. military scrip, and against direct military control. "Japan shouldn't be like Hawaii or the Philippines," Higashikuni told Ando later. "Japan was defeated but Japan was still Japan." Faced with a determined, self-confident, princely prime minister, the SCAP authorities had wavered, but they stood firm on the principle of removing from public office all those regarded as militarists. When they asked Higashikuni to remove his own interior minister on such grounds, Higashikuni refused, and, on October 5, 1945, resigned. Konoye, now an embarrassment to Hirohito, was not included in the next government, headed by Mamoru Shigemitsu, formerly Higashikuni's foreign minister. Konoye was still blithely unaware of the gathering clouds around him. On October 8 he obtained a meeting with George Atcheson, MacArthur's top civilian adviser with ambassadorial status, to discuss the new Japanese constitution. On October 11 Hirohito brought Konoye into the Privy Seal Secretariat as an adviser on constitutional reform, almost certainly to give him something to do and keep him out of harm's way. On October 17,

Konoye held a press conference on constitutional reform, largely attended by U.S. and British correspondents, in which he hinted that the emperor would gladly become a constitutional monarch along British lines.

But very shortly afterward, the word went out from SCAP that Konoye was in deep trouble. Highly responsive to MacArthur by this time, Hirohito became increasingly inaccessible to Konoye, and SCAP declared him persona non grata—no SCAP staffer was to have any dealings with him at all.

A month later Konoye was interrogated for three hours by the U.S. Strategic Bombing Survey team. Though a British embassy official, D. MacDermot, forwarding the transcript of Konoye's interrogation to the Foreign Office, later wrote that "one of the American generals who has interviewed Konoye several times described him to me as a rat who was quite prepared to sell anyone to save himself, and even went so far as to call his master, the Emperor, 'the major war criminal'," the actual transcript contains no such allegations.

On the contrary: in his misguided sense of loyalty to Hirohito, Konoye failed to spell out the differences between them in 1941, failed to give his version of his resignation in October 1941, failed above all to rise above generalities—all in his obsessive concern to protect the emperor. The closest he got to implicit criticism of Hirohito was in answer to a question asking him to spell out what "efforts" were made to terminate the war. "Just as finally the end of the war was brought about by the Emperor," Konoye replied, "so at that time efforts were made to persuade the Emperor, particularly through Kido, who was close to him, to put an end to the war"— implying that the final decision had been Kido's rather than Hirohito's, and that the emperor, had he wished, could have put an end to the war earlier.

Partly because Konoye was determined to keep his answers vague in order not to implicate the emperor, partly because he was ill at ease and unused to being cross-examined, he made a deplorable impression. Throughout, he hedged and prevaricated, blaming the military and his faulty memory, never once spelling out the dramatic details of his break with Hirohito in September 1941, his confrontation with Tojo in October, or his comments to his staff at the time, which would have corroborated his version of events. Partly out of princely arrogance, partly because he was unprepared for the committee's onslaught, he failed to provide a cogent defense of his own actions from September 1941 onward, or any indication of the sweeping nature of the change that came over him in the last three months before Pearl Harbor. The circumstances of the interrogation were also unusual: unlike other witnesses, Konoye was questioned not in Tokyo but aboard a U.S. Navy gunboat in Tokyo harbor. His interrogators pointedly called him "Mr. Konoye." "It was horrible," he told Tomita afterward, "like a prosecuting attorney taking a deposition from a criminal." He couldn't understand it. "Perhaps," he told Tomita, "the attitude of the U.S. Occupation staff is affected by the fact that there are so many Jews in MacArthur's Headquarters. . . . They are not just antipathetic towards the Imperial Family but seek some pretext to destroy it. They also seem to be plotting the communisation of Japan." He pointed out to Tomita that, ironically, while the militarists had treated him like a traitor from 1941 onward for trying to prevent a war, he was now being treated like a war criminal by SCAP.

On November 22 Konoye finally met Hirohito, and submitted his outline for a constitutional reform. He also formally asked Hirohito to remove his princely title. The emperor by this time had become distant, less interested in any of Konoye's plans or problems, aware that Konoye was now on SCAP's blacklist.

By November 1945, despite his successful initial meeting with MacArthur, Hirohito was not fully reassured as to his own fate: SCAP investigators were closing in on suspected war criminals in high places. They actually arrested a member of the imperial family, the elderly, inoffensive Prince Nashimoto, the chief priest at the sacred Ise shrine, and the last person to have had a say in the running of the war. Perhaps some SCAP officials wanted to show Hirohito he was not quite off the hook himself.

Konoye took this very badly: "Does not the Government do anything when an Imperial Prince is imprisoned?" Konoye asked Tomita. "The way things are, I doubt whether the [Japanese] press would do anything if the Emperor himself were arrested. I must ask Nashimoto why he didn't kill himself for the sake of the Emperor and Japan." (After a few weeks in detention, Prince Nashimoto was released; throughout, he had faced his ordeal with unexpected cheerfulness, carrying out his prisoner's chores with a broad smile, treating the whole experience as a huge joke.)

Then, on December 6, came the final blow: Konoye was ordered by SCAP to report to Sugamo Prison as a war criminal suspect on December 16.

Kido, similarly notified, was more serene. "Everything is as expected," he noted in his diary, "and I am not disturbed." The only thing that mattered, he told Konoye, was to keep the emperor from being charged—and who better could ensure this than he and Konoye?

Konoye disagreed. If he tried to explain why he had acted as he had as prime minister, he told Kido, this would not prevent the emperor from being charged. "The responsibility of the Supreme Command would still lie with the Emperor as Commander-in-Chief," he said. "If the United States has already made up its mind to punish the Emperor, I feel helpless to defend him." Perhaps he also felt that he could not spell out the rationale of his own behavior from 1937 onward without heavily implicating Hirohito, and that the prospect of betraying the emperor in this way was intolerable. In any case, he told friends, he couldn't bear the humiliation of standing in court as a war criminal suspect. He again returned to his immediate prewar record. To a *Mainichi* reporter, he said: "Before the war I was ridiculed for being indecisive, during the war I was rebuked as an escapist peacemaker, and after the war accused of being a war criminal. I am a child of fate."

In contrast, Kido displayed no such introspection. Though he suspected, even before December 6, that he was likely to be named as a war criminal suspect, he didn't let this interfere with his overriding responsibility: lifelong service to the emperor. He continued to provide Hirohito with good advice. On September 29 (two days after his visit to MacArthur) Hirohito complained to him about virulent attacks on him in the American press. "I can pretend not to notice," he told Kido. "I can also reveal my true feelings through a newspaper reporter or to MacArthur directly." Kido advised him to do no such thing. "Americans in general," he told the emperor, "have considerable misunderstanding of Japan's attitude. So if we try to defend ourselves, it could make matters worse." It was important to ignore the attacks and let everything die down. Hirohito followed his advice.

On November 12, Hirohito expressed the wish to commune with his ancestors at the Ise shrine to inform them of his calamitous defeat and beg their forgiveness. Again, it was Kido who arranged it with SCAP, obtaining MacArthur's special clearance for the trip, and carefully supervised the travel arrangements. It was Hirohito's first trip outside Tokyo since the end of the war and Kido worried about possible hostile demonstrations. He was relieved when, at Numazu station, where the imperial train stopped for six minutes, there were none, for "if a mob threw stones, there was nothing we could do." But "the six minutes passed quickly. It wasn't the stereotyped prewar welcome. Some people stood and bowed, but they were natural. I was glad to see the people and the Imperial Family coming close together." At another station, "a widow displayed a picture of her late army officer husband. I watched her face and thought she was a true Japanese and my eyes were moist."

After formally quitting his job as Lord Privy Seal, but staying on as a "special temporary employee of the Imperial Household," Kido had received various presents from the emperor: twenty thousand yen in cash, a barrel of imperial sake and canned goods. "The great sacred mercy makes me shed tears," Kido noted. He received more presents on November 24, when, along with other former peers, he submitted his formal request to become a commoner.

Unlike Konoye, who was kept at arm's length and ignored, Kido received further marks of esteem from Hirohito after December 6: five days before going to jail, Kido was summoned to dine with the emperor. Kido declined at first, on the grounds that as he was under suspicion as a suspected war criminal, he could "contaminate" the emperor.

Hirohito replied to the chamberlain who conveyed this apology that "in the eyes of the Americans he may be a criminal but he is a devoted servant of his country. If he is reluctant to come, have the food sent to him." A palace car came to fetch Kido from his home for his last dinner with Hirohito.

Kido received more gifts, including "a big table" from the empress, and doughnuts she had made herself. Kido noted that in the course of their conversation the emperor told him "various stories in all directions"—he rambled on, disjointedly, clearly upset by Kido's impending fate.

There was one last meeting, the day before Kido reported to Sugamo Prison. Hirohito's final words to him were "This time I am very sorry. Take care of your health. I think you understand my feelings completely as we have talked to each other always. So please explain it fully to them [the other prisoners]."

In this characteristically oblique way, the emperor was conveying a crucial message to Kido: he was to be his eyes and ears inside the prison, using his intuitive knowledge to interpret the emperor's viewpoint, and make sure it was understood. Unsaid but implicit was Hirohito's mute plea to protect him, come what may, from involvement in the trial.

In his country home, ignored and rejected by Hirohito, Konoye was making very different preparations: he made peace with his brother, a musician who had spent the war years in Germany, and from whom he had been estranged; he settled his family and private affairs, and dictated a brief political testament. "I have made many political blunders, beginning with the China war," it began,

> and I feel my responsibility for them deeply. The air is ringing with false charges and misunderstanding. Whatever you say, people accuse you of evasion and lying. I refuse to engage in mudslinging with people who will say anything to boost themselves. It makes no difference to me if people do not understand me. I am convinced that some time in the future I will be judged with justice and exonerated.
>
> The fervor and hatred that accompany war, the excessive arrogance of the victors and the extreme servility of the losers, the rumors because of intentionally false accusations and misunderstandings—all these together are called "public opinion." Eventually, I hope that in the court of the Gods, a just judgment will be passed on me. I find it intolerable, however, to stand in an American court as a so-called war criminal.
>
> The very fact that I did feel responsibility for the China war made the task of effecting a settlement [with the U.S.] all the more crucial to me.
>
> Concluding that the only remaining chance to achieve a settlement of the war in China was to reach an understanding with the U.S., I did everything in my power to make the negotiations a success. It is regrettable that I am now suspected by the same U.S. of being a war criminal.
>
> I believe those who know me well know what my aspirations were. I believe that even in the U.S. I have friends who understand me.

At a dinner with his two closest friends on December 14 Konoye allowed some of his bitterness toward Hirohito to seep through. He calmly informed them of his intention to die. "Tell the Emperor," he said, "to do the same when they come and get him."

At dawn on December 15 he killed himself; a prince of the royal blood was not supposed to spill it, so Konoye swallowed a cyanide capsule. His funeral was sparsely attended. As his biographer, Yoshitake Oka, noted, "a number of people who should have been there excused themselves. In the normal course of events, ten thousand people would have shown up. There were a few hundred." The emperor never attended funerals, barring those of his immediate family, but on this occasion he did not even send a representative, or write an immediate note of condolence to his family. As Mark Gayn, a correspondent in Tokyo for the *Chicago Sun*, wrote at the time, "the Emperor, unsure he would not himself be brought to trial as a war criminal, will not blacken himself by sympathy for a man upon whom for so long he had depended for guidance." According to one reliable contemporary report, Hirohito's only apparent reaction to Konoye's death was annoyance: he promptly spread the word that all those summoned to Sugamo Prison should unfailingly obey.

Apart from his political testament, Konoye left behind an underlined copy of Oscar Wilde's *De Profundis,* a work—and a writer—he much admired. The passage he had underlined on New Year's Day, 1945, read: "The people used to say of me that I was too individualistic. . . . Indeed, my main crime came not from too great individualism of life, but from too little"—another oblique reference to the real cause of his death: his determination to protect Hirohito at all costs, in character with his conception of his princely role.

Perhaps Konoye, with his keen sense of irony, would have appreciated the absurdity of his own death. Forty-three years later, Robert Fearey, a former SCAP official, gave me this account of the events leading up to it: shortly before Konoye's notification that he would stand trial as a war criminal, he said, "Atcheson called me into his office, and told me, 'I've had a call from General MacArthur and he has noticed that all these major war criminals have been arrested and tried, or are about to be tried, in Germany, and here we have arrested no major war criminals in Japan, they're still walking the streets. This isn't right. So would you please draw me a list of ten to twelve—or whatever the number was—of people who should be arrested, and then arrest them.' Together with Herb Norman, a Canadian working for the intelligence branch of SCAP, we drew up a list of ten people we thought should be arrested as major war criminals, and gave it to Atcheson, who gave it to MacArthur, and the next day they were arrested, headlines all over the place.

"Maybe a week later, MacArthur said, 'There must be more than ten.' So I produced another list, and on it was Prince Konoye, not because we felt he was a war criminal who should be tried and convicted, but because he had been prime minister at critical phases over many years when Japan had gone into north China, and his involvement was important from the military point of view. The understanding between us was that we would get word to Prince Konoye that we did not regard him as a war criminal like the others, that we only wanted him as a material witness and felt we had to do this because of the positions he had held."

In other words, Konoye was included in the second war criminal suspects' list only because of his knowledge of the past. "I am afraid," Fearey added, "that word of this did not get to Prince Konoye in time. Someone forgot to tell him."

CHAPTER TWENTY-FOUR

The very day Kido and Konoye received their notification to report to Sugamo Prison as war criminal suspects, the American contingent of the International Military Tribunal for the Far East (IMTFE) left the United States by air for Tokyo. Their leader, Joseph B. Keenan, a gangbusting attorney who had helped topple Al Capone and was to become the IMTFE's chief prosecutor, knew nothing about Japan. Truman picked him for the job because he wanted him as far away from Washington as possible. A close friend of FDR and of J. Edgar Hoover, he was no favorite of Truman, who took this drastic step so that he should no longer haunt the White House corridors.

It turned out to be a disastrous choice. A lecherous secret drinker who was frequently unintelligible in court in the afternoons, Keenan alienated some of the best American legal brains already at work at SCAP in Tokyo. His Perry Mason courtroom manner irritated the president of the court, Sir William Flood Webb, an able but crotchety Australian, who had already presided over one war criminal trial in the Philippines and was chief justice of the State of Queensland. It also completely baffled the Japanese defense lawyers. Keenan showed contempt for Japanese customs in little ways, such as refusing to take his outdoor shoes off when he entered Japanese homes or restaurants.

A striking physical resemblance to the great Hollywood comedian W. C. Fields provoked hilarity, but otherwise there was nothing funny about Keenan. He was a meddler as well as a consistent publicity-grabbing bully, slavishly subservient to MacArthur at all times. Under him, the so-called independence of the judiciary was a mockery. This highly idiosyncratic, unattractive figure dominated IMTFE proceedings from 1946 to 1948, making life miserable for all those who crossed him.

Before leaving for Tokyo, Keenan had told reporters in Washington that, in his view, Hirohito clearly deserved to stand trial. According to an Associated Press story shortly before his departure, "Keenan disclosed Emperor Hirohito may join in the prisoners dock as a war criminal." As Robert Donihi, a junior member of Keenan's prosecution team, recalls, "Emperor Hirohito was the subject of special interest before we left the U.S. and as far as the other sixteen of us were concerned, he was 'number one' on the list in consideration for trial. Right up to the time our plane left, we were led to think we were going to try the emperor. It was virtually as we boarded the plane that we learned, from a letter delivered to Keenan by President Truman practically at the airport, that we should lay off Hirohito, and that meant laying off the whole Imperial Household as well. I was told, personally: Do not attempt to interrogate any of them."

Truman's letter to Keenan was part of a policy battle fought out between bureaucrats in Washington and Tokyo. Only a few days previously (November 29) a top-secret directive from the joint chiefs of staff to MacArthur indicated that they at least had an open mind about the emperor's responsibilities. Referring to Hirohito "as a person and not to the Emperor institution as such," their note read:

> Whether Hirohito is to be tried as a war criminal is of great interest to the United States. The U.S. Government's position is that Hirohito is not immune from arrest, trial, and punishment as war criminal.
>
> It may be assumed that when it appears that the Occupation can proceed satisfactorily without him, the question of his trial will be raised.
>
> It may also be assumed that if such a proposal will serve a purpose, it may be raised by one or more of our allies. It's clear

we mustn't delay in collecting the evidence, necessary whether he is eventually tried or not, since any decision not to try him should be made in the light of all available facts. . . . Assembly of evidence must be conducted with strict security safeguards to avoid disclosure either of the evidence itself or of the fact that such evidence is being assembled.

This was certainly not MacArthur's view, and may have led to the hasty note delivered to Keenan as he boarded the plane to Tokyo. With considerable frankness Atcheson spelled out the pros and cons of prosecuting Hirohito. In a report to the State Department dated January 8, 1946, he wrote:

It's clear Hirohito is not immune from trial as a war criminal but treatment of him as a war criminal cannot be divorced from our overall objective in Japan. If we are prepared not only for indefinite occupation but huge expenditures on economic aid, and also on increasing the size of forces in Japan for any contingency that may arise, then we can adopt a strongly aggressive political policy, try the Emperor as a war criminal and encourage the complete abolition of the Emperor system. Even some Japanese argue that if he had sufficient power to stop the war, he had the authority to prevent it.

But, Atcheson pointed out, the emperor was "useful, obeyed by officials and people. . . . I am reliably informed that Hirohito is considering abdication at some time in the not too distant future. An important element in such planning is the fear he may be named as a war criminal. This would result in the elimination of a leader to whom Japan is accustomed, and to whom, strangely enough, most of the common people are grateful for bringing them peace. Thus if we decide to continue to use the Emperor indefinitely he should be given some indication that we regard his continuing on the throne desirable."

MacArthur followed this up with his own views in a letter to the joint chiefs of staff dated January 25, making Atcheson's points with caricatural emphasis. His extraordinary letter is worth quoting almost in full:

If he is tried, great changes must be made in occupational plans and due preparation therefore should be accomplished in preparedness before the actual action is initiated. His indictment will unquestionably cause a tremendous convulsion among the Japanese people, the repercussions of which cannot be overestimated. He is the symbol which unites all the Japanese. Destroy him and the nation will disintegrate.

The whole of Japan can be expected, in my opinion, to resist the action either by passive or semi-active means. They are disarmed and therefore represent no special menace to trained and equipped troops. But it is not inconceivable that all government agencies will largely cease, and a condition of underground chaos and disorder amounting to guerilla warfare in the mountains or outlying areas result. I believe all hope of introducing modern democratic methods would disappear and that when military control finally ceased some form of intense regimentation probably along communistic lines would arise from the mutilated masses. This would present an entirely different problem of occupation from that now prevalent. It would be absolutely essential to greatly increase the occupational forces. It is quite possible that a minimum of one million troops would be required which would have to be maintained for an indefinite number of years.

By brandishing the threat of administrative chaos, guerrilla warfare, the growth of Japanese Communism and the need to maintain a one-million-man garrison in Japan on a war footing for years to come, MacArthur effectively killed the idea of putting Hirohito on trial.

Whether he actually believed in his dire predictions or simply blackmailed Truman and the chiefs of staff into submitting to his own will is another matter. Even Grew, that archdefender of the imperial system, had been less sanguine. In July 1944, after the OSS had reported rumors that Hirohito was about to leave Tokyo for the comparative safety of Manchuria, Grew noted that "one could argue that if he flees the country he will be considered to have abdicated. The question whether the [occupation] military government should therefore set up another member of the Imperial family as the Emperor's successor or should treat the Emperor-institution as having been terminated should be decided after our occupation of Tokyo." Around this time, Washington even toyed with the idea of encouraging an exile Japanese group along Free French lines, called the International Japanese People's Liberation Alliance, to be underwritten by the OSS and the Office of War Information (OWI) and later used as the nucleus of a free "democratic" postwar government. The project was dropped not because it was feared that the end of the emperor system would lead to armed chaos, but because the OSS feared the Alliance would be dominated by Communist exiles.

Both the Atcheson and the MacArthur letters were deliberately ambiguous: MacArthur enumerated the consequences, as he said he saw them, of ending the emperor system. But at no time was this radical solution given serious thought. What many people, including Hirohito's own intimates, had in mind was Hirohito's abdication in favor of Akihito, and the setting up of a regency under Chichibu, Takamatsu or Mikasa, Hirohito's younger brothers. Had this taken place, there is no suggestion among them that it would have led to any of the consequences outlined by Atcheson and MacArthur. In the recent past, Chichibu, Takamatsu and Konoye had all contemplated the Hirohito abdication option without ever raising the possibility of hell breaking loose as a result. Leading Japanese historians, and many Japanese who experienced the trauma of surrender at first hand, agree in retrospect that a state of complete apathy prevailed immediately after Hirohito's August 15 speech, and that Hirohito's removal from the throne would not have led to any violent or lasting upheaval, especially if a regency had been established. Even the romantic boy-emperor conspiracy devised by Nakano Spy School and Imperial Navy stalwarts—among the toughest, most uncompromising advocates of continuing clandestine action after the war—showed their plans were long-term and nonviolent.

In short, everything points to MacArthur blatantly using his position as supreme commander to compel not only Truman but also America's allies to accept Hirohito's continued presence on the throne because this was what he wanted, especially after meeting the emperor on September 27, 1945. And it was MacArthur, more than any other single person, who officialized the theory of the emperor as puppet. In another report, MacArthur wrote that it would be "a disaster to indict Hirohito as a war criminal since he had been from the beginning to the end a puppet, a complete 'Charlie McCarthy' who had neither begun the war nor stopped it. At every point he had acted automatically on advice and he could not have done otherwise. The Cabinet meeting which ended the war was as much staged as those which began it."

This, over the years, became the officially accepted view: it ignored some of the evidence to the contrary readily available in the Kido diaries, and some key portions of the *Sugiyama Memorandum*. But comparing Hirohito to Hollywood ventriloquist Edgar Bergen's top-hatted doll also meant denying the emperor his one claim to greatness: the manner in which he ended the war. It was a price Hirohito's apologists were prepared to pay.

As Donihi pointed out, the emperor's immunity to prosecution had to extend to members of his family, for it would not have been possible to spare the emperor while pursuing his close relatives. So several princely figures who might otherwise have found themselves in the dock as "class A" criminals were spared, among them Prince Asaka, who commanded troops during the rape of Nanking.

There was another deal made behind the scenes that turned the IMTFE proceedings into a ghoulish farce. Before leaving Ping Fan, as the Soviets advanced into Manchuria in the final four days of the war, the infamous General Ishii, of Unit 731 fame, had some forty live *maruta,* held there in readiness for experiments, injected with prussic acid and cremated, their ashes and thousands of containers containing specimens dumped in the Sungari River. From Harbin, Ishii fled to Pusan, Korea, returning to Tokyo just after the end of the war. He took a room in the Wakamatsu Hotel, opposite the Tokyo Military Hospital in the Shinjuku district; there, while Empress Nagako was watching B-29s ferry in U.S. occupation troops, Ishii was busy disposing of the grisly *maruta* specimens kept until then in the Tokyo Military Hospital.

If ever anyone deserved to be labeled a "class A" war criminal suspect, it was Ishii. U.S. Army Colonel Murray Sanders, sent to Tokyo immediately after the war to investigate Unit 731's activities, many years later told a reporter from TVS* that his Unit 731 contact

---

*"Television South," a major independent British production company.

in Tokyo, Colonel Ryohi Nahito, after considerable pressure, "laid out the table of organization: it started with the Emperor and branched off into various departments—the war ministry, chief of staff, army medical affairs department, etc."

Through Nahito, Ishii, by now in hiding, petitioned Sanders for full immunity in return for all the Unit 731 scientific data on chemical and biological warfare. As Colonel Sanders (who died in 1986) told TVS: "MacArthur agreed to immunity for all in return for all the [Unit 731] information. I had MacArthur's word we would not prosecute." In January 1946 Ishii emerged from hiding. A year later, two U.S. scientists, Edwin Hill and Joseph Victor, came to Japan and debriefed Ishii and others. Their report contains the following euphemism: "Such information could not be obtained in our own laboratories because of scruples attached to human experimentation."

MacArthur kept his word, and Keenan raised no objections: at no time were Ishii, or any of his subordinates, arraigned before IMTFE. The Unit 731 issue did surface, very briefly, during the IMTFE court proceedings. A U.S. prosecutor, referring to documents supplied by China, noted early in the trial that "the enemy's TAMA [Japanese code name for Unit 731] Detachment carried off their civilian captives to a medical laboratory, where their reactions to poisonous serums were tested. This detachment was one of the most secret units. The number of persons slaughtered by this detachment cannot be ascertained."

Webb asked for further evidence: "This is something entirely new; are you going to leave it at that?"

"We do not at this time anticipate introducing evidence on that subject," the prosecutor replied. Webb concluded there was none, and dismissed this particular indictment, calling it, doubtless in good faith, "mere assertion unsupported by any evidence." Unit 731's role was never mentioned again.

Ishii died of cancer at a ripe old age; several Unit 731 specialists have written that, after a "decent interval," he was invited to lecture to U.S. Army specialists at Fort Detrick, Maryland, the U.S. Army's chemical warfare headquarters, and this has never been officially denied.

Since Hirohito was not on trial, and since the defendants did their best to shield him at all times, his name was rarely mentioned during the interminable IMTFE proceedings. Before the actual start of the trial (on May 3, 1946), Keenan had made his attitude very clear: when Sir William Webb asked him why the emperor hadn't been indicted, Keenan replied that everyone knew that throughout the prewar period "the Emperor had been in the power of gangsters." At a preparatory meeting of prosecutors, he also stressed his "hands off" policy where the emperor was concerned. A British member of his team asked, "Is that a decision or a proposal?" Keenan replied, "The policy has been decided. I am asking for your agreement." When the British lawyer said, "I can't go along with this sort of thing," Keenan replied, "It's in the interest of all the allied nations to carry out occupation policy smoothly; that is also the will of SCAP. If you gentlemen are unable to agree with SCAP policy, feel free to pack your bags and go home." In the course of time, some did.

A few months into the trial, however, the question arose: Should the emperor be called upon to testify? Hardly unexpectedly, both MacArthur and Keenan were adamantly opposed to this. In November 1947 Webb absented himself from Tokyo on leave; the decision not to involve the emperor in any way was taken in his absence. Webb was privately of the opinion that Hirohito should have been in court along with the other accused, and there was no love lost between him and Keenan.

A final attempt to involve Hirohito in IMTFE proceedings was made in the course of the trial by Edward P. Monaghan, of the prosecution team's investigative division. In a note to Keenan, Monaghan pointed out that there were reliable reports that Hirohito had kept a diary ever since he was a child. Since this diary would throw considerable light on the events leading up to Pearl Harbor, Monaghan suggested that the palace be subpoenaed to turn over the emperor's diary to the court. Keenan's reaction was predictable: in a handwritten note appended to Monaghan's request, marked "Confidential," he wrote:

> there are important matters of policy involved in suggestion; it concerns matters other than the need for dependable evidence. If any action should be taken on this it would be only after specific orders from the highest authority in SCAP. I believe that there are strong reasons why any such request should be denied.

Keenan's official reply, marked "Confidential," was as follows:

> The obvious matters of policy involved in procuring a thing as personal as a diary from the Emperor of Japan are so outstanding that at any stage of the proceedings it would have been difficult to have obtained consent to any demand for production of same.
>
> Particularly at this stage of our proceedings, with our case in chief already in, we could not expect to have serious considerations given thereto. It is, therefore, my conclusion that the matter should be dropped.
>
> Joseph B. Keenan,
Chief of Counsel, I.P.S.

For all his determination to protect Hirohito, even Keenan occasionally got carried away in the heat of cross-examination. Whenever this happened, realizing that the reply to his question might implicate Hirohito, he would, almost comically, cut himself short and abort his own line of questioning. A classic example of this occurred during his cross-examination of Kido. By rights, the prosecutor assigned to Kido should have been asking the questions, but Keenan, despite his imperfect knowledge of the Kido dossier, was not about to let a subordinate occupy center stage when a well-known figure was on the witness stand.

Keenan was trying to prove that Kido knew about Pearl Harbor. An IMTFE report (based on a *New York Times* story) had stated that the emperor, in admiral's uniform, had spent the night of December 7–8, 1941, monitoring radio transmission from Admiral Yamamoto's flagship. Keenan must have remembered this.

KEENAN: I am suggesting there was a little gathering over there at the Palace, to find out how this attack on Pearl Harbor was going?

KIDO: I know nothing about that.

KEENAN: That is all.

He was, however, expert in putting words into the accused's mouths that would exonerate the emperor and reinforce MacArthur's puppet thesis. An example of this came while questioning Kido about the September 6, 1941, *gozen kaigi.*

In reply to Keenan's question ("Did the Emperor have anything to do with the decision of the September 6 Imperial Conference?") Kido indulged in a lengthy, convoluted, hedging explanation. Keenan cut him short.

KEENAN: All right, then, the answer is that it wasn't really a decision of the Emperor at all. It was a decision formally made in his name but made by other people. Is not that perfectly plain?

KIDO: In plain language, yes.

The only time IMTFE court proceedings looked as if they might call Hirohito's entire role into question came toward the end, on December 31, 1947. By this time public interest in the trial had waned, both in Japan and abroad. Tojo was in the middle of a long statement, winding up his own defense proceedings, and had just stated that Hirohito had consented, "though reluctantly, to the war," when a Japanese defense lawyer for Kido interrupted him. "Did you ever make any suggestion or take action against the Emperor's will for peace?" he asked.

Tojo was taken aback. "No," he said, "I didn't. "None of us [Japanese] would dare act against the Emperor's will."

The reply may not have been significant to the handful of Western reporters present, but to the experts it was a crucial, and damning, admission: it made nonsense of the "emperor as puppet" theory so dear to MacArthur—and to Keenan—implying as it did that had Hirohito really wanted to prevent war, he could have acted accordingly, and been obeyed by all, including archmilitarists like Tojo. Webb immediately pounced on Tojo's reply; with some glee, he said (and his remark, though addressed to the court as a whole, was unmistakably directed at Keenan), "Well, you know the implications from that reply." The following day the chief Soviet prosecutor, outside the courtroom, requested that Hirohito be indicted as soon as possible.

All this could not have occurred at a less propitious time: six days previously, on Christmas Day, 1947, with Keenan's blessing, one of his Japanese aides, Ryukushi Tanaka, had called on Prince Takamatsu, told him that the emperor had nothing to worry about and that the court proceedings would come to an end without ever involving him. Keenan ingratiatingly intended this information to be unofficially conveyed to Hirohito himself.

Ryukushi Tanaka was the same huge, bullet-headed army officer who had monitored the departure of Chinese warlord Chang Tso-lin's train from Peking in 1928 and had been, in the thirties, the control of Eastern Jewel, the famous Japanese spy. He had fallen on hard times in recent years. Because of a long-standing feud with Tojo, and genuine doubts about the wisdom of going to war against the United States, he had been placed in the reserves, and his anguish at the course of events had led to insomnia, depression and a spell in a mental hospital. "As a result," he wrote later, "I was branded as a lunatic by my enemies."

In 1946 Tanaka had been routinely questioned by IMTFE staff, and a young American lieutenant, Robert Honidi,* realized his immense potential as prosecution witness. He introduced him to Keenan, who attached him to his personal staff. Tanaka became Keenan's court jester, pimp and adviser on Japanese matters. In his new role as archcollaborator, he was viewed as an abject traitor and turncoat by the Japanese establishment and the now demobilized military hierarchy. But his usefulness to the emperor as well as to Keenan was never denied, for Tanaka professed intense feelings of personal loyalty to Hirohito and claimed that his only reason for becoming a prosecution witness in the first place had been to protect the emperor's name. He provided damning evidence against Tojo and other hard-line generals, invariably adopting the MacArthur-Keenan line that the emperor had been nothing but a puppet, manipulated at all times by the military.

Now, with the puppet theory suddenly in jeopardy, Keenan stepped in with terrierlike energy and zeal. He had his Japanese secretary phone Tanaka, who lived in the country, and summoned him back to Tokyo in the middle of the night.

Tanaka, many years later, told what happened next in an article in

---

*Not to be confused with IMFTE's civilian prosecutor Robert Donihi, mentioned earlier in the chapter.

a Japanese magazine dated August 1965. Professor Hata, who has himself made a special study of both Tanaka and the events he described, and fleshed out Tanaka's account with his own additional investigation, confirms that, for all Tanaka's controversial personality, his account is completely accurate.

On January 1, 1948, an agitated Keenan told Tanaka the only way out was to get to Tojo in Sugamo Prison and get him to retract his statement. "A few days later," Tanaka wrote, "I went to court and met Tojo and asked him to do this. But Tojo was stubbornly against my suggestion. He said: 'What I said is what I believe about the Imperial family and I cannot go back on it.' "

Tanaka then sought a meeting with Tojo's Japanese defense counsel. "To my embarrassment," wrote Tanaka, "another of his lawyers tried to prevent this from taking place."

There was only one course left, and that was to have the palace itself put pressure on Tojo. "On the evening of January 3," Tanaka wrote, "with a Keenan aide, I went to see Yasumasa Matsudaira,* the Imperial Household Minister." (Professor Hata supplies additional detail here. Tanaka, he says, went round to Matsudaira's house late at night, hammered on the door in vain, and finally climbed over the wall to gain entry.)

Matsudaira agreed to cooperate: he told Tanaka he himself would visit the court. With his innate understanding of the way Tojo's mind worked, and fully aware of Kido's special role as the emperor's representative inside Sugamo Prison, Matsudaira knew that the person to put pressure on Tojo was Kido. The following day, January 4, he saw Kido, explaining everything. Kido agreed to help.

"Kido talked to Tojo and told him of Keenan's intention [to protect Hirohito at all costs]," Tanaka wrote. "He was still reluctant but Kido tried very hard to persuade him and eventually Tojo understood and reluctantly agreed."

On January 6 a carefully rehearsed charade was played out in the IMTFE court. Keenan was asking Tojo questions about Pu-yi, the Manchukuo puppet emperor, and suddenly digressed, as Tojo had been warned he would.

---

*Not to be confused with the former Imperial Household minister Tsuneo Matsudaira.

KEENAN: While we are discussing the subject matter of Emperors, it might be an appropriate moment to ask you a few questions on the relative positions of yourself and the Emperor of Japan on the matter of waging war in December of 1941. You have told us that the Emperor on repeated occasions made known to you that he was a man of peace and did not want war, is that correct?

TOJO: I was then speaking to you of my feeling toward the Emperor as subject, and that is a quite different matter from the problem of responsibility, that is, the responsibility of the Emperor.

KEENAN: Well, you did make war against the United States, Great Britain and the Netherlands, did you not?

TOJO: War was decided on in my cabinet.

KEENAN: Was that the will of Emperor Hirohito, that war should be instituted?

TOJO: It may not have been according to his will, but it is a fact that because of my advice and because of the advice given by the High Command, the Emperor consented—though reluctantly—to the war.

INTERPRETER: The first part should be corrected: it might have been against the Emperor's will.

TOJO: The Emperor's love and desire for peace remained the same right up to the very moment when hostilities commenced, and even during the war his feelings remained the same. The Emperor's feeling in this regard can be clearly ascertained from the Imperial Rescript on December 8, 1941, declaring war. . . . That is to say, the Imperial Rescript contains words to this effect: this war is indeed unavoidable and is against my own desires.

As Seiichi Yamazaki, Keenan's personal secretary, noted later, "What people saw there was just a fake play . . . conducted by the mutual agreement of Keenan and Tojo." Arnold Brackman, author of *The Other Nuremberg,* then a young UP correspondent in Tokyo present in court at the time, wrote later: "Thus, the most volatile crisis during the trial was contained as a result of a secret agreement between the Allied chief of counsel and the most-wanted war criminal in the dock." Though it has never been proved, many experts believe that a generous private settlement to Tojo's family was part of the deal.

Two days later, on January 8, Keenan was the guest of honor at a banquet hosted for him at Atami, the hot springs resort, by four leading Japanese members of the "peace faction," including the ex-prime minister Reijiro Wakatsuki and General Ugaki. Tanaka was present. Here Keenan announced, "The Emperor's innocence has been determined." There was much emotional rejoicing, and innumerable sake toasts were drunk. Afterward, Keenan called for the services of a geisha. Ruefully, Tanaka noted that he ended up paying for the girl, because, Keenan said, "I'm your guest here."

Tanaka was also shown new consideration: on January 15 he was invited to meet young Crown Prince Akihito. Imperial Household Minister Matsudaira was present. He told Tanaka that the emperor had read articles about Tanaka in the Japanese press, and "shown displeasure" in the past at Tanaka's role. But now, Matsudaira said, he had explained Tanaka's real role to the emperor. "Everything is now all right."

On November 12, 1948, Webb finally handed down the court's verdict: none of the accused was acquitted. Seven, sentenced to death by hanging, included Tojo, for whom the sentence could hardly have come as a surprise; Matsui, the general who had been nominally in charge at the rape of Nanking in 1937; and Koki Hirota, the former prime minister, who many SCAP officials felt should not have been indicted in the first place. A petition on Hirota's behalf quickly raised three hundred thousand signatures. Kido was sentenced to life imprisonment.

All those sentenced behaved with extraordinary dignity and stoicism. Tojo's lawyer reported: "His mind is eased very much by the verdict, knowing that he has given no additional trouble to the Emperor." The Japanese press was less respectful. "What are the feelings of the Emperor?" asked the *Kokusai Times*. "He cannot continue to conceal his responsibility for war crimes." A few provincial papers called for his abdication as an apology to the Japanese people. The most scathing editorials, expectedly, came from *Akahata* (Red Flag), the Communist daily. But some of the bitterest criticism arising out of Hirohito's immunity came from one of IMTFE's defense counsel, Owen Cunningham—and from members of the tribunal, including Webb himself. "If the prosecution wanted the truth as to individual responsibilities, why did they not call the Emperor of Japan to the witness stand?" Cunningham asked. "Did they not have the courage to do so? . . . No one can accept the prosecution's theory that the Emperor was the puppet of Tojo." In a dissenting opinion, the French member of IMTFE, Henri Bernard, wrote: "It cannot be denied, the declaration [of war] had a principal author who escaped all prosecution and of whom, in any case, the present defenders could only be considered as accomplices."

It was Webb's own opinion, not read out in court but distributed to the press, that caused the most stir: "The immunity of the Emperor, as contrasted with the part he played in launching the war in the Pacific, is I think a matter which the Tribunal should take into consideration in imposing sentences," he wrote. He compared the emperor to "the leader in the crime" granted immunity from prosecution. "His immunity was, no doubt, decided upon in the best interests of all the Allied powers." Refuting an argument not advanced in court but used by Hirohito himself in his initial meeting with MacArthur, Webb went on: "No ruler can commit the crime of launching aggressive war and then validly claim to be excused for so doing because his life would otherwise have been in danger."

It was known that there had been acrimonious argument among the judges on the number of death sentences to be pronounced, and that Webb, who had been against any death penalties whatever, on the grounds that all the accused, whatever their own responsibilities, had been "accomplices," had been overruled. MacArthur could have commuted the sentences, but chose not to interfere.

Hirohito was known to be stunned by the verdicts, especially the life sentence on Kido. But he was determined, by this time, to remain on the throne. In a deliberate move to show that he would not be swayed by adverse Japanese press comment, or calls to abdicate, he sent Hidenori Terasaki, one of his personal interpreters—the same Terasaki who, as a Washington-based diplomat and intelligence chief, had engineered the last-minute Roosevelt letter to him—to see William J. Sebald, MacArthur's political adviser. He conveyed a personal message from the emperor to MacArthur. Notwithstanding the sentences passed at IMTFE, he had "definitely" decided not to abdicate.

On the night of December 22 the hangings started. All but Hirota shouted *"Banzai!"*—their final homage to the emperor. It was all over by 0230 hours, December 23. That day, Hirohito closeted himself alone in the palace library, seeing no one. It happened to be Crown Prince Akihito's fifteenth birthday, but all celebrations were canceled.

Before leaving Japan, shortly afterward, Keenan was received in audience by Hirohito and the empress, given a signed photograph and a handbag for his wife. A well-known Tokyo art gallery owner in the Ginza gave him a topaz "for his effort in contributing to the Emperor's innocence."

CHAPTER TWENTY-FIVE

"The peaceful beginning of the occupation of Japan," wrote Kazuo Kawai, the American-educated political scientist, "will always remain something of a mystery. The United States expected resistance and treachery. To their amazement, both sides discovered that the other was not what they had been led to believe."*

The postwar behavior of the emperor of Japan, and his adaptability, came as the biggest surprise of all. Almost overnight, his uniforms and white chargers were seen no more, and his bewildered Japanese subjects discovered the existence of a resolutely civilian emperor, full of middle-class virtues and gauche affability, whom they could stare at and even talk to with impunity.

Overnight, too, the still-powerful Imperial Household Ministry (later to become an "Agency") started projecting the image of an imperial family of almost caricatural ordinariness: pictures were released showing Hirohito, with his wife and son, seated round a plain dining-room table, enjoying a simple meal, reading *The Stars and*

---

*Kazuo Kawai, *Japan's American Interlude* (Chicago: University of Chicago Press, 1960).

Stripes, the U.S. military newspaper, or watering flowers in the garden. There were even pictures of his humble, somewhat frayed indoor slippers. The change was less publicized, but equally dramatic, among lesser members of the imperial family. Shortly after the war nothing differentiated Prince Mikasa, for instance, from other students at Tokyo University. He wore shabby clothes, and rode around town on a bicycle. Prince Takamatsu tended his own vegetable garden.

Cynical Tokyo-based correspondents who witnessed all this knew that it was deliberately contrived, for behind the emperor's new look was a July 1946 directive from the SNWCC (State/Navy/War/Coordinating Committee) in Washington to MacArthur, defining the "preservation of the Imperial system" as official U.S. policy. "A direct attack on the Imperial system," this report read, "would weaken the democratic elements and, on the contrary, strengthen the extremists, both communist and militarist. The Supreme Commander is therefore ordered to assist secretly in popularizing and humanizing the Emperor. This will not be known to the Japanese people."

Hirohito dutifully went along with the change, at what must have been considerable personal cost. When, in the heady first few days of the occupation, a U.S. army sergeant found the emperor's white charger in the palace stable and rode him cowboy style through the palace grounds, Hirohito resented this not just as an invasion of privacy but as as an intolerable example of lèse-majesté, a humiliating personal affront that, he felt, should have been severely punished. But the need to cooperate—and collaborate—overrode all other considerations. The new constitution, American-imposed and reading like a translation from a foreign language (Konoye's draft, experts said later, would have been an improvement), guaranteed human rights and political liberties, put an end to Japan's "right of belligerency," disbanding all her armed forces, and turned Japan into a parliamentary democracy. The emperor became a constitutional monarch with only ceremonial powers, on the British model, "a symbol of the state and of the unity of the people." On New Year's Day, 1946, in a broadcast speech, he formally renounced his "divinity." Shintoism ceased being a state religion. "Feudalism" in all its forms was eradicated. Many Japanese, including those acceptable to SCAP, felt that in many ways the liberal practices foisted on Japan went too far. As Shigeru Yoshida, shortly to be Japan's durable postwar prime minister, later wrote in his memoirs, SCAP "initially allowed the trade union movement workers a degree of freedom in political activity that was not warranted by any economic need."

Hirohito did what he had to do, both to make the occupation as palatable as possible for his people and to ensure the survival of the emperor system in the occupation framework. In return, SCAP began aiding Japan economically on a huge scale, sending her massive quantities of food in the first years, and also did its utmost to restore the emperor's image. Not only was he immune from prosecution for war crimes, but SCAP collaborated in forging the historical image of Hirohito that has persisted to this day. *Stars and Stripes* was careful not to run stories on the emperor's wartime role; the brutal, and at times racist, anti-Hirohito propaganda that had been a feature of World War II was replaced by propaganda of another sort, extolling the emperor as a democratic-minded, peace-loving, decent sort of chap, caught up against his will in a regrettable militaristic adventure he had always deplored. Reporters like Russell Brines, AP's correspondent in Tokyo before and after the war, had sufficient prewar experience to know that this was a distortion of the facts, but the Hirohito issue, he wrote, was "too hot to handle: his trial would hardly have accomplished much, except to salve international wounded feelings or, perhaps, to keep the record straight."*

As they came to see the emperor at close quarters in the immediate postwar months, the foreign press corps in Tokyo, many of them former war correspondents themselves, who had been copiously exposed to wartime propaganda, found it difficult to adjust to the new situation. Most reacted with scorn, disbelief and patronizing condescension. To Mark Gayn, of the *Chicago Sun,* Hirohito came across as "a pathetic little man, compelled to do a distasteful job, desperately trying to control his disobedient voice and face and body," and Gayn described him on one of his earliest appearances as "about five feet two, in a badly cut, gray striped suit, with trousers a couple of inches too short. . . . He has a pronounced facial tic, and his right shoulder twitches constantly. When he walks, he throws his right leg a little sideways, as if he has no control over it. He was obviously excited and ill at ease, and uncertain what to do with his arms and hands."† To

---

*Russell Brines, *MacArthur's Japan* (New York: Lippincott, 1948).
†Mark Gayn, *Japan Diary* (New York: William Sloane, 1948).

Russell Brines, the emperor was "short, slight, round-shouldered," with such poor coordination "that he seemed constantly on the verge of toppling over."

The contrast between Hirohito's martial wartime image and his pathetically clumsy public appearances encouraged some of the less experienced members of the foreign press in the wholly mistaken belief that the emperor *was* a figure of fun, that he might well have been a puppet of the military machine. At one of his first public appearances, Brines noticed, under pouring rain "the Emperor of Japan and his soggy subjects stared at each other in mutual embarrassment. Then he reached suddenly for his battered fedora, thought better of it, dropped his hand and tried to smile. He then grinned, seized his hat and waved it lustily. The crowd cheered and everybody relaxed. . . . The huge contrast between his current appearance and the military presence [the Japanese] had gotten used to puzzled the public. He was a little man who had to be told by his entourage what to do."

Because of the discretion of Japanese newsreel makers and, later, of TV networks, the emperor's off-the-cuff remarks on these walkabouts were generally not recorded, or, at least, broadcast. One newsreel, however, shows him desperately attempting to make small talk with a factory worker.

"I gather you were in the bombing," Hirohito said.

"Nope," the worker replied, without using any of the formal, ultrarespectful form of speech that was usually de rigueur, "I wasn't."

"Ah so desuka," said Hirohito, visibly at a loss as to how to extricate himself. "Well . . . [losing interest in the proceedings, and it showed] we must all pull together."

In retrospect, Hirohito managed with infinite patience and a good deal of hard work the transition from "divine" ruler to constitutional monarch with only ceremonial powers, from uttering sibylline speeches to deferential courtiers in an archaic language to facing steelworkers on SCAP-encouraged walkabouts in factories. No wonder he sought refuge in polite clichés and empty formulas: he had to learn to speak a new language. The first time he went up to a small boy and asked him, "Where are your father and mother?" court officials were amazed—he had actually managed to speak to him in colloquial Japanese! Later, Hirohito was to tell his officials that his trouble was that he lacked the vocabulary for use in everyday life. He never did master the art of small talk, and, later, with the advent of television, TV crews filming him were ordered to turn off the sound to avoid possible embarrassment and ridicule. For all his new visibility, he still managed to keep aloof. He was used to American generals shaking him by the hand, or GIs asking him for autographs. He couldn't prevent this kind of familiarity, though he never got used to it and hated it, but he was determined to keep his own people at the proper distance. A court chamberlain described how, on a factory inspection tour, Hirohito came face-to-face with a labor union delegation. Their leader thrust out his hand, and said, "I would like to shake your hand on behalf of all Japanese workers." Hirohito kept his arms at his sides. He retreated a step, and, bowing slightly, said, "Let's do it the Japanese way." The Japanese worker bowed back: the formalities had been preserved. Hirohito's physical coordination may sometimes have been lacking, but he was not always the figure of fun Americans so scornfully described. An equally revealing moment, on film, came years later, in 1975, during the emperor's visit to Disneyland. An adult Mickey Mouse moved close to him, and seemed about to lay a friendly, reassuring arm on the startled emperor. With split-second timing and unexpected agility, Hirohito stepped smartly aside. A Mickey Mouse did not lay an arm on an emperor, even in the interests of better U.S.-Japanese relations.

His faculty for stating the obvious, on his early walkabouts, became legendary. In Hiroshima, on his first official visit outside Tokyo, he looked around him through his thick glasses and said sententiously, "There seems to have been considerable damage here." As Russell Brines noted, "He always said things like that." Among the press, his walkabouts became known as *ah so desuka* visits because that was his invariable response to any situation.*

Brines, with his experience of prewar Japan, knew that Hirohito "was far from the impotent or ignorant puppet that he was portrayed as being." But most of the other correspondents failed to realize that the scuffed shoes, the ill-fitting suits, the almost clownish demeanor were all part of an elaborate defense mechanism: they were ways of indicating that the emperor, in this unprecedented and painful situation, was facing up to the occupation in characteristic Japanese fashion.

Ah so desuka: "Indeed," "Is that so," "How interesting."

"The Japanese had learnt to protect themselves while bowing to authority," wrote Kawai. "They rolled with the punch." Hirohito showed them how.

In private he was far less humble, and more articulate. In a letter to his son, Akihito, dated September 9, 1945, he revealed both his inner strength and his true feelings about the lost war:

> Thank you for your letter. I'm pleased to know your spirit is strong. Japan is facing a lot of trouble but I am all right, don't worry.
>
> I should have mentioned earlier about the decision I made this time but I hesitated to do so because I couldn't contradict your teacher too much. Let me explain about the reason for Japan's defeat: the Japanese people rely on imperial Japan too much and looked down on the United States and Britain and our military put too much emphasis on the spirit and forgot about science.
>
> At the time of the Meiji Emperor, there were brilliant generals in the army and navy but this time Japan was just like Germany in World War One.
>
> The military were arrogant and didn't look at the situation from a wider point of view. They only knew how to go forward, not how to retreat.
>
> I thought that if we continue the war, we would be unable to protect the three divine items and have to kill people. So, swallowing our tears, I chose the way to save the Japanese race from extinction. It's getting cold so please take care of yourself,
>
> from father

So, soon after the surrender speech, here in a letter to a twelve-year-old that would escape the scrutiny of SCAP he was conveying his dismay that he had been betrayed by incompetent military commanders who had underestimated the fighting capacity of the enemy. No mention of his personal responsibility in acquiescing to, and starting, the war; no apparent guilt; a disparaging reference to his generals. The image-building was not confined to SCAP.

In the immediate aftermath of surrender, Hirohito also returned to his pet subject: his high regard for the British royal family, and his wretchedness at having had to declare war on Britain. He found it necessary to jog Kido's memory, on September 26, 1945: "Don't you recall, when I issued the declaration of war, I mentioned to Tojo that this was a very painful decision for me. . . . I felt as though my intestines had been severed by a knife." A year later he returned to the subject. On a visit to Japan in January 1946 Sir George Sansom, a British diplomat with earlier experience of Japan, was invited to meet Hirohito for a private audience, but thought it advisable to decline; before he left, however, the Imperial Household minister sent him Hirohito's personal message to King George VI, hoping for early restoration of normal relations between Japan and Britain, stressing that he had "done his utmost to avoid war" and apologizing for British suffering in lives and property losses caused by the war. There was a very good reason for this highly unusual piece of diplomacy: Hirohito was aware that Lord Mountbatten, a frequent visitor to Buckingham Palace, held strong views about Japan in general and Hirohito in particular, despite the fact that he had been part of the Prince of Wales' retinue on the visit to Japan in 1922, a recipient of the then Crown Prince's lavish hospitality. Mountbatten had been among those who had wanted Hirohito to sign the surrender document himself, and as the U.S. Army general Henry H. Arnold noted at the time, Mountbatten thought the entire imperial family were "morons, inbred and degenerate," and believed "the royal family should all be liquidated."*

Hirohito's sudden exposure to crowds of all kinds, after years of imperial seclusion, must have been an almost unbearably traumatic experience: NHK's Shizuto Haruna, the same sound engineer who had recorded Hirohito's surrender speech, recalls one of the emperor's early postwar walkabouts in the Mitsukoshi department store. Because of the crowd of (mostly American) press, Hirohito was unable to reach the microphone stand, and Haruna found himself thrusting a microphone into the emperor's face in one of the aisles, jostling with other radio journalists, some of them large Americans in uniform, and getting so close to the emperor that a palace chamberlain grabbed his jacket from behind to pull him away. This, as the diminu-

*Philip Ziegler, *Mountbatten* (London: Collins, 1985).

tive Haruna suddenly recalled as he pushed and shoved, was the same "living God" whose voice had never been heard by the public prior to August 15, 1945, on whom ordinary citizens had not even dared to gaze, the "divine monarch" he had not even been able to look at during the fateful August 14 recording session.

There were many such instances of onetime lèse-majesté becoming part of the accepted royal routine: Communist demonstrators gathered at Hibiya Park to boo the emperor. Yoshio Shiga, the Japanese Communist party leader and editor of *Akahata,* attacked Empress Nagako for "leading Japanese womanhood on the path of reaction and feudalism." There were even "rice riots" around the Imperial Palace, organized by the newly legal JCP to compel the Imperial Household to release its stocks to the people. As one American reporter recalled, the demonstrators fell silent when a car, with Empress Nagako inside, made its way through the crowd to enter the palace gates, and some of them even bowed.

Of course Hirohito was aware of the extraordinary changes imposed on Japan by defeat and the subsequent occupation. At the end of 1946 he wrote a poem urging his people not to forget their past:

> *The pine is brave*
> *that changes not its color,*
> *bearing the snow.*
> *People too*
> *like it should be.*

He was, as Brines pointed out, "telling them to bear the 'snow' of occupation without being transformed by it."

Gayn, who enjoyed extremely good relations with Japanese Communist leaders in this immediate postwar period, paints a depressing picture of a "highly reactionary" group around MacArthur determined to protect the prewar status quo while paying lip service to change; Gayn quotes MacArthur's influential aide, Brigadier Bonner Fellers, as saying, "Hirohito is no more of a war criminal than Roosevelt. As a matter of fact, if you examine the record closely . . ." Gayn felt that the walkabouts, the deliberate projection under American sponsorship of Hirohito as a democratic constitutional monarch, keenly interested in his subjects' welfare, was "a shameful conspiracy against the Japanese people."

There was one American with privileged access to the imperial family from 1947 onward, the only foreigner within the palace walls to witness the emperor's transformation at first hand: Elizabeth Gray Vining, a Quaker and author of children's books, was selected by the Imperial Household to become Crown Prince Akihito's English teacher. It was Hirohito's idea, she wrote later. "An American tutor was not imposed by the Occupation, and [the Emperor] didn't even consult the prince's official educational specialists." Hirohito had specified he wanted "a woman, a Christian, but not a fanatic"—the most important requisite of all being that whoever was selected must have had no experience of prewar Japan.*

Originally on a two-year contract, she proved so satisfactory to the imperial family that it was renewed twice, and would have been a third time had she accepted. She worked hard, for in addition to her hours with Akihito she ending up giving English lessons to the empress and to other members of the imperial family as well. Arriving in Tokyo in October 1946, she found conditions inside the palace reflected the poverty and destruction outside: there were Quonset huts inside the palace grounds, the Peers' School was cold, damp and dirty, the emperor and empress still lived in the library above their air raid shelter, and that winter young Prince Akihito suffered from chilblains.

The empress may have been less impressed with Elizabeth Vining than Hirohito, for halfway through her Japan stint, Empress Nagako approached SCAP and suggested that instead of continuing to receive instruction from her, Crown Prince Akihito be educated in the United States "in an American school" and then go to Britain (Oxford?) as a student. Senior SCAP officials debated this possibility at length. Finally William J. Sebald, MacArthur's political adviser, told the State Department in Washington:

> "I am against Prince Akihito's schooling in the U.S. I am inclined to believe it would be an almost impossible adjustment for one who has been brought up in the atmosphere of Japanese Court life. To be suddenly placed, at an early age, and with only rudimentary English, in an alien country and among boarding school boys would be a traumatic experience.

---

*Elizabeth Gray Vining, *Windows for the Crown Prince* (New York: Lippincott, 1952).

Sebald cited possible "reactions [among the boys] owing to the war.
. . . Because of the possibility of embarrassing incidents in the US
arising out of racial discrimination, quite aside from the hangover
from wartime animosities, the prince's sojourn here could be a source
of constant concern." He also worried that Akihito could develop an
anti-American bias as the result of unpleasant experiences in the
United States, like the former Japanese foreign minister, Yosuke Matsuoka, "who became violently anti-American as a result of indignities
in his youth as a student of a coastal North-Western University." For
these reasons, he also advised that Akihito go to Britain as a university
student rather than to the United States, because it would lessen
charges of "U.S. colonialism."

In the event, Vining stayed with her "Jimmy," as she called him in
the classroom. At first, she found Akihito shy, introspective and somewhat narrow-minded and humorless. Communication was difficult:
"His interests in those [early] days were almost entirely confined to
fish and I felt they needed broadening," she wrote. But under her
expert tutelage he was transformed into an outgoing, fun-loving extrovert, mingling with commoners of his own age on easy terms.
Apart from his passion for fish, tennis and riding, he was "fond of
travel, history, adventure, cowboys. He dislikes school stories, stars,
plants, aeroplanes, machines of any kind."

Vining turned out to be the ideal courtier—discreet, deferential,
always on call when needed. This is probably why her book is so
singularly uninformative. Though tantalizingly full of references to
intimate dinners with Hirohito and the rest of the imperial family,
games of "snap" with the emperor and so on, these events are invariably described with the discretion of an Imperial Household employee: they were "happy informal evenings with the Empress so
gracious and charming, the Emperor smiling benevolently on his
children and making occasional comments"—we are never told what
these comments were.

Vining drew all her knowledge of pre-occupation Japan from Japanese sources within the palace, never questioning what she was told.
For this reason, despite herself, her remarks are sometimes revealing.
In her book, for instance, she refers to Marquis Kido, then languishing
in Sugamo Prison after his outstanding services to the emperor, as
"the Lord Privy Seal who had been closest of all to the Emperor and

who was *generally said to have deceived the Emperor by withholding important information from him"* (author's italics).

Since Vining had only episodic contacts with SCAP, and was careful not to act as its "eyes and ears" within the palace or take any guidance from SCAP officials, this monstrous slur on the man to whom Hirohito owed so much could only have been the result of what was passed on to her by top palace sources, possibly by the imperial family members themselves. It was all part of the image-building process and the rewriting of history. Since Hirohito had to be perceived as completely blameless, all crimes committed in earlier times had nothing to do with him: his subordinates alone were to blame. Whether Kido himself ever discovered how his lifelong, devoted service to the emperor was travestied in this way in the interests of Hirohito's new image is unlikely, but even Kido, as time went on, must have been surprised by what he read in the newspapers. He still kept a diary. From it we learn that in October 1951 he conveyed a note to the Imperial Household minister, Matsudaira, for Hirohito's special attention. Kido had come to believe that the emperor was responsible for the war, and should therefore abdicate. Kido added that if this occurred, "the families of the dead and the war criminals would feel rewarded." Otherwise, the imperial family "would turn out to be the only ones to have evaded all responsibility for the war." Shortly afterward, with Japan a sovereign country after its 1951 peace treaty with the United States, Kido, along with all other remaining IMTFE prisoners, was freed. For the rest of his life he kept a dignified silence about the past, his contacts with the imperial family now few and far between.

In later years the horror of war and his friendship for Britain became Hirohito's familiar leitmotifs in his annual sessions with the small group of "court correspondents" licensed by the Imperial Household Agency to cover the emperor's activities. On August 29, 1963, he told them: "I have no comment to make: I rather regret my past sixty years. I couldn't do anything great. From now on, I want to make a great effort to help the people, contribute to international understanding and world peace." Nine years later, in 1971, he told them: "I had a similar feeling on my Golden Anniversary. When I think back, I feel really ashamed." Again and again, he referred to his friendly Buckingham Palace connection. "My most memorable time was during my visit to the British Royal Family," he said in 1969.

"The Prince of Wales was roughly my age. It was like a second home. King George V kindly explained British constitutional politics to me. Since then I have always thought how I should behave as the leader of a constitutional monarchy. . . . When I went to Europe, I thought: we should not go to war. When the war started, I was always thinking how I could end it." Returning again and again, in these brief, formal meetings, to his European trip, he said the Verdun battlefield "was even grimmer than I expected. I thought: this must never happen again." Asked in 1975 about his best—and his worst—experience, he replied, "I was on the throne a long time, and had many experiences of all kinds. My most meaningful experience was my European trip with the Empress, and then the United States trip I'm about to go on." He mentioned the Tokyo Olympics (1960) and the Osaka Fair as a few of the highlights of his life. "The worst, of course, without doubt, was everything connected with the second world war." In September that same year, he told his "court correspondents," "I always wish I could live like the general public, though it's rather difficult under the present situation. I think I am not so different from ordinary people." On January 22, 1984, the occasion of his wedding Diamond Jubilee, he praised the invisible assistance of the Empress. "When I think back, a lot happened in the past sixty years, but the Empress was always cheerful, made my family happy and supported my mind. I'm really thankful." Two months later he said that he enjoyed most "meeting my grandchildren, walking, observing animals and plants. What I really hated during sixty years are matters relating to the second world war. What I feel most pleased about is to see that Japan has recovered from the defeat and established a prosperous society by its own efforts."

During the occupation years the emperor's personal fortune came under public scrutiny for the first time ever. MacArthur did break up the prewar zaibatsu, and the imperial fortune was regarded as the Imperial Household Zaibatsu. SCAP released its findings to the press. Hirohito's assets consisted of 1.5 billion yen, made up of holdings in lumber and real estate as well as 330 million yen in cash. Jewelry was not included, and SCAP added that "Imperial property was markedly undervalued."

Yomiuri Hochi published its own evaluation of the emperor's fortune, listing 2 million yen's worth of jewelry, 3 million yen's worth of silver and 309 million yen in gold bullion. "The Imperial House-

hold," it wrote, "is a financial clique whose interests are connected
with those of imperialism by the holding of national bonds and shares
of various chartered banks, monopolistic companies and aggressive
commercial concerns. The Imperial family is also the biggest landowner." It suggested that the extensive palace grounds be opened up
to the public "to help with the housing shortage."

Yomiuri Hochi also listed overseas stocks held by the Imperial
Household in Korean and Taiwanese banks, the assets of the South
Manchurian Railway (owned largely by the emperor) and the Oriental Colonial Company. Among the assets owned by the Imperial
Household, it listed the Imperial Hotel opposite the palace, the Hokkaido Coal-mining and Steamship Company, the NYK and OSK companies, Konto Electric Supply, a large number of Mitsubishi shares,
six railway companies, the Japan Lumber Company and the Hakone
hot springs, as well as overseas debentures totaling 25 million yen.
There were also reports that the Imperial Household held up to 60
percent of the stock of the Bank of Japan and 22 percent of the
Yokohama Specie Bank, which specialized in overseas investments in
Japanese-occupied areas during the war.

The Imperial Household was stripped of most of these assets, but
there were some that escaped SCAP's scrutiny. As the war turned
against Japan, in 1943 and 1944, it was widely rumored that the
emperor, responding to expert advice and acting through overseas
intermediaries, had transferred some of his assets abroad, into Swiss
and Latin American banks in countries like Argentina that were sympathetic to the Axis. A SCAP report dated July 19, 1948, said that
"Japanese public and private assets located in neutral and Latin American countries have not been adequately controlled and are a proper
interest of SCAP." Some SCAP specialists believed that Imperial
Household assets spirited out of Japan in the war years totaled $111
million (1945 value)—$23 million in Switzerland and $38 million in
Latin America, mostly from Yokohama Specie Bank holdings abroad.
Nothing was ever done to recover these missing millions, and by 1951
the occupation had come to an end. Throughout, MacArthur showed
a marked disinclination to investigate the emperor's hidden overseas
assets.

Becoming a constitutional monarch meant becoming a salaried official. The yearly sum granted Hirohito for salary and all expenses in
1945 came to 32 million yen. Of this, 8 million yen (about U.S.

$650,000 in 1945) was the emperor's salary, the rest went into running the palaces and officials' salaries. The emperor's land, farms, lumber and other tangible assets were handed over to the the state. The Imperial Palace, and the priceless Akasaka Palace site, where close members of the imperial family continue to live to this day, were not affected. Far harder hit than the emperor himself were his relatives: while members of his immediate family continued to draw stipends, the imperial family payroll was restricted to a handful of people: almost overnight, princely cousins found themselves, owing to SCAP's land reform and crippling capital levies on their other assets, deprived of their farms, real estate, and, of course, of the police and army protection that had been routinely provided. They were given a final lump-sum payment, out of the emperor's own fortune, but all those young enough to do so had to work for a living. Since the traditional calling for princes, before surrender, had been an army or navy career, some career changes were traumatic, and some princely living standards dropped dramatically.

Ordinary Japanese reacted to all this with considerable interest. In the U.S. Military Archives at Suitland, Maryland, where the SCAP records are kept, there are three large cardboard boxes somewhat mistakenly labeled "military intelligence." They contain thousands of letters written to MacArthur during the occupation years, all translated. They must have provided intelligence of a crude kind, for some of them consist of anonymous denunciations of former "militarists" or "thought police" holding down jobs in the new administration, or embarking on new and lucrative careers as black marketeers and racketeers. Many deal with Hirohito and the emperor system, and most of them ask MacArthur not to treat him as a war criminal. Though a small minority branded Hirohito as "the worst war criminal of all," the majority of letter writers asked MacArthur to "forgive" him. Typical was a letter from a former kamikaze pilot volunteer, "friendly to the United States": "The Imperial family is beyond criticism. This is the national Japanese feeling, for the last 3,000 years. So if you tamper with the imperial system or the Emperor himself . . . this will be the world's biggest tragedy." Other writers complained that despite the changes, some schools were still indulging in "extreme Shintoist military education." The process of turning Japan into a democracy, one Tokyo citizen wrote, was like "trying to grow cherry blossoms on a plum tree."

Gradually, as the Japanese came to terms with their new political environment, the emperor's public schedule eased somewhat: by 1948 he was no longer front-page news, except when something startling happened, like the opening of the Diet session of 1948— taboos were broken, for commoners were allowed to look down on Hirohito from the visitors' gallery, and Komakichi Matsuoka, a leader of the House of Representatives, refused to meet him beforehand. Some Diet members didn't bow to the emperor, and the president of the Senate failed to attend an audience with him before the inauguration ceremonies. By and large, however, Japanese newspaper editors were careful to eliminate even factual stories that reflected adversely on the emperor and the imperial court.

Imperceptibly, as Japan gradually recovered from the destruction and shambles of defeat, the lot of the Japanese people improved, and the Imperial Household itself became less austere. As early as 1947 Elizabeth Vining described her farewell lunch at the palace in her honor before returning to the United States on leave. There was "French gourmet food," and with dessert, "an eagle carved out of ice to feed an eaglet," symbolizing the American tutor bringing refreshment to the Crown Prince. Later, in 1949, she attended another imperial family party, and this time a string orchestra played at lunch. As Mrs. Matsudaira, widow of the former Japanese ambassador in London and Washington, and Prince Chichibu's mother-in-law, whispered to Elizabeth Vining during dinner, "It's all come back."

CHAPTER TWENTY-SIX

By 1950 the predictions of the navy and Spy School plotters who had briefly decided to hide and raise a boy emperor at war's end had come true in one respect: the cold war between the Soviet Union and the United States had begun in earnest, and, since June 25, a hot war was raging in Korea. John Foster Dulles, America's hyperactive assistant to Secretary of State Dean Acheson, and Truman's peripatetic envoy, felt that Japan was too valuable an ally in the cold war against the Soviet Union to be indefinitely treated as a second-class, occupied nation, and that the time had come for her to assume major international responsibilities. Though he was careful never to overstep his constitutionally defined role, Hirohito played an important if little-known part in bringing about this positive attitude.

As Professor Hata points out, over the years a certain amount of friction had become apparent between the emperor and MacArthur. The Supremo's favorite Japanese was no longer the emperor but Shigeru Yoshida, the prime minister whom MacArthur met no less than seventy-six times during his six years in Tokyo. MacArthur never traveled outside Tokyo, except for a weekend in Yoshida's country home, and lived and worked in an overwhelmingly American environment; in all, he met only sixteen Japanese during his entire tenure of office as supreme commander.

Yoshida and MacArthur agreed on almost everything—including the need to adhere strictly to Japan's postwar constitution banning the reestablishment of its armed forces, and to respect her economic priorities. But Hirohito shared Dulles's view that Japan should be allowed to rearm, and even be host nation not only to the United States but to other forces in the Western camp as well; both men wanted Japan to become a full-fledged member of the Western Alliance, long before this notion became acceptable to the rest of the world.

By this time, of course, Hirohito's ceremonial status and diminished role meant that he had no means of bringing pressure to bear, even indirectly, on the Japanese government, but his personal views did carry considerable weight, especially with prominent Americans. Hirohito and Dulles met several times, and it was as a result of these meetings, Professor Hata believes, that Dulles was reinforced in his conviction that Japanese rearmament and membership in the Western Alliance, necessary to Western security as a whole, would also be acceptable to the Japanese people. In 1950–51, the CIA was predicting the Soviet Union's imminent entry into the Korean War; if this happened, Japan needed to rearm—fast.

Dulles, of course, got his way. As Yoshida later wrote, "Rearmament was for Japan out of the question at that time."* But the United States insisted, and written into the U.S.-Japan Security Treaty— signed immediately after the conclusion of the San Francisco Peace Treaty, which brought Japan's occupation status to an end—was the preamble that the United States, "in the interests of peace and security, is precisely willing to maintain certain of its armed forces in and around Japan, in the expectation, however, that Japan will itself increasingly assume responsibility for its own defense against direct and indirect aggression." There is no doubt that this was only reluctantly accepted by Yoshida, conscious of the additional economic burden the "self-defense forces" would entail, while Hirohito himself was far more enthusiastic about the principle of Japanese rearmament. Hata

---

Fifty Years of Light and Dark (Mainichi Shimbun Publishing Company, 1985).

is also convinced that Hirohito was far less concerned than Yoshida about the future of Okinawa, the offshore island administered after the war by the United States, and used as an important U.S. military base. Hirohito, he says, was prepared to concede such rights indefinitely.

The circumstances of MacArthur's departure from Tokyo, on April 16, 1951, also showed how far Hirohito had moved since that historic, humiliating September 27, 1945, meeting. SCAP wanted Hirohito to see MacArthur off at the airport. This, palace officials felt, was out of the question. On the contrary, they wanted MacArthur to call on Hirohito at the palace to take his leave. MacArthur refused pointblank. Eventually, a compromise solution was accepted: Hirohito agreed to call on MacArthur at the U.S. Embassy residence where they had met for the first time. The niceties were preserved: Hirohito presented MacArthur, on departure, with two valuable silver vases.

Later (on April 22, 1952) Hirohito was to tell Dulles that MacArthur's resignation came as a "big shock" but that he had been reassured by Dulles's proven determination to protect Japan from Communist encroachment. "Is there a danger," Hirohito asked, "that the United States will change its policy towards communism in Asia which is bolstered by the Soviet Union?" Dulles reassured him there would be no change. The San Francisco Treaty heralded Japan's return to the international community of nations: in 1956 she became the eightieth member of the United Nations; in 1958 the last U.S. ground troops left Japan; in 1969 Okinawa became once more part of Japan.

Though the discreet Dulles-Hirohito meetings marked the emperor's return to international respectability, it was a long time before he reentered the world scene publicly. In the intervening years, he grew old gracefully, performing the duties of a ceremonial head of state, attending poetry-reading competitions, athletic meetings, sumo wrestling championships and visiting every Japanese province except Okinawa. After 1971 he visited Bonn, Brussels, Paris and London. The only major anti-Hirohito demonstration, staged by Asian students, was in Bonn. In 1975 he made a much publicized and highly successful state visit to the United States.

By the seventies the Japanese "economic miracle" had transformed the nation; by the early seventies Tokyo was one of the most modern—and largest—capitals in the world. Though the skeletons of victims of the 1945 air raids continued to surface in excavations during the 1970s Tokyo building boom, the war years seemed very remote indeed, even to those who had lived through them. It was impossible, now, not to look down on the emperor: along the vestigial palace moat, separated by only a few hundred yards of carefully tended lawns, huge modern skyscrapers towered over the Imperial Palace grounds. Out of respect for the imperial family, however, there were no neon lights or advertising billboards, those hallmarks of modern Japan.

In advance of the emperor's 1975 U.S. visit, and especially for American consumption, a *Pictorial History* was published by Kodansha, the large Japanese publishing house. Photos showed Hirohito in still slightly baggy dark suits and rather gaudy silk ties, but also in white shorts and straw hat, very much the middle-class Japanese seaside vacationer. The empress, "an accomplished artist," was also featured in the book, her paintings and kimono designs fulsomely praised.

The *Pictorial History* included a rare, informal glimpse of Hirohito, interesting not only for the details it revealed about his daily life, but for the image it intentionally projected of him as an almost caricaturally ordinary person. The text read:

> He is an avid TV fan, one of the many indications that far from being shackled by tradition and cut off from ordinary life, he is in good touch. His day begins at 7 A.M. Apparently he rises earlier but refrains from leaving his room to avoid disturbing those who wait on him. At 7 A.M. on the dot he presses the buzzer by his bed to let the attendants know he is up.
>
> His bedroom, which no attendant is allowed to enter in his presence, is in the Western style, with an ordinary bed and red carpeting. Fukiaga palace, his private residence, has only one room done in the Japanese style—the Empress' sitting-room.
>
> He wears old, comfortable suits. He is careless of dress, tends to leave things where he took them off, likes gray, dislikes brown, wears suspenders, is not dismayed that some suits are shiny with wear. The Empress selects his ties.
>
> She joins her husband in the living-room for Western-style breakfast—bread, oatmeal, eggs, vegetable salad and milk from the Imperial dairy farm. He watches the NHK TV drama serial at 8:15 A.M., and is also a keen viewer of sumo

wrestling, tennis, baseball, glued to the set but only for the last hour of the day's sport. He videotapes important events, and watches TV news. At 10 A.M., he leaves for the Outer Palace, weather permitting he walks to work. The Empress invariably sees him off, at the bottom of the steps, bows politely as he lifts his hat in response, then she watches until he starts to disappear round the corner 50 yards away, when she bows again. At this point, the Emperor always turns and waves his hat at her.

Lunch, said the *Pictorial History,* consists of "sushi, sandwiches or noodles, often in his office, and dinner is early—at 6 P.M. His doctors insist on a low-fat diet, with plenty of green vegetables. All vegetables and fruit come from the Imperial farm, and are organically grown without any chemical additives. His French-trained chef prepares a mixture of Western and Japanese dishes, and menus are established two weeks in advance." The *Pictorial History* omits the fact—confirmed by court reporters with access to palace officials—that the practice of food tasting, an age-old imperial custom originally introduced to prevent would-be murderers from poisoning the emperor, was still adhered to: a court physician sampled a tiny portion of whatever was served. The imperial stools were analyzed daily.

After dinner the emperor and empress "watch TV, read till 9:30 P.M. and so to bed. For the curious," the *Pictorial History* added archly, "it might be of interest that the Emperor has absolute sovereignty over the channel selection but knows which programs the Empress enjoys." Occasionally, it said, "Hirohito listens as his wife sings Schubert 'lieder,' accompanying herself on the piano." On Sundays "they go for a two-hour stroll, the grandchildren visit at least once a week. His biology research is on Thursdays and Saturdays." Whenever he goes to the country, "he carries a magnifying glass around his neck."

By British royal family standards, even before age and illness restricted his activities, Hirohito had a singularly leisurely life. Until poor health prevented it, he continued reading state documents—some of which required his ceremonial seal, three and half inches high and made of solid gold. Though three different stamps ("read," "endorsed," "approved") were affixed to all the papers that came under his scrutiny, endorsement and approval were, of course, mere formalities.

Perhaps inevitably, after the relative informality of the occupation years, with brash American servicemen photographing Hirohito and even demanding autographs from him, the age-old palace formalities were gradually reintroduced. The Imperial Household Agency officials, always sticklers for protocol, their real power curtailed and now restricted exclusively to palace functions, saw to that. Their intense conservatism and insistence on archaic protocol was a constant source of irritation to the younger members of the imperial family, including Akihito himself. "They still behaved," says one member of the imperial family, "as though they were living in the thirties."

Some rituals were immutable: French Ambassador Bernard Dorin described to me how, in 1987, he was carefully rehearsed in the art of the slight, medium and deep bows before being admitted into the imperial presence to present his credentials. The Imperial Household Agency chamberlain taking him through his paces told him to keep his eyes downcast in Hirohito's presence, for "one does not look at the Sun." The emperor's welcoming speech was in archaic Japanese and he inquired after the health of "my esteemed brother, President Mitterrand."

Before he became ill, Hirohito received briefings on foreign affairs twice a week; in the last years of his life, he spent summers in his new country house in Hasu, winters in Shimoda, also in a brand-new mansion. Until poor health put a stop to it, he continued to attend athletic meets and poetry competitions, planted trees and occasionally received foreign guests, but by and large, his official workload was slight.

There is none of the subliminal promotion of industry that forms such an important part of the activities of British royalty, especially on visits abroad. Japanese imperial family members are far too polite to say so openly, but it's clear they regard the unabashed royal promotion of British goods as hopelessly vulgar. They are also baffled by the British royal family's press coverage: while there is a great deal of interest in whom Hirohito's grandson will marry, for instance, the Japanese press handles things differently: a small group of correspondents, specially vetted by the Imperial Household Agency, are kept on a very tight rein. They have a small clubhouse within the palace grounds, and their job is largely confined to reproducing official press communiqués (prepared in a large "newsroom" in the Imperial Household Agency building) in their respective papers. The paparazzi phenomenon around the imperial family simply does not exist; the discreet but vigilant Japanese police screen around the imperial family sees to that. Besides, members of the imperial family scarcely ever indulge in the kind of behavior that delights the tabloids; they live far more secluded lives, and access to the Akasaka Palace grounds, that huge walled-in compound where the emperor's closest relatives live, is severely restricted. Ultrasophisticated electronic surveillance protects all imperial residences, and special clearance has to be obtained from the Imperial Household Agency to film even *outside* the palaces; any breach of the regulations leads to the speedy appearance of police cars.

If anything, says court reporter Toshiya Matsuzaki, the atmosphere inside the palace became increasingly formal as the emperor became older and older. Every year, right up to 1989, the year he died, Hirohito invited the surviving members of his Peers' School class to tea, but the occasion had none of the bantering informality it would have had elsewhere, and was in fact, one contemporary of the emperor's admitted, rather an ordeal, for the emperor's small talk was as limited as ever, and conversation inevitably focused on classmates who had died in the intervening twelve months.

Court correspondents, even those who covered the palace beat for decades, were never recognized by name, though some of them, at retirement time, found themselves recipients of the Order of the Rising Sun, junior grade.

In public, Hirohito seemed good-natured, but in the privacy of the palace, one court reporter says, tantrums were frequent, and his bad temper was feared. A stickler for strictly observed routine, he was angry when it was disturbed; on his rare official engagements, he required a detailed schedule long in advance and was irritated when changes were made. Like almost all royals, he insisted on punctuality: once, when a valet brought him his frock coat (required for the formal opening of the Diet) at the very last minute, he became very angry indeed.

In many respects, says another court reporter who observed him since just after the war, Hirohito really was the absentminded scientist, indifferent to the way he looked, only relaxing in the company of other scientists, comfortable only in old clothes or in his laboratory gear, and never happier than when talking to fellow experts about prehistoric cuttlefish or the habits of sea spiders. "He really was meant to be a university professor," says a former ambassador who observed him at close quarters. Most of Hirohito's lighthearted moments had to do in some way or other with biology and science. A delegation from the Royal Society, that prestigious British scientific association, called on him just before his trip to Britain in 1971, after he had been formally reinstated as a member (his name had been struck off after Pearl Harbor), and he conducted his fellow scientists on an extensive tour of his palace laboratory. "He took a malicious delight in placing a live chameleon on my neck to see how it would change color," says a member of that delegation. He was also capable of quite earthy enjoyment of biological details. During his subsequent visit to the London Zoo, in 1971, he showed great interest in the pandas there, and was particularly curious about their unsuccessful mating habits. The head keeper's reply, "They mistook the orifice," delighted him. Though he didn't actually burst into raucous laughter, he clearly indicated, by his facial expression, that he found this a comically apt description. In general, those who met him say he was perfectly at ease only with marine biologists of his own stature with whom he was able to share a common interest. In a scientific conversation with a visiting Soviet marine biologist, a court interpreter recalled, there was a near breakdown in communication because, in the absence of a Russian translator, no exchange seemed possible. Hirohito surprised his entourage—and the visitor—by breaking into halting Latin. Soon he and the Russian were exchanging names of prehistoric underwater animals in the kind of Latin used exclusively by scientists, and got on famously. But small talk was always an effort. At one reception, an Imperial Household Agency official went up to a Japanese-speaking ambassador, and said, "Please go and talk to him, he's such a nice old gentleman."

During his trip to Europe as crown prince, in 1921, Hirohito ordered a pair of shoes from John Lobb, the royal bootmaker in London, and then, with typical thrift, had this pair copied by the famous Otsuka shoe shop in Tokyo, which made shoes for him subsequently. Likewise with his suits: before the war, patterns were sent to a Savile Row tailor, but since the emperor could not be touched, the results were sometimes grotesque. A Tokyo tailor made the emperor's suits from 1941 onward. Before the end of the war, the imperial "By Appointment" signs were as coveted by leading Japanese shopkeepers as they are in Britain, but this practice was discontinued in 1950. The Imperial Household Agency decided that "in the interests of democracy" and to avoid the risk of excessive commercialization, the emperor should not make his preferences known. But special brands of "imperial sake" and "imperial cigarettes" continued to be manufactured, to be distributed as gifts.

Television really did play an enormous part in his postwar life. There were aspects of Japanese everyday life he could only have learned about from watching TV. In his occasional chats with court correspondents Hirohito admitted as much, even discussing soap operas with them. His favorite was *Oshin,* a well-made series about the life of an ordinary Japanese family at the turn of the twentieth century. "I didn't realize how hard those times were," Hirohito told court reporters, "especially for women." One court reporter asked him if he didn't find what he saw on TV strange. "Not at all," Hirohito answered. "I've found it very useful." Had he not been an assiduous TV watcher, he would probably have answered differently when, on his seventy-eighth birthday, a court reporter asked him if he found life was tiring. "It's more exhausting to be a 'salaryman' in the Marunouchi district riding a packed train for hours every day," Hirohito replied.

On his trips abroad, especially to the United States, Hirohito's simple sense of fun delighted his guests: visiting the Rockefeller estate in Williamsburg, he was told that legend had it that anyone sitting under a certain tree was sure of becoming rich. He immediately made a beeline for it, grinning. He showed genuine interest in anything to do with agriculture, driving a combine harvester, picking up and closely examining a piglet on a farm with every sign of enjoyment. He overcame his dislike of small talk in his meeting with Gerald Ford (they talked about American football and the Japanese passion for baseball) and Hirohito explained the finer points of sumo wrestling to him. "I watch the championships every year," he said, "but I never back one team against another, not in public at least."

Quintessentially Japanese in his love of exotic fish dishes, Hirohito was particularly fond of eels, sea slugs and sea cucumber. His one regret was that Imperial Household regulations forbade him to sample the famous *fugu,* the Japanese delicacy that has to be handled by expert cooks because the fish contains lethal poison that must be removed. One of the rare glimpses of truly informal, unposed family life was provided by a member of the Imperial Household, who overheard the emperor, the empress and the imperial physician, Dr. Sugimura, discuss the pros and cons of eating *fugu*. "May I eat *fugu*?" Hirohito asked his doctor.

Certainly not, Sugimura replied.

"Why not?" Hirohito asked. "This particular *fugu* was given to me by my son. Surely there's no danger involved when they're handled by expert *fugu* chefs."

A long discussion followed. Dr. Sugimura was adamant, the emperor insistent. Finally Empress Nagako put a stop to it. "That's enough about *fugu*," she told both men. "Please stop arguing about it."

Elizabeth Vining described Crown Prince Akihito as a charming but obedient schoolboy brought up in almost the same isolation as his father (she tried in vain to persuade court officials that he would be better off living with his parents, or at least sharing a house with his younger brother), and few people outside his immediate family circle feel they really know Akihito, beyond the fact that he is an expert on fish, an excellent tennis player and skier, and the first crown prince ever to marry a commoner. Though Michiko Shoda, daughter of a rich flour-mill owner, was known to be one of the leading contenders for marriage to Akihito, her commoner status was at first regarded as an insuperable bar, and it's well known that neither Empress Nagako nor the hidebound Imperial Household Agency chiefs were pleased, and, in the early years of her marriage, at least, found subtle ways of conveying their disapproval.

Mainichi Shimbun's book commemorating the fiftieth year of Hirohito's rule showed how respectful the Japanese media remain toward the imperial family: the *Mainichi,* in common with other leading newspapers, agreed on an embargo on the whole subject of Akihito's chosen fiancée until the official announcement was made. As the *Mainichi* authors relate, a reporter rushed to the newsroom shouting, " 'It was Michiko-san after all.' He was sobbing. The editor also was in tears."

The *New York Times'* then resident Tokyo correspondent, Clyde Haberman, attended a press conference given by Prince Akihito and Princess Michiko in 1986, shortly before their departure for a brief U.S. visit. "As they chatted," he wrote, "they were surrounded by government bureaucrats of various pinstripes. Shepherded to and fro by chamberlains, they looked like glass-encased butterflies." But both are reported to have minds of their own: Michiko has had several run-ins with Imperial Household officials, and insisted on bringing up her son Naruhito, now twenty-nine, at home; Akihito is also said to be determined, as emperor, to retire large numbers of crusty Imperial Household officials and make the Imperial Palace a more informal place, more in touch with everyday life at the close of the twentieth century. But traditions die exceedingly hard: Prince Naruhito, first in the line of succession, has been of marriageable age for years, but is certainly not entirely free to marry the bride of his choice: a committee composed of leading Imperial Household officials, the prime minister, Emperor Akihito and other family representatives is expected to approve a list of suitable candidates, and the requirements are draconian: Naruhito's bride has to have perfect sight, an impeccable background and past with no hint of scandal (or previous boyfriend), and she must be no taller than her husband-to-be.

The discretion shown toward Akihito by the Japanese press also extends to Hirohito's second son, Prince Hitachi (a courtesy title, this—his name at birth was Masahito) and to Hirohito's three surviving daughters—Kazuko, Atsuko and Takako. Kazuko, fifty-nine in 1988, has been, since her widowhood, the high priestess of the sacred Ise shrine; Atsuko is the wife of a prominent businessman of aristocratic lineage; Takako married a banker, and lived with her husband in Washington, D.C., for several years. The emperor's daughters were all compelled by tradition to relinquish their imperial titles on marriage, and they seldom attract the attention of Japan's deferential gossip columnists. Though Hirohito gave his formal approval to their marriages, protocol forbade him to attend their actual wedding ceremonies, which took place outside the Imperial Palace.

For most of his life Hirohito had been remarkably fit, but on April 29, 1987, during a banquet held in his honor on his birthday, he felt nauseated, and left the table. His condition declined, and later that year he underwent major surgery. The operation took place in the Imperial Palace clinic, a small but ultramodern hospital, and while the medical reports were uninformative, it was clear that he had undergone an operation for stomach cancer; part of his colon was removed. Though he recovered sufficiently to wave to crowds on the occasion of his birthday in 1988, and managed to fulfill some official functions, such as the ceremonial planting of rice that year, he was clearly a very sick man. Newspapers reported that Hirohito was suffering from a slowly evolving but inoperable tumor of the pancreas. The Imperial Household Agency refused to comment, and his 1987 operation highlighted the agency's still extraordinarily secretive character.

Hirohito himself was kept in ignorance of his condition, so when he started reading newspapers as he was convalescing he learned more from them than he had from Imperial Household Agency officials, and became extremely angry. One court reporter said that Imperial Household officials were stunned by his tongue-lashing. Dr. Moriaka, the surgeon who operated on the emperor, later complained to journalists that he wasn't able to examine Hirohito alone: court officials and court-appointed physicians got in his way. Court reporters were told that Hirohito's first words to his staff after resuming consciousness were to tell them to switch on the TV set so he could watch the sumo wrestling. On their first visit to him, his granddaughters presented him with a giant teddy bear.

I watched him at one of his last public appearances, his eighty-seventh birthday, April 29, 1988. On that day tens of thousands of Japanese, mostly in groups, were ushered into the palace in eager but tightly disciplined groups, herded into the rectangular space outside its low-lying postwar wing, an understated piece of architecture that looks like the outside of a school, or maybe a particularly expensive gymnasium. On a loudspeaker a policewoman announced the imminent arrival of the emperor. His immediate family lined up behind a bulletproof glass bay, and then, shuffling slightly, Hirohito appeared. "How good of you to come," he said over the loudspeaker. "I thank you and wish you happiness in your lives." This was repeated three times at forty-five-minute intervals—the time it took to clear the grounds of the palace and bring in fresh visitors. The emperor looked tired, his face and hands covered in liver spots, so thin one could see the skull beneath the skin, and his delivery was slightly slurred—ill-fitting false teeth appeared to be the trouble.

Contingency plans in the event of Hirohito's death had been in existence for years. Inevitably, they were updated after his 1987 operation. In government and TV circles the date of death was code-named X Day (the date of the empress's death was referred to as Y Day) and with typical Japanese thoroughness almost everything was meticulously planned, in a series of conferences attended by government and Imperial Household Agency representatives, and, later, by editors and TV network executives.

The elaborate instructions that went out to all TV networks covered the eventuality of the emperor's dying during the night. In this case a special program was to be be broadcast immediately, until the end of broadcasting time that day; if death occurred after 6:00 A.M., the special program was to continue for the next twenty-four hours (for Y Day the programs were slightly shorter).

During this time there were to be no commercials, no commercially sponsored condolences, and no songs, comedies, drama or sport; in the following mourning period, lasting at least a week, programs were to be suitably tailored to take the emperor's death into account. The major broadcasting networks already had in readiness hours and hours of special programs about the emperor and his life and times. The initial announcement of the emperor's death was to be restricted to the time and cause of death, and the emperor's age, with no detailed discussion of the ailments leading up to it. TV anchormen were to wear black, reporters dark blue or dark gray suits; cameramen were allowed navy blue blazers. Black ties were to be worn by all. A list of special interviewees had been drawn up a long time in advance, and TV insiders say that many of those initially approached subsequently declined: they were concerned that if they said anything that might be considered disrespectful about Hirohito, the extremist right-wing groups that profess fanatical devotion to the emperor—and want a return to a more authoritarian emperor system—might take reprisals.

Publishing companies made equally detailed preparations: newspapers and magazines all had their special issues ready. Banks, stock markets, movie houses, theaters and nightclubs were to remain closed during the official mourning period.

The emperor's death was of vital concern to the printing, publishing, paper and incense trade for one uniquely Japanese reason. With Hirohito's death on January 7, 1989, the Showa era came to an end, and Hirohito was renamed Emperor Showa. All official Japanese stationery, letterheads, calendars, documents, bills, etc., up to that day carried the Showa date: 1988, for instance, was the sixty-second year of Showa, which began in 1926, when Hirohito came to the throne. This meant that, overnight, all diaries, documents and official letterheads had to be reprinted.

Already, at the time of Emperor Taisho's death in 1926, this brought about a huge upheaval in the publishing and printing trades and caused the ruin of many small-time purveyors of New Year cards, for, as Taisho's death was announced on Christmas Day, out of respect for the late emperor almost all Japanese refrained from sending New Year greetings cards that failed to take his death into account and thus could have been interpreted as a disrespectful attitude.

In Hirohito's case, speculation about his health led to certain stock market upheavals as early as 1987. With incense being consumed in enormous quantities, shares in a small chemical firm manufacturing incense—which had lain dormant for years—suddenly rocketed, and stayed high; shares in paper, publishing and printing firms also rose in anticipation. By and large, Japanese diary manufacturers, in anticipation of Hirohito's death before December 31, 1988, refrained from marketing Showa calendars for 1989.

Far more important than stock market fluctuations, however, were the political decisions that were to be taken in the wake of Hirohito's death. The emperor's burial ceremonies traditionally occur several weeks after the actual death, and the problems facing the Takeshita government were many. A source of considerable controversy not only in political circles but throughout Japan was the ritual envisaged for both the many burial ceremonies and the enthronement. Was he to be buried as an ordinary citizen—as the opposition parties wanted—or in a series of elaborate Shinto ceremonies, as the direct descendant of the sun-goddess Amaterasu? The nature of the enthronement ceremonies was also under review: when Taisho died, Hirohito presided over no less than sixty religious ceremonies, and it was nearly two years before the enthronement took place. But in 1926 and 1928, the emperor was still a "living God." The Imperial Household Agency, and the politicians, had to agree on a ceremonial that would be sufficiently awesome to take account of the mystical bond between the emperor and the Japanese people, yet also take account of his postwar status as an ordinary human being.

The nature of the funeral and enthronement ceremonies provided a crucial test: had Japan made a clean sweep of its presurrender past, or was there still a strong element, particularly among the conservative Liberal Democratic party rank and file, influential enough to insist on archaic ceremonies that underlined Japan's uniqueness as a country of "divine" origins?

Akihito almost certainly favored a simple citizen's funeral ceremony for his father, and an equally low-key enthronement ceremony for himself, but the LDP conservatives and the traditionalist Imperial

Household Agency represent a formidable coalition, and wanted ceremonies to compare with those of 1926 and 1928. There were several
reasons for this. For all Japan's postwar recovery and emergence as a
leading world power, the Showa era was also a low point in her
history; hugely colorful, traditional ceremonies marking the beginning of another imperial "era" would, in their view, help exorcise the
past; the LDP has increasingly felt that the imperial system, even in
its modified postwar form, is a binding element in Japanese society,
and that the emphasis should be on more, not less, respect for the
monarchical system. It believes that this is a feeling shared by Japan's
"silent majority," and that to skimp on pageantry and the ceremonial
simply fuels the anger of the people while at the same time alienating
ordinary middle-of-the-road voters.

The funeral ceremonies on February 24, 1989, attended by 163
heads of state and government (including Britain's Prince Philip,
Belgium's King Baudouin, King Juan Carlos of Spain and King Carl
Gustav XVI of Sweden, Presidents Corazon Aquino, George Bush
and François Mitterrand as well as King Hussein of Jordan) turned out
to be a judicious mixture of civil and Shintoist rites, the latter held
behind an opaque black curtain and watched only by the late emperor's family, palace officials and Shinto priests. The empress—confined to a wheelchair for several months—was too sick to attend.

The Shintoist rites took place inside Shinjuku Gyoen, a park once
reserved for imperial use. Sea bream, birds, mountain potatoes and
melons were offered to the spirit of the late emperor; his favorite
personal effects, including his microscope and his Mickey Mouse
watch, were buried with him.

Stringent security precautions had been in force throughout Tokyo
for at least a week. Tiny groups of left-wingers protested, but there
was no major mishap, except for the rain and freezing cold. Some two
hundred thousand people, far fewer than the expected crowd of eight
hundred thousand, lined the five-mile procession route. As the London *Financial Times* noted, "great pains were taken to satisfy the
demands of nationalists who wanted a traditional Shinto ceremony
and others who insisted on a clear separation of church and state.
. . . Bored mourners retreated frequently from the funeral hall to
adjacent marquees for tea, where the conversations were often so
lively that officials circulated with signs pleading for silence."

In the Japanese calendar, Emperor Showa's funeral took place on the forty-eighth day of Heisei, the name of the new era, as designated by Emperor Akihito. Heisei means "achieving peace." Whatever changes occur in Japan during the Heisei era, it is unlikely to be as memorable as Showa—the very name a reminder of Japan's extraordinary rise, fall and resurrection, and of one man's miraculous survival.

EPILOGUE

While there have been relatively few books about Emperor Hirohito, there have been scores about Japan's economic miracle and her postwar emergence as a world power. It's a cliché that Japan, from the sixties on, acquired immensely more clout as an exporter and industrial innovator than she gained through the brutal conquest and occupation of most of Asia from 1931 to 1945. Not even the most rabid Japanese nationalist would today suggest that the emperor of Japan has a divine right to rule the world through *hakko ichiu,* but it's universally recognized that Japanese names like Honda, Mitsubishi, Sanyo, Sony and Toyota do, indeed, straddle "the eight corners of the world," as do Japanese banks (nine out of ten of the world's largest), real estate conglomerates, hotel and even restaurant and hairdressing salon chains, and the yen itself.

It would be absurd to argue that the emperor system has been directly responsible for this extraordinary leap forward. Since January 1946, Hirohito's status as the "symbol of unity of the Japanese people" has been so understated that few of the seminal books chronicling Japan's astonishing recovery even mention him. Just as Hirohito once noted, in one of his brief, somewhat stilted conversations with Japanese "court correspondents," that he never allowed himself to express in public his preference for individual sumo wrestlers, so he never "put out more flags" for any of Japan's major conglomerates. On his 1975 trip to the United States, he visited Disneyland and model farms, not factories with Japanese connections. As mentioned before, in the interests of nonfavoritism and democracy, the Imperial Household Agency even put a stop to highly prized "By Appointment" certificates.

For all this discretion and reluctance to beat the Japanese drum, the emperor system, even in its muted, postwar incarnation, has been a constant factor in Japanese politics and society: it is almost as if the old imperial values have been taken over by the major Japanese conglomerates and adapted to present-day economic realities. As the tide of war turned inexorably against Japan in January 1944, Kido had noted in his diaries: "Looking over the future trend of the world, I believe that we must preserve and cultivate our real power in the State for about a hundred years before embarking on conquest again." It has taken Japan considerably less than a hundred years to achieve its goals, and again and again one is confronted with strange, sometimes risible, parallels between prewar traditional rites and present-day practices. The Yasukuni Shrine, dedicated to the spirits of all dead warriors, has a parallel in mercantile, "salaryman" Japan, where the ashes of many deserving lifelong employees of major corporations are laid to rest in "corporation shrines." At annual pilgrimages conducted to these sites, the "heroic conduct" of these hardy ex-fighters is celebrated; their exploits in promoting the greatness and profitability of the firms to which they devoted their lives, their health often impaired by excessive work, travel and drinking in the pursuit of markets, profits and contracts, are recalled with all the hyperbole of heroic wartime Japan.

The salarymen's incestuous after-hours drinking in downtown bars, swapping in-house gossip and going over their firms' battle tactics, is a little like the ritual toasts exchanged by old-time Japanese warriors. The aims, objectives and overall strategy of leading Japanese corporations may not be as explicitly laid out as in a prewar order of battle, but the decision-making procedures, the consensus phenomenon and the final, elaborate "summit meetings" within a major corporation can be compared to the various steps leading up to the old-time *gozen kaigi,* the sacred imperial conference. Just as the emperor, at such meetings, made his influence felt indirectly by hints and pertinent questions, guiding from the sidelines but reluctant to challenge official policy head-on, so the top leaders of Japan's huge conglomerates act not as individualistic decision-makers or innovators but more as figureheads representing a corporate whole, using their power as discreetly and as subtly as Hirohito did in the events leading up to Pearl Harbor.

Sometimes, in the course of Japan's economic miracle, the past intruded with almost comical intensity. Take, for instance, the moment Corporal Shoichi Yokoi returned to Japan after twenty-eight years in hiding in the jungles of Guam, obeying to the letter his commanding officer's 1944 injunction to hide out in the jungles and evade capture by the enemy. On February 2, 1972, on Japanese soil, and fighting back his tears, Yokoi insisted on carrying out his military duties to the last. "Yokoi Shoichi, reporting back from Guam," he told the astounded TV teams awaiting him at Tokyo airport, "shamefully alive, to report how the war was lost. I have brought back the rifle [still in working order, and intact except for the absence of its wooden butt, eaten by termites] given me by His Gracious Majesty. I am now returning it to His Imperial Majesty. I am deeply ashamed at my failure to serve His Majesty." (Hirohito's predictable reaction: "It must have been very hard for him. I hope he gets a good rest now.")

Those Japanese who had not experienced World War II could not understand Yokoi's behavior. Yokoi, in turn, was shocked to discover that the "chrysanthemum curtain" no longer prevented the Japanese press from publishing photographs of the emperor. Traditionalists and, inevitably, the ultranationalist right-wing groups felt inordinately proud of Yokoi, the obscure NCO from the supply company of the 38th Regiment, who had used his skills as a tailor to fashion shoes and clothes out of twine and bark, and had survived far longer than Robinson Crusoe in a far more hostile environment, intent all these years on fighting a one-man war and, above all, on avoiding the ultimate shame of capture.

But had there ever been, in the Japanese consciousness, the notion of surrender? In a perceptive introduction to a book on Shoichi Yokoi, Russell Braddon argues not.* As he points out, nowhere in Hirohito's surrender speech was surrender, or even defeat, specifi-

---

*The Last Japanese Soldier, translated by Ruri Corley Smith with an introduction by Russell Braddon (London: Tom Stacey, 1972).

cally mentioned—only that "the fighting had to stop." And as the *New York Times'* Clyde Haberman reflected, in a valedictory piece on leaving his three-year Tokyo assignment, "Anyone living in Japan could be forgiven the impression that World War Two began on August 6, 1945, when the United States dropped an atom-bomb on Hiroshima. Precious little is said about the misery that Japan had inflicted throughout Asia for years. . . . Hiroshima and Nagasaki enabled the Japanese to convince themselves that they, possibly along with the Jews, were the war's prime victims."

This in turn explains why the Japanese educational system is intent on perpetuating a version of events that not only absolves Japan from any blame for the horrors of World War II but also promotes the concept of Japan as victim. Former Education Minister Fujio Masayuki also felt that Japan's textbooks were "not sufficiently patriotic." That Japan had nothing to be ashamed of during the war is the message rammed home by any number of prominent ruling-party Liberal Democratic politicians. On April 22, 1988, Land Agency Minister Seisuko Okuno told assembled veterans' representatives at a ceremony at the Yasukuni Shrine that Japan's war with China was not "a war of aggression. Japan fought in order to secure its safety." In any case, he went on, "the white races had turned Asia into a colony. . . . Japan was by no means the aggressor nation." Because the Japanese government was intent on better relations with China, the ensuing outcry forced Okuno to resign. What few people realized was that a senior representative of Emperor Hirohito was present on this occasion, and that the presentation of sacred imperial gifts to the Yasukuni Shrine (bales of precious raw silk out of which banners would be made) was indeed the pretext for the ceremony in the first place.

In another context, the innocent spectacle of well-scrubbed, uniformed Japanese schoolchildren photographed in groups outside the Imperial Palace (such visits occur successively all day long) becomes a little less innocent once one is aware of the considerable censorship of textbooks and the unresolved controversy in the procrastinating Japanese courts on this major issue.

Any Japanese textbook attempting to tell the unvarnished truth about Japan from the thirties on is liable to heavy rewriting, and since the Textbook Certification Commission vets all textbooks for middle schools, headmasters have no real choice. Some of the Education

Ministry alterations imposed on history-book writers were exposed in the *Japan Law Review* of August 1970.

Commenting on a proposed history textbook on the Sino-Japanese war, for instance, an anonymous official wrote: "In treatment of the causes of the Sino-Japanese war, it reads as if Japan did something wrong. Mention the wrongs on the other side." In another comment, he wrote: "The illustrations of 'anti-Japanese slogans' in China are humiliating to the nation. This is a Japanese textbook." Perhaps the single most scandalous gap in schoolbooks dealing with World War II is the omission of any detailed account of Unit 731. Despite the spate of popular, highly documented, best-selling books on the subject, the Education Ministry still acts as though allegations of experiments on human guinea pigs were unproven. In any case, the ministerial argument runs, "To write about reconsideration of the war is unnecessary since present-day pupils had nothing to do with it. They were born long afterwards." This patently absurd argument, which, carried to its logical conclusion, justifies the nonteaching of history to any schoolchildren, is in marked contrast with Germany's constant soul-searching about the Nazi era, and in the course of investigating material for this book, I could not fail to note how unaware many sophisticated, highly educated Japanese under thirty were of their own recent past.

In Japan, any questioning of the official "line" is likely to lead to charges of "leftism," and so scared is the Japanese public of rightist bullyboys, acting with seeming impunity, that the already strong compulsion to conform is reinforced. It was this same tendency that set Japan on its calamitous prewar course in the thirties. Now, institutionally and officially, at least, Japan is a democracy, but the unofficial, behind-the-scenes influence of rightist groups, with extremely sophisticated fund-raising techniques, is far stronger than in any other democratic country, and—under the surface—the LDP, the mainstream, ruling political party, has more in common with the John Birch Society or Frenchman Jean-Marie Le Pen's National Front than is commonly realized. The LDP and France's National Front differ more on economic than on political issues: it's Le Pen's vote-catching belief that the personal income tax can be dispensed with that differentiates him most from his Japanese counterparts. On immigration—with their faith in the notion of the built-in superiority of the white and

"Yamato" (Japanese) races, and the need for a solid, patriotic nationalist underpinning to further their countries' greatness—the two parties are in almost perfect accord. No LDP spokesman would ever
publicly recognize this, but many resident diplomats in Tokyo tacitly
acknowledge the fact. Again, such is the fear of Japan's financial clout
that such remarks are invariably off the record.

So "modern" is Japan, and so ingrained our Western belief in
computers as the instruments of communication, that there's a widespread belief that a country at the forefront of technology cannot
possibly be politically retrograde. Because there are many reasons in
the West not to offend the Japanese, their highly selective interpretation of the past, and collective attitude to revisionists in their midst,
seldom make headlines. It even comes as a surprise for most non-
Japanese to learn to what extent the tub-thumping nationalist groups,
which want a restoration of the prewar emperor system, are able to
influence policy and keep any "revisionist" opinions from being aired.
When a distinguished *Asahi Journal* editor, Yetsuka Chikushi, decided
to go "behind the chrysanthemum curtain" to run a piece about the
emperor's wartime responsibilities, he soon began receiving anonymous phone calls threatening his children's lives. Rather than be party
to a crime, or air the scandal in public, his superiors quietly transferred
him to New York as a senior correspondent of the *Asahi Shimbun*.
Professor Kyoshi Inouye of Kyoto, who highlighted some of the
entries in the Kido diaries and the *Sugiyama Memorandum* in a book
casting new light on the emperor's wartime role,* was also subjected
to threats, his house daubed with painted insults, and remained under
police protection for several years.

The Japanese nationalists' desire to return to a balmy pre-Hiro-
shima era, affirming the sacred nature of the emperor as an inescapable
part of Japan's national heritage, without which there can be no true
greatness, has been variously seen as hopelessly romantic nostalgia
(exemplified by Yukio Mishima and his theatrical end) and as a clash
between those who accept Japan's new internationalism and those
who reject it. It's unlikely that new Mishimas will emerge: he always
seemed to me to be a product of his time, his romantic quest a
rationalization of his guilt at having avoided wartime military service.

---

*Kyoshi Inouye, *The Emperor's Responsibilities* (Tokyo: Gendai Hyoronsha, 1975).

For all his artistic greatness, Mishima is, in a sense, irrelevant; what we see in present-day Japan is a totally illogical, irrational attitude toward the emperor system, not just among arrant nationalists, but right across the Japanese spectrum.

On the one hand is the "official" doctrine affirming the myth of Hirohito's innocence. It extends beyond Japan, to most Western academic circles, and is backed by the generations of diplomats following the Joseph C. Grew "line," for almost all Western ambassadors in Tokyo—charmed by the younger members of the imperial family they have been privileged to meet, and absorbed in this fascinating, in many respects forward-looking, elitist society—dismiss any other view as revisionist nonsense. "Revisionism" is a word with ugly connotations, unless used as *New York Times* reviewer Ronald Sanders does as "a kind of writing that differs, on grounds of scholarly objectivity, from popular assumptions and myths." In that case, he points out, "all serious historical writing is revisionist."

Japanese attitudes toward the emperor are, indeed, based on popular conceptions and myths that are not only questionable but, above all, inconsistent, for while every effort is made to isolate him from the 1931–45 events, it is now increasingly fashionable to maintain that the events themselves were preordained and were nothing to be ashamed of. In a book on the fiftieth anniversary of the Showa era, *Mainichi Shimbun,* the big newspaper conglomerate, referred to the events leading up to Pearl Harbor as follows:

> We would be indiscreet to maintain Japan was forced into war by subtle U.S. diplomatic manoeuvers. But with President Ford defending the U.S. right to intervene militarily in the Middle East if the U.S. is threatened with the strangulation of oil supply in 1975, then what was so unusual about Japan defending the same right in 1941?*

Such an assertion pleases Japanese readers, little versed in the background to events (for Japanese history books carry next to nothing about what really happened). It ignores, of course, the fact that Japan needed oil mainly to sustain its huge military buildup. And the anal-

---

Fifty Years of Light and Dark (Tokyo: Mainichi Shimbun, 1975).

ogy would be valid only if, prior to 1973, the year of the oil crisis, the United States had overrun large parts of Central and South America and behaved with extreme cruelty there for years. The point could also be made that though President Ford may have barked, the United States did not bite: the hallmark of American policy in the Middle East has been, in fact, a growing disengagement, which many critics regard as unworthy of a nation with international responsibilities.

In the same way, the emperor's role as father figure to the great Japanese "family" has seldom been questioned. Just before Hirohito's U.S. trip in 1975, *Newsweek*'s Bernard Krisher was granted a rare interview. He asked, "What are the particular ingredients Your Majesty feels have contributed to the 2000-year survival of the Imperial tradition?"* Hirohito answered, "Because, throughout history, the Imperial Family has always given first thought to the welfare of the people." In the light of the incredible sacrifices imposed on the Japanese from 1937 onward, in terms of unremitting work, shortages, austerity, and finally lives lost and homes destroyed, it was an extraordinary reply. Even more extraordinary, perhaps, was that it was accepted at its face value, both in Japan and the United States, and that no indignant editorial underlined the questionable nature of such an assertion.

To want to have it both ways is human: in contemporary Japan, this reaches caricatural proportions. No country has ever exploited the rules governing free trade more than Japan. At the same time, to justify the stringent limits on foreign imports, Japanese officials and lobbyists, with a straight face, invoke Japan's "uniqueness": imports of European skis are limited because they are "unsuitable" for Japan, given the "uniqueness" of Japanese snow; imports of American and Charolais beef are equally unsuitable, because of the "uniqueness" of the Japanese digestive system; Japanese rice is ten times more costly than the world price, but imports are banned "because rice is the core of our spiritual civilization." Japanese neurologists have even postulated the "uniqueness" of the Japanese brain, and scientists have erected whole theories on such "uniqueness" stemming from distant evolution itself—the so-called European races evolving from chimpanzees, the Japanese from "Oriental" primates such as orangutans.

Newsweek, September 29, 1975.

One of the taboos every foreign businessman, however ignorant of Japanese customs, is drilled to observe is that it is bad form ever to refer to Japanese ethnic origins. It's accepted by leading anthropologists that behind the legends of Amaterasu and her divine progeny is the reality of the colonization of what is now Japan by Chinese and Korean invaders. Japanese susceptibilities are such that this must never be mentioned, even in sophisticated company. Japanese attitudes toward the Koreans in their midst should by rights attract the indignant attention of antiracists and do-gooders of all kinds. Twenty thousand Koreans died at Hiroshima, but only long after the end of the war was a monument finally erected to them—and it stands outside Hiroshima's Peace Park.

The individual behavior of some Japanese reflects this double scale of values. On his visits to foreign capitals, former premier Yasuhiro Nakasone was an "internationalist," almost a liberal. At home, he was a staunch nationalist, who encouraged the setting up of the Japanology Institute, whose director, Takeshi Umehara, believes that Western civilization is like a disease threatening the modern world. Until his death, no foreign artist was more adulated in France than the Japanese painter Foujita. No Franco-Japanese event in Paris was complete without him, and this highly publicity-conscious, fashionable painter never let slip an opportunity to air his views on the need for close bonds between the two countries. He was, to judge from newspaper cuttings, "Monsieur Japon" in Paris. It would come as something of a surprise to many of the well-meaning French socialites who lionized him and bought his paintings to learn how rabidly Foujita had used his painterly talents as a propagandist of Japanese militarism and pro-Axis victory. Yet, with the war over, he assumed his place in French high society as though nothing had happened. Only veteran journalists like Robert Guillain, who lived out the war years in Tokyo, noticed how quickly Foujita jettisoned his past. As former *New York Times* correspondent Clyde Haberman wrote (August 28, 1988), "No country can turn on a dime like Japan."

This, perhaps, is a function of Japanese "uniqueness": that it justifies a double scale of values, and that no moral stigma can be attached to any behavior relating to "foreigners." Since this "uniqueness" is the foundation on which Japanese society is built, and since it determines Japanese relations with the outside world, the emperor system assumes far more importance than, say, the British, Dutch or Swedish monarchy in relation to its people. As Yuji Kishida, a Freudian psychologist (quoted by Ian Buruma in the *New York Times*) wrote: "The Japanese are able to cope with modernization not because their identity is based on firm principles but because of the illusion that all Japanese are connected by blood. . . . Japanese identity is threatened when foreigners are assimilated in our midst. . . . the core of this belief is the fact that all Japanese believe they are related by blood to the Emperor. . . . as long as we believe that, the Japanese identity won't be threatened."*

Thus the emperor's real past becomes something of a family secret, not to be divulged to outsiders. Part of the Japanese "uniqueness" has been the ability not only to accept over the years a version of history, and of the Emperor's role, that is palpably, demonstrably false, but to impose it on the rest of the world.

New York Times, April 12, 1987.

BIBLIOGRAPHY

Agawa, Hiroyuki. *The Reluctant Admiral.* New York: Kodansha, 1982.

Beasley, W.G. *A Modern History of Japan.* Rutland, Vt.: Tuttle, 1963.

Bergamini, David. *Japan's Imperialist Conspiracy.* New York: Morrow, 1971.

Brackman, Arnold C. *The Other Nuremberg.* New York: Morrow, 1987.

Brocade Banner: The Story of Japanese Nationalism. Civil Intelligence Section, GHQ Far Eastern Command, September 1946.

Brines, Russell. *MacArthur's Japan.* New York: Lippincott, 1948.

Butow, Robert. *Tojo and the Coming of the War.* Princeton, N.J.: Princeton University Press, 1961.

Coffey, Thomas M. *Imperial Tragedy.* New York: World Publishing Co., 1970.

Connors, Lesley. *The Emperor's Adviser, Kinmochi Saionji.* Croom Helm and Nissan Institute for Japanese Studies, Tokyo, 1987.

Craigie, Sir Robert. *Behind the Japanese Mask.* London: Hutchinson, 1945.

Day, David. *The Great Betrayal.* London: Angus & Robertson, 1988.

Department of Defense. Magic Intercepts (5 vols.). Washington, D.C.

Feis, Herbert. *The Road to Pearl Harbor.* Princeton, N.J.: Princeton University Press, 1975.

Futara, Yoshimori, and Setsuko Saweda. *The Crown Prince's European Tour.* Osaka: Mainichi, 1925.

Gayn, Mark. *Japan Diary.* New York: William Sloane Associates, 1948.

Grew, Joseph C. *Ten Years in Japan.* London: Hammond, 1945.

Guillain, Robert. *I Saw Tokyo Burning.* London: John Murray, 1981.

————. *Orient Extrême.* Paris: Arlea le Seuill, 1988.

Harada, Kumao. *Prince Saionji and the Political Situation.* Tokyo: Iwanami Shoten, 1956.

Hata, Ikuhito. *The Emperor's Five Decisions.* New York: Kodansha, 1984.

IMTFE (International Military Tribunal for the Far East). "Documents Presented in Evidence," prosecution exhibits and trial excerpts, National Archives, Washington, D.C.

Inouye, Kyoshi. *The Emperor's Responsibilities.* Tokyo: Gendai Hyoronsha, 1975.

James, D. Clayton. *The Years of MacArthur.* Boston: Houghton Mifflin, 1985.

Japan Times, Japan Times & Advertiser and *Nippon Times,* microfilms, 1940–41.

Johnson, Chalmers. *An Instance of Treason.* Rutland, Vt.: Tuttle, 1977.

Kanroji, Osanaga. *The Emperor and Poems and Horses.* Tokyo: Shuken Asahi, 1967.

————. *Hirohito: An Intimate Portrait.* Los Angeles: Gateway Publishers, 1975.

Kato, Matsuo. *The Lost War.* New York: Knopf, 1946.

Kawai, Kazuo. *Japan's American Interlude.* Chicago: University of Chicago Press, 1960.

Kido, Koichi. *Nikki.* Tokyo: Daigaku Shuppankai, 1966.

————. *Kenkyukai.* Tokyo: Daigaku Shuppankai. 1971.

Kodama, Yoshiro. *I Was Defeated.* Tokyo: Booth and Fukuda, 1957.

Kurosawa, Akira. *Something Like an Autobiography.* New York: Knopf, 1982.

Lewin, Ronald. *The American Magic: Codes, Ciphers and the Defeat of Japan.* New York: Farrar, Straus & Giroux, 1982.

Mainichi Shimbun. *Fifty Years of Light and Dark.* 1985.

Manning, Paul. *Hirohito: The War Years.* New York: Dodd, Mead, 1986.

May, Henry John. *Little Yellow Gentlemen.* London: Cassells, 1937.

Minear, Richard. *Victor's Justice.* Princeton, N.J.: Princeton University Press, 1971.

Montgomery, Michael. *Imperialist Japan.* London: Charles Helm, 1988.

Morley, James William, ed. *The Fatal Choice: Japan's Advance into Southeast Asia.* New York: Columbia University Press, 1980.

Mosley, Leonard. *Hirohito, Emperor of Japan.* Englewood Cliffs, N.J.: Prentice-Hall, 1967.

Oka, Yoshitake. *Konoe Fumimaro: A Political Biography.* Tokyo: University of Tokyo Press, 1983.

Pacific War Research Society. *Japan's Longest Day.* New York: Kodansha International, 1968.

Packard, Jerrold M. *Sons of Heaven.* New York: Scribner's, 1987.

Prange, Gordon W. *Pearl Harbor: The Verdict of History.* New York: McGraw-Hill, 1986.

Price, Willard. *Japan and the Son of Heaven,* Duell, Sloan and Pearce, 1945.

Shiroyama, Saburo. *War Criminal: The Life and Death of Koki Hirota.* New York: Kodansha, 1977.

Spector, Ronald H. *Eagle Against the Sun: The American War with Japan.* New York: Free Press, 1984.

Steinberg, David Joel. *Philippine Collaboration in World War Two.* Manila: Solidaridad Publishing House, 1970.

Storry, Richard. *A History of Modern Japan.* New York: Pelican, 1961.

Sugiyama Memorandum. Tokyo: Hara Shobo, 1967.

Television South. *Did the Emperor Know?* (documentary).

Terasaki, Gwen. *A Bridge to the Sun.* London: Michael Joseph, 1958.

Toland, John. *The Rising Sun.* New York: Random House, 1970.

Tolischus, Otto. *Tokyo Record.* New York: Reynal & Hitchcock, 1943.

Vining, Elizabeth Gray. *Windows for the Crown Prince.* New York: Lippincott, 1952.

Wilcox, Robert. *The Secret War.* New York: Morrow, 1987.

Yoshida, Shigeru. *Memoirs.* Boston: Houghton Mifflin, 1962.

Young, A. Morgan. *Imperial Japan.* New York: Morrow, 1938.

APPENDIX

The emperor's surrender speech (recorded August 14, 1945) broadcast August 15, 1945.

To Our good and loyal subjects:

After pondering deeply the general trends of the world and the actual conditions obtaining in Our Empire today, We have decided to effect a settlement of the present situation by resorting to an extraordinary measure.

We have ordered Our Government to communicate to the Governments of the United States, Great Britain, China and the Soviet Union that Our Empire accepts the provisions of their Joint Declaration.

To strive for the common prosperity and happiness of all nations as well as the security and well-being of Our subjects is the solemn obligation which has been handed down by Our Imperial Ancestors, and which We lay close to heart. Indeed, We declared war on America and Britain out of Our sincere desire to ensure Japan's self-preservation and the stabilization of East Asia, it being far from Our thought either to infringe upon the sovereignty of other nations or to embark on territorial aggrandizement. But now the war has lasted for nearly four years. Despite the best that has been done by everyone—the gallant fighting of military and naval forces, the diligence and assiduity of Our servants and the devoted service of Our one hundred million people—the war situation has developed not necessarily to Japan's advantage, while the general trends of the world have all turned against her interest. Moreover, the enemy has begun to employ a new and most cruel bomb, the power of which to do damage is indeed incalculable, taking the toll of many innocent lives. Should We continue to fight, it would not only result in an ultimate collapse and obliteration of the Japanese nation, but also it would lead to the total extinction of human civilisation. Such being the case, how are We to save the millions of Our subjects; or to atone Ourselves before the hallowed spirits of Our Imperial Ancestors? This is the reason why We have ordered the acceptance of the provisions of the Joint Declaration of the Powers.

We cannot but express the deepest sense of regret to our Allied nations of East Asia, who have consistently cooperated with the Empire towards the emancipation of East Asia. The thought of those officers and men as well as others who have fallen in the fields of battle, those who died at their posts of duty, or those who met with untimely death and all their bereaved families, pains Our heart night and day. The welfare of the wounded and the war-sufferers, and of those who have lost their homes and livelihood, are the object of Our profound solicitude. The hardships and sufferings to which Our nation is to be subjected hereafter will be certainly great. We are keenly aware of the inmost feelings of all ye, Our subjects. However, it is according to the dictate of time and fate that We have resolved to pave the way for a grand peace for all the generations to come by enduring the unendurable and suffering what is insufferable.

Having been able to safeguard and maintain the structure of the Imperial State, We are always with ye, Our good and loyal subjects, relying upon your sincerity and integrity. Beware most strictly of any outbursts of emotion which may engender needless complications, or any fraternal contentions and strife which may create confusion, lead ye astray and cause ye to lose the confidence of the world. Let the entire nation continue as one family from generation to generation, ever firm in its faith of the imperishableness of its divine land, and mindful of its heavy burden of responsibilities, and the long road before it. Unite your total strength to be devoted to the construction of the future. Cultivate the ways of rectitude; foster nobility of spirit; and work with resolution so as ye may enhance the innate glory of the Imperial State and keep pace with the progress of the world.

Imperial Seal affixed.

THE 14TH DAY OF THE 8TH MONTH OF THE 20TH YEAR OF SHOWA.

INDEX

ABOUT THE AUTHOR

EDWARD BEHR was educated at the Lycée Janson de Sailly, St. Paul's School and Magdalene College, Cambridge. He then joined Reuters as a correspondent based in Paris. Four years later, he became Jean Monnet's press aide before joining Time-Life as a correspondent in Paris, Beirut and New Delhi. He covered the Algerian war from 1957 to 1962, and his book *The Algerian Problem* became required State Department reading. After covering the 1962 Indochina war for *Time* (and narrowly escaping capture by the Chinese on the Tibetan border), he became a roving correspondent for the *Saturday Evening Post,* then joined *Newsweek* in 1965.

As Asia bureau chief based in Hong Kong, he covered China's Cultural Revolution and the Vietnam war. His experiences led to *The Thirty-sixth Way,* and his best seller *Anyone Here Been Raped and Speaks English?*

As Paris bureau chief, then as European and cultural editor of *Newsweek International*, he covered the events of May 1968 in Paris, and in August of the same year he witnessed the occupation of Czechoslovakia by the Soviets. In 1981 he wrote a political thriller, *Getting Even.* More recently he wrote *The Last Emperor,* the tie-in book to Bernardo Bertolucci's Oscar-winning film, and it was research into the life of Pu-yi, the puppet emperor of the Japanese-dominated Manchukuo, that led him to research the life of Emperor Hirohito.

Edward Behr is married and lives in Paris and Ramatuelle.